PEARSON
ReadyUp!™
INTERVENTION

PEARSON

Glenview, Illinois • Boston, Massachusetts • Chandler, Arizona • New York, New York

PEARSON

ISBN-13: 978-0-328-86981-7
ISBN-10: 0-328-86981-3
6 19

LEVEL B • TABLE OF CONTENTS

PART 1: FOUNDATIONAL SKILLS

PRINT CONCEPTS

PHONOLOGICAL AWARENESS

PHONICS AND WORD RECOGNITION

RF.1.3.a *Know the spelling-sound correspondences for common consonant digraphs.*

FLUENCY

PART 2: READING, WRITING, AND LANGUAGE

READING LITERATURE

WRITING

LANGUAGE

TABLE OF CONTENTS

ReadyUp! Intervention Program Overview

Targeted, Flexible Intervention

ReadyUp! Intervention is designed to help teachers target and address students' intervention needs, whether they require minor remediation or intensive instruction.

Targeted Intervention Every lesson is based on Common Core State Standards. Teachers can use the Table of Contents (p. iii) or Skills Trace (p. T10) to quickly find the lessons that correspond to particular grade-level standards or the broader skill concepts their students struggle to master. The program offers flexibility through multiple entry and exit points to accommodate students' differing intervention needs and rates of mastery.

Scaffolded Instruction Lessons are scaffolded in one of two ways, depending on the nature of the skills addressed.

- Discrete skills are scaffolded into small, manageable minilessons for thorough coverage and focused practice.
- Broader skills progress from easier minilessons to harder minilessons, offering a range of entry points for students as well as scaffolded practice to help them develop understanding and demonstrate proficiency.

Data-Driven Assessment Two levels of assessment checks—after discrete minilessons and after a series of related lessons—allow teachers to quickly monitor students' progress throughout the program.

Comprehensive Intervention Coverage in Two Parts

ReadyUp! Intervention offers lessons that cover the spectrum of students' intervention needs, from foundational skills to reading literature, reading informational text, writing, and language.

Key Elements of Reading Intervention Lessons

Part 1: Foundational Skills Focus The first part of *ReadyUp! Intervention* focuses on the Common Core State Standards (CCSS) Foundational Skills and provides in-depth instruction, practice, and assessment in Print Concepts, Phonological Awareness, Phonics and Word Recognition, and Fluency (including comprehension, oral reading, and vocabulary).

Teacher Pages

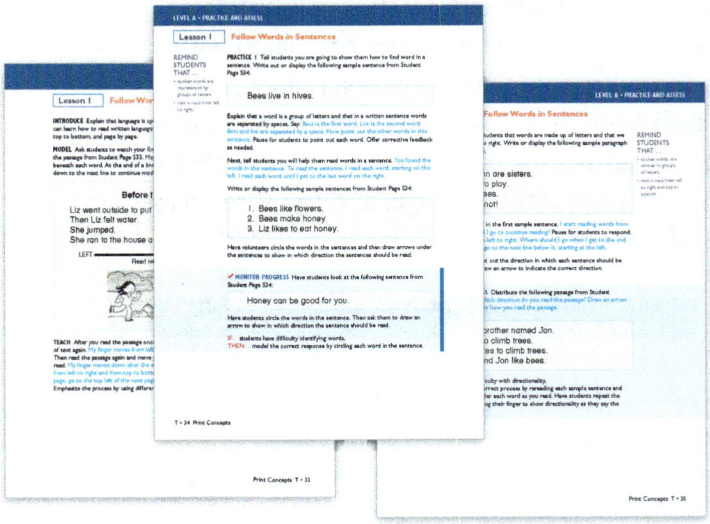

Student Pages

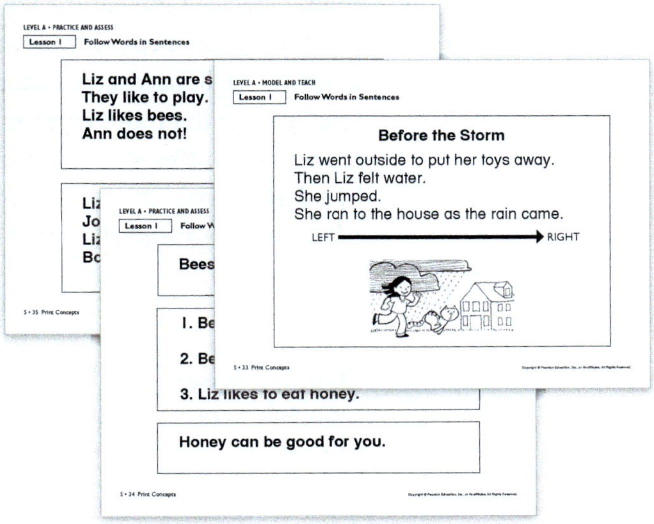

Part 2: Reading, Writing, and Language Focus The second part of *ReadyUp! Intervention* focuses on the Common Core State Standards for Reading Literature, Reading Informational Text, Writing, and Language.

Teacher Pages

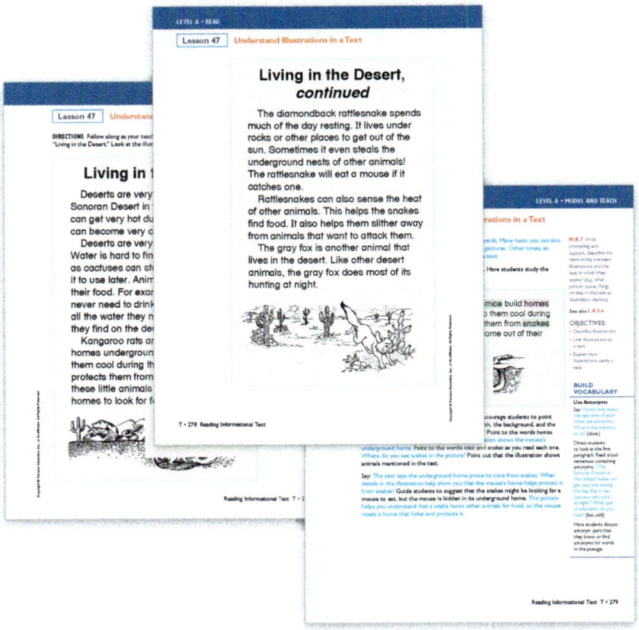

Student Pages

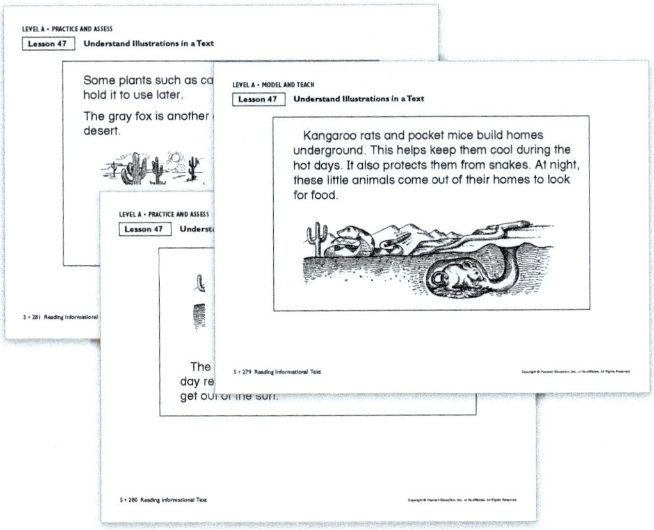

Lesson Overview

Teacher Pages

Format and Features Lessons follow an easy-to-use, consistent format, yet they are designed to be flexible. Each lesson offers multiple entry points, guided practice, independent practice, and progress monitoring to ensure mastery.

Model and Teach The first page of each lesson sets key objectives based on the Common Core State Standards. The Model and Teach page introduces the skill or concept through a reading context. The model, combined with intensive skill instruction across the subsequent lesson pages, reinforces students' understanding of key skills both in isolation *and* in context, helping students transfer skill knowledge to developing reading and writing proficiency. In other words, the Model and Teach page sets the stage, and the three pages of practice scaffold the teaching of the skills that have been introduced.

Introduce section identifies and defines the skill.

Model section and passage help teachers model the skill in context.

Teach section allows teachers to explain, expand on, and clarify the initial skill instruction.

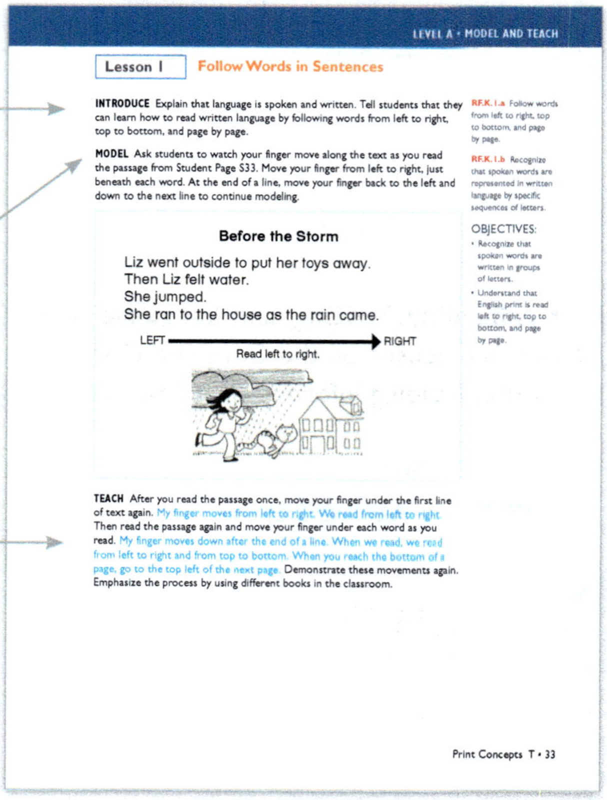
LEVEL A • MODEL AND TEACH

Lesson 1 Follow Words in Sentences

INTRODUCE Explain that language is spoken and written. Tell students that they can learn how to read written language by following words from left to right, top to bottom, and page by page.

MODEL Ask students to watch your finger move along the text as you read the passage from Student Page S33. Move your finger from left to right, just beneath each word. At the end of a line, move your finger back to the left and down to the next line to continue modeling.

Before the Storm

Liz went outside to put her toys away.
Then Liz felt water.
She jumped.
She ran to the house as the rain came.

LEFT → RIGHT
Read left to right.

TEACH After you read the passage once, move your finger under the first line of text again. My finger moves from left to right. We read from left to right. Then read the passage again and move your finger under each word as you read. My finger moves down after the end of a line. When we read, we read from left to right and from top to bottom. When you reach the bottom of a page, go to the top left of the next page. Demonstrate these movements again. Emphasize the process by using different books in the classroom.

RF.K.1.a Follow words from left to right, top to bottom, and page by page.

RF.K.1.b Recognize that spoken words are represented in written language by specific sequences of letters.

OBJECTIVES:
- Recognize that spoken words are written in groups of letters.
- Understand that English print is read left to right, top to bottom, and page by page.

Print Concepts T • 33

Practice and Assess Each lesson includes Practice and Assess pages that follow a gradual release of responsibility model to scaffold learning. Most lessons include three Practice and Assess pages that either increase in difficulty or teach different aspects of a complex skill. Routines, activities, and assessment (Monitor Progress and Independent Practice) are included at point of use within each lesson.

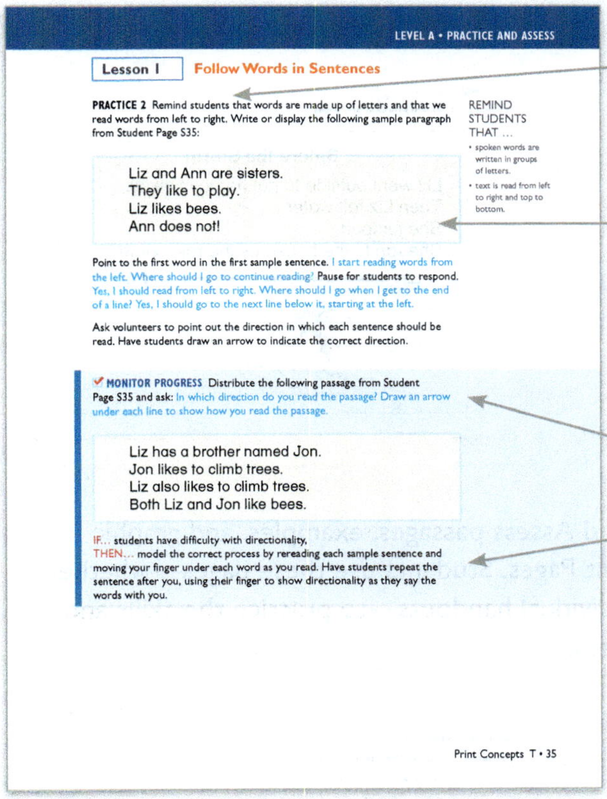

LEVEL A • PRACTICE AND ASSESS

Lesson 1 **Follow Words in Sentences**

PRACTICE 2 Remind students that words are made up of letters and that we read words from left to right. Write or display the following sample paragraph from Student Page S35:

REMIND STUDENTS THAT . . .

- spoken words are written in groups of letters.
- text is read from left to right and top to bottom.

Liz and Ann are sisters.
They like to play.
Liz likes bees.
Ann does not!

Point to the first word in the first sample sentence. *I start reading words from the left. Where should I go to continue reading?* Pause for students to respond. *Yes, I should read from left to right. Where should I go when I get to the end of a line? Yes, I should go to the next line below it, starting at the left.*

Ask volunteers to point out the direction in which each sentence should be read. Have students draw an arrow to indicate the correct direction.

MONITOR PROGRESS Distribute the following passage from Student Page S35 and ask: *In which direction do you read the passage? Draw an arrow under each line to show how you read the passage.*

Liz has a brother named Jon.
Jon likes to climb trees.
Liz also likes to climb trees.
Both Liz and Jon like bees.

IF... students have difficulty with directionality,
THEN... model the correct process by rereading each sample sentence and moving your finger under each word as you read. Have students repeat the sentence after you, using their finger to show directionality as they say the words with you.

Print Concepts T • 35

Guided practice helps students develop skills.

Routines, passages, and examples are included at point of use.

Monitor Progress helps teachers quickly assess student proficiency and determine next steps.

Student Pages

Projectable and Printable Pages The models, passages, examples, and graphic organizers on Teacher Lesson Pages are also included as student-facing pages. Student Pages can be projected digitally for group work. They can also be printed so students have their own copies for reading and writing.

Model and Teach Each Model and Teach passage also appears as a Student Page. Students can follow along as the teacher reads the passage aloud, noting how the focused skill is introduced in context. As students gain reading proficiency, they can use the passages for repeated readings as well as for comprehension practice.

Student Pages allow students to follow along, read, and annotate the model passage.

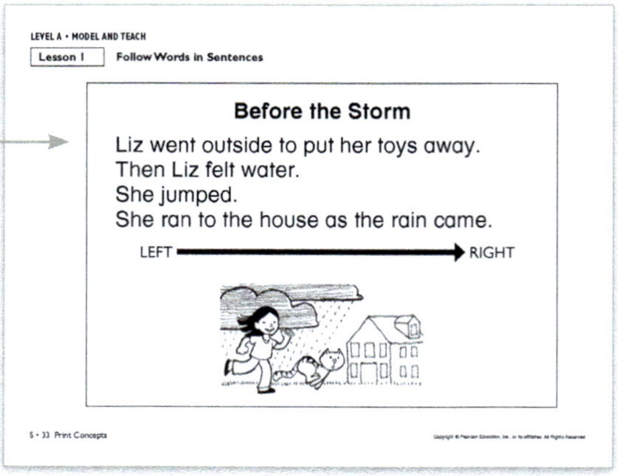
LEVEL A • MODEL AND TEACH

Lesson 1 Follow Words in Sentences

Before the Storm

Liz went outside to put her toys away.
Then Liz felt water.
She jumped.
She ran to the house as the rain came.

S • 33 Print Concepts

Practice and Assess Practice and Assess passages, examples, and graphic organizers also appear as Student Pages. Students use these pages—whether displayed for the group or as individual handouts—to practice the skills and demonstrate independent mastery.

Student Pages allow students to engage in the lesson through a variety of whole-group, small-group, and individual work that supports learning.

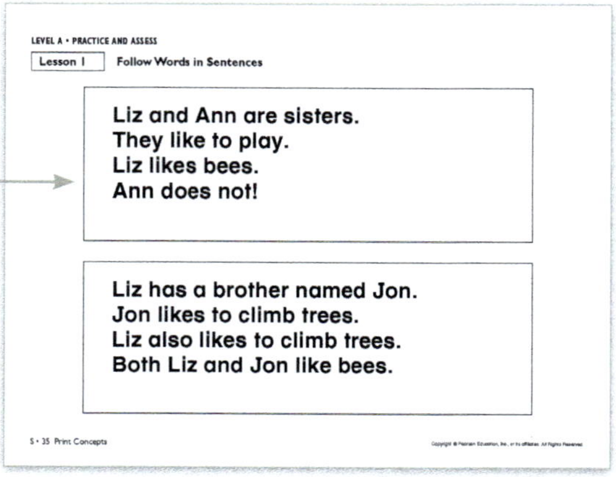
LEVEL A • PRACTICE AND ASSESS

Lesson 1 Follow Words in Sentences

Liz and Ann are sisters.
They like to play.
Liz likes bees.
Ann does not!

Liz has a brother named Jon.
Jon likes to climb trees.
Liz also likes to climb trees.
Both Liz and Jon like bees.

S • 35 Print Concepts

Read Passages and Build Vocabulary

Read Passages All Reading Literature and Reading Informational Text close reading lessons are preceded by a two-page reading passage. Teachers can read these passages aloud and give students copies to follow along or read and reread on their own. The Read passages offer a variety of brief texts on engaging, grade-appropriate literary, science and technology, and social studies topics, and they give students opportunities to apply close reading skills. Students are encouraged to annotate their copies of the passages as they analyze details and interact with the text and illustrations.

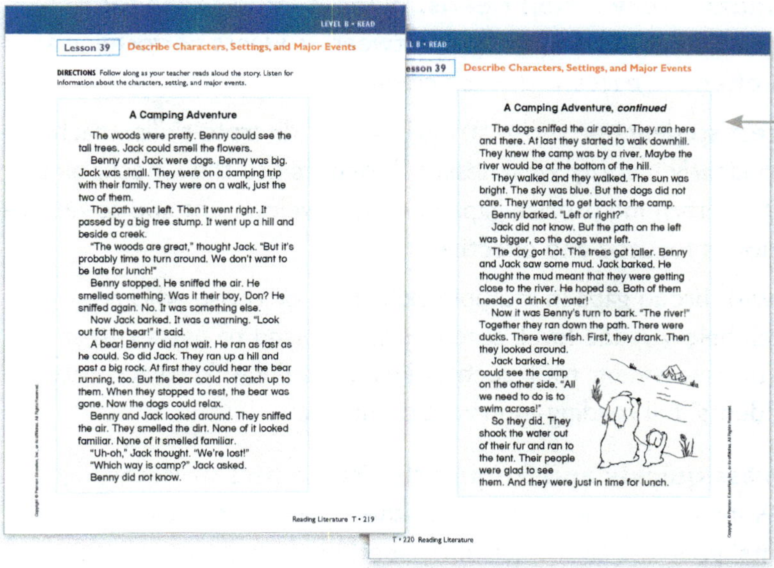
LEVEL B • READ

Lesson 39 Describe Characters, Settings, and Major Events

DIRECTIONS Follow along as your teacher reads aloud the story. Listen for information about the characters, setting, and major events.

A Camping Adventure

The woods were pretty. Benny could see the tall trees. Jack could smell the flowers.

Benny and Jack were dogs. Benny was big. Jack was small. They were on a camping trip with their family. They were on a walk, just the two of them.

The path went left. Then it went right. It passed by a big tree stump. It went up a hill and beside a creek.

"The woods are great," thought Jack. "But it's probably time to turn around. We don't want to be late for lunch!"

Benny stopped. He sniffed the air. He smelled something. Was it their boy, Don? He sniffed again. No. It was something else.

Now Jack barked. It was a warning. "Look out for the bear!" it said.

A bear! Benny did not wait. He ran as fast as he could. So did Jack. They ran up a hill and past a big rock. At first they could hear the bear running, too. But the bear could not catch up to them. When they stopped to rest, the bear was gone. Now the dogs could relax.

Benny and Jack looked around. They sniffed the air. They smelled the dirt. None of it looked familiar. None of it smelled familiar.

"Uh-oh," Jack thought. "We're lost!"

"Which way is camp?" Jack asked.

Benny did not know.

Reading Literature T • 219

LEVEL B • READ

Lesson 39 Describe Characters, Settings, and Major Events

A Camping Adventure, *continued*

The dogs sniffed the air again. They ran here and there. At last they started to walk downhill. They knew the camp was by a river. Maybe the river would be at the bottom of the hill.

They walked and they walked. The sun was bright. The sky was blue. But the dogs did not care. They wanted to get back to the camp.

Benny barked. "Left or right?"

Jack did not know. But the path on the left was bigger, so the dogs went left.

The day got hot. The trees got taller. Benny and Jack saw some mud. Jack barked. He thought the mud meant that they were getting close to the river. He hoped so. Both of them needed a drink of water!

Now it was Benny's turn to bark. "The river!" Together they ran down the path. There were ducks. There were fish. First, they drank. Then they looked around.

Jack barked. He could see the camp on the other side. "All we need to do is to swim across!"

So they did. They shook the water out of their fur and ran to the tent. Their people were glad to see them. And they were just in time for lunch.

T • 220 Reading Literature

Read passages help students engage with longer texts to practice close reading.

Build Vocabulary In all Reading Literature and Reading Informational Text close reading lessons, the Model and Teach section includes a brief Build Vocabulary feature. The feature gives students targeted practice with strategies to help determine the meaning of words and phrases in context. After a Think Aloud, students demonstrate how to determine the meaning of a new word or phrase in context by applying the strategy on their own.

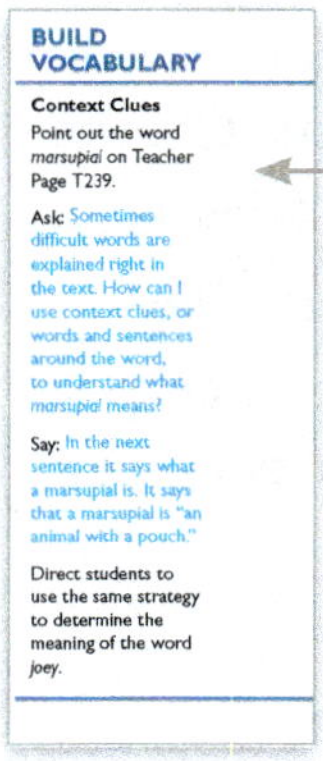
BUILD VOCABULARY

Context Clues

Point out the word *marsupial* on Teacher Page T239.

Ask: Sometimes difficult words are explained right in the text. How can I use context clues, or words and sentences around the word, to understand what *marsupial* means?

Say: In the next sentence it says what a marsupial is. It says that a marsupial is "an animal with a pouch."

Direct students to use the same strategy to determine the meaning of the word *joey*.

Build Vocabulary features introduce vocabulary strategies, model the strategy, and have students apply it independently.

Formative Assessment

Monitor Progress and Checkpoint Assessments Ongoing formative assessment guides intervention and ensures that struggling readers master the skills they need to learn without spending time on the skills they already know. Within the *ReadyUp! Intervention* program, formative assessment opportunities are quick, efficient, and data-driven. Formative assessment occurs within each Practice minilesson (Monitor Progress and Independent Practice) and after a series of related lessons within a strand (Checkpoint Assessments). For effective assessment, use these steps.

1. **Identify individual intervention needs.** Without intervention focused precisely on each student's needs, the gap between students performing at and below level often increases with each grade.
   - For the youngest students or those struggling with discrete skills, teachers may be able to clearly identify weaknesses. Teachers use the Checkpoint Assessments to determine precise gaps in skills development and to ensure that intervention is focused and effective.
   - For students with broad gaps in multiple skill areas or those who are performing well below grade level, teachers are advised to use a research-based diagnostic assessment tool, such as Pearson's DRA®2, to accurately determine students' full reading-intervention needs.
2. **Monitor progress quickly and frequently.** As teachers work through intervention lessons with students, they use the Monitor Progress activities to check students' progress and determine whether each student should advance or whether reteaching is needed. If students continuously struggle with the Monitor Progress and Independent Practice formative assessments, teachers can adjust the pace of the intervention (see p. T24).
3. **Check that students are retaining and developing knowledge.** Teachers use the Checkpoint Assessments to guide pacing and determine intervention entry and exit points.
   - As students develop skills across multiple lessons, teachers use the Checkpoint Assessments to ensure that students have retained the skills and can apply them in new and diverse contexts. Checkpoint Assessment data help teachers determine when to review skills, adjust instruction and pacing as needed, and gauge intervention exit points.
   - For any level and intensity of intervention, the Checkpoint Assessments offer a quick way to determine key skills proficiency.

Monitor Progress Monitor Progress assessment occurs after each minilesson. The final minilesson culminates in Independent Practice, in which students demonstrate what they have learned independently.

IF.../THEN... directives guide intervention based on Monitor Progress results.

> ✓ **MONITOR PROGRESS** Distribute the following passage from Student Page S35 and ask: *In which direction do you read the passage? Draw an arrow under each line to show how you read the passage.*
>
> Liz has a brother named Jon.
> Jon likes to climb trees.
> Liz also likes to climb trees.
> Both Liz and Jon like bees.
>
> IF... students have difficulty with directionality,
> THEN... model the correct process by rereading each sample sentence and moving your finger under each word as you read. Have students repeat the sentence after you, using their finger to show directionality as they say the words with you.

Checkpoint Assessments Two-page Checkpoint Assessments occur after similar lessons within a strand. Assessment instructions, scoring, and remediation options are included with each Checkpoint Assessment.

Short, targeted assessments determine students' proficiency across multiple lessons of instruction.

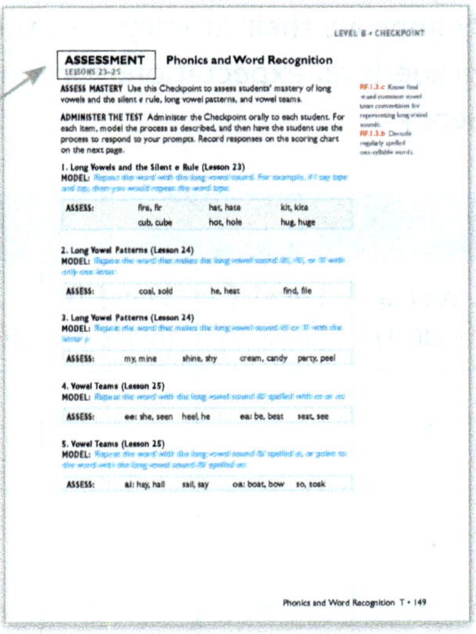
LEVEL B • CHECKPOINT

ASSESSMENT LESSONS 23–25 **Phonics and Word Recognition**

ASSESS MASTERY Use this Checkpoint to assess students' mastery of long vowels and the silent e rule, long vowel patterns, and vowel teams.

ADMINISTER THE TEST Administer the Checkpoint orally to each student. For each item, model the process as described, and then have the student use the process to respond to your prompts. Record responses on the scoring chart on the next page.

RF.1.3.c Know final -e and common vowel team conventions for representing long vowel sounds.
RF.1.3.b Decode regularly spelled one-syllable words.

1. Long Vowels and the Silent e Rule (Lesson 23)
MODEL:
ASSESS: fire, fir | hat, hate | kit, kite | cub, cube | hot, hole | hug, huge

2. Long Vowel Patterns (Lesson 24)
MODEL:
ASSESS: coal, sold | he, heat | find, file

3. Long Vowel Patterns (Lesson 24)
MODEL:
ASSESS: my, mine | shine, shy | cream, candy | party, peel

4. Vowel Teams (Lesson 25)
MODEL:
ASSESS: ee: she, seen | heel, he | ea: be, beat | seat, see

5. Vowel Teams (Lesson 25)
MODEL:
ASSESS: ai: hay, hail | sail, say | oa: boat, bow | so, soak

Phonics and Word Recognition T • 149

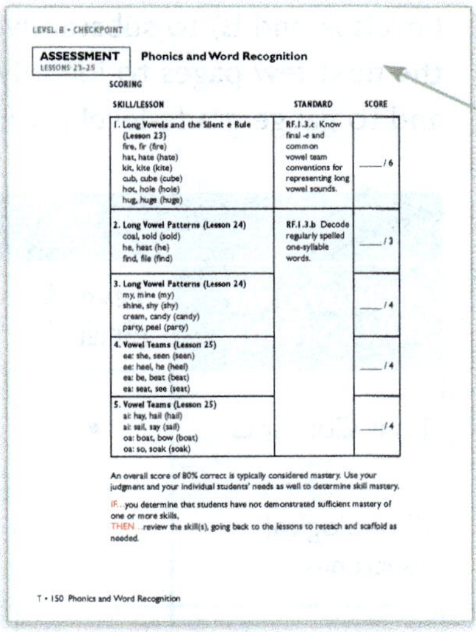
LEVEL B • CHECKPOINT

ASSESSMENT LESSONS 23–25 **Phonics and Word Recognition**

SCORING

SKILL/LESSON	STANDARD	SCORE
1. Long Vowels and the Silent e Rule (Lesson 23) fire, fir (fire) hat, hate (hate) kit, kite (kite) cub, cube (cube) hot, hole (hole) hug, huge (huge)	RF.1.3.c Know final -e and common vowel team conventions for representing long vowel sounds.	___ / 6
2. Long Vowel Patterns (Lesson 24) coal, sold (sold) he, heat (he) find, file (find)	RF.1.3.b Decode regularly spelled one-syllable words.	___ / 3
3. Long Vowel Patterns (Lesson 24) my, mine (my) shine, shy (shy) cream, candy (candy) party, peel (party)		___ / 4
4. Vowel Teams (Lesson 25) ee: she, seen (seen) ee: heel, he (heel) ea: be, beat (beat) ea: seat, see (seat)		___ / 4
5. Vowel Teams (Lesson 25) ai: hay, hail (hail) ai: sail, say (sail) oa: boat, bow (boat) oa: so, soak (soak)		___ / 4

An overall score of 80% correct is typically considered mastery. Use your judgment and your individual students' needs as well to determine skill mastery.

IF... you determine that students have not demonstrated sufficient mastery of one or more skills,
THEN... review the skill(s), going back to the lessons to reteach and scaffold as needed.

T • 150 Phonics and Word Recognition

Scoring instructions help teachers assess students' mastery of skills and shape future instruction.

Skills Overview

Foundational Skills Trace

In Part 1, the *ReadyUp! Reading Intervention* program provides a clear sequence of discrete lessons that cover the full range of CCSS Foundational Skills critical to reading success. Students' intervention needs vary widely. Many students require differing levels of intervention in particular skill areas, and teachers may need to reteach or introduce skills that are typically taught well below a student's current grade level.

The Foundational Skills Trace shows when concepts are introduced in the program as well as how they develop and expand across grades. At a glance, teachers can see the prerequisite skills students need to learn prior to addressing grade-level standards. Teachers can then determine entry points and customize an intervention path to focus on skills a student has not yet mastered, while avoiding reteaching skills the student may already know.

The CCSS strands vary by grade level. Use a student's current grade-level proficiency to begin determining intervention needs. Then use the CCSS strands to determine main areas for foundational skills intervention, and identify skills and skill concepts requiring review or in-depth instruction. Students struggling with phonics and fluency may require intervention in basic Print Concepts and Phonological Awareness (Grade K and Grade 1 skills, in Levels A and B) to substantively improve their literacy. Use the skills trace on the next few pages to identify grade-level expectations for foundational skills and to gauge grade-level proficiency.

	LEVEL					
FOUNDATIONAL SKILLS STRAND	**Level A** (Grade K)	**Level B** (Grade 1)	**Level C** (Grade 2)	**Level D** (Grade 3)	**Level E** (Grade 4)	**Level F** (Grade 5)
Print Concepts	•	•				
Phonological Awareness	•	•				
Phonics and Word Recognition	•	•	•	•	•	•
Fluency	•	•	•	•	•	•

Focus on Decoding Follow each horizontal skill concept band to the left to determine prerequisite skills. For example, if a student struggles with Lesson 1, *Understand Sentences,* for Level B Print Concepts, begin intervention instruction with Level A Print Concepts, Lesson 2, or, if needed, with Level A, Lesson 1.

Levels A–B (Grades K–1)
Print Concepts and Phonological Awareness

STRAND AND TOPIC	LEVEL A (GRADE K)					LEVEL B (GRADE 1)				
Print Concepts										
Features of Print	L1 Follow Words in Sentences	L2 Understand Words and Sentences				L1 Understand Sentences				
Alphabetic Code	L3 Learn the Letters in the Alphabet 1	L4 Learn the Letters in the Alphabet 2								
Phonological Awareness										
Rhyme	L5 Identify Rhyme in Words	L6 Produce Rhyme in Words								
Syllables	L7 Blend and Count Syllables in Spoken Words	L8 Segment and Count Syllables in Spoken Words								
Onset and Rime	L9 Blend Onset and Rime	L10 Segment Onset and Rime								
Initial, Final, and Medial Sounds	L11 Identify Same and Different Initial Sounds	L12 Identify Same and Different Final Sounds	L13 Identify Same and Different Medial Sounds	L14 Isolate Initial, Final, and Medial Sounds		L8 Isolate Initial, Final, and Medial Sounds in Single-Syllable Words				
Adding, Substituting, and Changing Phonemes	L15 Add Initial Phonemes	L16 Add Final Phonemes	L17 Delete or Change Initial Phonemes	L18 Delete or Change Final Phonemes	L19 Change Medial Phonemes					
Blending and Segmenting	L20 Blend Two to Three Phonemes into Words					L9 Segment and Blend Sounds	L10 Blend and Segment Three- and Four-Phoneme Words	L11 Blend, Segment, and Count Five or More Phonemes	L12 *R*-Controlled Vowels	L13 Consonant Digraphs
Short Vowel Sounds						L2 Identify Short *a, i,* and *o*	L3 Identify Short *e* and *u*			
Long Vowel Sounds						L4 Identify Long *a, i,* and *o*	L5 Identify Long *e* and *u*	L6 Review Short and Long Vowel Sounds	L7 Distinguish Short and Long Vowel Sounds	
More Vowel Sounds						L14 Diphthongs and Variants	L15 Schwa /ə/ Sound			

All Print Concepts and Phonological Awareness skills are covered in Levels A and B (Grades K and 1).

Level A (Grade K)
Phonics and Word Recognition and Fluency

STRAND AND TOPIC	LEVEL A (GRADE K)				
Phonics and Word Recognition					
Consonants: Sounds and Graphemes	L21 Connect Sounds and Letters: Consonants 1	L22 Connect Sounds and Letters: Consonants 2	L23 Connect Sounds and Letters: Consonants 3	L24 Spelling: Soft Consonant Sounds	
Vowels: Sounds and Graphemes (Short Vowels)	L25 Short *a*	L26 Short *i*	L27 Short *o*	L28 Short *e*	L29 Short *u*
Vowels: Sounds and Graphemes (Long Vowels)	L30 Long *a*, *i*, and o	L31 Long *e* and *u*			
Vowels: Sounds and Graphemes (Vowel Teams and Patterns)					
High-Frequency Words	L32 High-Frequency Words 1	L33 High-Frequency Words 2	L34 High-Frequency Words 3	L35 Similarly Spelled Words	
Decoding (Segmenting and Blending)					
Syllable Patterns					
Prefixes, Suffixes, and Inflectional Endings					
Irregular Spellings					
Fluency					
Comprehension	L36 Activate Prior Knowledge	L37 Make Predictions About Text	L38 Understand Read-Aloud, Echo-Read, and Choral-Read Text		
Oral Reading (Accuracy and Rate)					
Oral Reading (Expression)					
Vocabulary (References)					
Vocabulary (Context Clues)					
Vocabulary (More Strategies)					

Level B (Grade 1)
Phonics and Word Recognition and Fluency

STRAND AND TOPIC	LEVEL B (GRADE 1)				
Phonics and Word Recognition					
Consonants: Sounds and Graphemes	L16 Common Consonant Digraphs 1 • /sh/ *sh* • /th/ *th* • /f/ *ph, gh*	L17 Common Consonant Digraphs 2 • /ch/ *ch* • /ch/ *tch* • /wh/ *wh*	L18 Common Consonant Digraphs 3 • /j/ *dge* • /ng/ *ng*, /ngk/ *nk* • /k/ *ck*	L19 Common Consonant Digraphs 4 • /n/ *kn* • /r/ *wr* • /m/ *mb*	
Vowels: Sounds and Graphemes (Short Vowels)					
Vowels: Sounds and Graphemes (Long Vowels)	L23 Long Vowels and the Silent *e* Rule	L24 Long Vowel Patterns • Long *e, o,* and *i* (Spelled *e, o, i*) • Long *i* (Spelled *y*) • Long *e* (Spelled *y*)	L25 Vowel Teams • Long *e* (Spelled *ee, ea*) • Long *a* (Spelled *ai*) • Long *o* (Spelled *oa*)		
Vowels: Sounds and Graphemes (Vowel Teams and Patterns)					
High-Frequency Words	L30 Irregular Spellings • Sound /d/ (Spelled *ld*) • Sound /k/ (Spelled *lk*) • Sound /w/ (Spelled *o*)				
Decoding (Segmenting and Blending)	L20 Decode Regularly Spelled VC and CVC Words	L21 Decode Words: Initial Blends • Initial *l* and *r* Blends • Initial *s* Blends • Three-Letter Initial *s* Blends	L22 Decode Words: Final Blends • *nd, nt, mp, ft* • *lt, ld, lp* • *sk, sp, st*		
Syllable Patterns	L26 Understand Syllables • Count Syllables • Closed Syllables • Open Syllables	L27 Syllable Patterns • VC/CV • V/CV • VC/V	L28 Syllable Patterns: *R*-Controlled Vowels		
Prefixes, Suffixes, and Inflectional Endings	L29 Inflectional Endings • *-s, -es* • *-ed* • *-ing*				
Irregular Spellings					
Fluency					
Comprehension	L31 Determine Genre and Purpose				
Oral Reading (Accuracy and Rate)	L32 Read Accurately	L33 Read with Appropriate Rate			
Oral Reading (Expression)	L34 Read with Appropriate Expression				
Vocabulary (References)	L35 Use a Dictionary and Glossary				
Vocabulary (Context Clues)	L36 Use Context Clues: Definition				
Vocabulary (More Strategies)					

Level C (Grade 2)
Phonics and Word Recognition and Fluency

STRAND AND TOPIC	LEVEL C (GRADE 2)				
Phonics and Word Recognition					
Consonants: Sounds and Graphemes					
Vowels: Sounds and Graphemes (Short Vowels)					
Vowels: Sounds and Graphemes (Long Vowels)	L1 Distinguish Short and Long Vowels	L2 More Vowel Teams 1 • Long *a* (Spelled *ay*) • Long *i* (Spelled *ie, igh*) • Long *o* (Spelled *ow*)			
Vowels: Sounds and Graphemes (Vowel Teams and Patterns)	L3 More Vowel Teams 2 • Short *e* (Spelled *ea*) • Sound /o͝o/ (Spelled *oo*) • Long *e* (Spelled *ie, ey*)	L4 Vowel Patterns with /o͞o/ • Sound /o͞o/ (Spelled *oo*) • Sound /o͞o/ (Spelled *ew*) • Sound /o͞o/ (Spelled *ue, ui*)	L5 Vowel Patterns with /aw/	L6 Vowel Diphthongs	
High-Frequency Words					
Decoding (Segmenting and Blending)					
Syllable Patterns	L7 Syllable Patterns • Syllable Types • C + *-le* • VCCCV	L8 Syllable Patterns: Long Vowels • CVVC • V/V • VVCV			
Prefixes, Suffixes, and Inflectional Endings	L9 Decode Words with Prefixes	L10 Decode Words with Suffixes			
Irregular Spellings	L11 Inconsistent Spellings • Schwa Sound /ə/ in First Syllable • Schwa Sound /ə/ in Second Syllable • /f/ *ff*, /l/ *ll*, /s/ *ss*	L12 Irregular Spellings • Spelling Pattern *ough* /uf/ • Spelling Patterns *gn* /n/ and *mn* /m/ • Spelling Patterns *st* /s/ and *rh* /r/			
Fluency					
Comprehension	L13 Make and Confirm Predictions				
Oral Reading (Accuracy and Rate)	L14 Read Accurately with Appropriate Rate	L15 Use Punctuation Cues for Appropriate Phrasing			
Oral Reading (Expression)	L16 Read with Appropriate Expression				
Vocabulary (References)					
Vocabulary (Context Clues)	L17 Use Context Clues: Synonyms and Antonyms				
Vocabulary (More Strategies)	L18 Understand Multiple-Meaning Words				

Level D (Grade 3)
Phonics and Word Recognition and Fluency

STRAND AND TOPIC	LEVEL D (GRADE 3)				
Phonics and Word Recognition					
Consonants: Sounds and Graphemes					
Vowels: Sounds and Graphemes (Short Vowels)					
Vowels: Sounds and Graphemes (Long Vowels)					
Vowels: Sounds and Graphemes (Vowel Teams and Patterns)					
High-Frequency Words					
Decoding (Segmenting and Blending)	L3 Decode Multisyllable Words	L4 Decode Compound Words • Compounds • More Compounds • Compounds with Longer Word Parts			
Syllable Patterns					
Prefixes, Suffixes, and Inflectional Endings	L1 Understand Prefixes and Suffixes • Isolate Prefixes • Isolate Suffixes • Determine Meaning of Affixes	L2 Decode Words with Latin Suffixes • *-able* • *-er, -or, -ist* • *-ment, -ty, -ity*			
Irregular Spellings	L5 Irregular Spellings: Endings • Ending *-ed, -ing:* Double Final Consonant • Endings *-er, -est* • Endings *-ed, -ing:* Drop Final *e*	L6 Plurals • Plural *-s* • Plural *-es* • Plural *f* or *fe* to *v*	L7 More Endings and Plurals • Ending *-es:* Spelling Change *y* to *i* • Ending *-ed:* Spelling Change *y* to *i* • Irregular Plurals	L8 Contractions • Contractions *n't, 'm* • Contractions *'s, 'd* • Contractions *'re, 've, 'll*	L9 Possessives and Abbreviations • Singular Possessives • Plural Possessives • Abbreviations
Fluency					
Comprehension	L10 Activate Prior Knowledge	L11 Ask and Answer Questions	L12 Retell and Summarize		
Oral Reading (Accuracy and Rate)	L13 Read Accurately with Appropriate Rate	L14 Use Punctuation Cues for Appropriate Phrasing			
Oral Reading (Expression)	L15 Read with Appropriate Expression				
Vocabulary (References)					
Vocabulary (Context Clues)	L16 Use Context Clues: Examples				
Vocabulary (More Strategies)	L17 Determine Meaning of Unfamiliar Words	L18 Understand Homographs			

Focus on Fluency and Comprehension Use each horizontal skill concept band to the left to determine prerequisite skills. Grade-level standards for students at Level E (Grade 4) and Level F (Grade 5) shift from decoding text to fluently reading and comprehending text. If students need intervention with print concepts, sound-letter correspondences, or basic phonics concepts, see references to skills in Levels A–D (Grades K–3) to guide instruction.

Level E (Grade 4)
Phonics and Word Recognition and Fluency

STRAND AND TOPIC	LEVEL E (GRADE 4)					
Phonics and Word Recognition						
Decoding	L1 Decode Compound Words	L2 Decode Words Using Roots				
Fluency						
Comprehension (Purpose and Understanding)	* See Part 2 (Reading, Writing, and Language)					
Comprehension (Literature)						
Comprehension (Informational Text)						
Comprehension (Vocabulary/ Meaning)						
Oral Reading (Accuracy and Rate)	L3 Accuracy and Rate					
Oral Reading (Appropriate Phrasing/ Punctuation Cues)	L4 Appropriate Phrasing and Punctuation Cues					
Oral Reading (Expression and Intonation)	L5 Expression and Intonation					
Overall Fluency						
Vocabulary (Context Clues)	L6 Use Context Clues 1	L7 Use Context Clues 2	L8 Use Context Clues 3	L9 Understand Multiple-Meaning Words		
Vocabulary (Word Relationships)	L10 Understand Synonyms	L11 Understand Antonyms				
Vocabulary (Greek and Latin Affixes and Roots)						
Vocabulary (Affixes and Roots)	L12 Understand Prefixes *un-, dis-, mis-*	L13 Understand Prefixes *pre-, re-*	L14 Understand Suffixes *-ful, -less*			
Vocabulary (References)						

Level F (Grade 5)

Phonics and Word Recognition and Fluency

STRAND AND TOPIC	LEVEL F (GRADE 5)					
Phonics and Word Recognition						
Decoding	L3 Decode Words Using Greek and Latin Roots	L4 Decode Multisyllabic Words				
Fluency						
Comprehension (Purpose and Understanding)	* See Part 2 (Reading, Writing, and Language)					
Comprehension (Literature)						
Comprehension (Informational Text)						
Comprehension (Vocabulary/ Meaning)						
Oral Reading (Accuracy and Rate)	L3 Accuracy and Rate					
Oral Reading (Appropriate Phrasing/ Punctuation Cues)	L4 Appropriate Phrasing and Punctuation Cues					
Oral Reading (Expression and Intonation)	L5 Expression and Intonation					
Overall Fluency	L6 Fluency 1	L7 Fluency 2				
Vocabulary (Context Clues)						
Vocabulary (Word Relationships)						
Vocabulary (Greek and Latin Affixes and Roots)	L8 Understand Greek and Latin Prefixes	L9 Understand Greek and Latin Suffixes	L10 Understand Greek and Latin Roots			
Vocabulary (Affixes and Roots)	L11 Understand Suffixes *-ly, -al*	L12 Understand Suffixes *-able, -ive; -ous, -ish*	L13 Understand Suffixes *-ness, -ion*			
Vocabulary (References)	L14 Use a Dictionary, Glossary, and Thesaurus					

Reading, Writing, and Language Skills Trace

In *ReadyUp! Intervention,* Part 1: Foundational Skills lessons focus on the fundamental elements of decoding. In Part 2: Reading, Writing, and Language, intervention lessons focus on a deeper analysis of both literary and informational texts and on writing and language. The Part 2 skills are intended to be taught initially alongside and then as a continuation of the reading foundational skills as students move from basic decoding toward deeper understanding of text.

Reading Literature and Informational Texts As students master decoding, they move toward an increasingly sophisticated skill level in reading analysis, writing, and language development. These skills move in a continuum across the grade levels in CCSS, and *ReadyUp!* follows that depth and breadth from level to level. Use the Skills Trace on the following pages to identify prerequisite skills for each reading standard within a strand to adjust intervention to meet students' current needs and goals.

Writing Intervention lessons for writing target the skills and concepts that offer the greatest payoff for struggling students. Students focus on the basics of understanding writing tasks and processes, including research and technology. Each Practice and Assess page within the lessons tailors the instruction to one of the three main modes (opinion, informative/explanatory, or narrative), so students understand how to apply the skills across writing genres. Use the Skills Trace to target key topics for writing intervention or remediation as well as to gauge students' progress.

Language Intervention lessons for language development similarly target skills and concepts that prove hardest to master and/or are most crucial for struggling students. Students can immediately transfer these targeted skills to other real-life writing tasks both in and out of school.

Vocabulary The CCSS address both vocabulary acquisition and use as students determine word meanings, acquire new words, and use these new words in their own speaking and writing. In *ReadyUp! Intervention,* students acquire vocabulary skills through in-depth, stand-alone lessons throughout the strands. In addition, students apply vocabulary strategies as they access frequent point-of-use Build Vocabulary features in the Part 2 Reading lessons.

Reading Literature Skills Trace

STRAND AND TOPIC		LESSONS BY LEVEL						
		LEVEL A (GRADE K)	**LEVEL B** (GRADE 1)	**LEVEL C** (GRADE 2)	**LEVEL D** (GRADE 3)	**LEVEL E** (GRADE 4)	**LEVEL F** (GRADE 5)	**LEVEL G** (GRADE 6)
Key Ideas and Details	**RL.1**	L39 Ask and Answer Questions	L37 Ask and Answer Questions About a Story	L19 Ask and Answer Questions About a Text	L19 Ask and Answer Questions About a Text	L15 Make Inferences	L15 Draw Conclusions	L1 Cite Text Evidence
	RL.2	L40 Retell Stories	L38 Retell Stories	L20 Recount Stories	L20 Determine Central Message or Moral	L16 Determine Theme	L16 Determine Theme	L2 Determine Theme
	RL.3		L39 Describe Characters, Settings, and Major Events	L21 Describe Characters	L21 Describe Characters	L17 Understand Character L18 Understand Plot L19 Understand Setting	L17 Compare and Contrast Characters, Setting, and Events	L3 Understand Development in a Narrative
Craft and Structure	**RL.4**		L40 Identify the Meaning of Words	L22 Describe the Meaning of Words and Phrases	L22 Distinguish Between Literal and Nonliteral Language	L20 Recognize Idioms, Adages, Proverbs, and Allusions	L18 Interpret Figurative Language	L4 Determine Connotation, Denotation, and Tone
	RL.5	L41 Recognize Types of Texts		L23 Learn Story Structure	L23 Describe Structure in Literature	L21 Compare and Contrast Structure and Point of View	L19 Analyze Structure in Literature	L5 Analyze Narrative Structure
	RL.6	L42 Identify the Role of Storytellers	L41 Analyze Characters' Experiences	L24 Compare Characters' Points of View	L24 Distinguish Between Points of View		L20 Describe Point of View	L6 Explain Point of View
Integration of Knowledge and Ideas	**RL.7**	L43 Understand Illustrations in a Story		L25 Use Information from Illustrations	L25 Interpret Illustrations		L21 Analyze Visual Elements in Literature	L7 Compare and Contrast Experiences of a Text
	RL.9			L26 Compare and Contrast Two Versions of a Story	L26 Compare and Contrast in Literature	L22 Compare and Contrast Literature	L22 Compare and Contrast Literature	L8 Compare and Contrast Literature

Reading Informational Text Skills Trace

STRAND AND TOPIC		LESSONS BY LEVEL						
		LEVEL A (GRADE K)	LEVEL B (GRADE 1)	LEVEL C (GRADE 2)	LEVEL D (GRADE 3)	LEVEL E (GRADE 4)	LEVEL F (GRADE 5)	LEVEL G (GRADE 6)
Key Ideas and Details	**RI.1 RI.2**	L44 Identify Main Topic and Key Details	L42 Identify Main Topic and Key Details	L27 Identify Main Ideas	L27 Find the Main Idea	L23 Determine the Main Idea and Details	L23 Determine Multiple Main Ideas	L9 Determine Central Ideas
	RI.3		L43 Connect Information in a Text	L28 Describe Relationships Between Ideas	L28 Describe the Relationship Between Ideas	L24 Explain Ideas from Informational Texts	L24 Understand Cause-Effect Relationships L25 Understand Compare-Contrast Relationships	L10 Analyze Development of Ideas
Craft and Structure	**RI.4**	L45 Define Unfamiliar Words		L29 Understand Academic and Domain-Specific Words	L29 Understand Academic and Domain-Specific Words	L25 Learn Academic and Domain-Specific Words	L26 Understand Domain-Specific Vocabulary	L11 Determine the Meaning of Words and Phrases
	RI.5			L30 Use Text Features	L30 Use Text Features	L26 Describe Text Structure	L27 Compare Structure in Two Texts	L12 Analyze Structure
	RI.6	L46 Examine the Presentation of Information		L31 Identify Main Purpose	L31 Understand Point of View	L27 Compare and Contrast Accounts	L28 Analyze Multiple Accounts	L13 Determine Author's Point of View and Purpose
Integration of Knowledge and Ideas	**RI.7**	L47 Understand Illustrations in a Text	L44 Understand Illustrations	L32 Examine Images in a Text	L32 Use Illustrations to Understand a Text	L28 Interpret Visual, Oral, and Quantitative Information		L14 Integrate Information
	RI.8		L45 Determine Reasons	L33 Describe Points and Supporting Reasons	L33 Describe Logical Connections Between Sentences and Paragraphs	L29 Analyze Author's Reasons and Evidence	L29 Analyze Author's Reasons and Evidence	L15 Analyze Author's Reasons and Evidence
	RI.9	L48 Compare Texts	L46 Compare Two Texts	L34 Compare Two Texts	L34 Compare Two Texts	L30 Compare and Contrast Two Texts	L30 Draw Evidence and Integrate Information	L16 Compare and Contrast Texts

Writing Skills Trace

STRAND AND TOPIC		LESSONS BY LEVEL						
		LEVEL A (GRADE K)	LEVEL B (GRADE 1)	LEVEL C (GRADE 2)	LEVEL D (GRADE 3)	LEVEL E (GRADE 4)	LEVEL F (GRADE 5)	LEVEL G (GRADE 6)
Plan and Develop Writing	W.4 W.5	L49 Ask and Answer Questions About a Prompt	L47 Use a Prompt to Identify a Writing Topic		L35 Analyze a Prompt	L31 Analyze a Writing Prompt	L31 Plan Response to a Prompt	L17 Analyze and Plan Before Writing
				L35 Write Clear Sentences	L36 Plan and Draft a Piece of Writing	L32 Create Coherent Paragraphs	L32 Use Clear Organization	L18 Produce Clear, Coherent Writing
Research	W.6 W.7 W.8	L50 Use a Topic to Recall and Gather Information	L48 Recall and Gather Information About a Topic	L36 Collaborate on Planning and Developing Writing		L33 Research a Topic	L33 Paraphrase Sources	L19 Quote and Paraphrase from Sources
				L37 Gather Information on a Topic	L37 Research a Writing Assignment			L20 Use Technology in Writing
Strengthen and Revise Writing	W.5	L51 Add Details to Writing	L49 Add Specific Details to Support Ideas				L34 Strengthen Opening and Concluding Statements	L21 Revise and Rewrite Drafts
				L38 Revise and Focus Paragraphs	L38 Revise Organization in a Piece of Writing	L34 Link Ideas with Transitions	L35 Revise, Edit, and Rewrite	
				L39 Edit and Publish Writing	L39 Revise Language in a Piece of Writing	L35 Revise Sentences for Clarity and Precision		

Detailed instruction on and practice with main writing modes (W.1, W.2, and W.3) are covered within most lessons.

Language Skills Trace

STRAND AND TOPIC		LESSONS BY LEVEL						
		LEVEL A (GRADE K)	LEVEL B (GRADE 1)	LEVEL C (GRADE 2)	LEVEL D (GRADE 3)	LEVEL E (GRADE 4)	LEVEL F (GRADE 5)	LEVEL G (GRADE 6)
Grammar and Usage	**L.1**	L52 Understand Nouns, Verbs, and Prepositions	L50 Use Subject-Verb Agreement	L40 Understand Nouns, Verbs, and Agreement	L40 Understand Subject-Verb and Pronoun-Antecedent Agreement	L36 Use Progressive Tense Verbs and Modals	L36 Use Correct Verb Tense	L22 Use Pronouns Correctly
					L41 Understand Coordinating and Subordinating Conjunctions	L37 Use Frequently Confused Words Correctly		
Capitalization, Punctuation and Spelling	**L.2**	L53 Capitalize and Punctuate Sentences	L51 Produce and Expand Sentences	L41 Use Contractions and Possessives		L38 Punctuate Quotations and Direct Speech	L37 Use Commas Correctly	
			L52 Understand Spelling Patterns		L42 Use Conventional Spellings and Suffixes			
Language and Craft	**L.3**			L42 Use Formal and Informal English			L38 Expand, Combine, and Reduce Sentences for Style and Effect	L23 Vary Sentence Patterns for Meaning Style, and Effect
Word Relationships	**L.5**	L54 Sort Words into Categories						L24 Use Word Relationships

Intervention and Your Students

ReadyUp! Intervention includes the common threads of effective reading intervention programs: a focus on planning, pacing, and adapting to students' needs; supportive activities to build language, fluency, and home-school connections; and a current research base on proven intervention philosophy and practice.

Planning

ReadyUp! Intervention offers a consistent lesson format to make instruction, practice, and assessment during intervention clear and easy to use. Student models, activities, routines, and assessments are provided at point of use and follow a gradual-release model. The pace of the lessons is naturally dependent on the needs of each student. The chart below provides a suggested pacing for lessons, many of which might typically take about one week.

Weekly Lesson Plan

DAY 1	MODEL AND TEACH	**INTRODUCE** ("I do")	• Introduce general concept or skill to students.
		MODEL ("I do")	• Identify the skill in context, through an annotated reading model. • Reinforce that the foundational skills are intrinsic to overall reading fluency. • Model fluency through regular read-alouds. • Give repeated practice with decodable, developmentally appropriate text.
		TEACH ("I do")	• Explain the skill in context. • Teach the skill explicitly.
DAY 2	PRACTICE AND ASSESS	**PRACTICE 1** ("We do")	• Guide practice of the most basic aspects of the skill through reteaching and routines. • Display or distribute Student Pages to give students guided practice.
		MONITOR PROGRESS ("We do")	• Assess students' progress. • Review or reteach as needed.
DAY 3		**PRACTICE 2** ("We do")	• Guide practice of intermediate aspects of the skill through reteaching and routines. • Display or distribute Student Pages to give students guided practice.
		MONITOR PROGRESS ("We do")	• Assess students' progress. • Review or reteach as needed.
DAY 4		**PRACTICE 3** ("We do")	• Guide practice of the most difficult aspects of the skill through reteaching and routines. • Display or distribute Student Pages to give students guided practice.
		INDEPENDENT PRACTICE ("You do")	• Assess students' independent progress. • Review or reteach as needed. • Move on to next lesson.

Pacing

ReadyUp! Intervention is intended to be used in addition to the core curriculum and may be used in a variety of ways. The lesson format is consistent but adaptive and easy to implement. It can be flexibly used both for students needing brief, targeted intervention for particular skills and for students requiring broader and more intensive intervention across strands and even across multiple grade levels. Teachers can focus on intervention lessons that complement and reinforce grade-level instruction taught in their core curriculum. Alternatively, they may focus on reviewing (or introducing) prerequisite skills from earlier grades needed for students to approach and achieve grade-level reading expectations.

Customizing Intervention Models Teachers can adapt the program in ways that best fit the intervention needs of their students, adjusting for the percentage of students in class requiring intervention and the resources available in their classroom, school, and district. The models below offer several ways to use *ReadyUp! Intervention.*

Intervention Models

- **One-on-one intervention**
- **Small groups (outside of class)**
- **Small groups (in class)**

Level of Intervention Needed (**LOW** → **HIGH**)	One-on-One Extensive Intervention (classroom teacher)		One-on-One Intervention (literacy specialists/aides)
		Small Groups (groups organized by intervention needs of students)	
	Small Groups (in class to reteach/review core instruction)		Small Groups (before or after class to reteach/review core instruction)
	Number of Students Requiring Intervention **LOW** → **HIGH**		

Adapting to Students' Needs

ReadyUp! Intervention follows a consistent format, but the sequence and number of lessons in the program are not prescriptive. Intervention should be quick and efficient, targeted to the skills and concepts that are proving barriers to grade-level reading proficiency. If a straightforward concept is introduced and quickly mastered in a session or two, teachers should move on. On the other hand, some lessons may require several sessions for instruction, modeling, and to practice skills before students will show mastery. The number of sessions, their duration, and the intervention model used should be tailored to students' needs. For example, students needing intensive intervention may require 30-minute daily sessions for instruction, practice and progress monitoring. For students needing minimal intervention, two to three 30-minute small-group sessions may be enough to teach the concept and provide sufficient guided practice and assessment.

Customizing Intervention As students' proficiency improves, teachers may wish to have students focus on only the second or third minilesson after concepts are taught and modeled. The goal is to make intervention as quick and efficient as possible. Pacing should be adapted as students' skill level increases.

Intensive Intervention

- 30-minute sessions of daily instruction one-on-one or in small groups

Moderate Intervention

- 30-minute sessions, 2–3 times/week, one-on-one or in small groups

Minimal Intervention

- 30-minute sessions, 2–3 times/week, stations in class
- 30-minute sessions, 2–3 times/week, in small groups, to preteach or reteach

IF... students continue to struggle, THEN... adjust pacing by

1. determining gaps in knowledge and teaching prerequisite skills.
2. increasing number of sessions per week.
3. decreasing the number of students in sessions.

IF... students improve quickly, THEN... adjust pacing by

1. using the Checkpoint Assessments to gauge student mastery, teaching entire lessons only if needed.
2. decreasing the number of sessions per week.
3. increasing the number of students in sessions.

Building Language

A sound knowledge of how language works is critical to reading and writing. Familiarizing students with word-building activities can help them recognize and pronounce words, decode words in text, and improve spelling and writing.

Word-Building Activities Word building helps students develop an understanding of the alphabetic principle and reinforces a generative understanding of words and language as students create and manipulate words. Word-building practice has been shown to help students shift from partial alphabet decoding to full alphabetic decoding,[1] which in turn leads to improvements in word recognition.[2]

Word building involves creating simple cards or tiles to build words. The teacher instructs students to form a particular word using the cards. The teacher then has students add, delete, or replace a letter, such as changing the initial *t* in *tap* to an *m*, forming the new word, *map*. Students focus on changing the initial, final, and medial letters (or phonemes, such as *ch*). After each word is "built," the teacher and students read the word aloud, with the teacher offering corrective feedback as needed. As students' phonological awareness and phonics knowledge increases, they are able to build increasingly sophisticated words, as well as sort words by their features, expanding their understanding from letters and phonemes to words and their morphemes, affixes, and inflected endings. The process helps students transfer knowledge between decoding (reading) and encoding (spelling and writing) to reinforce understanding in both areas. For additional word-building activities and ideas for the classroom, see Patricia Cunningham's series, *Making Words*.

t	a	p
m	a	p
m	o	p
p	o	p
p	o	t
p	i	t
	i	t

Elkonin Boxes and letter tiles help students create words and manipulate them to create new words.

1. Ehri, Linnea C. 2005. "Learning to Read Words: Theory, Findings, and Issues." *Scientific Studies of Reading* 9 (2): 167–188.

2. McCandliss, Bruce, Isabel Beck, Rebecca Sandak, and Charles Perfetti. 2003. "Focusing Attention on Decoding for Children with Poor Reading Skills: Design and Preliminary Tests of the World Building Intervention." *Scientific Studies of Reading* 7: 75–104.

Building Fluency

Reading fluency is inextricably linked to reading comprehension. As students develop fluency, or automaticity with decoding, they are able to focus more attention on comprehension, or understanding the meaning of a text. Repeated readings of the same text help students develop automaticity, and this technique is emphasized throughout *ReadyUp! Intervention*. As teachers gauge students' fluency, they should keep in mind that comprehension is the true goal of automaticity in decoding and proficiency in oral reading.

Mastering Full Alphabet Decoding To develop fluency, students must first develop full alphabetic knowledge and be proficient in full alphabet decoding. Students who use only the first and last parts of a word to identify it are using partial alphabetic decoding. Students who only partially decode may seem to read fluently and quickly at first, but they will struggle as texts become more complex and include more unfamiliar words (and fewer visual cues). Students who partially decode should be encouraged to slow down and fully decode each word, focusing on improving accuracy as opposed to rate. As students achieve full alphabetic decoding, their rate will improve as well.

Miscue Analysis Once students are capable of independently reading passages, teachers can use miscue analysis to diagnose students' reading proficiency. To perform a miscue analysis, give the student an unfamiliar passage to read aloud. As the student reads, mark the following types of errors on your own copy of the passage. Log students' miscues to determine areas in which they need additional review and support.

Miscue	Explanation	Example	Analysis
correction	Student corrects error without prompting.	I even saw a fox! was/saw	Self correcting is a good strategy, but check that the student is not reading too quickly.
omission	Student leaves out a word(s).	I saw a (bat) fly and a kangaroo jump.	Check that the student is not reading too quickly. Omission may also signal that sight-word recognition is weak.
insertion	Student inserts a word(s) that isn't in the text.	We went to the zoo. too I saw a bat fly ^ and a kangaroo jump.	The student may be reading too quickly. Check that insertions do not detract from meaning.

Miscue	Explanation	Example	Analysis
repetition	Student repeats a word or section of text.	I saw a bat fly and a kangaroo jump.	Repetition of a word or phrase often means the student is struggling to comprehend meaning.
reversal	Student reverses order of the print (e.g., saying "of" instead of "for").	I heard a duck quack.	Check for reversals that change the meaning. The student may need to slow down.
substitution	Student reads a different word from the one in the text.	want We went to the zoo.	The student may not understand the word. Check whether the substituted word is logical or simply a guess. Focus on full alphabet decoding.

How to Measure Fluency Reading passages are differentiated to cover a range of reading levels within a classroom.

LEVEL/GRADE	MINILESSON	WCPM
A (Grade K)	N/A	N/A
B (Grade 1)	1	Choral read
B (Grade 1)	2	20–35
B (Grade 1)	3	35–50
C (Grade 2)	1	50–65
C (Grade 2)	2	65–80
C (Grade 2)	3	80–95
D (Grade 3)	1	70–85
D (Grade 3)	2	85–100
D (Grade 3)	3	100–115
E (Grades 4)	1	95–105
E (Grades 4)	2	105–115
E (Grades 4)	3	115–125
F (Grade 5)	1	110–120
F (Grade 5)	2	120–130
F (Grade 5)	3	130–140

Adapted from Hasbrouck, Jan, and Gerald Tindal. 2005. "Oral Reading Fluency: 90 Years of Measurement." Web. 3 August 2015. http://eric.ed.gov/?id=ED531458.

Teachers can use the following routine with students individually or in student pairs. It is important to emphasize that learning to read fluently takes practice and that doing repeated readings and keeping track of reading times helps students see how their reading improves with practice. The goal of fluency practice is not to read fast, but to read accurately, at an appropriate rate, and with expression. Automaticity with print enables students to devote more mental energy to comprehension.

1. Introduce Timed Repeated Readings Tell students that today they will read a passage multiple times. Each time they read, they (or you) will keep track of how many words they read correctly in one minute. Say that you will time their reading for one minute. They will underline any words they don't know as they read. When the time is up, students will draw a line after the last word they read.

2. Measure Fluency After one minute, tell students that it is time to figure out how many words they read correctly. Show them how to use the numbers at the right of the passage to identify the total number of words they read. Then have them count the words they underlined. To figure out how many words they read correctly, tell students to take the total number of words they read and subtract the number of underlined words. For example, if their total is 65 words and they underlined 5 words, they will subtract 5 from 65. That means they read 60 words correct per minute (60 WCPM). Have students read the same selection three times and record their best score on their charts.

3. Track Progress Use the chart below to track fluency and especially to show students how repeated readings and practice in general improves their scores.

Fluency Progress Chart

Name ______________________________

115																														
110																														
105																														
100																														
95																														
90																														
85																														
80																														
75																														
70																														
65																														
60																														
55																														
50																														
45																														
40																														
35																														
30																														
25																														
20																														
	1	2	3	4	5	6	7	8	9	10	11	12	13	14	15	16	17	18	19	20	21	22	23	24	25	26	27	28	29	30

Building a Home-School Connection

Successful intervention is dependent on regular communication between teachers and students' parents or guardians. Sharing learning goals and expectations as well as any potential concerns is critical. Through clear, consistent, and regular communication, teachers can outline how they are working with students in class and what additional intervention instruction will address gaps in learning. They can share which techniques are most effective with each student and offer suggestions for how to expand learning gains to engage students outside the classroom. When teachers share clear expectations and regular progress updates, parents and guardians can better reinforce their student's learning while also offering their own questions and observations to guide further instruction. Shared knowledge is empowering—it gives parents and guardians more leverage as advocates for and contributors to their student's learning, both in recognizing and addressing concerns and in developing curious, enthusiastic, and motivated learners.

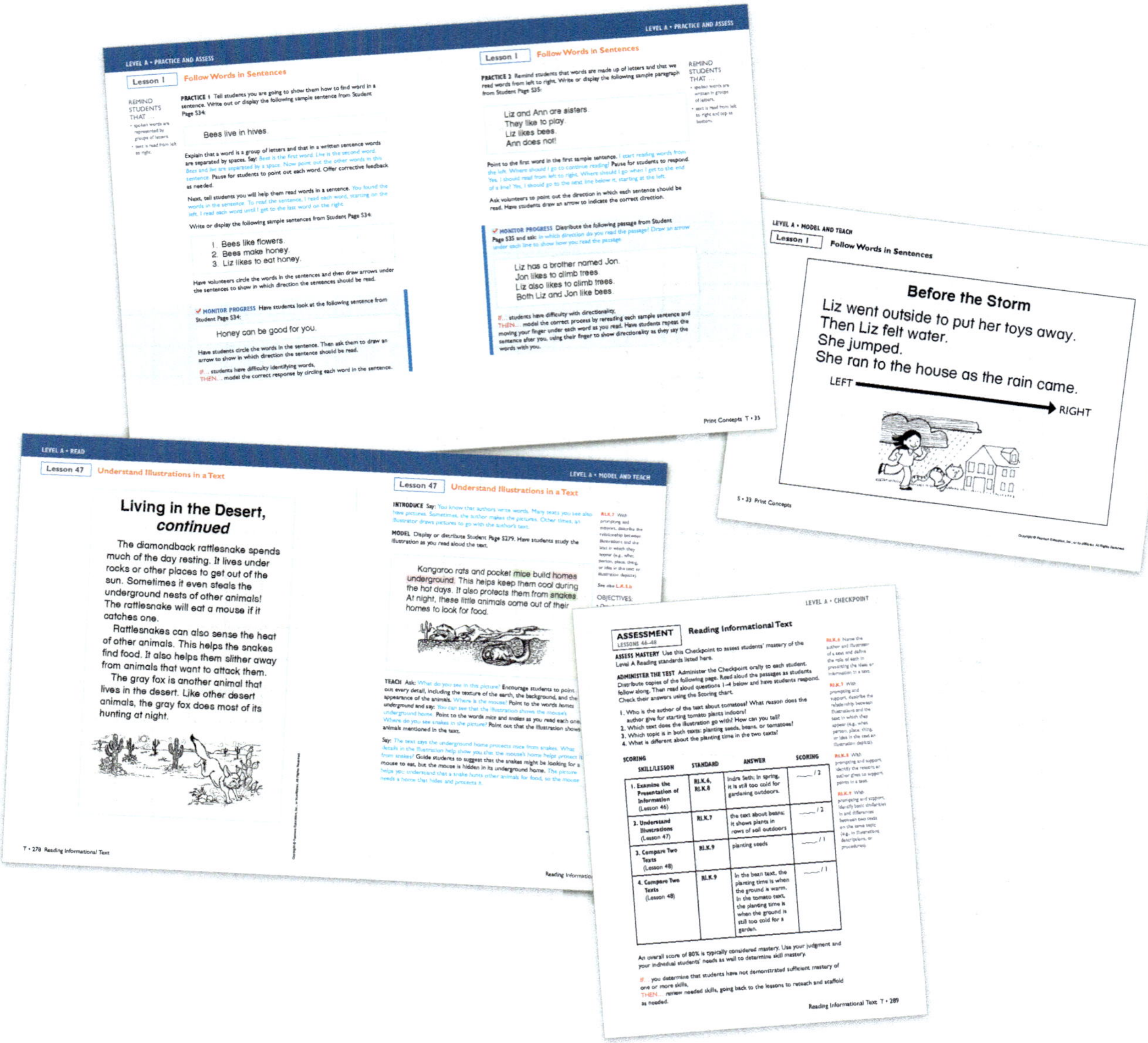

Understanding the Research Base

Effective, targeted intervention is research based in best-practices instruction. The more teachers understand the reasons for particular skills and strategies, the more effective they can be in facilitating student mastery of critical learning goals.

Developing a Research-Based Approach According to the Common Core State Standards, "no set of grade-specific standards can fully reflect the great variety in abilities, needs, learning rates, and achievement levels of students in any given classroom." Instead of being an isolated measure of grade-level proficiency, standards should be used as markers along the path to college and career readiness. The way students learn to read and develop critical thinking skills depends on many different factors, including age, primary language, cultural heritage, and experiences (*FirstSchool* 2014). To address the needs of all students, a curriculum must be flexible. The skill sequence should be progressive but integrated, with each grade's skills building on previous grade-level instruction. The sequence for each grade makes connections and prerequisites among skills clear, within and across grades, to make scaffolding and targeted intervention appropriately flexible and efficient.

To facilitate skills mastery, research supports a gradual release of responsibility. Teachers model first, and then they guide practice. Eventually students work in groups and then independently (Frey and Fisher 2011). This approach matches the common "I do it," "We do it," "You do it together," and "You do it alone" model for lessons (Fisher and Frey 2014).

Teaching Skills in Context Engaging and motivating context allows for effective reading instruction (Shanahan et al. 2010). When a skill is presented in context, students know exactly why they need to practice that particular skill and how that skill fits into general reading proficiency. Context, therefore, gives students a real-world example of the skill in practice and motivates students to engage in the lesson. All lessons in the program include a model passage or stimulus to anchor the lesson. This modeling reinforces the fact that literacy skills are in service to mastery of real-world texts and tasks.

Using Formative Assessment to Guide Intervention Instruction
Teachers use assessment to set goals for students, monitor progress toward those goals, give feedback on that progress, and adjust teaching as needed (Allal 2010). By observing how students respond to this ongoing formative assessment, teachers can adjust or focus activities in each lesson. Research shows that effective formative assessment strives to answer the questions *Where am I going? Where am I now?* and *Where to next?* (Frey and Fisher 2011). By answering these questions, students know exactly why they are being assessed, what skills they need to address to improve, and what skills they will need for future classroom work.

Understanding the Research Base: Bibliography

Allal, Linda. 2010. "Assessment and the Regulation of Learning." Penelope Peterson, Eva Baker, and Barry McGaw (Eds.), *International Encyclopedia of Education Vol. 3* (3rd ed.), 348–352. Oxford: Elsevier.

California Department of Education. 2014. *ELA/ELD Framework*. Sacramento, California: California Department of Education. Ch. 1, 33–34; Ch. 3, 39–40; Ch. 4; Ch. 5; Ch. 12, 16.

FirstSchool: Transforming PreK–3rd Grade for African American, Latino, and Low-Income Children. Ed. Ritchie, Sharon, and Laura Gutmann. 2014. New York: Teachers College Press.

Fisher, Douglas, and Nancy Frey. 2014. *Better Learning Through Structured Teaching: A Framework for the Gradual Release of Responsibility (Second Ed).* Alexandria, VA: ASCD.

Frey, Nancy, and Douglas Fisher. 2011. *The Formative Assessment Action Plan: Practical Steps to More Successful Teaching and Learning.* Alexandria, VA: ASCD.

Hudson, Roxanne. 2011. "Fluency Problems: When, Why, and How to Intervene." Rollanda E. O'Connor and Patricia F. Vadasy (Eds.), *Handbook of Reading Interventions,* 169–197. New York: Guilford.

National Association for the Education of Young Children. 2009. *Developmentally Appropriate Practice in Early Childhood Programs Serving Children from Birth Through Age 8.* Washington, D.C.: National Association for the Education of Young Children. 5-6.

National Governors Association Center for Best Practices and Council of Chief State School Officers. 2010. *Common Core State Standards for English Language Arts and Literacy in History/Social Studies, Science, and Technical Subjects.* Washington, DC: Authors. 6.

Shanahan, Timothy, K. Callison, C. Carriere, N. K. Duke, P. D. Pearson, C. Schatschneider, and J. Torgesen. 2010. *Improving Reading Comprehension in Kindergarten Through 3rd Grade: A Practice Guide* (NCEE 2010-4038). Washington, DC: National Center for Education Evaluation and Regional Assistance, Institute of Education Sciences, U.S. Department of Education.

FOUNDATIONAL SKILLS

PART 1

Lesson 1 Understand Sentences

RF.1.1.a Recognize the distinguishing features of a sentence (e.g., first word, capitalization, ending punctuation).

OBJECTIVES:

- Recognize that a sentence is a group of words that expresses a thought or question.
- Recognize that a sentence begins with a capitalized word and ends with a punctuation mark.

INTRODUCE Remind students of what they already know about sentences. A sentence is a group of words that says something or asks a question. Hold up a book that is open to a page with a sentence. Remember that we read words in a sentence from left to right.

Today we will learn more about sentences. A sentence always begins and ends the same way. Point to the first word in the sentence. It begins with a capital letter. Point to the punctuation mark at the end. It ends with a punctuation mark.

MODEL Display or share copies of the following passage, "Plants," from Student Page S33 and read it aloud. Point to each capital letter and punctuation mark as you read aloud.

Plants

Begins with a capital letter

Do all plants need water?
Yes.
But plants are different.
Some plants need a little water.
Some need a lot.

Ends with a punctuation mark

TEACH Point to the first letter in each sentence. The first word in every sentence is capitalized.

Point to the punctuation mark at the end of each sentence. Every sentence ends with a punctuation mark.

Point to the question mark. A sentence that asks a question ends with a question mark. This sentence asks if all plants need water.

Point to the periods. A sentence that says something ends in a period. These sentences answer the question and give us more information. They tell us that different plants need different amounts of water.

Lesson 1

Understand Sentences

REMIND STUDENTS THAT...

- sentences begin with a capital letter.

PRACTICE 1 Remind students that sentences are groups of words that tell or ask about something. The first word in a sentence is always capitalized. Then write or display the following passage from Student Page S34.

All plants need water.
So how can a plant live in a dry place?
How does it get the water it needs?

Read aloud the first sentence with students. Point to the word *All* and underline it. *All* is the first word in the sentence. It starts with a capital *A*. Circle the capital.

Read aloud the second sentence. What is the first word in this sentence? Pause for students to respond. Yes, the first word is *So*. Underline it. Show me the capital letter. Ask a volunteer to circle it.

Read aloud the last sentence with students. What is the first word in this sentence? Ask a volunteer to underline it. Show me the capital letter. Ask another volunteer to circle it.

✔ **MONITOR PROGRESS** Distribute the following passage from Student Page S34. Have students underline the first word in the sentence and circle the capital letter.

A cactus is a kind of plant that lives in a dry place.
It needs little water.
Why?
A cactus can store water inside.
It can live a long time with no water.

IF...students have difficulty recognizing that sentences begin with a capitalized word,
THEN...briefly review distinguishing between capital and lowercase letters by writing the lowercase and uppercase form of several letters and modeling identifying the capital letter.

Lesson 1 Understand Sentences

PRACTICE 2 Remind students that sentences always end with a punctuation mark. Then write or display the following passage from Student Page S35.

> Can you have a cactus at home?
> Yes, you can.
> Some people have many at home.
> Will you get one?
> Before you do, learn how to look after it.

Read aloud the first sentence. Does this sentence tell about something or ask something? Give students a moment to respond. Right, it asks a question. Circle the question mark. A question mark is one type of punctuation mark. We use it at the end of sentences that ask a question.

Read aloud the next sentence. Does this sentence tell about something or ask something? Pause for students to respond. Right, it tells something. It answers the question. Circle the period. A period is another type of punctuation mark. We use it at the end of sentences that tell about something. Repeat the process with the other sentences.

REMIND STUDENTS THAT...

- sentences end with a punctuation mark.
- sentences express a thought or ask a question.

✓ MONITOR PROGRESS Distribute the following passage from Student Page S35. Have students identify whether each sentence is a question or statement. Then have them circle the punctuation mark at the end of the sentence.

> Can you look after my cactus?
> Do not put it in a dark and cold place.
> Put it someplace warm.
> Do not give it so much water.
> It can rot.

IF...students have difficulty recognizing that sentences end with a punctuation mark,
THEN...write a short sentence twice, once with a punctuation mark and once without it, and model choosing the sentence that ends with a punctuation mark.

Lesson 1 Understand Sentences

REMIND STUDENTS THAT...

- the first word in a sentence is always capitalized.
- sentences end with a punctuation mark.
- sentences express a thought or ask a question.

PRACTICE 3 Remind students that sentences express a thought or ask a question. We will look at sentences with mistakes in capitalization or punctuation. Write or display the following passage from Student Page S36.

> is a place with a lot of water good for plants
> No.
> So much water can be bad.
> some plants have many ways to live in wet places
> these plants try not to take in some of the water.
> The plants are waxy.
> so some water falls off

Read aloud the first sentence. How do all sentences begin? Right, all sentences begin with a capital letter. Does this sentence begin with a capital letter? No. Circle the error and write a capital *I* above it.

How do all sentences end? Right, all sentences end with a punctuation mark. Does the first sentence end with a punctuation mark? No. Model choosing the correct punctuation mark. Do I use a period or a question mark? If the sentence is telling about something, I use a period. If it is asking a question, I use a question mark. Reread the sentence. This sentence is a question. I need to use a question mark. Write a question mark at the end of the sentence. Guide students to identify the remaining errors.

✓ **INDEPENDENT PRACTICE** Have students write two short sentences or display the following sentences from Student Page S36. Have them work with partners and use the checklist below to identify any errors in partners' sentences.

> i water my plants.
> They like water
> My brother likes plants
> Will he water my plants

Checklist:
✓ Does the sentence begin with a capital letter?
✓ Does the sentence end with a punctuation mark?
✓ Do questions end with question marks?

IF...students have difficulty identifying the errors,
THEN...model finding the errors with another sample sentence.

Lesson 1 **Understand Sentences**

Plants

Do all plants need water?
Yes.
But plants are different.
Some plants need a little water.
Some need a lot.

Lesson 1 Understand Sentences

All plants need water.
So how can a plant live in a dry place?
How does it get the water it needs?

A cactus is a kind of plant that lives in a dry place.
It needs little water.
Why?
A cactus can store water inside.
It can live a long time with no water.

Lesson 1 Understand Sentences

Can you have a cactus at home?
Yes, you can.
Some people have many at home.
Will you get one?
Before you do, learn how to look after it.

Can you look after my cactus?
Do not put it in a dark and cold place.
Put it someplace warm.
Do not give it so much water.
It can rot.

Lesson 1 Understand Sentences

is a place with a lot of water good for plants
No.
So much water can be bad.
some plants have many ways to live in wet places
these plants try not to take in some of the water.
The plants are waxy.
so some water falls off

i water my plants.
They like water
My brother likes plants
Will he water my plants

ASSESSMENT
LESSON 1

Print Concepts

ASSESS MASTERY Use this Checkpoint to assess students' mastery of the features of a sentence.

ADMINISTER THE TEST Display or print copies of p. T38, and administer the Checkpoint to each student. For each item, model the process and have students respond. Record responses on the scoring chart below.

1. Understand Sentences: Correct Beginning (Lesson 1)
MODEL: I will show you three sentences. You tell me if each sentence has the correct beginning. If the sentence begins with a capital letter, say *yes*. If it does not, say *no*.

2. Understand Sentences: Correct Punctuation (Lesson 1)
MODEL: I will show you three sentences. You tell me if each sentence has the correct punctuation. If the sentence ends with the correct punctuation mark, say *yes*. If it does not, say *no*.

3. Understand Sentences: Correct Parts of a Sentence (Lesson 1)
MODEL: I will show you three sentences. You tell me if each sentence has all the correct parts. If the sentence begins with a capital letter and ends with the correct punctuation, say *yes*. If it does not, say *no*.

RF.1.1.a Recognize the distinguishing features of a sentence (e.g., first word, capitalization, ending punctuation).

SCORING

SKILL/LESSON	SCORE
1. Understand Sentences (Lesson 1) this is a pine tree. (no) it is big! (no) Can you see the top of it? (yes)	_____ / 3
2. Understand Sentences (Lesson 1) Are you hot (no) We can sit in the shade. (yes) Where is a big tree (no)	_____ / 3
3. Understand Sentences (Lesson 1) Did you water the plant? (yes) The plant can dry up (no) its color can fade. (no)	_____ / 3

An overall score of 80% correct is typically considered mastery. Use your judgment and your individual students' needs as well to determine skill mastery.

IF... you determine that students have not demonstrated sufficient mastery of one or more skills,
THEN... review the skill(s), going back to the lessons to reteach as needed.

ASSESSMENT
LESSON 1

Print Concepts

this is a pine tree.
it is big!
Can you see the top of it?

Are you hot
We can sit in the shade.
Where is a big tree

Did you water the plant?
The plant can dry up
its color can fade.

Lesson 2 Identify Short *a, i,* and *o*

INTRODUCE Present the topic. Today we will listen to the middle sounds in words. We will practice hearing three sounds: /ă/, /ĭ/, and /ŏ/.

MODEL Display and read aloud "The Rock Pit" from Student Page S39. This passage has words that have the same beginning sound, /p/, and the same ending sound, /t/. Their middle sounds are different. Listen as I say the words: *Pat, pit,* and *pot.*

RF.1.2.a Distinguish long from short vowel sounds in spoken single-syllable words.

OBJECTIVE:
- Identify short *a, i,* and *o* in spoken words.

The Rock Pit

Short *a* sound
Short *i* sound
Short *o* sound

Pat has a pit.
She dumps a pot of rocks in the pit.
The rock pit is cool and deep.
In the pit, the rocks drop down, down, down.

middle sound /ă/	middle sound /ĭ/	middle sound /ŏ/
Pat	pit	pot

TEACH Point to the annotations on the text. I will say each word slowly. After I say a word, we will say the word together slowly. Listen for the sound in the middle. The first word is *Pat.* Draw out the vowel as you say the word. Say it with me slowly: /p//ă//t/. The middle sound is /ă/.

The next word is *pit.* Say the sounds slowly with me: /p//ĭ//t/. What is the middle sound? Pause. Yes, the middle sound is /ĭ/. Now listen to the third word: *pot.* Say the sounds slowly with me: /p//ŏ//t/. What is the middle sound? Pause. Yes, the middle sound is /ŏ/.

We know other words with these middle sounds. For example, the words *hat, bat,* and *sat* have the middle sound /ă/. What other words do you know with that sound? Pause for responses. The middle sound /ĭ/ is in the words *kid, sit,* and *win.* What are some other words with /ĭ/? Pause for responses. What are some words you know with the /ŏ/ sound like the one in *pot* and *rock*? Invite responses.

Lesson 2 Identify Short *a, i,* and *o*

REMIND STUDENTS THAT...

- words are made up of different sounds.
- they can hear the middle sound in a word by saying the word slowly.

PRACTICE 1 First, model listening for a middle phoneme. I am going to say a word very slowly so I can hear its middle sound. Listen with me: *cap*. I will say the sounds in the word: /k/ (pause) /ă/ (pause) /p/. The middle sound is /ă/.

Now listen as I slowly say another word. Listen for the middle sound: /k//ă//t/. The word is *cat*. It has the same middle sound as *cap*.

I will say one more word. Listen for the middle sound: *cape*, /k//ā//p/. Does it have the same middle sound as *cap* and *cat*? Pause for responses. No, it has a different middle sound. Only *cap* and *cat* have the middle sound /ă/.

I will say two words. You tell me if the middle sounds are /ă/ in both words, or if the middle sounds are different. Guide practice using the following word pairs from Student Page S40.

tan, tab (same)	pet, pat (different)
mad, made (different)	clap, snap (same)
man, pal (same)	van, vane (different)
sat, sad (same)	nap, nab (same)
back, bake (different)	plan, plaid (same)
snuck, snack (different)	ran, rack (same)

✔ **MONITOR PROGRESS** Read each set of three words from Student Page S40. Have students tell you which word has the middle /ă/ sound.

<u>pat</u>, pet, pit	snip, <u>snap</u>, snake
pale, pull, <u>pal</u>	<u>bat</u>, hut, not
fist, fade, <u>fast</u>	gate, game, <u>gab</u>

IF... students have trouble identifying the word with the middle /ă/ sound,
THEN... slowly say the sounds in each word and have students repeat after you. Isolate the middle sound in each word to help students pinpoint the one with the middle /ă/ sound.

Lesson 2 Identify Short *a, i,* and *o*

PRACTICE 2 First, model listening for a middle phoneme. I am going to say a word very slowly so I can hear its middle sound. Listen with me: *did.* I will say the sounds in the word: /d/ (pause) /ĭ/ (pause) /d/. The middle sound is /ĭ/.

Now listen as I slowly say another word. Listen for the middle sound: /k//ĭ//t/. The word is *kit.* It has the same middle sound as *did.*

I will say one more word. Listen for the middle sound: *kite,* /k//ī//t. Does it have the same middle sound as *did* and *kit?* Pause for responses. No, it has a different middle sound. Only *did* and *kid* have the middle sound /ĭ/.

I will say two words. You tell me if the middle sounds are /ĭ/ in both words, or if the middle sounds are different. Guide practice using the following word pairs from Student Page S41.

tick, bill (same)	wet, with (different)
fit, fight (different)	sick, sit (same)
pin, him (same)	clip, vine (different)
pitch, tip (same)	fish, fill (same)
dim, dime (different)	wrist, rib (same)
zip, swipe (different)	give, gift (same)

REMIND STUDENTS THAT…

- words are made up of different sounds.
- they can hear the middle sound in a word by saying the word slowly.

✔ **MONITOR PROGRESS** Read each set of three words from Student Page S41. Have students tell you which word has the middle /ĭ/ sound.

put, pot, <u>pit</u>	<u>flip</u>, flap, fly	<u>fin</u>, fan, fun
pal, <u>pill</u>, pile	<u>hit</u>, hut, hot	rhyme, room, <u>rim</u>

IF… students have trouble identifying the word with the middle /ĭ/ sound, THEN… slowly say the sounds in each word and have students repeat after you. Isolate the middle sound in each word to help students pinpoint the one with the middle /ĭ/ sound.

Lesson 2 Identify Short *a, i,* and *o*

REMIND STUDENTS THAT...

- words are made up of different sounds.
- they can hear the middle sound in a word by saying the word slowly.

PRACTICE 3 First, model listening for a middle phoneme. I am going to say a word very slowly so I can hear its middle sound. Listen with me: *not.* I will say the sounds in the word: /n/ (pause) /ŏ/ (pause) /t/. The middle sound is /ŏ/.

Now listen as I slowly say another word. Listen for the middle sound: /k//ŏ//t/. The word is *cot.* It has the same middle sound as *not.*

I will say one more word. Listen for the middle sound: *coat,* /k//ō//t. Does it have the same middle sound as *not* and *cot?* Pause for responses. No, it has a different middle sound. Only *not* and *cot* have the middle sound /ŏ/.

I will say two words. You tell me if the middle sounds are /ŏ/ in both words, or if the middle sounds are different. Guide practice using the following word pairs from Student Page S42.

pop, pod (same)	tot, told (different)
hop, hope (different)	sock, sob (same)
not, knock (same)	job, joke (different)
mop, job (same)	dot, hop (same)
batch, botch (different)	shop, doll (same)
stop, stole (different)	knot, flop (same)

✔ **INDEPENDENT PRACTICE** Read each set of three words from Student Page S42. Have individual students identify which word has the middle /ŏ/ sound.

pat, <u>pot</u>, pit	<u>clock</u>, click, cloak
<u>lots</u>, loots, likes	moat, <u>mom</u>, map
tape, type, <u>top</u>	<u>rod</u>, red, road

IF... students have trouble identifying the word with the middle /ŏ/ sound, THEN... slowly say the sounds in each word and have students repeat after you. Isolate the middle sound in each word to help students pinpoint the one with the middle /ŏ/ sound.

Lesson 2 **Identify Short *a*, *i*, and *o***

The Rock Pit

Pat has a pit.
She dumps a pot of rocks in the pit.
The rock pit is cool and deep.
In the pit, the rocks drop down, down, down.

middle sound /ă/ Pat	**middle sound /ĭ/ pit**	**middle sound /ŏ/ pot**

Teacher: This Student Page is intended as an *optional extension* of the lesson. After teaching the phonological awareness lesson orally, you can distribute or display this page to connect the phonological awareness skills (sounds) to phonics skills (sound-spelling).

Lesson 2 Identify Short *a*, *i*, and *o*

tan, tab	pet, pat
mad, made	clap, snap
man, pal	van, vane
sat, sad	nap, nab
back, bake	plan, plaid
snuck, snack	ran, rack

pat, pet, pit	snip, snap, snake
pale, pull, pal	bat, hut, not
fist, fade, fast	gate, game, gab

Teacher: This Student Page is intended as an *optional extension* of the lesson. After teaching the phonological awareness lesson orally, you can distribute or display this page to connect the phonological awareness skills (sounds) to phonics skills (sound-spelling).

Lesson 2 Identify Short *a*, *i*, and *o*

tick, bill	wet, with
fit, fight	sick, sit
pin, him	clip, vine
pitch, tip	fish, fill
dim, dime	wrist, rib
zip, swipe	give, gift

put, pot, pit	flip, flap, fly	fin, fan, fun
pal, pill, pile	hit, hut, hot	rhyme, room, rim

Teacher: This Student Page is intended as an *optional extension* of the lesson. After teaching the phonological awareness lesson orally, you can distribute or display this page to connect the phonological awareness skills (sounds) to phonics skills (sound-spelling).

Lesson 2 Identify Short *a*, *i*, and *o*

pop, pod	tot, told
hop, hope	sock, sob
not, knock	job, joke
mop, job	dot, hop
batch, botch	shop, doll
stop, stole	knot, flop

pat, pot, pit	clock, click, cloak
lots, loots, likes	moat, mom, map
tape, type, top	rod, red, road

Teacher: This Student Page is intended as an *optional extension* of the lesson. After teaching the phonological awareness lesson orally, you can distribute or display this page to connect the phonological awareness skills (sounds) to phonics skills (sound-spelling).

Lesson 3 Identify Short e and *u*

RF.1.2.a Distinguish long from short vowel sounds in spoken single-syllable words.

OBJECTIVES:

- Identify short e in spoken words.
- Identify two pronunciations of short *u* in spoken words.

INTRODUCE Present the topic. Today we will listen to the middle sounds in words. We will practice hearing three sounds: /ĕ/, /ŭ/, and /o͝o/.

MODEL Read aloud "The Bench" from Student Page S43. This passage has words that have similar beginning and ending sounds. Their middle sounds are different, though. Listen as I say the words: *bench, brush, bush.*

The Bench

Let's sit on the bench. — Short e sound
It is the bench next to the big bush.
Look!
Someone painted the bench red!
The painters left behind a brush. — Short *u* sound

middle sound /ĕ/	middle sound /ŭ/	middle sound /o͝o/
bench	brush	bush

TEACH If you wish, display Student Page S43. Gesture to the displayed chart. I will say each word slowly. After I say a word, we will say the word together *very* slowly. Listen for the sound in the middle. The first word is *bench*. Draw out the vowel as you say the word. Say it with me slowly: /b//ĕ//n//ch/. The middle sound is /ĕ/.

We know other words with this middle sound. For example, the words *get, pet,* and *wet* have the middle sound /ĕ/. What other words do you know with that sound? Invite responses.

The next word is *brush*. Say the sounds slowly with me: /b//r//ŭ//sh/. What is the middle sound? Pause. Yes, the middle sound is /ŭ/.

We know other words with this middle sound. For example, the words *run, fun,* and *sun* have the middle sound /ŭ/. What are some other words you know with the /ŭ/ sound in the middle? Invite responses.

The last word is *bush*. Say the sounds with me: /b//o͝o//sh/. The middle sound is /o͝o/. You can hear the same middle sound, /o͝o/, in the words *wood, hoof,* and *pull*.

Lesson 3 Identify Short *e* and *u*

REMIND STUDENTS THAT...

- words are made up of different sounds.
- they can hear the middle sound in a word by saying the word slowly.

PRACTICE 1 First, model listening for a middle phoneme. I am going to say a word very slowly so I can hear its middle sound. Listen with me: *bed*. I will say the sounds in the word: /b/ (pause) /ĕ/ (pause) /d/. The middle sound is /ĕ/.

Now listen as I slowly say another word. Listen for the middle sound: /b//ĕ//s//t/. The word is *best*. It has the same middle sound as *bed*.

I will say one more word. Listen for the middle sound: *beast*, /b//ē//s//t/. Does it have the same middle sound as *bed* and *best*? Pause for responses. No, it has a different middle sound. Only *bed* and *best* have the middle sound /ĕ/.

I will say two words. You tell me if the middle sounds are /ĕ/ in both words, or if the middle sounds are different. Guide practice using the following word pairs from Student Page S44.

ten, tell (same)	peck, peek (different)
red, reed (different)	pep, kept (same)
bet, bend (same)	head, said (same)
shell, shack (different)	next, press (same)
men, pen (same)	steep, step (different)
fell, feel (different)	vest, chest (same)

✔ **MONITOR PROGRESS** Read each set of three words from Student Page S44. Have students tell you which word has the middle /ĕ/ sound.

seat, <u>set</u>, sit	<u>belt</u>, bean, bank
puck, <u>peck</u>, peak	<u>let</u>, lot, loot
will, wheel, <u>well</u>	neat, not, <u>net</u>

IF... students have trouble identifying the word with the middle /ĕ/ sound, THEN... slowly say the sounds in each word and have students repeat after you. Isolate the middle sound in each word to help students pinpoint the one with the middle /ĕ/ sound.

Lesson 3 Identify Short *e* and *u*

PRACTICE 2 First, model listening for a middle phoneme. I am going to say a word very slowly so I can hear its middle sound. Listen with me: *cup*. I will say the sounds in the word: /k/ (pause) /ŭ/ (pause) /p/. The middle sound is /ŭ/.

Now listen as I slowly say another word. Listen for the middle sound: /k//ŭ//t/. The word is *cut*. It has the same middle sound as *cup*.

I will say one more word. Listen for the middle sound: *cute*, /k//ū//t/. Does it have the same middle sound as *cup* and *cut*? Pause for responses. No, it has a different middle sound. Only *cup* and *cut* have the middle sound /ŭ/.

I will say two words. You tell me if the middle sounds are /ŭ/ in both words, or if the middle sounds are different. Guide practice using the following word pairs from Student Page S45.

bun, cub (same)	jet, jut (different)
tube, tub (different)	rush, club (same)
run, plum (same)	puff, poof (different)
fluff, flood (same)	just, tuck (same)
tough, suit (different)	hunch, lunch (same)
look, luck (different)	tub, glove (same)

REMIND STUDENTS THAT...

- words are made up of different sounds.
- they can hear the middle sound in a word by saying the word slowly.

✓ **MONITOR PROGRESS** Read each set of three words from Student Page S45. Have students tell you which word has the middle /ŭ/ sound.

root, rat, <u>rut</u>	<u>plug</u>, pond, prove
<u>gust</u>, goose, guest	bat, <u>hut</u>, not
duke, <u>duck</u>, deck	you, <u>young</u>, yell

IF... students have trouble identifying the word with the middle /ŭ/ sound, THEN... slowly say the sounds in each word and have students repeat after you. Isolate the middle sound in each word to help students pinpoint the one with the middle /ŭ/ sound.

Lesson 3 Identify Short *e* and *u*

REMIND STUDENTS THAT...

- words are made up of different sounds.
- they can hear the middle sound in a word by saying the word slowly.

PRACTICE 3 Focus on the /o͝o/ sound in *full* and *look*. I am going to say the word *look* very slowly so I can hear its middle sound. Listen: /l/ (pause) /o͝o/ (pause) /k/. The middle sound is /o͝o/.

Now listen as I slowly say the word *full*. Listen for the middle sound: /f/ /o͝o/ /l/. The word is *full*. It has the same middle sound as *look*.

I will say one more word. Listen for the middle sound: *fool*, /f/ /o͞o/ /l/. Does it have the same middle sound as *look* and *full*? Listen closely as I say the words again: *look, full, fool*. Pause for responses. No, *fool* has a different middle sound. Only *look* and *full* have the middle sound /o͝o/.

I will say two words. You tell me if the middle sounds are /o͝o/ in both words, or if the middle sounds are different. Guide practice using the following word pairs from Student Page S46.

hoof, look (same)	talk, took (different)
shoot, should (different)	nook, put (same)
could, good (same)	bull, book (same)
shook, new (different)	foot, hood (same)
pull, cook (same)	wood, food (different)

✔ **INDEPENDENT PRACTICE** Read each set of three words from Student Page S46. Have individual students identify which word has the middle /o͝o/ sound.

<u>put</u>, pot, pat	<u>book</u>, boot, but
<u>crook</u>, croak, crock	step, <u>stood</u>, slid
luck, <u>look</u>, lick	<u>push</u>, pest, posh
<u>good</u>, grunt, gum	crash, bash, <u>bush</u>

IF... students have trouble identifying the word with the middle /o͝o/ sound, THEN... slowly say the sounds in each word and have students repeat after you. Isolate the middle sound in each word to help students pinpoint the one with the middle /o͝o/ sound.

Lesson 3 **Identify Short *e* and *u***

The Bench

Let's sit on the bench.
It is the bench next to the big bush.
Look!
Someone painted the bench red!
The painters left behind a brush.

middle sound /ĕ/	middle sound /ŭ/	middle sound /o͝o/
	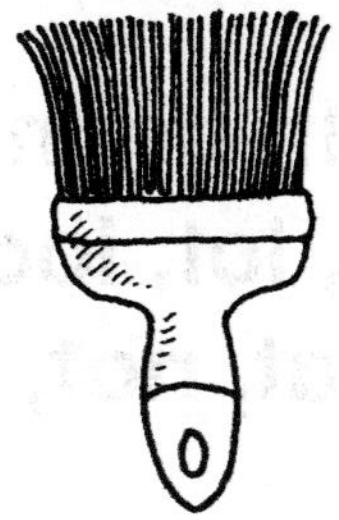	

Teacher: This Student Page is intended as an *optional extension* of the lesson. After teaching the phonological awareness lesson orally, you can distribute or display this page to connect the phonological awareness skills (sounds) to phonics skills (sound-spelling).

Lesson 3 Identify Short e and *u*

ten, tell	**peck, peek**
red, reed	**pep, kept**
bet, bend	**head, said**
shell, shack	**next, press**
men, pen	**steep, step**
fell, feel	**vest, chest**

seat, set, sit	**belt, bean, bank**
puck, peck, peak	**let, lot, loot**
will, wheel, well	**neat, not, net**

Teacher: This Student Page is intended as an *optional extension* of the lesson. After teaching the phonological awareness lesson orally, you can distribute or display this page to connect the phonological awareness skills (sounds) to phonics skills (sound-spelling).

Lesson 3 Identify Short e and *u*

bun, cub	jet, jut
tube, tub	rush, club
run, plum	puff, poof
fluff, flood	just, tuck
tough, suit	hunch, lunch
look, luck	tub, glove

root, rat, rut	plug, pond, prove
gust, goose, guest	bat, hut, not
duke, duck, deck	you, young, yell

Teacher: This Student Page is intended as an *optional extension* of the lesson. After teaching the phonological awareness lesson orally, you can distribute or display this page to connect the phonological awareness skills (sounds) to phonics skills (sound-spelling).

Lesson 3 Identify Short e and *u*

hoof, look
shoot, should
could, good
shook, new
pull, cook

talk, took
nook, put
bull, book
foot, hood
wood, food

put, pot, pat
crook, croak, crock
luck, look, lick
good, grunt, gum

book, boot, but
step, stood, slid
push, pest, posh
crash, bash, bush

Teacher: This Student Page is intended as an *optional extension* of the lesson. After teaching the phonological awareness lesson orally, you can distribute or display this page to connect the phonological awareness skills (sounds) to phonics skills (sound-spelling).

ASSESSMENT
LESSONS 2–3

Phonological Awareness

ASSESS MASTERY Use this Checkpoint to assess students' mastery of the short *a*, *i*, *o*, e, and *u* sounds.

RF.1.2.a Distinguish long from short vowel sounds in spoken single-syllable words.

ADMINISTER THE TEST Administer the Checkpoint orally to each student. For each item, model the process as described, and then have the student use the process to respond to your prompts. Record responses on the scoring chart on the facing page.

1. Identify Short *a*, *i*, and *o* (Lesson 2)

MODEL: Listen for the sounds /ă/, /ĭ/, and /ŏ/ in words. I will give you a sound. Then I will say two words. You will tell me which word has the sound I gave. For example, if I say /ă/, *plate*, *pat*, you would say *pat* because *pat* has the /ă/ sound.

ASSESS:	/ă/: man, main	/ĭ/: rhyme, rim	/ŏ/: got, goat

2. Identify Short *a*, *i*, and *o* (Lesson 2)

MODEL: Listen for the sounds /ă/, /ĭ/, and /ŏ/ in words. I will give you a sound. Then I will say three words. You will tell me which word has the sound I gave. For example, if I say /ŏ/, *not*, *nose*, *note*, you would say *not* because *not* has the /ŏ/ sound.

ASSESS:	/ĭ/: fight, fin, fine	/ŏ/: joke, job, join	/ă/: tail, take, tan

3. Identify Short e and *u* (Lesson 3)

MODEL: Listen for the sounds /ĕ/, /ŭ/, and /o͝o/ in words. I will give you a sound. Then I will say two words. You will tell me which word has the sound I gave. For example, if I say /ĕ/, *men*, *mean*, you would say *men* because *men* has the /ĕ/ sound.

ASSESS:	/ĕ/: red, read	/ŭ/: gloom, glum	/o͝o/: broke, brook

4. Identify Short e and *u* (Lesson 3)

MODEL: Listen for the sounds /ĕ/, /ŭ/, and /o͝o/ in words. I will give you a sound. Then I will say three words. You will tell me which word has the sound I gave. For example, if I say /ŭ/, *soon*, *sun*, *song*, you would say *sun* because *sun* has the /ŭ/ sound.

ASSESS:	/o͝o/: cool, cook, cone
	/ĕ/: led, lead, lean
	/ŭ/: boom, bun, bone

ASSESSMENT
LESSONS 2–3

Phonological Awareness

SCORING

SKILL/LESSON	SCORE
1. Identify Short *a*, *i*, and *o* (Lesson 2) /ă/: man /ĭ/: rim /ŏ/: got	_____ / 3
2. Identify Short *a*, *i*, and *o* (Lesson 2) /ĭ/: fin /ŏ/: job /ă/: tan	_____ / 3
3. Identify Short e and *u* (Lesson 3) /ĕ/: red /ŭ/: glum /o͝o/: brook	_____ / 3
4. Identify Short e and *u* (Lesson 3) /o͝o/: cook /ĕ/: led /ŭ/: bun	_____ / 3

An overall score of 80% correct is typically considered mastery. Use your judgment and your individual students' needs as well to determine skill mastery.

IF…you determine that students have not demonstrated sufficient mastery of one or more skills,
THEN… review the skill(s), going back to the lessons to reteach and scaffold as needed.

Lesson 4 Identify Long *a*, *i*, and *o*

INTRODUCE Present the topic. Today we will listen to the middle sounds in words. We will practice hearing three sounds: /ā/, /ī/, and /ō/.

MODEL Read aloud "Kate's Party" from Student Page S49. This passage has words that have the same beginning sound, /k/. Their middle sounds are different, though. Listen as I say the words: *cake, kite, cone.*

Kate's Party

My sister Kate is having a party.
Our dad makes a big white cake.
Our mom brings ice cream, and she hands us a cone.
I bring a kite. It's a gift for Kate!

Long *a* sound

Long *o* sound

Long *i* sound

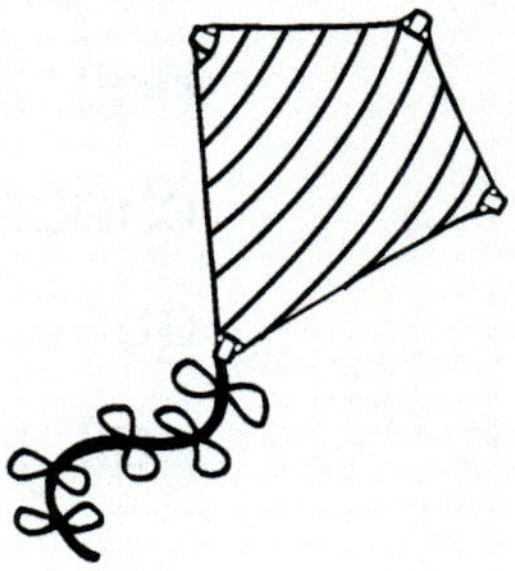

middle sound /ā/	middle sound /ī/	middle sound /ō/
cake	kite	cone

TEACH If you wish, display Student Page S49. I will say each word slowly. After I say a word, we will say the word together slowly. Listen for the sound in the middle. The first word is *cake.* Draw out the vowel as you say the word. Say it with me slowly: /k//ā//k/. The middle sound is /ā/.

The next word is *cone.* Say the sounds slowly with me: /k//ō//n/. What is the middle sound? Pause. Yes, the middle sound is /ō/: *cone.* Now listen to the third word: *kite.* Say the sounds slowly with me: /k//ī//t/. What is the middle sound? Pause. Yes, the middle sound is /ī/.

We know other words with these middle sounds. For example, the words *bake, shade,* and *tame* have the middle sound /ā/. What other words do you know with that sound? Pause for responses. What are some words you know with the /ō/ sound like the one in *boat* and *cold?* Invite responses. The middle sound /ī/ is in the words *bike, time,* and *light.* What are some other words with /ī/? Pause for responses.

RF.1.2.a Distinguish long from short vowel sounds in spoken single-syllable words.

OBJECTIVE:

- Identify long *a, i,* and *o* in spoken words.

Lesson 4 Identify Long *a*, *i*, and *o*

REMIND STUDENTS THAT...

- words are made up of different sounds.
- they can hear the middle sound in a word by saying the word slowly.

PRACTICE 1 First, model listening for a middle phoneme. I am going to say a word very slowly so I can hear its middle sound. Listen with me: *cave*. I will say the sounds in the word: /k/ (pause) /ā/ (pause) /v/. The middle sound is /ā/.

Now listen as I slowly say another word. Listen for the middle sound: /m//ā//k/. The word is *make*. It has the same middle sound as *cave*.

I will say one more word. Listen for the middle sound: *mask*, /m//ă//sk/. Does it have the same middle sound as *cave* and *make*? Pause for responses. No, it has a different middle sound. Only *cave* and *make* have the middle sound /ā/.

I will say two words. You tell me if the middle sounds are /ā/ in both words, or if the middle sounds are different. Guide practice using the following word pairs from Student Page S50.

save, shake (same)	clam, blame (different)
rain, ran (different)	date, face (same)
plate, brave (same)	hail, have (different)
tail, sail (same)	chase, that (different)
lean, lane (different)	quail, stain (same)
wake, wall (different)	pail, pace (same)

✔ **MONITOR PROGRESS** Read each set of three words from Student Page S50. Have students tell you which word has the middle /ā/ sound.

dot, <u>daze</u>, dug	<u>snake</u>, snuck, snack
pump, pig, <u>page</u>	<u>bait</u>, bat, bite
brag, bright, <u>break</u>	gas, <u>game</u>, glow

IF... students have trouble identifying the word with the middle /ā/ sound, THEN... slowly say the sounds in each word and have students repeat after you. Isolate the middle sound in each word to help students pinpoint the one with the middle /ā/ sound.

Lesson 4 Identify Long *a, i,* and *o*

PRACTICE 2 First, model listening for a middle phoneme. I am going to say a word very slowly so I can hear its middle sound. Listen with me: *side.* I will say the sounds in the word: /s/ (pause) /ī/ (pause) /d/. The middle sound is /ī/.

Now listen as I slowly say another word. Listen for the middle sound: /b/ /ī/ /t/. The word is *bite.* It has the same middle sound as *side.*

I will say one more word. Listen for the middle sound: *tip,* /t/ /ĭ/ /p/. Does it have the same middle sound as *side* and *bite?* Pause for responses. No, it has a different middle sound. Only *side* and *bite* have the middle sound /ī/.

I will say two words. You tell me if the middle sounds are /ī/ in both words, or if the middle sounds are different. Guide practice using the following word pairs from Student Page S51.

tide, tried (same)	fine, fin (different)
fit, flight (different)	sign, ripe (same)
pile, child (same)	cliff, climb (different)
nice, dime (same)	rhyme, rice (same)
guide, gift (different)	height, slight (same)
sweet, swipe (different)	pride, price (same)

REMIND STUDENTS THAT...

- words are made up of different sounds.
- they can hear the middle sound in a word by saying the word slowly.

✔ **MONITOR PROGRESS** Read each set of three words from Student Page S51. Have students tell you which word has the middle /ī/ sound.

limb, him, <u>like</u>	from, <u>fright</u>, frame
bond, <u>bind</u>, bin	<u>nine</u>, none, nail
<u>mild</u>, mint, milk	van, vim, <u>vine</u>

IF... students have trouble identifying the word with the middle /ī/ sound, THEN... slowly say the sounds in each word and have students repeat after you. Isolate the middle sound in each word to help students pinpoint the one with the middle /ī/ sound.

Lesson 4 Identify Long *a, i,* and *o*

REMIND STUDENTS THAT...

- words are made up of different sounds.
- they can hear the middle sound in a word by saying the word slowly.

PRACTICE 3 First, model listening for a middle phoneme. I am going to say a word very slowly so I can hear its middle sound. Listen with me: *soap*. I will say the sounds in the word: /s/ (pause) /ō/ (pause) /p/. The middle sound is /ō/.

Now listen as I slowly say another word. Listen for the middle sound: /r//ō//d/. The word is *road*. It has the same middle sound as *soap*.

I will say one more word. Listen for the middle sound: *pot*, /p//ŏ//t/. Does it have the same middle sound as *soap* and *road*? Pause for responses. No, it has a different middle sound. Only *soap* and *road* have the middle sound /ō/.

I will say two words. You tell me if the middle sounds are /ō/ in both words, or if the middle sounds are different. Guide practice using the following word pairs from Student Page S52.

poke, slope (same)	phone, hope (same)
roll, doll (different)	cold, nose (same)
goal, stole (same)	foam, dome (same)
notch, note (different)	coal, clock (different)
both, bob (different)	joke, close (same)
hold, woke (same)	tool, told (different)

✔ **INDEPENDENT PRACTICE** Read each set of three words from Student Page S52. Have individual students identify which word has the middle /ō/ sound.

<u>chose</u>, chop, cheek	full, <u>froze</u>, fan
tin, <u>tone</u>, tilt	<u>home</u>, hum, moon
<u>broke</u>, book, back	pop, push, <u>pole</u>

IF... students have trouble identifying the word with the middle /ō/ sound, THEN... slowly say the sounds in each word and have students repeat after you. Isolate the middle sound in each word to help students pinpoint the one with the middle /ō/ sound.

Lesson 4 **Identify Long *a*, *i*, and *o***

Kate's Party

My sister Kate is having a party.
Our dad makes a big white cake.
Our mom brings ice cream, and she hands us a cone.
I bring a kite. It's a gift for Kate!

middle sound /ā/	middle sound /ī/	middle sound /ō/
		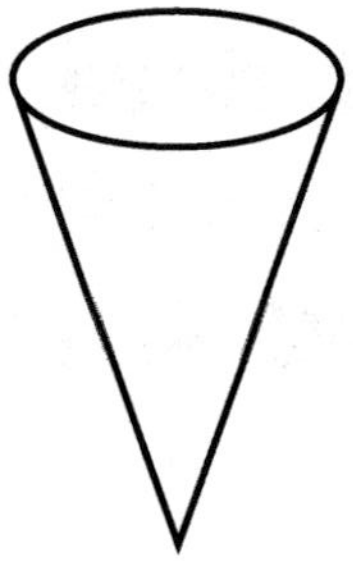

Teacher: This Student Page is intended as an *optional extension* of the lesson. After teaching the phonological awareness lesson orally, you can distribute or display this page to connect the phonological awareness skills (sounds) to phonics skills (sound-spelling).

Lesson 4 Identify Long *a*, *i*, and *o*

save, shake
rain, ran
plate, brave
tail, sail
lean, lane
wake, wall

clam, blame
date, face
hail, have
chase, that
quail, stain
pail, pace

dot, daze, dug
pump, pig, page
brag, bright, break

snake, snuck, snack
bait, bat, bite
gas, game, glow

Teacher: This Student Page is intended as an *optional extension* of the lesson. After teaching the phonological awareness lesson orally, you can distribute or display this page to connect the phonological awareness skills (sounds) to phonics skills (sound-spelling).

Lesson 4 Identify Long *a*, *i*, and *o*

tide, tried	fine, fin
fit, flight	sign, ripe
pile, child	cliff, climb
nice, dime	rhyme, rice
guide, gift	height, slight
sweet, swipe	pride, price

limb, him, like	from, fright, frame
bond, bind, bin	nine, none, nail
mild, mint, milk	van, vim, vine

Teacher: This Student Page is intended as an *optional extension* of the lesson. After teaching the phonological awareness lesson orally, you can distribute or display this page to connect the phonological awareness skills (sounds) to phonics skills (sound-spelling).

Lesson 4 Identify Long *a*, *i*, and *o*

poke, slope
roll, doll
goal, stole
notch, note
both, bob
hold, woke

phone, hope
cold, nose
foam, dome
coal, clock
joke, close
tool, told

chose, chop, cheek
tin, tone, tilt
broke, book, back

full, froze, fan
home, hum, moon
pop, push, pole

Teacher: This Student Page is intended as an *optional extension* of the lesson. After teaching the phonological awareness lesson orally, you can distribute or display this page to connect the phonological awareness skills (sounds) to phonics skills (sound-spelling).

Lesson 5 Identify Long e and *u*

INTRODUCE Present the topic. Today we will listen to the middle sounds in words. We will practice hearing three sounds: /ē/, /ū/, and /o͞o/.

MODEL Read aloud "Next Week." This passage has words with the three middle sounds we will learn about today. Listen as I say the words: *week, cube, boot.*

Next Week

Long e sound

Did you hear, did you hear, about next week?
The word on the street is that it will snow
three feet!
I like ice in a cube, but not in a sheet!
But I will put on my boots if the snow
gets that deep.

Long *u* sound

middle sound /ē/ week	middle sound /ū/ cube	middle sound /o͞o/ boot

TEACH If you wish, display Student Page S53. Say: I will say each word slowly. Then we will say the word together slowly. Listen for the sound in the middle. The first word is *week.* Draw out the vowel as you say the word. Say it with me slowly: /w//ē//k/. The middle sound is /ē/. We know other words with this middle sound. For example, the words *neat, seal,* and *cheap* have the middle sound /ē/. What other words do you know with that sound? Invite responses.

The next word is *cube.* Say the sounds slowly with me: /k//ū//b/. What is the middle sound? Pause. Yes, the middle sound is /ū/. It sounds like the word *you.* Let's say it again: /ū/. We know other words with this middle sound. For example, the words *cute* and *fuel* have the middle sound /ū/.

The last word is *boot.* Say the sounds with me: /b//o͞o//t/. The middle sound is /o͞o/. You can hear the same middle sound, /o͞o/, in the words *school* and *moon.*

RF.1.2.a Distinguish long from short vowel sounds in spoken single-syllable words.

OBJECTIVES:

- Identify long e in spoken words.
- Identify two pronunciations of long *u* in spoken words.

Lesson 5 Identify Long *e* and *u*

REMIND STUDENTS THAT...

- words are made up of different sounds.
- they can hear the middle sound in a word by saying the word slowly.

PRACTICE 1 First, model listening for a middle phoneme. I am going to say a word very slowly so I can hear its middle sound. Listen with me: *bead*. I will say the sounds in the word: /b/ (pause) /ē/ (pause) /d/. The middle sound is /ē/.

Now listen as I slowly say another word. Listen for the middle sound: /p//ē//k/. The word is *peek*. It has the same middle sound as *bead*.

I will say one more word. Listen for the middle sound: *pet*, /p//ĕ//t/. Does it have the same middle sound as *bead* and *peek*? Pause for responses. No, it has a different middle sound. Only *bead* and *peek* have the middle sound /ē/.

I will say two words. You tell me if the middle sounds are /ē/ in both words, or if the middle sounds are different. Guide practice using the following word pairs from Student Page S54.

read, feel (same)	sweet, sweat (different)
jeep, gem (different)	teen, heel (same)
leaf, sneak (same)	real, deal (same)
keep, cup (different)	squeeze, cheese (same)
wheat, beach (same)	steep, step (different)
fell, feel (different)	queen, seem (same)

✔ **MONITOR PROGRESS** Read each set of three words from Student Page S54. Have students tell you which word has the middle /ē/ sound.

sat, <u>seat</u>, set	<u>bean</u>, bet, back
peck, pick, <u>peak</u>	<u>please</u>, plant, play
wet, win, <u>wheel</u>	<u>neat</u>, nap, night

IF... students have trouble identifying the word with the middle /ē/ sound, THEN... slowly say the sounds in each word and have students repeat after you. Isolate the middle sound in each word to help students pinpoint the one with the middle /ē/ sound.

Lesson 5 Identify Long e and *u*

PRACTICE 2 First, model listening for a middle phoneme. I am going to say a word very slowly so I can hear its middle sound. Listen with me: *mule*. I will say the sounds in the word: /m/ (pause) /ū/ (pause) /l/. The middle sound is /ū/. It sounds like the word *you*. Listen again: *mule*.

Now listen as I slowly say another word. Listen for the middle sound: /h//ū//j/. The word is *huge*. It has the same middle sound as *mule*.

I will say one more word. Listen for the middle sound: *hug*, /h//ŭ//g/. Does it have the same middle sound as *mule* and *huge*? Pause for responses. No, it has a different middle sound. Only *mule* and *huge* have the middle sound /ū/.

I will say two words. You tell me if the middle sounds are /ū/ in both words, or if the middle sounds are different. Guide practice using the following word pairs from Student Page S55.

cute, mule (same)	mute, moat (different)
tub, fume (different)	cube, cue (same)
muse, fuel (same)	fuse, fuzz (different)
few, view (same)	hog, huge (different)

REMIND STUDENTS THAT...

- words are made up of different sounds.
- they can hear the middle sound in a word by saying the word slowly.

MONITOR PROGRESS Read each set of three words from Student Page S55. Have students tell you which word has the middle /ū/ sound.

cub, cab, <u>cube</u>	<u>cute</u>, cat, cot
<u>fuel</u>, fill, fall	mate, <u>mute</u>, must
high, <u>huge</u>, hug	moon, moan, <u>mule</u>

IF... students have trouble hearing the /y/ at the beginning of /ū/,
THEN... have them watch your face as you slowly say the sounds in *use* and *ooze*. Isolate the long vowel sounds, have students echo them, and have students tell if they sound the same or different.

Lesson 5 Identify Long e and *u*

REMIND STUDENTS THAT...

- words are made up of different sounds.
- they can hear the middle sound in a word by saying the word slowly.

PRACTICE 3 First, model listening for a middle phoneme. I am going to say a word very slowly so I can hear its middle sound. Listen with me: *pool*. I will say the sounds in the word: /p/ (pause) /o͞o/ (pause) /l/. The middle sound is /o͞o/.

Now listen as I slowly say another word. Listen for the middle sound: /t//o͞o//b/. The word is *tube*. It has the same middle sound as *pool*.

I will say one more word. Listen for the middle sound: *tub*, /t//ŭ//b/. Does it have the same middle sound as *pool* and *tube*? Pause for responses. No, it has a different middle sound. Only *pool* and *tube* have the middle sound /o͞o/.

I will say two words. You tell me if the middle sounds are /o͞o/ in both words, or if the middle sounds are different. Guide practice using the following word pairs from Student Page S56.

boot, tooth (same)	roam, rude (different)
suit, stuff (different)	moose, spoon (same)
goose, juice (same)	root, rat (different)
soon, food (same)	hoop, rule (same)
call, cool (different)	June, boost (same)
loose, less (different)	tune, loop (same)

INDEPENDENT PRACTICE Read each set of three words from Student Page S56. Have individual students identify which word has the middle /o͞o/ sound.

cat, cut, <u>cool</u>	<u>moon</u>, man, mine
book, <u>booth</u>, buck	limb, <u>plume</u>, plum
<u>duke</u>, duck, deck	<u>tool</u>, tell, tall

IF... students have trouble identifying the word with the middle /o͞o/ sound, THEN... slowly say the sounds in each word and have students repeat after you. Isolate the middle sound in each word to help students pinpoint the one with the middle /o͞o/ sound.

Lesson 5 **Identify Long e and *u***

Next Week

Did you hear, did you hear, about next week?
The word on the street is that it will snow three feet!
I like ice in a cube, but not in a sheet!
But I will put on my boots if the snow gets that deep.

middle sound /ē/	middle sound /ū/	middle sound /o͞o/
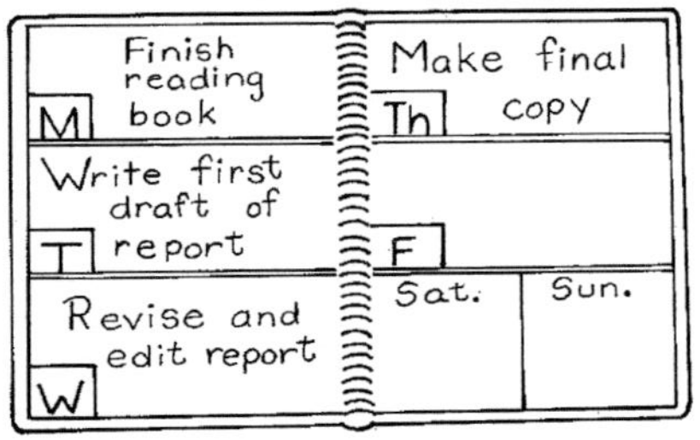	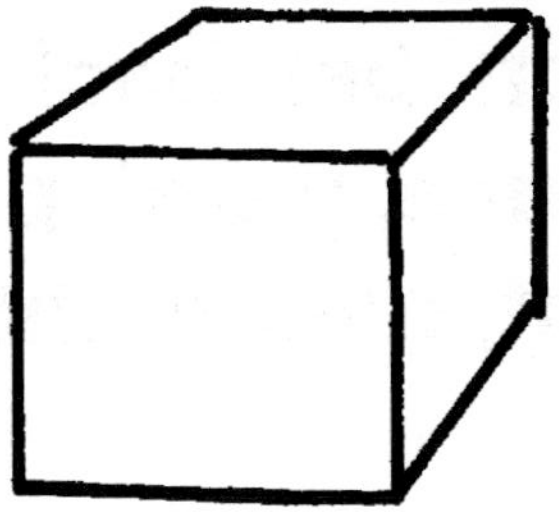	

Teacher: This Student Page is intended as an *optional extension* of the lesson. After teaching the phonological awareness lesson orally, you can distribute or display this page to connect the phonological awareness skills (sounds) to phonics skills (sound-spelling).

Lesson 5 Identify Long e and *u*

read, feel	sweet, sweat
jeep, gem	teen, heel
leaf, sneak	real, deal
keep, cup	squeeze, cheese
wheat, beach	steep, step
fell, feel	queen, seem

sat, seat, set	bean, bet, back
peck, pick, peak	please, plant, play
wet, win, wheel	neat, nap, night

Teacher: This Student Page is intended as an *optional extension* of the lesson. After teaching the phonological awareness lesson orally, you can distribute or display this page to connect the phonological awareness skills (sounds) to phonics skills (sound-spelling).

Lesson 5 Identify Long *e* and *u*

cute, mule	mute, moat
tub, fume	cube, cue
muse, fuel	fuse, fuzz
few, view	hog, huge

cub, cab, cube	cute, cat, cot
fuel, fill, fall	mate, mute, must
high, huge, hug	moon, moan, mule

Teacher: This Student Page is intended as an *optional extension* of the lesson. After teaching the phonological awareness lesson orally, you can distribute or display this page to connect the phonological awareness skills (sounds) to phonics skills (sound-spelling).

Lesson 5 Identify Long *e* and *u*

boot, tooth
suit, stuff
goose, juice
soon, food
call, cool
loose, less

roam, rude
moose, spoon
root, rat
hoop, rule
June, boost
tune, loop

cat, cut, cool
book, booth, buck
duke, duck, deck

moon, man, mine
limb, plume, plum
tool, tell, tall

Teacher: This Student Page is intended as an *optional extension* of the lesson. After teaching the phonological awareness lesson orally, you can distribute or display this page to connect the phonological awareness skills (sounds) to phonics skills (sound-spelling).

ASSESSMENT
LESSONS 4–5

Phonological Awareness

RF.1.2.a Distinguish long from short vowel sounds in spoken single-syllable words.

ASSESS MASTERY Use this Checkpoint to assess students' mastery of the long *a, i, o, e,* and *u* sounds.

ADMINISTER THE TEST Administer the Checkpoint orally to each student. For each item, model the process as described, and then have the student use the process to respond to your prompts. Record responses on the scoring chart on the next page.

1. Identify Long *a, i,* and *o* (Lesson 4)
MODEL: Listen for the sounds /ā/, /ī/, and /ō/ in words. I will give you a sound. Then I will say two words. You will tell me which word has the sound I gave. For example, if I say /ō/, *coat, cot,* you would say *coat* because *coat* has the /ō/ sound.

ASSESS:	/ā/: tap, tape	/ī/: dime, dim	/ō/: hope, hop

2. Identify Long *a, i,* and *o* (Lesson 4)
MODEL: Listen for the sounds /ā/, /ī/, and /ō/ in words. I will give you a sound. Then I will say three words. You will tell me which word has the sound I gave. For example, if I say /ā/, *tall, tail, talk,* you would say *tail* because *tail* has the /ā/ sound.

ASSESS:	/ō/: mop, mile, mole	/ā/: rake, rock, rack	/ī/: bike, back, bin

3. Identify Long e and *u* (Lesson 5)
MODEL: Listen for the sounds /ē/, /ū/, and /o͞o/ in words. I will give you a sound. Then I will say two words. You will tell me which word has the sound I gave. For example, if I say /o͞o/, *soon, sun,* you would say *soon* because *soon* has the /o͞o/ sound.

ASSESS:	/ē/: feel, fell	/ū/: cute, cut	/o͞o/: show, shoe

4. Identify Long e and *u* (Lesson 5)
MODEL: Listen for the sounds /ē/, /ū/, and /o͞o/ in words. I will give you a sound. Then I will say three words. You will tell me which word has the sound I gave. For example, if I say /ē/, *fed, feed, few,* you would say *feed* because *feed* has the /ē/ sound.

ASSESS:
/ū/: mule, mud, mile
/o͞o/: ram, room, roam
/ē/: peek, peck, pet

ASSESSMENT
LESSONS 4–5

Phonological Awareness

SCORING

SKILL/LESSON	SCORE
1. Identify Long *a, i,* and *o* (Lesson 4) /ā/: tape /ī/: dime /ō/: hope	____ / 3
2. Identify Long *a, i,* and *o* (Lesson 4) /ō/: mole /ā/: rake /ī/: bike	____ / 3
3. Identify Long *e* and *u* (Lesson 5) /ē/: feel /ū/: cute /o͞o/: shoe	____ / 3
4. Identify Long *e* and *u* (Lesson 5) /ū/: mule /o͞o/: room /ē/: peek	____ / 3

An overall score of 80% correct is typically considered mastery. Use your judgment and your individual students' needs as well to determine skill mastery.

IF...you determine that students have not demonstrated sufficient mastery of one or more skills,
THEN...review the skill(s), going back to the lessons to reteach and scaffold as needed.

Lesson 6 Review Short and Long Vowel Sounds

RF.1.2.a Distinguish long from short vowel sounds in spoken single-syllable words.

OBJECTIVES:

- Recognize short and long vowel sounds.
- Differentiate short and long vowel sounds.

INTRODUCE Present the topic. You know that different sounds make different words. For example, think about the word *tug*. Say it with me: *tug*. If you change the middle sound to /ă/, you make a new word: *tag*. Let's say it together: *tag*.

MODEL Display or share copies of Student Page S59. These are pictures of words with different middle sounds. I will say each word slowly. Say it with me, and then say the middle sound with me. Point to the picture for *wag*. Say the word slowly, drawing out the vowel. Have students repeat it with you. Then say together: The middle sound is /ă/. Continue with the remaining short vowels, then repeat the process with the long vowels.

wag middle sound /ă/	mitt middle sound /ĭ/	pot middle sound /ŏ/	nest middle sound /ĕ/	rug middle sound /ŭ/	book middle sound /o͝o/
	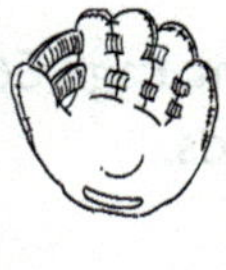				

tape middle sound /ā/	dime middle sound /ī/	coat middle sound /ō/	peel middle sound /ē/	fuel middle sound /ū/	spoon middle sound /o͞o/

TEACH Use the vertical alignment in the charts to demonstrate the difference in sound between the short and long versions of each vowel. Point to the picture for *wag* and say: This word has the middle sound /ă/. Say the sound with me: /ă/. Say the word: *wag*. Point to the picture for *tape*. This word has the middle sound /ā/. Say the sound with me: /ā/. Say the word: *tape*. Repeat for the remaining vowels.

Lesson 6 Review Short and Long Vowel Sounds

REMIND STUDENTS THAT...

- most words have middle sounds.
- they can hear the middle sound in a word by saying the word slowly.

PRACTICE 1 Use the routine to review medial short vowels. First, model listening for a middle phoneme. I will say a word slowly so I can hear its middle sound. Listen with me: *mat.* I will say the sounds in the word: /m/ (pause) /ă/ (pause) /t/. The middle sound is /ă/. Then segment a word, have students repeat the middle sound, and have them generate other words with the same middle sound.

Routine

1. Segment the word.	Listen as I say a word slowly: *tap.* The sounds are /t//ă//p/.
2. Isolate the middle sound.	The middle sound I hear is /ă/. Say it with me: /ă/.
3. Say a new word with the same middle sound.	What is another word with the same middle sound? How about *rap*? Tell me some others. Prompt students as necessary.

Use the following base words and prompts from Student Page S60 to help students generate words with medial short vowel sounds.

tap	rap, cap, map, lap, nap, hat, cat
tip	hip, dip, sit, pin, win, bit, hit, rip, fin
hop	mop, top, cot, dot, job, not, pot
ten	hen, pen, bed, red, jet, let, met, net, pet
cut	cup, but, hut, gum, bun, fun, mud
look	book, cook, hook, took, foot, hood

✓ **MONITOR PROGRESS** Have students isolate and voice the short vowel sounds in the following words from Student Page S60.

less (/ĕ/)	glad (/ă/)	sip (/ĭ/)
hot (/ŏ/)	bat (/ă/)	mend (/ĕ/)
book (/o͝o/)	miss (/ĭ/)	stop (/ŏ/)
dust (/ŭ/)	rush (/ŭ/)	look (/o͝o/)

IF... students have difficulty identifying the middle sound in a word,
THEN... slowly sound out the word, asking students to pay close attention to the positioning of your lips as you emphasize the word's middle sound.

Lesson 6 Review Short and Long Vowel Sounds

PRACTICE 2 Use the routine to review medial long vowels. First, model listening for a middle phoneme. I will say a word slowly so I can hear its middle sound. Listen with me: *pail*. I will say the sounds in the word: /p/ (pause) /ā/ (pause) /l/. The middle sound is /ā/. Then segment a word, have students repeat the middle sound, and have them generate other words with the same middle sound.

REMIND STUDENTS THAT...

- most words have middle sounds.
- they can hear the middle sound in a word by saying the word slowly.

Routine

1. Segment the word.	Listen as I say a word slowly: *cape*. The sounds are /k//ā//p/.
2. Isolate the middle sound.	The middle sound I hear is /ā/. Say it with me: /ā/.
3. Say a new word with the same middle sound.	What is another word with the same middle sound? How about *grape*? Tell me others. Prompt as necessary.

Use the following base words and prompts from Student Page S61 to help students generate words with medial long vowel sounds.

cape	cake, made, main, gate, save, wave
rice	right, bite, fight, nice, mice, light
coal	bowl, soap, note, pose, rose, joke
keen	bean, clean, deep, feed, green
cute	mule, cube, fuel, view, fuse
loop	loose, lose, room, move, cool

MONITOR PROGRESS Have students isolate and voice the long vowels in the following words from Student Page S61.

mood (/o͞o/)	huge (/ū/)	nail (/ā/)
kind (/ī/)	road (/ō/)	boot (/o͞o/)
sleep (/ē/)	soak (/ō/)	mute (/ū/)
need (/ē/)	wild (/ī/)	game (/ā/)

IF... students have difficulty identifying the middle sound in a word,
THEN... slowly sound out the word, asking students to pay close attention to the positioning of your lips as you emphasize the word's middle sound.

Lesson 6 Review Short and Long Vowel Sounds

REMIND STUDENTS THAT...

- by saying words slowly, they can hear the middle sounds.
- they can hear whether two or more words have the same or different middle sounds.

PRACTICE 3 Tell students that they will find words with specific middle sounds. I will say a sound. Then I will say two words. You will tell me which word has the middle sound that I said. For example, I will say the sound /ā/. Then I will say *cap, cape*. Which word has the sound /ā/? That's right; the word *cape* has the sound /ā/.

Continue the activity with these sounds and word pairs from Student Page S62, in random order.

/ă/ plan, plane (plan)	/ā/ date, sad (date)
/ĭ/ wise, hill (hill)	/ī/ chin, time (time)
/ŏ/ drop, droop (drop)	/ō/ pose, pod (pose)
/ĕ/ tease, ten (ten)	/ē/ gem, geese (geese)
/ŭ/ soon, sun (sun)	/ū/ hug, huge (huge)
/o͝o/ hook, hoot (hook)	/o͞o/ boom, book (boom)

INDEPENDENT PRACTICE Read each set of three words as shown on Student Page S62. Before reading each set of words, ask students to tell you which word has the vowel sound shown. For example: Which word has the middle sound /ā/: *bat, bait, bit?*

/ă/ bone, bin, <u>ban</u>	/ī/ tip, <u>type</u>, tap
/ŭ/ <u>tough</u>, tan, teen	/o͞o/ most, <u>move</u>, mop
/ē/ not, knit, <u>neat</u>	/ĕ/ <u>bell</u>, ball, bull
/ū/ school, <u>mule</u>, soon	/ō/ best, <u>boast</u>, bale
/ŏ/ <u>pop</u>, pep, pup	/ĭ/ <u>quit</u>, quart, quite
/ā/ soft, <u>safe</u>, self	/o͝o/ <u>cook</u>, coat, colt

IF... students have difficulty determining the correct medial sound for a set of words,
THEN... have them repeat the sound and then say each word slowly, listening carefully as they draw out the medial vowel sound in each word.

Lesson 6 Review Short and Long Vowel Sounds

wag	mitt	pot	nest	rug	book
				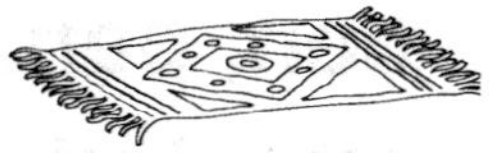	

tape	dime	coat	peel	fuel	spoon

Teacher: This Student Page is intended as an *optional extension* of the lesson. After teaching the phonological awareness lesson orally, you can distribute or display this page to connect the phonological awareness skills (sounds) to phonics skills (sound-spelling).

Lesson 6 Review Short and Long Vowel Sounds

tap	**rap, cap, map, lap, nap, hat, cat**
tip	**hip, dip, sit, pin, win, bit, hit, rip, fin**
hop	**mop, top, cot, dot, job, not, pot**
ten	**hen, pen, bed, red, jet, let, met, net, pet**
cut	**cup, but, hut, gum, bun, fun, mud**
look	**book, cook, hook, took, foot, hood**

less	**glad**	**sip**
hot	**bat**	**mend**
book	**miss**	**stop**
dust	**rush**	**look**

Teacher: This Student Page is intended as an *optional extension* of the lesson. After teaching the phonological awareness lesson orally, you can distribute or display this page to connect the phonological awareness skills (sounds) to phonics skills (sound-spelling).

Lesson 6 Review Short and Long Vowel Sounds

cape	**cake, made, main, gate, save, wave**
rice	**right, bite, fight, nice, mice, light**
coal	**bowl, soap, note, pose, rose, joke**
keen	**bean, clean, deep, feed, green**
cute	**mule, cube, fuel, view, fuse**
loop	**loose, lose, room, move, cool**

mood	**huge**	**nail**
kind	**road**	**boot**
sleep	**soak**	**mute**
need	**wild**	**game**

Teacher: This Student Page is intended as an *optional extension* of the lesson. After teaching the phonological awareness lesson orally, you can distribute or display this page to connect the phonological awareness skills (sounds) to phonics skills (sound-spelling).

Lesson 6 Review Short and Long Vowel Sounds

/ă/ plan, plane	**/ā/ date, sad**
/ĭ/ wise, hill	**/ī/ chin, time**
/ŏ/ drop, droop	**/ō/ pose, pod**
/ĕ/ tease, ten	**/ē/ gem, geese**
/ŭ/ soon, sun	**/ū/ hug, huge**
/o͝o/ hook, hoot	**/o͞o/ boom, book**

/ă/ bone, bin, ban	**/ī/ tip, type, tap**
/ŭ/ tough, tan, teen	**/o͞o/ most, move, mop**
/ē/ not, knit, neat	**/ĕ/ bell, ball, bull**
/ū/ school, mule, soon	**/ō/ best, boast, bale**
/ŏ/ pop, pep, pup	**/ĭ/ quit, quart, quite**
/ā/ soft, safe, self	**/o͝o/ cook, coat, colt**

Teacher: This Student Page is intended as an *optional extension* of the lesson. After teaching the phonological awareness lesson orally, you can distribute or display this page to connect the phonological awareness skills (sounds) to phonics skills (sound-spelling).

Lesson 7 Distinguish Short and Long Vowel Sounds

RF.1.2.a Distinguish long from short vowel sounds in spoken single-syllable words.

OBJECTIVES:

- Distinguish short and long initial vowel sounds.
- Distinguish short and long medial vowel sounds.
- Distinguish long final vowel sounds.

INTRODUCE You know that words are made up of sounds, and different sounds make different words. You can say a word slowly to hear its sounds. For example, say the word *name* slowly with me: /n//ā//m/. The sounds in *name* are /n/ (pause) /ā/ (pause) /m/. You can also say sounds quickly together to make a word: /n//ā//m/, *name*.

MODEL Display or share copies of the following passage, "My Favorite Food," from Student Page S63. These words contain many sounds we know. Listen for the sounds in the words. Read the passage at a measured pace.

My Favorite Food

I eat some pickles every day.
I usually choose dill, but not always.
Can you spare the time today?
We could go get a jar.
Okay?

TEACH I want a word that has the sound /ā/. I will say two words. You tell me which one has the /ā/ sound: *can* (pause) *day*. Which one has /ā/? Pause for responses. Continue the activity with the sounds and word pairs below, beginning with the long vowel sounds.

/ē/	eat, get	/ă/	day, can
/ī/	time, dill	/ĕ/	get, we
/ō/	not, go	/ĭ/	if, I
/ū/	you, some	/ŏ/	not, you
/o͞o/	could, choose	/ŭ/	go, but
/o͝o/	could, you		

Extend teaching by using some or all of the following one-syllable words in the passage: *I, eat, some, day, choose, dill, but, not, Can, you, time, We, could, go, get.* Ask: What sound do you hear in the word _____?

Lesson 7 Distinguish Short and Long Vowel Sounds

REMIND STUDENTS THAT...

- words are made of different sounds they can hear.
- they can hear the sound at the beginning a word by saying it slowly.

PRACTICE 1 Have students detect short and long vowels at the beginnings of words. I will say a word. I want you to tell me the sound you hear at the very beginning of the word. For example, if I say the word *ash*, you will say /ă/, the sound at the beginning of *ash*.

Voice each of the following words from Student Page S64 and ask: What is the sound at the beginning?

am	aim	age	act	add	ache
it	I	ice	itch	ink	I'll
odd	oat	ox	own	old	Oz
eel	elf	egg	east	edge	each
of	ooze	up	use	you	us

Display the following sentences from Student Page S64 and read them aloud. Then read each word that is or begins with a vowel. After each word, ask: What is the sound at the beginning of the word?

Ed asked an ox for oats to eat at eight.
Oh no! I used it up!

✔ **MONITOR PROGRESS** Randomly choose words from the lists and sentences above. Say a word and then ask: Which sound is at the beginning?

IF... students have trouble distinguishing between short and long vowel sounds,
THEN... slowly say the sounds in the word and have students repeat after you. Isolate the beginning sound and have students repeat it. Return to the word later in the practice.

Lesson 7 Distinguish Short and Long Vowel Sounds

PRACTICE 2 Have students detect short and long vowels in the middle of words. I will say a word. I want you to tell me the sound you hear in the middle. For example, if I say the word *cap*, you will say /ă/, the sound in the middle of *cap*.

Voice each of the following words from Student Page S65 and ask: What is the sound in the middle?

bat	bait	plate	rat	last	tame
sit	time	nice	switch	lick	find
hop	boat	fox	cloak	bold	dot
feel	shelf	neck	beast	help	seat
shove	cool	pup	cute	use	bus

Display the following sentences from Student Page S65 and read them aloud. Then read each word in each sentence and ask: What is the sound in the middle of the word?

Can Ruth make cute sheep hop?
Ben should hug his close friends.
Dave has six black socks that match.
Kyle's book says rocks melt.

REMIND STUDENTS THAT...

- words are made of different sounds they can hear.
- they can hear the middle sound in a word by saying the word slowly.

MONITOR PROGRESS Present the sounds and word pairs below. For each sound, ask: Which word has the _____ sound in the middle?

/ă/	hand, hail	/ā/	wall, wait
/ĭ/	trick, trike	/ī/	fine, fin
/ŏ/	shows, shop	/ō/	knock, nose
/o͝o/	look, pose	/o͞o/	most, moose
/ĕ/	beast, best	/ē/	says, sneeze
/ŭ/	rug, rude	/ū/	mud, huge

IF... students have trouble distinguishing between medial vowel sounds, THEN... slowly say the sounds in each word and have students repeat after you. Isolate the medial sounds and have students repeat them. Repeat the desired phoneme and match one of the words to it. Return to the word pair later in the practice.

Lesson 7 Distinguish Short and Long Vowel Sounds

REMIND STUDENTS THAT...

- words are made of different sounds they can hear.
- they can hear the final sound in a word by saying the word slowly.

PRACTICE 3 Have students identify long vowels and where they hear the sounds in words. I will say a word. Tell me the sound you hear at the end of the word. For example, if I say the word *day*, you will say /ā/.

Voice each of the following words from Student Page S66 and ask: What is the sound at the end?

sleigh /ā/	glow /ō/	shoe /o͞o/	try /ī/	we /ē/
clue /o͞o/	clay /ā/	pie /ī/	tree /ē/	no /ō/

Display the following sentences from Student Page S66 and read them aloud. Then read each word and ask: What is the sound at the very end of the word?

Clay may dry.	We see a blue shoe.
Try my glue.	Show snow to Lee.

Read the words below. After each word, ask students where they hear the long vowel sound. For example, ask: where did you hear /ā/: at the beginning, in the middle, or at the end of the word?

babe	ache	they	ice	fly	like
grow	oats	rope	each	free	keep
soon	ooze	true	fuel	mew	used

☑ **INDEPENDENT PRACTICE** Voice the long vowel sound (name the letter) and then read the corresponding word pair aloud. Ask students which word contains the sound you gave. Then have them identify whether the sound is at the beginning, middle, or end of the word.

A: <u>ate</u>, ax (beginning)
I: <u>cry</u>, crib (end)
O: not, <u>go</u> (end)
E: bell, <u>bee</u> (end)
U: <u>few</u>, fun (end)

IF... students have trouble distinguishing between short and long vowel sounds, THEN... repeat the long phoneme, slowly say the sounds in the words, and have students repeat both words after you. Model choosing the correct word.

Lesson 7 Distinguish Short and Long Vowel Sounds

My Favorite Food

I eat some pickles every day.
I usually choose dill, but not always.
Can you spare the time today?
We could go get a jar.
Okay?

/ē/	**eat, get**	**/ă/**	**day, can**
/ī/	**time, dill**	**/ĕ/**	**get, we**
/ō/	**not, go**	**/ĭ/**	**if, I**
/ū/	**you, some**	**/ŏ/**	**not, you**
/o͞o/	**could, choose**	**/ŭ/**	**go, but**
/o͝o/	**could, you**		

Teacher: This Student Page is intended as an *optional extension* of the lesson. After teaching the phonological awareness lesson orally, you can distribute or display this page to connect the phonological awareness skills (sounds) to phonics skills (sound-spelling).

Lesson 7 Distinguish Short and Long Vowel Sounds

am	aim	age	act	add	ache
it	I	ice	itch	ink	I'll
odd	oat	ox	own	old	Oz
eel	elf	egg	east	edge	each
of	ooze	up	use	you	us

Ed asked an ox for oats to eat at eight.

Oh no! I used it up!

Teacher: This Student Page is intended as an *optional extension* of the lesson. After teaching the phonological awareness lesson orally, you can distribute or display this page to connect the phonological awareness skills (sounds) to phonics skills (sound-spelling).

Lesson 7 Distinguish Short and Long Vowel Sounds

bat	bait	plate	rat	last	tame
sit	time	nice	switch	lick	find
hop	boat	fox	cloak	bold	dot
feel	shelf	neck	beast	help	seat
shove	cool	pup	cute	use	bus

Can Ruth make cute sheep hop?

Ben should hug his close friends.

Dave has six black socks that match.

Kyle's book says rocks melt.

Teacher: This Student Page is intended as an *optional extension* of the lesson. After teaching the phonological awareness lesson orally, you can distribute or display this page to connect the phonological awareness skills (sounds) to phonics skills (sound-spelling).

Lesson 7 Distinguish Short and Long Vowel Sounds

sleigh	glow	shoe	try	we
clue	clay	pie	tree	no

Clay may dry. **We see a blue shoe.**

Try my glue. **Show snow to Lee.**

Teacher: This Student Page is intended as an *optional extension* of the lesson. After teaching the phonological awareness lesson orally, you can distribute or display this page to connect the phonological awareness skills (sounds) to phonics skills (sound-spelling).

Lesson 8 Isolate Initial, Final, and Medial Sounds in Single-Syllable Words

RF.1.2.c Isolate and pronounce initial, medial vowel, and final sounds (phonemes) in spoken single-syllable words.

OBJECTIVES:

- Detect the initial sound in a spoken word.
- Detect the final sound in a spoken word.
- Detect the medial vowel sound in a spoken word.

INTRODUCE Remind students of their previous experience with hearing different sounds in words. Words have beginning sounds and ending—also called final—sounds. Most words have middle sounds, too. Today we will listen closely to words and then say just their beginning sounds. Then we will listen closely and say just their final sounds. Finally, we will listen closely and say just their middle sounds.

MODEL Listen as I say a word: *feet.* Blend the word slowly, emphasizing the beginning sound /f/. I ask myself, What is the beginning sound in *feet?* I say the word again: *feet.* The word *feet* begins with /f/. Follow the same procedure to model isolating the /h/ in *hit* and the /t/ in *tap.*

Keep the Beat

We hit the drum.
We tap our feet.
We clap and hum.
We keep the beat.

TEACH Display the above sentences from Student Page S67 as you continue. Now listen as I say another word: *drum.* I am going to say it again, and this time I will pay close attention to the final sound in the word: *drum.* I hear /m/ at the end of *drum.* The final sound is /m/. Repeat the procedure to model isolating the final sound in *hit.*

Listen again to the word *tap.* I am going to say it again and pay close attention to the middle sound. Draw out the vowel as you say the word: *tap.* I hear the middle sound /ă/. Repeat the procedure to model isolating the middle sound in *hit.*

Lesson 8

Isolate Initial, Final, and Medial Sounds in Single-Syllable Words

REMIND STUDENTS THAT...

- every word has a beginning sound.
- they can hear the beginning sound in a word by saying the word slowly.

PRACTICE 1 We are going to practice hearing the beginning sounds in words. After that, we will listen to two words and decide if their beginning sounds are the same or different.

Listen as I say a word: *sail*. Say it with me slowly: *sail*. Now, let's say the separate sounds in the word: /s//ā//l/. What was the first sound? Pause for responses. The first sound in *sail* is /s/. Let's say the beginning sound again: /s/.

Repeat the process with the following words from Student Page S68.

rice	bake	cut	peel	help	mark
day	pie	wear	zip	laugh	food
give	juice	new	save	ten	bear
voice	year	doll	ball	fair	lose

Now I will say two words. Tell me if their beginning sounds are the same or if they are different. Here are the words: *gift, big*. Are the beginning sounds the same? Pause for responses. No, the sounds are different. Here are two more words: *nice, new*. Are the beginning sounds the same? Pause. Yes, both words begin with /n/.

Continue the activity with the word pairs below.

porch, push (same)	whale, fish (different)
sort, fort (different)	big, bank (same)
read, write (same)	cool, day (different)
fur, feel (same)	now, mush (different)

MONITOR PROGRESS Have students isolate the initial sound in each of the following words.

like tough beak have sell done walk go melt

IF...students have trouble identifying a beginning sound,
THEN...first have students watch your mouth as you model isolating the correct sound. Repeat the sound and have students say it with you. Return to the word later in the practice.

Lesson 8

Isolate Initial, Final, and Medial Sounds in Single-Syllable Words

PRACTICE 2 We are going to practice hearing the ending sounds in words. After that, we will listen to two words and decide if their ending sounds are the same or different.

Listen as I say a word: *pick*. Say it with me slowly: *pick*. Now, let's say the separate sounds in the word: /p//ĭ//k/. What is the final sound? Pause for responses. The last sound in *pick* is /k/. Let's say the final sound again: /k/.

Repeat the process with the following words from Student Page S69.

lot	need	heap	tug	year	house
miss	grab	drive	map	joke	full
tough	badge	game	door	mix	froze
made	fluff	lean	hem	break	pot

Now I will say two words. Tell me if their final sounds are the same or if they are different. Here are the words: *throw, ball*. Are the ending sounds the same? Pause for responses. No, the sounds are different. Here are two more words: *clam, rhyme*. Are the ending sounds the same? Pause. Yes, both words end with /m/.

Continue the activity with the word pairs below.

flake, brick (same)	hole, head (different)
clap, mitt (different)	climb, boom (same)
sit, wait (same)	hiss, bird (different)
nab, bib (same)	line, swim (different)

REMIND STUDENTS THAT...

- every word has a final sound.
- they can hear the final sound in a word by saying the word slowly.

✔ **MONITOR PROGRESS** Have students isolate the final sound in each of the following words.

one hair wall ship bread mat cook team dress

IF...students have trouble identifying a final sound,
THEN...have students watch your mouth as you model isolating the correct sound. Have students repeat the sound after you. Return to the word later in the practice.

Lesson 8

Isolate Initial, Final, and Medial Sounds in Single-Syllable Words

REMIND STUDENTS THAT...

- many words have middle sounds.
- they can hear the middle sound in a word by saying the word slowly.

PRACTICE 3 We are going to practice hearing the middle sounds in words. After that, we will listen to two words and decide if their middle sounds are the same or different.

Listen as I say a word: *hat*. Say it with me slowly: *hat*. Now, let's say the separate sounds in the word: /h//ă//t/. The first sound is /h/. The last sound is /t/. What is the middle sound in *hat*? Pause for responses. The middle sound in *hat* is /ă/. Let's say the middle sound again: /ă/.

Repeat the process with the following words from Student Page S70.

race	pack	kneel	book	duke	tell
rip	bone	shake	pile	chop	pin
sun	leave	bed	lock	fool	move
mop	tug	goat	wheel	lace	tap

Now I will say two words. Tell me if their middle sounds are the same or if they are different. Here are the words: *time, tune*. Are the middle sounds the same? Pause for responses. No, the sounds are different. Here are two more words: *hen, said*. Are the middle sounds the same? Pause. Yes, both words have /ĕ/ in the middle.

Continue the activity with the word pairs below.

dab, gap (same)	nail, bell (different)
height, note (different)	with, hit (same)
seem, clean (same)	cute, fun (different)
cook, push (same)	not, sad (different)

✓ **INDEPENDENT PRACTICE** Have students isolate the medial sound in each of the following words.

sack	bite	heel	pose	red
boot	some	case	win	box

IF...students have trouble identifying a medial sound,
THEN...model isolating the correct sound. Return to the word later in the practice.

Lesson 8 **Isolate Initial, Final, and Medial Sounds in Single-Syllable Words**

Keep the Beat

We hit the drum.
We tap our feet.
We clap and hum.
We keep the beat.

Teacher: This Student Page is intended as an *optional extension* of the lesson. After teaching the phonological awareness lesson orally, you can distribute or display this page to connect the phonological awareness skills (sounds) to phonics skills (sound-spelling).

Lesson 8 Isolate Initial, Final, and Medial Sounds in Single-Syllable Words

rice	bake	cut	peel	help	mark
day	pie	wear	zip	laugh	food
give	juice	new	save	ten	bear
voice	year	doll	ball	fair	lose

Teacher: This Student Page is intended as an *optional extension* of the lesson. After teaching the phonological awareness lesson orally, you can distribute or display this page to connect the phonological awareness skills (sounds) to phonics skills (sound-spelling).

Lesson 8 Isolate Initial, Final, and Medial Sounds in Single-Syllable Words

lot	need	heap	tug	year	house
miss	grab	drive	map	joke	full
tough	badge	game	door	mix	froze
made	fluff	lean	hem	break	pot

Teacher: This Student Page is intended as an *optional extension* of the lesson. After teaching the phonological awareness lesson orally, you can distribute or display this page to connect the phonological awareness skills (sounds) to phonics skills (sound-spelling).

Lesson 8 Isolate Initial, Final, and Medial Sounds in Single-Syllable Words

race	pack	kneel	book	duke	tell
rip	bone	shake	pile	chop	pin
sun	leave	bed	lock	fool	move
mop	tug	goat	wheel	lace	tap

Teacher: This Student Page is intended as an *optional extension* of the lesson. After teaching the phonological awareness lesson orally, you can distribute or display this page to connect the phonological awareness skills (sounds) to phonics skills (sound-spelling).

ASSESSMENT
LESSONS 6–8

Phonological Awareness

ASSESS MASTERY Use this Checkpoint to assess students' mastery of short and long vowel sounds in single-syllable words.

ADMINISTER THE TEST Administer the Checkpoint orally to each student. For each item, model the process as described, and then have the student use the process to respond to your prompts. Record responses on the scoring chart on the next page.

RF.1.2.a Distinguish long from short vowel sounds in spoken single-syllable words.

RF.1.2.c Isolate and pronounce initial, medial vowel, and final sounds (phonemes) in spoken single-syllable words.

1. Review Short and Long Vowel Sounds (Lesson 6)

MODEL: I will say a word slowly so that you can hear the beginning sound, the middle sound, and the final sound. Tell me the middle sound you hear. For example, if I say the word *lane*, /l/ /ā/ /n/, you will say /ā/, because /ā/ is the middle sound in the word.

ASSESS:	raise	cheese	bike	phone	soon	huge
	chess	back	hot	bud	wish	good

2. Distinguish Short and Long Vowel Sounds (Lesson 7)

MODEL: I will ask you which of two words has the sound I want. For example, if I say, "I want a word with /ă/: *mask, made*," you will say *mask*, because *mask* has the /ă/ sound.

ASSESS:	/ă/	cape, cap	/ā/	wade, wad
	/ĭ/	lit, light	/ī/	cry, crow
	/ŏ/	not, note	/ō/	own, an
	/o͝o/	push, posh	/o͞o/	true, tree
	/ĕ/	yeast, yes	/ē/	heap, help
	/ŭ/	must, mood	/ū/	few, foe

3. Isolate Initial, Final, and Medial Sounds in Single-Syllable Words (Lesson 8)

MODEL: I will say a word and then ask you to tell me one of its sounds—its beginning sound, its middle sound, or its final sound. For example, if I say *pole* and ask you for its final sound, you will say /l/.

ASSESS:	part (beginning)	jab (final)	sit (middle)
	leg (middle)	fall (beginning)	north (beginning)
	date (beginning)	snow (final)	tuck (middle)

ASSESSMENT
LESSONS 6–8

Phonological Awareness

SCORING

SKILL/LESSON	SCORE
1. Review Short and Long Vowel Sounds (Lesson 6) /ā/; /ē/; /ī/; /ō/; /o͞o/; /ū/; /ĕ/; /ă/; /ŏ/; /ŭ/; /ĭ/; /o͝o/	_____ / 12
2. Distinguish Short and Long Vowel Sounds (Lesson 7) cap; wade lit; cry not; own push; true yes; heap must; few	_____ / 12
3. Isolate Initial, Final, and Medial Sounds in Single-Syllable Words (Lesson 8) /p/; /b/; /ĭ/ /ĕ/; /f/; /n/ /d/; /ō/; /ŭ/	_____ / 9

An overall score of 80% correct is typically considered mastery. Use your judgment and your individual students' needs as well to determine skill mastery.

IF…you determine that students have not demonstrated sufficient mastery of one or more skills,
THEN…review the skill(s), going back to the lessons to reteach and scaffold as needed.

Lesson 9 Segment and Blend Sounds

RF.1.2.b Orally produce single-syllable words by blending sounds (phonemes), including consonant blends.

OBJECTIVES:

- Segment one-syllable words.
- Count the sounds in words.
- Blend sounds into one-syllable words.

INTRODUCE Today we will take words apart and put them back together. We will start by listening to words to hear all of their sounds. We will count the separate sounds. After that, we will blend sounds together to make words.

MODEL Listen as I say a word and then slowly say each sound in the word: *in*, /ĭ//n/. The word *in* is made of the sounds /ĭ/ and /n/. Repeat the procedure to segment the words *set*, /s//ĕ//t/, and *fun*, /f//ŭ//n/.

Now model counting sounds. Listen as I say the sounds in *fun*. I will hold up a finger for each sound I hear. Slowly say *fun*, holding up one finger for each sound. There are three sounds. Now I will put the sounds back together. I will say them quickly to make the word: *fun*.

Fun!

We try to have fun.
We skip and we run.

We jump on the bed.
"Stop that!" Mom says.

TEACH Present the above passage, which appears on Student Page S73. Segment and count words with two, three, and four sounds. I will say a word slowly. Then we will say the sounds together. We will say the sounds one more time so we can count the sounds. The first word is *we*. Say the sounds slowly with me: /w//ē/. Let's use our fingers to count the sounds: /w/ (hold up one finger) /ē/ (hold up a second finger). There are two sounds. Let's say them together fast to make the word: *we*.

Repeat the process with *try* (/t//r//ī/) and *stop* (/s//t//ŏ//p/). Make sure students can segment and accurately count the sounds.

Lesson 9 Segment and Blend Sounds

REMIND STUDENTS THAT...

- by saying a word slowly, they can hear and count its sounds.

PRACTICE 1 Point out that some very short words have just one sound: *I* and *eye*, for example. Then focus on words with two sounds. Many short words have just two sounds. Here's a word like that: *no*. Say the word with me: *no*. Now, let's count the sounds. We'll say the word slowly and raise one finger for each sound we hear. Say *no* with students and then slowly speak its sounds: /n//ō/. Raise a finger for each sound. Which sounds did we say? (/n//ō/) How many sounds is that? Pause for responses.

Repeat the above process with the following words from Student Page S74.

is	if	at	it	to	do
we	key	go	off	so	lie
up	ill	say	on	pie	toe
an	up	eat	ate	hay	why

Move on to three-phoneme words. Now let's count sounds in words that have more than two sounds. I will say a word, and then we will say each sound in the word slowly. Listen to this word: *hop*. Now say each sound with me and hold up a finger for each sound: /h//ŏ//p/. How many sounds did we say? Pause for responses. That's right. *Hop* has three sounds. Repeat the process with the following words from Student Page S74.

tip	pin	rat	den	cot	home
love	night	book	neat	cake	soon

✔ **MONITOR PROGRESS** Have students say, segment, and count sounds in the words *be, egg, new, dog, time,* and *low.*

IF... students have trouble saying the sounds in a word,
THEN... model the correct response by slowly saying each sound. Repeat the word and have students say the sounds with you. Revisit the word later on to give students the opportunity to practice saying the sounds that make up the word.

Lesson 9 Segment and Blend Sounds

PRACTICE 2 We know how to say a word slowly so that we can hear each sound. Today we are going to practice saying more words and their sounds.

Point to or hold up a green object. Say *green* and then slowly say each sound: /g//r//ē//n/. The word *green* is made of the sounds /g/, /r/, /ē/, and /n/. Say the word slowly with me: *green. Green* has /g//r/ at the beginning.

Say: *sip, skip.* These words have some sounds that are alike, but their beginning sounds are not exactly the same. Let's say the words slowly and listen to the beginning sounds: *sip, skip.*

Point to a desk and say the word: *desk.* Listen to each sound in the word: /d//ĕ//s//k/. The word *desk* is made of the sounds /d/, /ĕ/, /s/, and /k/. Listen as I say the word again: *desk.* The word has /s//k/ at the end.

Say: *bet, best.* These words have some sounds that are alike, but their final sounds are not exactly the same. Let's say the words slowly and listen to the final sounds: *bet, best.*

Repeat the procedure with the following words from Student Page S75. Start with initial two-letter blends and conclude with final two-letter blends.

train	slip	spin	stay	try	great
grow	tree	spell	broom	flat	plum
end	just	raft	list	bend	most
milk	belt	fast	tent	lift	last

REMIND STUDENTS THAT...

- by saying a word slowly, they can hear and count its sounds.

MONITOR PROGRESS Say each of the following words aloud. Then have students say and segment each word.

treat	stool	grin	drop	break	plan
sand	help	tusk	soft	list	pant

IF... students have difficulty segmenting blends in a word,
THEN... say each sound in the word slowly as students pay close attention to the position of your tongue and lips. Emphasize the two distinct sounds in the blend as you say the word.

Lesson 9 Segment and Blend Sounds

REMIND STUDENTS THAT...

- they have listened to words to identify their separate sounds.
- to say a word, they say the separate sounds together quickly without stopping.

PRACTICE 3 We know that words are made up of sounds. Some very short words have just one sound, but most words have two or more sounds. Today we will put sounds together to make words.

I will say the sounds that make up a word: /s/ (pause) /ō/. Say the sounds with me: /s/ (pause) /ō/. Now I will blend the sounds together to make the word. To do this, I will say the sounds quickly without stopping: *so*. Blend the sounds with me: *so*.

Let's try another one. Here are the sounds: /s//l//ō/. Say the sounds with me: /s//l//ō/. Now blend the sounds with me. Say the word *slow* slowly but without pauses. Then say the word normally.

Repeat the process to blend the sounds in the word *most:* /m//ō//s//t/. Then have students continue practicing with these words from Student Page S76.

lip /l//ĭ//p/	slip /s//l//ĭ//p/	list /l///ĭ//s//t/
bed /b//ĕ//d/	bend /b//ĕ//n//d/	bread /b//r//ĕ//d/
fat /f//ă//t/	flat /f//l//ă//t/	fast /f//ă//s//t/
hum /h//ŭ//m/	drum /d//r//ŭ//m/	bump /b//ŭ//m//p/
fix /f//ĭ//k//s/	flick /f//l//ĭ//k/	fist /f//ĭ//s//t/
bowl /b/ō//l/	blow /b//l//ō/	bold /b//ō//l//d/
rain /r//ā//n/	train /t//r//ā//n/	paste /p//ā//s//t/

✓ **INDEPENDENT PRACTICE** Say the following sounds with students. Then have them blend the sounds into words.

/l//ī//t/ (light)	/f//l//ī//t/ (flight)
/s//ē//l/ (seal)	/s//t//ē//l/ (steal)
/b//o͞o//t/ (boot)	/b//o͞o//s//t/ (boost)
/f//ē//s//t/ (feast)	/s//p//o͞o//n/ (spoon)

IF... students have difficulty blending sounds into words,
THEN... have students say each sound separately to make sure that they can pronounce it correctly. Then have them practice saying the sounds more quickly and fluidly until they can blend the word successfully.

Lesson 9 **Segment and Blend Sounds**

Fun!

We try to have fun.
We skip and we run.

We jump on the bed.
"Stop that!" Mom says.

Teacher: This Student Page is intended as an *optional extension* of the lesson. After teaching the phonological awareness lesson orally, you can distribute or display this page to connect the phonological awareness skills (sounds) to phonics skills (sound-spelling).

Lesson 9 Segment and Blend Sounds

is	if	at	it	to	do
we	key	go	off	so	lie
up	ill	say	on	pie	toe
an	up	eat	ate	hay	why

tip	pin	rat	den	cot	home
love	night	book	neat	cake	soon

Teacher: This Student Page is intended as an *optional extension* of the lesson. After teaching the phonological awareness lesson orally, you can distribute or display this page to connect the phonological awareness skills (sounds) to phonics skills (sound-spelling).

Lesson 9 Segment and Blend Sounds

train	slip	spin	stay	try	great
grow	tree	spell	broom	flat	plum
end	just	raft	list	bend	most
milk	belt	fast	tent	lift	last

Teacher: This Student Page is intended as an *optional extension* of the lesson. After teaching the phonological awareness lesson orally, you can distribute or display this page to connect the phonological awareness skills (sounds) to phonics skills (sound-spelling).

Lesson 9 Segment and Blend Sounds

lip	**slip**	**list**
bed	**bend**	**bread**
fat	**flat**	**fast**
hum	**drum**	**bump**
fix	**flick**	**fist**
bowl	**blow**	**bold**
rain	**train**	**paste**

Teacher: This Student Page is intended as an *optional extension* of the lesson. After teaching the phonological awareness lesson orally, you can distribute or display this page to connect the phonological awareness skills (sounds) to phonics skills (sound-spelling).

Lesson 10 Blend and Segment Three- and Four-Phoneme Words

INTRODUCE You know that words are made of sounds. Some words have just two sounds, words like *egg*, *it*, and *ape*. Many words have three sounds or four sounds. Today we will blend three or four sounds into words. We will also take apart words and say their sounds.

MODEL Display or distribute Student Page S77. Read aloud "Lost Cap." Say: This passage includes words that have the same beginning sounds, /k/, and the same ending sounds, /p/. The first word has three sounds: /k//ă//p/, *cap*. The next word has four sounds: /k//ă//m//p/, *camp*. The last word also has four sounds: /k//l//ă//p/, *clap*.

Lost Cap

Last week at camp, I lost my cap. three sounds
I looked on the porch.
I looked in my tent. four sounds
I looked all over.
Then I looked on my vest.
When I found my cap, my friends started to clap!

cap	camp	clap

TEACH Listen again to the first word. Its sounds are /k/ (pause) /ă/ (pause) /p/. Say the sounds with me: /k/ (pause) /ă/ (pause) /p/. Now let's say the sounds quickly together to make the word: *cap*. Say the word with me again: *cap*.

Now listen to the sounds in the middle word: /k/ (pause) /ă/ (pause) /m/ (pause) /p/. There are two sounds at the end, /m/ and /p/. Say all the sounds in the word with me: /k/ (pause) /ă/ (pause) /m/ (pause) /p/. Now let's say the word: *camp*.

Listen to the sounds in the last word: /k/ (pause) /l/ (pause) /ă/ (pause) /p/. There are two sounds at the beginning, /k/ and /l/. Say all the sounds in the word with me: /k/ (pause) /l/ (pause) /ă/ (pause) /p/. Now let's say the word: *clap*.

RF.1.2.b Orally produce single-syllable words by blending sounds (phonemes), including consonant blends.

RF.1.2.d Segment spoken single-syllable words into their complete sequence of individual sounds (phonemes).

OBJECTIVES:

- Blend phonemes, including consonant blends, into single-syllable words.
- Segment single-syllable words, including words with consonant blends, into phonemes.

Lesson 10 Blend and Segment Three- and Four-Phoneme Words

REMIND STUDENTS THAT...

- words are made of different sounds they can hear.
- by saying the sounds together without stopping, they can say the word.
- by saying words very slowly, they can hear all the sounds in the words.

PRACTICE 1 Guide students to blend sounds into a CVC word. Tap your fingers on the desk and say: I will say a word: *tap*. Now I will say the sounds in the word very slowly: /t/ (pause) /ă/ (pause) /p/. I want you to say those sounds with me: /t/ (pause) /ă/ (pause) /p/. To turn those sounds into a word, we say the sounds together without stopping. Say the distinct sounds without pausing, and then say the word: /t//ă//p/, *tap*.

I will say some sounds. Together, we will turn the sounds into a word. Ready? Listen: /p/ (pause) /ŏ/ (pause) /d/. Say the sounds with me: /p/ (pause) /ŏ/ (pause) /d/. Now let's make a word from the sounds: /p//ŏ//d/, *pod*.

Repeat the process using the following words from Student Page S78.

hot	/h//ŏ//t/	sail	/s//ā//l/
wet	/w//ĕ//t/	leave	/l//ē//v/
fan	/f//ă//n/	coat	/k//ō//t/
lip	/l//ĭ//p/	move	/m//o͞o//v/
rug	/r//ŭ//g/	fight	/f//ī//t/

Now have students segment the same words with you in random order. For example: I will say a word: *hot*. Now I want us to say the sounds in the word: /h/ (pause) /ŏ/ (pause) /t/. Say the sounds with me: /h//ŏ//t/.

✓ **MONITOR PROGRESS** For Exercise 1, have students blend each set of phonemes into words. For Exercise 2, have students segment each of the words.

1. /s//ī//n/ (sign)	/k//ĭ//t/ (kit)	/m//ŭ//g/ (mug)
2. maze (/m//ā//z/)	feel (/f//ē//l/)	nod (/n//ŏ//d/)

IF... students have trouble blending the sounds into words,
THEN... choose a word to focus on and model blending its sounds slowly at first, then gradually picking up the pace. Have students echo you until they can blend the word successfully. If needed, provide other familiar words for additional practice with blending.

Lesson 10 Blend and Segment Three- and Four-Phoneme Words

PRACTICE 2 Guide students to blend sounds into words with final blends. Bump your fists together. I will say some sounds very slowly: /b/ (pause) /u/ (pause) /m/ (pause) /p/. To turn those sounds into a word, we say them together without stopping: /b//u//m//p/, *bump*. We made the word *bump* from the sounds.

Present Student Page S79. I will say some sounds. Together, we will turn the sounds into a word. Ready? Listen: /ă/ (pause) /s/ (pause) /k/. Say the sounds with me: /ă/ (pause) /s/ (pause) /k/. Now let's make a word from the sounds. Say the distinct sounds without pausing, and then say the word: /ă//s//k/, *ask*. Repeat the process using the remaining five words from the student page.

Want fast help?
Ask Old Ant.

Have students segment the same six words with you in random order. For example: I will say a word: *old*. Now I want to say the sounds in the word: /ō/ (pause) /l/ (pause) /d/. Say the sounds with me: /ō//l//d/. What are the sounds in the word *old*? (/ō//l//d/).

MONITOR PROGRESS Have students blend the phonemes in the first line into words. Then have them segment the words in the second line.

1. /s//ŏ//k/ (sock)	/m//ĕ//l//t/ (melt)	/w//ī//l//d/ (wild)
2. and (/ă//n//d/)	band (/b//ă//n//d/)	dust (/d//ŭ//s//t/)

IF... students have difficulty segmenting the words,
THEN... choose a word to focus on and slowly sound it out, elongating the pronunciation of each phoneme for emphasis. Have students echo you, and then return to the word later in the practice so that students can segment the word independently. If needed, provide other familiar words for additional practice.

REMIND STUDENTS THAT...

- words are made of different sounds they can hear.
- by saying the sounds together without stopping, they can say the word.
- by saying words very slowly, they can hear all the sounds in the words.

Lesson 10 Blend and Segment Three- and Four-Phoneme Words

REMIND STUDENTS THAT...

- words are made up of different sounds they can hear.
- by saying the sounds together without stopping, they can say the word.
- by saying words very slowly, they can hear all the sounds in the words.

PRACTICE 3 Guide students to blend sounds into words with initial blends. Slide a hand across your desktop. I will say some sounds very slowly: /s/ (pause) /l/ (pause) /ī/ (pause) /d/. To turn those sounds into a word, we say them together without stopping: /s//l//ī//d/, *slide*. We made the word *slide* from the sounds.

Great!
Fresh, clean snow!

Present Student Page S80. I will say some sounds. Together, we will turn the sounds into a word. Ready? Listen: /g/ (pause) /r/ (pause) /ā/ (pause) /t/. Say the sounds with me: /g/ (pause) /r/ (pause) /ā/ (pause) /t/. Now let's make a word from the sounds: /g//r//ā//t/, *great*. Repeat the process using the remaining three words from the student page.

Have students segment the same four words with you in random order. For example: I will say a word: *snow*. Now I want to say the sounds in the word: /s/ (pause) /n/ (pause) /ō/. Say the sounds with me: /s//n//ō/. What are the sounds in the word *snow*? (/s//n//ō/).

INDEPENDENT PRACTICE Have students blend the first six phonemes below into words. Then have them segment the six words that follow.

/p//l//ā//s/ (place)	/d//r//ī/ (dry)	/s//w//ĭ//m/ (swim)
/s//t//ŏ//p/ (stop)	/b//l//ō/ (blow)	/k//r//ē//p/ (creep)
glove (/g//l//ŭ//v/)	flip (/f//l//ĭ//p/)	spell (/s//p//ĕ//l/)
blue (/b//l//o͞o/)	smile (/s//m//ī//l/)	track (/t//r//ă//k/)

IF...students have difficulty blending phonemes or segmenting words,
THEN...demonstrate the blending or segmenting process with an appropriate word from the activity, slowing your pace to emphasize the word or individual phonemes as needed. Have students use the applicable process to blend or segment a different word from the activity. Revisit both words later to ensure that students have mastered the blending or segmenting process.

Lesson 10 **Blend and Segment Three- and Four-Phoneme Words**

Lost Cap

Last week at camp, I lost my cap.
I looked on the porch.
I looked in my tent.
I looked all over.
Then I looked on my vest.
When I found my cap, my friends started to clap!

cap	camp	clap
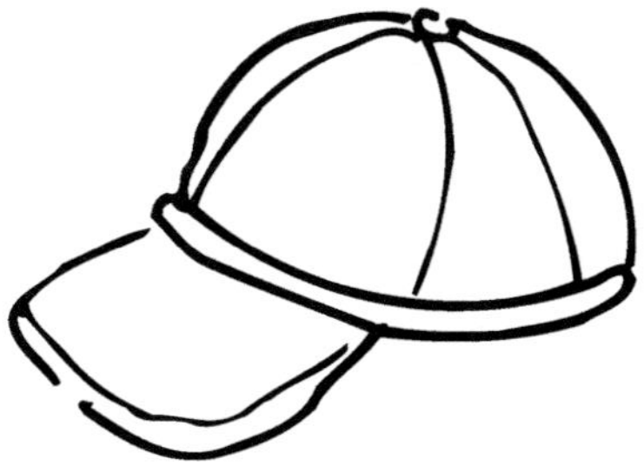		

Teacher: This Student Page is intended as an *optional extension* of the lesson. After teaching the phonological awareness lesson orally, you can distribute or display this page to connect the phonological awareness skills (sounds) to phonics skills (sound-spelling).

Lesson 10 Blend and Segment Three- and Four-Phoneme Words

hot	**sail**
wet	**leave**
fan	**coat**
lip	**move**
rug	**fight**

Teacher: This Student Page is intended as an *optional extension* of the lesson. After teaching the phonological awareness lesson orally, you can distribute or display this page to connect the phonological awareness skills (sounds) to phonics skills (sound-spelling).

Lesson 10 Blend and Segment Three- and Four-Phoneme Words

Want fast help?
Ask Old Ant.

Teacher: This Student Page is intended as an *optional extension* of the lesson. After teaching the phonological awareness lesson orally, you can distribute or display this page to connect the phonological awareness skills (sounds) to phonics skills (sound-spelling).

Lesson 10 Blend and Segment Three- and Four-Phoneme Words

Great!
Fresh, clean snow!

Teacher: This Student Page is intended as an *optional extension* of the lesson. After teaching the phonological awareness lesson orally, you can distribute or display this page to connect the phonological awareness skills (sounds) to phonics skills (sound-spelling).

Lesson 11 Blend, Segment, and Count Five or More Phonemes

RF.1.2.b Orally produce single-syllable words by blending sounds (phonemes), including consonant blends.

RF.1.2.d Segment spoken single-syllable words into their complete sequence of individual sounds (phonemes).

OBJECTIVES:

- Blend five or more phonemes into single-syllable words.
- Segment single-syllable words of five or more phonemes.
- Count the phonemes in a word.

INTRODUCE You know that every word is made up of sounds. The sounds /s//t//ă//m//p/ blend together to make the word *stamp,* for example. Today we will blend sounds together to make words. We will also take apart words and count their sounds.

MODEL Listen to these sounds: /f/, /r/, /ĕ/, /n/, /d/. Now I will blend the sounds to make a word. Repeat the sounds. Then say them distinctly but more quickly, and finally say the word. Listen again: /f/, /r/, /ĕ/, /n/, /d/; /f//r//ĕ//n//d/; *friend.*

Now I will take apart a word and count the sounds. The word is *stripe.* As I say the sounds, I will hold up one finger for each sound. Slowly say each sound: /s/, /t/, /r/, /ī/, /p/. Use your other hand to point to one raised finger for each sound. The word *stripe* has five sounds: /s/, /t/, /r/, /ī/, /p/.

The Clean Floor

They swept with brooms.
They swept twelve rooms.
They scrubbed some streaks.
The clean floor squeaks!

TEACH Present Student Page S81. Listen as I say six sounds: /s//k//w//ē//k//s/. I will say the sounds again: /s//k//w//ē//k//s/. Now we will all say the sounds together to make a word. Lead students to gradually blend the phonemes into the word *squeaks.* Repeat with *scrubbed* and *streaks.*

Now we will count the sounds in a word. The word is *swept.* Listen as I say each sound: /s//w//ĕ//p//t/. I will say the sounds again, and I want you to count them with me: /s/, /w/, /ĕ/, /p/, /t/. Hold up a finger for each sound. Then point to each finger. The word *swept* has five sounds. I can also count the sounds by making marks on the board. Sound out *swept* again, making a tic mark on the board for each sound. Repeat with *brooms* and *twelve.*

Lesson 11

Blend, Segment, and Count Five or More Phonemes

REMIND STUDENTS THAT...

- words are made of different sounds they can hear.
- by saying the sounds in a word quickly without stopping, they can say the word.

PRACTICE 1 I will say the sounds that make up a word: /s/, /t/, /r/, /ī/, /k/. Now I will blend the sounds together to make the word. To do this, I will say the sounds quickly without stopping: *strike*.

Now let's blend sounds together to make a word. I will say the sounds. Then you and I will say the sounds together two times. Finally, we will say them quickly without stopping. We will make the word.

The sounds are /p/, /l/, /ă/, /n/, /t/. Let's say the sounds together: /p/, /l/, /ă/, /n/, /t/. Say the sounds distinctly but more quickly, and finally say the word: /p//l//ă//n//t/, *plant*. Repeat the blending of *strike* and *plant* as needed to make sure students are able to remember and enunciate the individual sounds. Then use the same procedure to have students blend the phonemes below into words.

/s//k//r//ā//p/	(scrape)	/t//r//ŭ//k//s/	(trucks)
/s//p//ĕ//n//d/	(spend)	/s//n//ă//p//s/	(snaps)
/p//r//ĭ//n//t/	(print)	/b//r//ā//k//s/	(breaks)
/s//t//r//ā//t/	(straight)	/s//t//r//ē//t//s/	(streets)
/g//ĕ//s//t//s/	(guests)	/s//p//ōō//n//z/	(spoons)
/f//r//ŏ//s//t/	(frost)	/s//k//r//ŭ//b/	(scrub)

Present these two sentences from Student Page S82, which are made up of six words that students just created by blending phonemes.

Trucks scrape streets. Guests scrub spoons.

✔ **MONITOR PROGRESS** Have students blend two words that begin with the same three phonemes:

/f//l//ā//k//s/ (flakes) /f//l//ā//m//z/ (flames)

If they are successful, have students blend the following phonemes:

/k//l//ĭ//k//s/	(clicks)	/s//k//r//ē//m//z/	(screams)
/r//ĕ//s//t//s/	(rests)	/b//l//ŏ//k//s/	(blocks)

IF... students have trouble blending five or more phonemes into words,
THEN... have them blend the first three phonemes in a word, and then slowly add in each remaining phoneme to complete the word.

Lesson 11 Blend, Segment, and Count Five or More Phonemes

PRACTICE 2 Work with five-phoneme words. Point to the top of your head and say: This is my scalp. Listen as I say the word: *scalp*. The sounds in the word are /s/, /k/, /ă/, /l/, /p/. How many sounds is that? I will say the sounds again and hold up one finger for each sound. Repeat the sounds, holding up a finger for each one. Then use your other hand to count the fingers you have held up. One, two three, four, five. There are five sounds in *scalp*.

Listen as I say a word. Then say the sounds slowly with me and hold up a finger for each sound. Have students segment and count the five sounds in the following words. As students proceed, they will realize that all the words have five sounds. Focus their attention on careful, clear segmenting.

blond	(/b//l//ŏ//n//d/)	crisp	(/k//r//ĭ//s//p/)
prince	(/p//r//ĭ//n//s/)	drips	(/d//r//ĭ//p//s/)
screen	(/s//k//r//ē//n/)	grasp	(/g//r//ă//s//p/)
slant	(/s//l//ă//n//t/)	floats	(/f//l//ō//t//s/)
flaps	(/f//l//ă//p//s/)	blimp	(/b//l//ĭ//m//p/)
sprays	(/s//p//r//ā//z/)	trust	(/t//r//ŭ//s//t/)
grand	(/g//r//ă//n//d/)	stunt	(/s//t//ŭ//n//t/)

Present the following sentence from Student Page S83, which contains four of the five-phoneme words that students just segmented.

The blond prince did a grand stunt.

REMIND STUDENTS THAT…

- by saying a word slowly, they can hear all of its sounds.
- they can use their fingers to count the sounds they hear in a word.

✔ **MONITOR PROGRESS** Have students segment and count the sounds in the following words.

crust	(/k//r//ŭ//s//t/)	speaks	(/s//p//ē//k//s/)
creeps	(/k//r//ē//p//s/)	strays	(/s//t//r//ā//z/)
blast	(/b//l//ă//s//t/)	stand	(/s//t//ă//n//d/)

IF… students have trouble segmenting and counting five-phoneme words, THEN… have them first segment and count the three-phoneme word *stay*, progress to the four-phoneme word *stray*, and finally segment and count the five-phoneme word *strays* from the activity. Provide guidance and assistance as needed.

Lesson 11 Blend, Segment, and Count Five or More Phonemes

REMIND STUDENTS THAT...

- by saying a word slowly, they can hear all of its sounds.
- they can count the sounds they hear in a word.

PRACTICE 3 Work with words of six or seven phonemes. Put a hand to your brow and squint as if you are looking into the sun. Say: I'm squinting my eyes. Listen to the word *squint* as I say the word's sounds: /s/, /k/, /w/, /ĭ/, /n/, /t/. How many sounds is that? I'll say the sounds again and make a mark on the board for each sound. Repeat the sounds, making a mark on the board for each one. Then point to and count each mark. There are six sounds in *squint*.

Have a volunteer make marks on the board or on a sheet of paper as you segment words and count sounds together. Listen as I say a word. Then say the sounds slowly with me and make a mark for each sound. Segment and count the sounds in these words.

strands (/s//t//r//ă//n//d//z/, 7)
strange (/s//t//r//ā/n//j/, 6)
splits (/s//p//l//ĭ//t//s/, 6)
strict (/s//t//r//ĭ//k//t/, 6)
crusts (/k//r//ŭ//s//t//s/, 6)
streams (/s//t//r//ē//m//z/, 6)
sprints (/s//p//r//ĭ//n//t//s/,7)
clumps (/k//l//ŭ//m//p//s/, 6)

Present the following sentence from Student Page S84, which contains four of the six-phoneme words that students just segmented.

Strange crusts and clumps of dirt float down streams.

✓ **INDEPENDENT PRACTICE** Have students use pencils to make tally marks on sheets of paper as they segment the following words. Then have them identify how many sounds each word has.

spreads (/s//p//r//ĕ//d//z/, 6)
scrolls (/s//k//r//ō//l//z/, 6)
crafts (/k//r//ă//f//t//s/, 6)

IF... students identify less than six phonemes in any of the words,
THEN... have them repeat the segmenting process at a significantly slower rate to distinguish each of the six individual phonemes.

Lesson 11 **Blend, Segment, and Count Five or More Phonemes**

The Clean Floor

They swept with brooms.
They swept twelve rooms.
They scrubbed some streaks.
The clean floor squeaks!

Teacher: This Student Page is intended as an *optional extension* of the lesson. After teaching the phonological awareness lesson orally, you can distribute or display this page to connect the phonological awareness skills (sounds) to phonics skills (sound-spelling).

Lesson 11 Blend, Segment, and Count Five or More Phonemes

Trucks scrape streets. Guests scrub spoons.

Teacher: This Student Page is intended as an *optional extension* of the lesson. After teaching the phonological awareness lesson orally, you can distribute or display this page to connect the phonological awareness skills (sounds) to phonics skills (sound-spelling).

Lesson 11 Blend, Segment, and Count Five or More Phonemes

The blond prince did a grand stunt.

Teacher: This Student Page is intended as an *optional extension* of the lesson. After teaching the phonological awareness lesson orally, you can distribute or display this page to connect the phonological awareness skills (sounds) to phonics skills (sound-spelling).

Lesson 11 Blend, Segment, and Count Five or More Phonemes

Strange crusts and clumps of dirt float down streams.

Teacher: This Student Page is intended as an *optional extension* of the lesson. After teaching the phonological awareness lesson orally, you can distribute or display this page to connect the phonological awareness skills (sounds) to phonics skills (sound-spelling).

Lesson 12 *R*-Controlled Vowels

INTRODUCE Today we will listen to the sounds in words that have /r/ after the vowel. The sounds are /ar/ as in *star*, /or/ as in *door*, and /er/ as in *bird*.

MODEL Read aloud "The Baby" from Student Page S85. These are words that have the same beginning sounds, /b/, and the same ending sounds, /n/. Their middle sounds are different. Listen as I say the words: *barn, born, burn.*

The Baby

When the baby was born, Dad and I were
out in the barn.
We heard the news.
We jumped and hugged!
Even the animals seemed to smile.
We left the barn to burn a candle in the window.
We could not wait to meet the new baby!

/or/ sound

/ar/ sound

/er/ sound

barn	born	burn

TEACH Point to the image of the barn. This is a barn. *Barn* has the middle sound /ar/. Other words with this sound are *are* (as in, we *are* here) and *farm*. What other words do you know that have the /ar/ sound? Pause for responses.

Point to the word *born*. The word *born* has the middle sound /or/. Other words with this sound are *or* (as in, we study *or* we play) and *floor*. What other words do you know that have the /or/ sound? Pause for responses.

Point to the word *fire*. We burn things in a fire. *Burn* has the middle sound /er/. Other words with this sound are *fur* (as in, a bear has *fur*) and *work*. What other words do you know that have the /er/ sound? Pause for responses.

Today we learned about three sounds: /ar/, /or/, and /er/.

RF.1.2.d Segment spoken single-syllable words into their complete sequence of individual sounds (phonemes).

OBJECTIVES:

- Recognize that vowel sounds change when the vowel is followed by /r/.
- Segment words that contain *r*-controlled vowels.

Lesson 12 R-Controlled Vowels

REMIND STUDENTS THAT…

- words are made of different sounds they can hear.
- by saying a word slowly, they can hear all of its sounds.

PRACTICE 1 Use Student Page S86 to help students recognize the /ar/ sound. Say: I will say a word slowly so I can hear its sounds: *car*. I will say the sounds in the word: /k/ (pause) /ar/. *Car* ends with the /ar/ sound.

Point to the harp and say: This is a *harp*. Say the word slowly with me to hear the sounds: /h//ar//p/. The middle sound in *harp* is /ar/. Repeat the process to isolate the medial /ar/ sound in *guard, cart,* and *shark* and the initial /ar/ in *arm*.

Now I will say two words. Clap when you hear the /ar/ sound in a word. Say each word pair normally, then repeat and pause after each word for students to clap. Clap: *far, fur; stump, start; mark, make; lodge, large; chart, child; stir, star; charm, shirt; heard, hard; bark, bake*.

MONITOR PROGRESS Say the following pairs of words and have students tell you which of the two words has the /ar/ sound.

heart, hurt	yore, yarn	art, eat
sneak, snarl	park, pat	jet, jar
start, stop	cord, card	farm, firm

IF… students have trouble distinguishing the /ar/ sound,
THEN… have students watch your mouth as you make the /ar/ sound, and then pronounce the words in unison several times.

Lesson 12 R-Controlled Vowels

PRACTICE 2 Use the images on Student Page S87 to help students recognize the /or/ sound. Model listening for a phoneme. I will say a word slowly so I can hear its sounds. Listen with me: *door.* I will say the sounds in the word: /d/ (pause) /or/. *Door* ends with the /or/ sound.

Now let's listen for the /or/ sound together. Point to the horse and say: This is a *horse.* Say the word slowly with me to hear the sounds: /h//or//s/. The middle sound in *horse* is /or/. Repeat the process to isolate the medial /or/ in *fort* and *corn,* the final /or/ in *score,* and the single phoneme in *oar.*

door	horse	fort
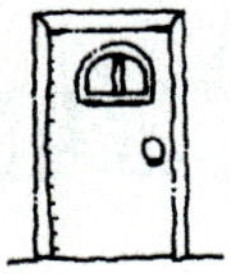		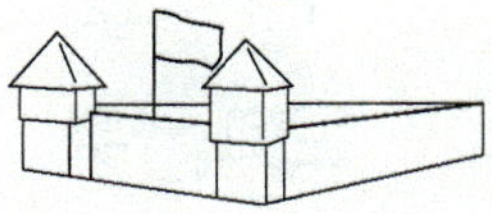
corn	score	oar
	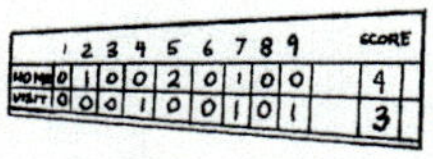	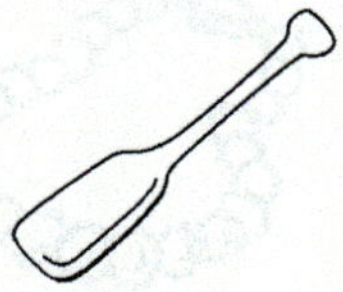

Now I will say two words. Clap when you hear the /or/ sound in a word. For example, if I say, *store* (pause) *stare, you would clap for the /or/ sound in store.* Proceed with the word pairs below. Say each pair normally, then repeat and pause after each word for students to clap.

rare, roar	chart, chore	perch, porch
short, shirt	tear, torn	stork, streak
hear, horn	were, war	more, mire

MONITOR PROGRESS Say each word pair. Have students say which has the /or/ sound. For example, say: *mare, more.* Which word has /or/? (more)

sport, spurt	car, core	lore, lair
sneak, snore	fork, flake	curt, court
pore, peer	firm, form	tour, tore

IF... students misidentify the word with the /or/ sound,
THEN... have students repeat each word in the pair very slowly, listening carefully for the word that contains the /or/ sound.

REMIND STUDENTS THAT...

- words are made of different sounds they can hear.
- by saying a word slowly, they can hear all of its sounds.

Lesson 12 R-Controlled Vowels

REMIND STUDENTS THAT…

- words are made of different sounds they can hear.
- by saying a word slowly, they can hear all of its sounds.

PRACTICE 3 Use Student Page S88 to help students recognize the /er/ sound. Say: I will say a word slowly so I can hear its sounds. Listen with me: *stir.* I will say the sounds in the word: /s/ (pause) /t/ (pause) /er/. *Stir* ends with the /er/ sound.

Point to the shirt and say: This is a *shirt*. Say the word slowly with me to hear the sounds: /sh//er//t/. The middle sound in *shirt* is /er/. Repeat the process to isolate the medial /er/ in *herd, pearls,* and *fern* and the initial /er/ in *earth*.

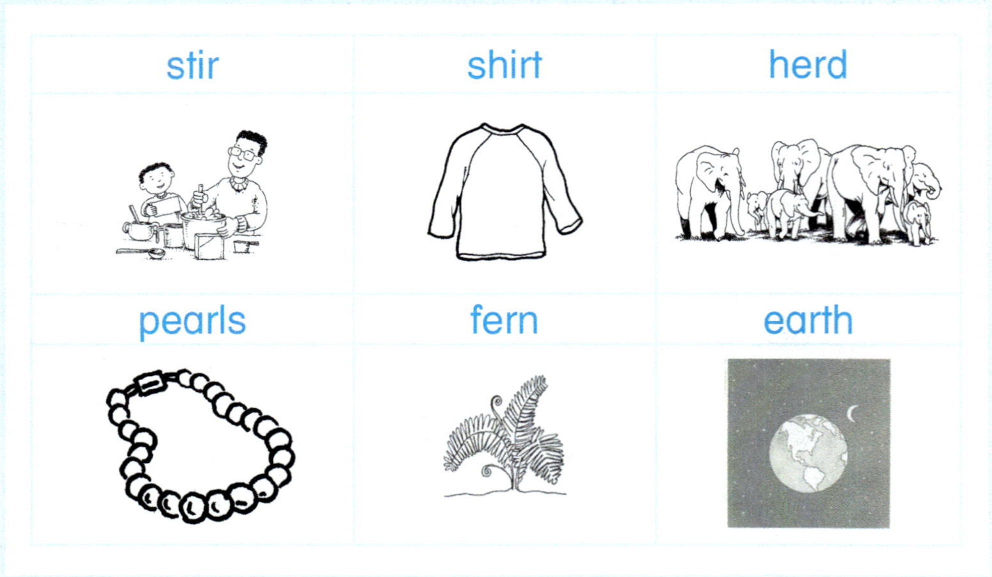

Now I will say two words. Clap when you hear the /er/ sound in a word. For example, if I say, *turn* (pause) *tame,* you would clap for the /er/ sound in *turn.* Say each word pair below normally, then repeat and pause after each word for students to clap: *word, wire; urge, age; cove, curve; hair, her; lean, learn; perch, punch; wake, work; hurt, heart; squat, squirt.*

INDEPENDENT PRACTICE Say the following pairs of words and have students tell you which one has the /er/ sound. For example, say: *voice, verse.* Which word has /er/? (verse)

air, urn	girl, goal	shore, sure
blur, bare	wild, world	gem, germ
purse, pool	dart, dirt	spurt, sport

IF… students cannot identify which word in the pair has the /er/ sound,
THEN… have students practice pronouncing several familiar /er/ words, and then return to the word pair later on to have students try again.

Lesson 12 ***R*-Controlled Vowels**

The Baby

When the baby was born, Dad and I were out in the barn.
We heard the news.
We jumped and hugged!
Even the animals seemed to smile.
We left the barn to burn a candle in the window.
We could not wait to meet the new baby!

barn	born	burn

Teacher: This Student Page is intended as an *optional extension* of the lesson. After teaching the phonological awareness lesson orally, you can distribute or display this page to connect the phonological awareness skills (sounds) to phonics skills (sound-spelling).

Lesson 12 *R*-Controlled Vowels

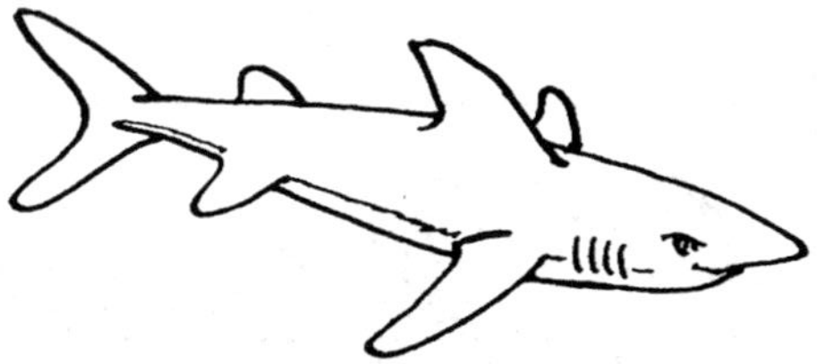

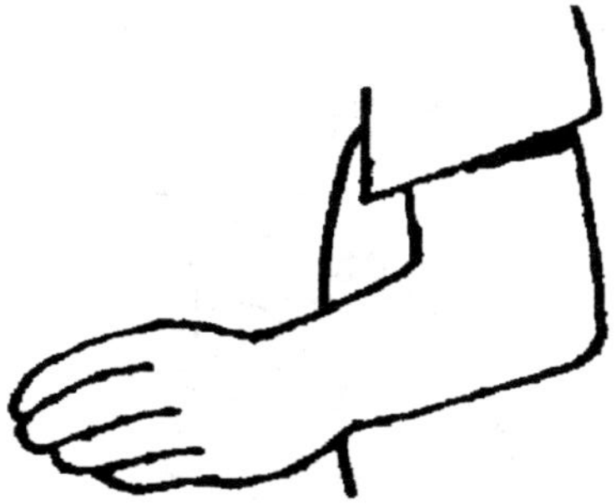

Teacher: This Student Page is intended as an *optional extension* of the lesson. After teaching the phonological awareness lesson orally, you can distribute or display this page to connect the phonological awareness skills (sounds) to phonics skills (sound-spelling).

Lesson 12 *R*-Controlled Vowels

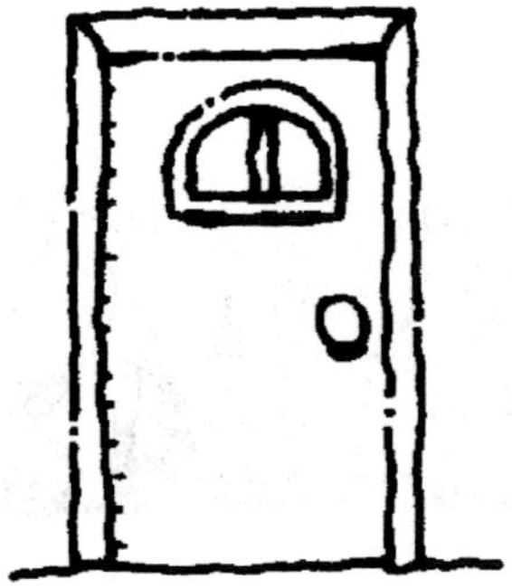

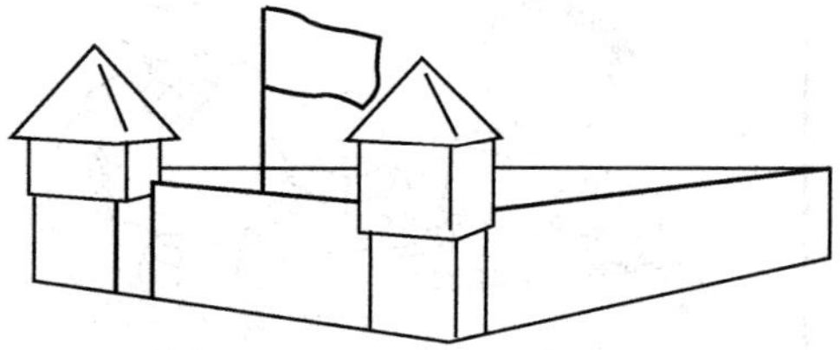

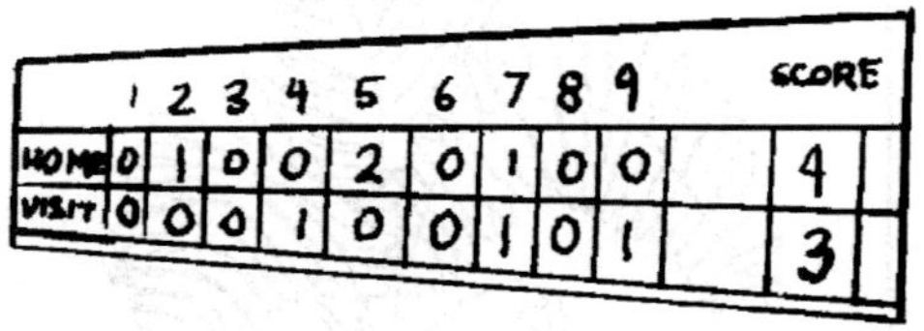

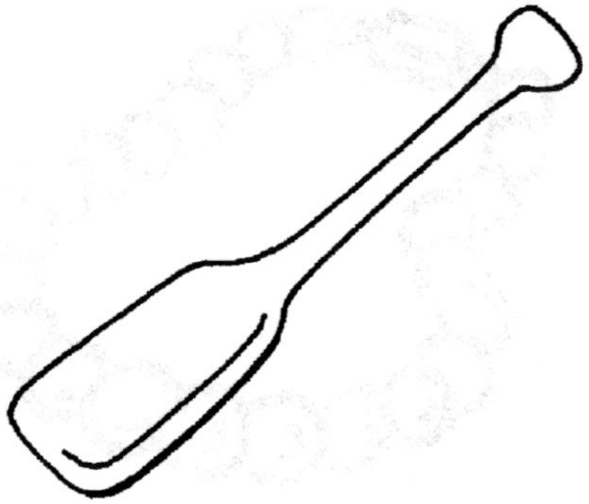

Teacher: This Student Page is intended as an *optional extension* of the lesson. After teaching the phonological awareness lesson orally, you can distribute or display this page to connect the phonological awareness skills (sounds) to phonics skills (sound-spelling).

Lesson 12 *R*-Controlled Vowels

Teacher: This Student Page is intended as an *optional extension* of the lesson. After teaching the phonological awareness lesson orally, you can distribute or display this page to connect the phonological awareness skills (sounds) to phonics skills (sound-spelling).

Lesson 13 Consonant Digraphs

RF.1.2.d Segment spoken single-syllable words into their complete sequence of individual sounds (phonemes).

OBJECTIVES:

- Recognize the sounds of common consonant digraphs.
- Segment words that contain consonant digraphs.

INTRODUCE You know that words are made of sounds. Today we will listen for the sounds in *shoe* and *chew*—the /sh/ and /ch/ sounds. We will also listen for the /th/ sound in *think* and the /ng/ sound in *young*.

MODEL Present the illustrated sentences from Student Page S89. Point to the picture of the dogs. Listen as I read about this picture. Read the sentence. I hear /ng/ at the end of *young* and *wrong*. I hear /ch/ at the beginning of *chewed*. I hear /sh/ at the beginning of *shoes*. Listen again. Repeat the sentence.

The young pups chewed the wrong shoes!	She thought of a white sheep sitting on a chair.

TEACH Point to the picture of the sheep and read the sentence. I will say some of these words slowly. *She; she* has /sh/ at the beginning. Say the sound with me: /sh/. The next word is *thought; She thought*. The word *thought* has /th/ at the beginning. Say /th/ with me: /th/.

Listen as I say *sheep*: /sh//ē//p/. What sound do you hear at the beginning of the word? Pause for responses. *Sheep* has /sh/ at the beginning.

Listen for the ending sound in this word: *sitting*. Let's say the word together: *sitting*. What sound do you hear at the end? Pause for responses. Let's say the sound together: /ng/.

Where is the sheep sitting? Pause for responses. The sheep is sitting on a chair. What sound is at the beginning of *chair*? Pause for responses. The /ch/ sound is at the beginning of *chair*. Let's say it together: /ch/.

Lesson 13 Consonant Digraphs

REMIND STUDENTS THAT...

- words are made of different sounds they can hear.
- by saying a word slowly, they can hear its sounds.

PRACTICE 1 Help students hear and distinguish the /sh/ and /ch/ sounds. Listen to these words: *I wish for a fish.* What sound do you hear at the end of *wish* and *fish?* Pause for responses. Let's make the /sh/ sound together: /sh/. Now let's think of words that start with /sh/. How about *shout?* What are some others? Invite responses.

Now listen to these words: *I chew some cheese.* What sound do you hear at the beginning of *chew* and *cheese?* Pause for responses. Let's make the /ch/ sound together: /ch/. Now let's think of words that end with /ch/. How about *touch?* What are some others? Invite responses.

I will say some words. Say the sounds you hear in each word. For example, if I say *teach,* you will say /t/ /ē/ /ch/. Have students segment these words.

couch /k/ /ow/ /ch/	chick /ch/ /i/ /k/	shark /sh/ /ar/ /k/
leash /l/ /ē/ /sh/	chest /ch/ /e/ /s/ /t/	rich /r/ /i/ /ch/
crush /k/ /r/ /u/ /sh/	shield /sh/ /ē/ /l/ /d/	shelf /sh/ /e/ /l/ /f/
chill /ch/ /i/ /l/	pouch /p/ /ow/ /ch/	chase /ch/ /ā/ /s/

If desired, present Student Page S90 and have students segment the words *couch, chick, shark,* and *leash* again. Then have them identify which two words have the /ch/ sound and which two have the /sh/ sound.

ch		sh	

MONITOR PROGRESS Have students segment these word pairs and identify which word has the /sh/ sound and which one has the /ch/ sound.

shoe, chew	chin, shin
much, mush	wish, which

IF... students have trouble distinguishing the two sounds,
THEN... have them slowly say each sound with you, noting the different position of the lips and tongue as they make each sound. Provide familiar /sh/ and /ch/ words to help students practice distinguishing the two sounds.

Lesson 13 Consonant Digraphs

PRACTICE 2 Listen to these words: *We sew with thread.* What sound do you hear at the end of *with?* Pause for responses. What sound do you hear at the beginning of *thread?* Pause for responses. We hear /th/ at the end of *with* and at the beginning of *thread.* Say the sound with me: /th/.

I will say some words. Say the sounds you hear in each word. For example, if I say *with,* you will say /w//i//th/. Have students segment these words.

bath /b//a//th/ both /b//ō//th/ thick /th// i//k/

Listen as I say a new word: *spring.* What sound do you hear at the end of *spring?* Pause for responses. Say the sound with me: /ng/. This sound comes at the end of many words we know. I will say more words. Say the sounds you hear in each word. For example, if I say *king,* you will say /k//i//ng/. Have students segment these words.

bang /b//a//ng/ bring /b//r// i//ng/ sting /s//t// i//ng/

If desired, present Student Page S91 and have students segment the words *thread, tooth,* and *spring* again. Then have them identify which words have the /th/ sound and which word has the /ng/ sound.

th		ng
	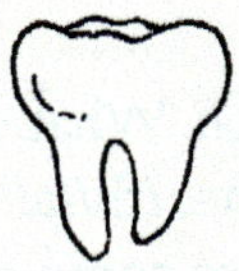	

MONITOR PROGRESS Have students segment these words.

through /th//r//ōō/ truth /t//r//ōō//th/
song /s//o//ng/ string /s//t//r// i//ng/

Repeat each word with students. After each one, ask: Does [*through*] have the /th/ sound or the /ng/ sound?

IF... students cannot determine if a word has the /th/ or the /ng/ sound,
THEN... have them segment the word again at a significantly slower pace, guiding them to listen carefully for the correct sound.

REMIND STUDENTS THAT...

- words are made of different sounds they can hear.
- by saying a word slowly, they can hear its sounds.

Lesson 13 Consonant Digraphs

REMIND STUDENTS THAT...

- words are made of different sounds they can hear.
- by saying a word slowly, they can hear its sounds.

PRACTICE 3 Review the digraph sounds alone, and then combine them with other consonants and digraphs. I will say some words. After each word, tell me the sound at the beginning. For example, if I say *think*, you will say /th/. Have students identify the initial sounds in these words.

shell thumb champ cheek short third

Now tell me the final sound for each word I say. For example, if I say *push*, you will say /sh/. Have students identify the final sounds in these words.

ping both reach flash bang peach

Read aloud this passage from Student Page S92. Help students identify words that have the /ch/, /th/, and /ng/ sounds.

The chinchilla inches along.
There!
I can measure its length.

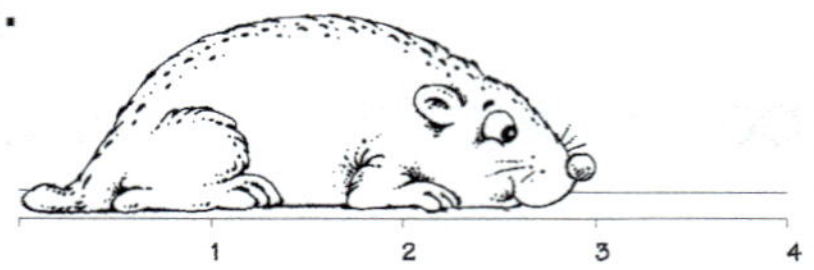

Explain that sometimes these sounds are combined with other sounds at the ends of words. Listen to this word: *lunch*. Say the word slowly with me to hear the sounds: /l//u//n//ch/. The last sound in *lunch* is /ch/. Have students segment these words.

inch itch wrench pinch pitch tenth

Now listen to these words: *thank you*. What sounds can we hear in the word *thank*? Say the sounds slowly with me: /th//a//ng//k/. This word begins with /th/. Inside, it has the /ng/ sound. Here are some other words with the /ng/ sound inside. Say the sounds in the words with me:

drink /d//r//i//ng//k/ length /l//e//ng//th/

✔ **INDEPENDENT PRACTICE** Have students segment each of these words and then determine whether the word has the /sh/, /ch/, /th/, or /ng/ sound.

flash shove charm fang threw

IF... students have trouble isolating a digraph sound,
THEN... model the correct response by segmenting the word, have the student repeat the word with emphasis on the digraph sound, and return to the word later in the practice.

Lesson 13 Consonant Digraphs

The young pups chewed the wrong shoes!	She thought of a white sheep sitting on a chair.

Teacher: This Student Page is intended as an *optional extension* of the lesson. After teaching the phonological awareness lesson orally, you can distribute or display this page to connect the phonological awareness skills (sounds) to phonics skills (sound-spelling).

Lesson 13 Consonant Digraphs

ch		sh	
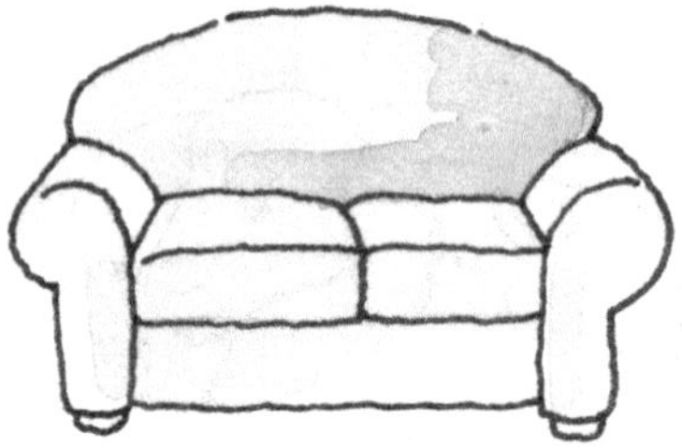			

Teacher: This Student Page is intended as an *optional extension* of the lesson. After teaching the phonological awareness lesson orally, you can distribute or display this page to connect the phonological awareness skills (sounds) to phonics skills (sound-spelling).

Lesson 13 Consonant Digraphs

th		ng
	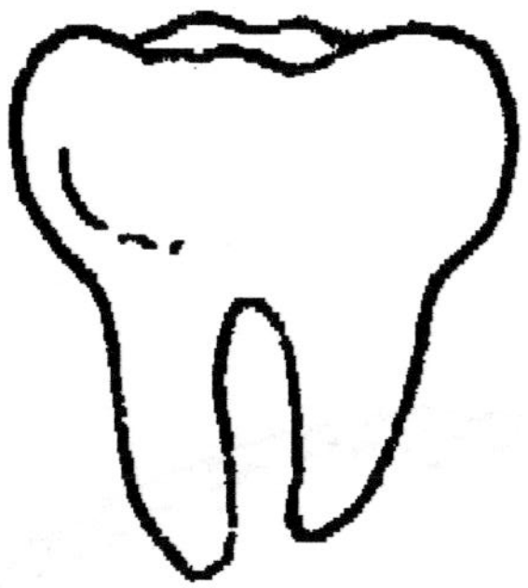	

Teacher: This Student Page is intended as an *optional extension* of the lesson. After teaching the phonological awareness lesson orally, you can distribute or display this page to connect the phonological awareness skills (sounds) to phonics skills (sound-spelling).

Lesson 13 Consonant Digraphs

The chinchilla inches along.
There!
I can measure its length.

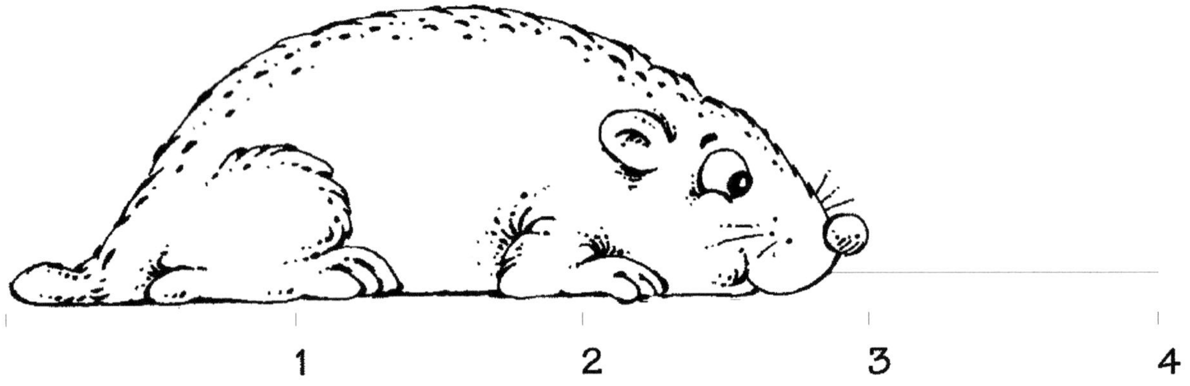

Teacher: This Student Page is intended as an *optional extension* of the lesson. After teaching the phonological awareness lesson orally, you can distribute or display this page to connect the phonological awareness skills (sounds) to phonics skills (sound-spelling).

ASSESSMENT
LESSONS 9–13

Phonological Awareness

ASSESS MASTERY Use this Checkpoint to assess students' mastery of blending and segmenting sounds in words.

ADMINISTER THE TEST Administer the Checkpoint orally to each student. Model the process as described, and then have the student use the process to respond to your prompts. Record responses on the chart on the next page.

1. Segment and Blend Sounds (Lesson 9)
MODEL: I will say the sounds that make a word. You will say the word. If I say /ĭ//t/, you will say *it.* Then I will say a word. You will say each sound in the word. If I say *hat,* you will say /h//ă//t/.

ASSESS:	/s//l//ă//m/	/t//ă//s//k/	/f//ĭ//n//d/	/w//ē/	
	from	look	pay	glow	nest

2. Blend and Segment Three- and Four-Phoneme Words (Lesson 10)
MODEL: I will say the sounds that make a word. You will say the word. If I say /r//ī//t/, you will say *right.* Then I will say a word. You will say each sound in the word. If I say *smile,* you will say /s//m//ī//l/.

ASSESS:	/p//ŏ//t/	/s//p//ĭ//n/	/p//ō//l//z/
	skip	melt	cub
	sleep	hand	pail

3. Blend, Segment, and Count Five or More Phonemes (Lesson 11)
MODEL: I will say a word. You will say each sound in the word and then count the sounds. If I say *straight,* you will say /s//t//r//ā//t/ and count five sounds. Then I will say the sounds that make a word. You will blend them together to say the word. If I say /s//t//r//ā//t/, you will say *straight.*

ASSESS:	friend	twelve	trust	sprayed
	/s//p//r//ĭ//n//t//s/	/g//r//ā//t//s/	/p//l//ă//n//z/	

4. *R*-Controlled Vowels (Lesson 12)
MODEL: I will name a sound and say two words. You will tell me which word has the sound I named. If I say /or/, *more, share,* you will say *more.*

ASSESS:	/ar/	dare, star	jar, burr	for, charm
	/or/	shore, sure	hair, wore	forth, cloth
	/er/	birth, bark	thirst, most	porch, perch

RF.1.2.b Orally produce single-syllable words by blending sounds (phonemes), including consonant blends.

RF.1.2.d Segment spoken single-syllable words into their complete sequence of individual sounds (phonemes).

ASSESSMENT
LESSONS 9–13

Phonological Awareness

5. Consonant Digraphs (Lesson 13)

MODEL: I will say a word and ask you to give me its final sound. If I say *each*, you will say /ch/. Then I will say a word and ask you to give me its beginning sound. If I say *shoe*, you will say /sh/.

ASSESS:	final:	splash	lurch	sling	health
	beginning:	throat	show	cheer	

SCORING

SKILL/LESSON	STANDARD	SCORE
1. Segment and Blend Sounds (Lesson 9) slam; task; find; we; /f//r//ŭ//m/; /l//o͞o//k/; /p//ā/; /g//l//ō/; /n//ĕ//s//t/	**RF.1.2.b** Orally produce single-syllable words by blending sounds (phonemes), including consonant blends.	_____ / 9
2. Blend and Segment Three- and Four-Phoneme Words (Lesson 10) pot; spin; poles; /s//k//ĭ//p/; /m//ĕ//l//t/; /k//ŭ//b/; /s//l//ē//p/; /h//ă//n//d/; /p//ā//l/	**RF.1.2.b** Orally produce single-syllable words by blending sounds (phonemes), including consonant blends. **RF.1.2.d** Segment spoken single-syllable words into their complete sequence of individual sounds (phonemes).	_____ / 9
3. Blend, Segment, and Count Five or More Phonemes (Lesson 11) /f//r//ĕ//n//d/, 5; /t//w//ĕ//l//v/, 5; /t//r//ŭ//s//t/, 5; /s//p//r//ā//d/, 5; sprints; grates; plans		_____ / 7
4. R-Controlled Vowels (Lesson 12) star; jar; charm; shore; wore; forth; birth; thirst; perch		_____ / 9
5. Consonant Digraphs (Lesson 13) /sh/; /ch/; /ng/; /th/; /th/; /sh/; /ch/		_____ / 7

An overall score of 80% correct is typically considered mastery. Use your judgment and your individual students' needs as well to determine skill mastery.

IF...you determine that students have not demonstrated sufficient mastery of one or more skills,
THEN...review the skill(s), going back to the lessons to reteach and scaffold as needed.

Lesson 14 Diphthongs and Variants

RF.1.2.d Segment spoken single-syllable words into their complete sequence of individual sounds (phonemes).

OBJECTIVES:

- Recognize the sounds of common diphthongs and variants.
- Segment words that contain diphthongs and variants.

INTRODUCE Remind students that they have learned to listen carefully for sounds in words. Today, we're going to listen carefully for three sounds in words: /oi/, /ow/, and /o͞o/. Say the sounds with me: /oi/, /ow/, and /o͞o/.

MODEL Provide some familiar examples of words with the /oi/, /ow/, and /o͞o/ sounds. I will say words with the sounds /oi/, /ow/, and /o͞o/. First, I will say words with the /oi/ sound. Say it with me: /oi/. The word *oil* has this sound. So do the words *boil* and *soil*. Let's say these words together: *oil, boil, soil*. Each of these words has the /oi/ sound.

Repeat the above process by presenting the words *cloud, cow,* and *town* for the /ow/ sound and the words *look, took,* and *book* for the /o͞o/ sound.

TEACH Read aloud the sentences below from Student Page S95. Before you read each one, say: I will read a sentence. Listen for words that have the [/oi/, /ow/, /o͞o/] sound. Read each sentence slowly, emphasizing the diphthong in *boil, oil, cow, town, took,* and *book*.

Boil the water before you add oil.	I saw a cow in town.	He took a book with him.

Draw students' attention to the image of the pot of boiling water. You *boil* the water before you add *oil*. Say the words with me: *boil, oil.* Do you hear the /oi/ sound? Say it with me: /oi/. Repeat the process for the remaining two illustrated sentences.

Lesson 14 Diphthongs and Variants

REMIND STUDENTS THAT...

- words are made of different sounds they can hear.
- some words contain the /oi/ sound.
- by saying a word slowly, they can hear the /oi/ sound.

PRACTICE 1 Review previously introduced words with the /oi/ sound. Remember that some words have the /oi/ sound. *Oil* is one word we learned that has this sound. Listen for the /oi/ sound as I say the word: *oil*. Let's say it together: *oil*. What is another word that has the /oi/ sound? Yes! *Boil* is another word that has the /oi/ sound. Use the same process to reinforce the /oi/ sound in *boil*.

Introduce new words that have the /oi/ sound. I will say a new word. Listen carefully to the word as I say it: *toy*. Say it with me: *toy*. Do you hear the /oi/ sound? Let's say it again slowly: /t//oi/. Use the same process to introduce the word *boy*.

Read aloud the following passage from Student Page S96. Then say: Now I will read the story again. Listen carefully for the /oi/ sound. Raise your hand when you hear a word with the /oi/ sound.

Oh, Boy!

A girl and a boy went to the store.
The boy got oil to make cookies.
The girl got a toy boat.
They will have fun today!

MONITOR PROGRESS Describe this game to the class: I will say a word. If the word has the /oi/ sound, clap your hands. If the word does not have the /oi/ sound, don't clap your hands. Demonstrate the game by saying *boil* and *boat*, clapping your hands after *boil* and refraining from clapping after *boat*.

Use the following words to play the game:

oil	coat	sew	soil
toy	town	ball	joy

IF... students cannot identify words that have the /oi/ sound,
THEN... have students repeat the word very slowly, segmenting the sounds and listening closely for the /oi/ sound.

Lesson 14 Diphthongs and Variants

PRACTICE 2 Review previously introduced words with the /ow/ sound. Remember that some words have the /ow/ sound. *Cow* is one word we learned that has this sound. Listen for the /ow/ sound as I say the word: *cow*. Say it with me: *cow*. What is another word that has the /ow/ sound? Right! The word *town* has the /ow/ sound. Use the same process to reinforce the /ow/ sound in *town*.

Introduce new words that have the /ow/ sound. Listen carefully to this word: *brown*. Do you hear the /ow/ sound? Let's say it together slowly: /br//ow//n/. Use the same process to introduce the word *clown*.

Say: Listen as I read a poem. Read aloud "Right in the Middle of Town" from Student Page S97. Then say: Now I will read the poem again. Listen carefully for the /ow/ sound. Raise your hand when you hear a word with the /ow/ sound.

REMIND STUDENTS THAT…

- words are made of different sounds they can hear.
- some words contain the /ow/ sound.
- by saying a word slowly, they can hear the /ow/ sound.

Right in the Middle of Town

I saw a clown
Ride a cow
Right in the middle of town.
What color was that silly cow?
That silly cow was brown.

✔ **MONITOR PROGRESS** Read aloud the word pairs below. For each pair, have students identify which word has the /ow/ sound.

<u>cow</u>, can	dot, <u>down</u>	club, <u>clown</u>
close, <u>cloud</u>	<u>brown</u>, broom	<u>town</u>, tub
from, <u>frown</u>	<u>loud</u>, lead	

IF… students misidentify the word that has the /ow/ sound,
THEN… have them say each word in the pair softly to themselves, segmenting the sounds in each word to pinpoint the correct word.

Lesson 14 Diphthongs and Variants

REMIND STUDENTS THAT...

- words are made of different sounds they can hear.
- some words contain the /o͝o/ sound.
- by saying a word slowly, they can hear the /o͝o/ sound.

PRACTICE 3 Review previously introduced words with the /o͝o/ sound. Remember that some words have the /o͝o/ sound. *Book* is one word we learned that has this sound. Listen for the /o͝o/ sound as I say the word: *book*. Let's say it together: *book*. What is another word that has the /o͝o/ sound? Yes! The word *took* also has the /o͝o/ sound. Use the same process to reinforce the /o͝o/ sound in *took*.

Introduce new words that have the /o͝o/ sound. Listen carefully as I say a word: *put*. Do you hear the /o͝o/ sound in *put*? Say it with me: *put*. Use the same process to introduce the word *look*.

Read aloud the following passage from Student Page S98. Then say: Now I will read the story again. Listen carefully for the /o͝o/ sound. Raise your hand when you hear a word with the /o͝o/ sound.

Jack and Mia

Jack has a favorite book.
He put it in his wagon.
Mia has a tiny dog.
She put it in her wagon.
They took their wagons to the park.
Now look what fun they are having!

INDEPENDENT PRACTICE Read aloud the following sets of words. For each set, have students identify which word has the /o͝o/ sound.

took, take, tone	bowl, bone, book	pop, put, pet
look, lock, lake	show, shook, shake	feet, fort, foot

IF... students have difficulty identifying the word that has the /o͝o/ sound, THEN... have students read each set of words aloud and then repeat each word very slowly, segmenting the sounds carefully and listening for the /o͝o/ sound.

Lesson 14 Diphthongs and Variants

Boil the water before you add oil.	I saw a cow in town.	He took a book with him.

Teacher: This Student Page is intended as an *optional extension* of the lesson. After teaching the phonological awareness lesson orally, you can distribute or display this page to connect the phonological awareness skills (sounds) to phonics skills (sound-spelling).

Lesson 14 Diphthongs and Variants

Oh, Boy!

A girl and a boy went to the store.
The boy got oil to make cookies.
The girl got a toy boat.
They will have fun today!

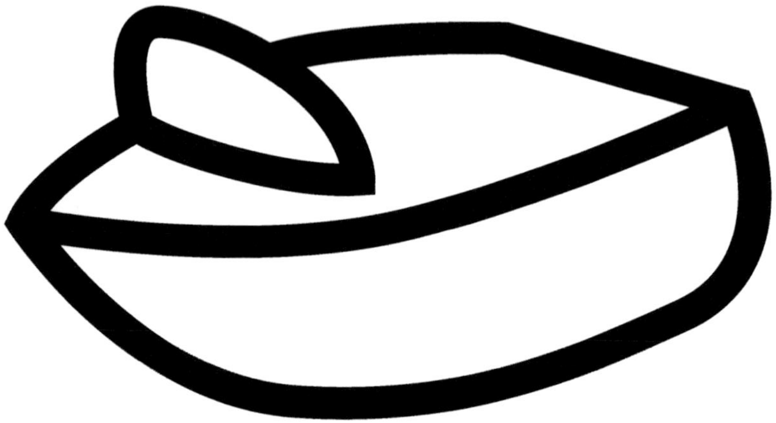

Teacher: This Student Page is intended as an *optional extension* of the lesson. After teaching the phonological awareness lesson orally, you can distribute or display this page to connect the phonological awareness skills (sounds) to phonics skills (sound-spelling).

Lesson 14 **Diphthongs and Variants**

Right in the Middle of Town

I saw a clown
Ride a cow
Right in the middle of town.
What color was that silly cow?
That silly cow was brown.

Teacher: This Student Page is intended as an *optional extension* of the lesson. After teaching the phonological awareness lesson orally, you can distribute or display this page to connect the phonological awareness skills (sounds) to phonics skills (sound-spelling).

Jack and Mia

Jack has a favorite book.
He put it in his wagon.
Mia has a tiny dog.
She put it in her wagon.
They took their wagons to the park.
Now look what fun they are having!

Teacher: This Student Page is intended as an *optional extension* of the lesson. After teaching the phonological awareness lesson orally, you can distribute or display this page to connect the phonological awareness skills (sounds) to phonics skills (sound-spelling).

Lesson 15 Schwa /ə/ Sound

INTRODUCE Remind students that they have learned to listen carefully for sounds in words. The most common sound in English is the /ə/ (unstressed "/uh/") sound. Any vowel can create this sound. The schwa sound often appears in the unstressed syllable of a word. Today, we're going to listen carefully for a new sound: /ə/, as in the first syllable of the words *about* and *again* or the last syllable of the words *melon* and *basket*. Help students recognize the /ə/ sound as you say the words. Point out that it can be difficult to hear the /ə/ sound, but it is in many words.

MODEL Read the passage aloud. Point out the /ə/ words.

At the Fruit Stand

Marta went to the fruit stand.
She saw a nice, ripe melon.
"Oh no!" Marta said.
She had left her basket at home.
"Later I will try again," she said.

TEACH Demonstrate listening for the /ə/ sound. Begin by having students listen for syllables. Listen as I say the syllables that make up the word. As you say each syllable, clap your hands: *mel* (clap) *on* (clap). What word did I say? Repeat with *basket* and *again*.

After the oral exercise, you may wish to display the passage on Student Page S99 to extend the concept and show the different spellings of the /ə/ sound.

RF.1.2.d Segment spoken single-syllable words into their complete sequence of individual sounds (phonemes).

OBJECTIVES:

- Segment words into syllables.
- Segment words to identify how sounds can be different in different syllables.
- Identify the /ə/ sound in spoken words.
- Distinguish words with the /ə/ sound.

Lesson 15 Schwa /ə/ Sound

REMIND STUDENTS THAT...

- they can segment words into syllables.
- they can identify stressed and unstressed syllables.

PRACTICE 1: Identify Stressed and Unstressed Syllables Review syllable stresses. In some words, syllables have strong sounds. Listen to the word *shortcut*. Clap to emphasize syllables: *short* (clap) *cut* (clap). We hear the /or/ in the first syllable and the /ŭ/ in the second syllable. Both syllables are strong.

Now listen to the word *table: ta* (clap) *ble* (clap). Is one syllable stronger than the other? Yes, the first syllable. ***Ta**ble*. The first syllable is stronger, or "stressed." The second syllable is "unstressed." The /ə/ sound only appears in unstressed syllables.

Next, say each word in the word list below, and have volunteers tell which syllables are stressed and unstressed.

level (stressed/unstressed)
away (unstressed/stressed)
open (stressed/unstressed)
buckle (stressed/unstressed)
careful (stressed/unstressed)
buses (stressed/unstressed)

After you work through the exercise orally, you may wish to display Student Page S100 to extend the lesson, pointing out the syllables and where the /ə/ sound appears.

✔ **MONITOR PROGRESS** Check students' progress with the words below. Listen carefully while I say each word. Tell me which syllable is *unstressed*.

picture (second)	lower (second)	about (first)
lemon (second)	button (second)	cattle (second)

IF... students cannot determine which syllable is unstressed,
THEN... review syllables and exaggerate the stressed syllable. Remind them that the stressed syllable sounds stronger than the unstressed syllable. Return to problematic words later in the lesson.

Lesson 15 Schwa /ə/ Sound

PRACTICE 2: Identify Syllables with /ə/ Review syllable stresses. In some words, syllables have strong sounds. Listen to *exit.* We hear the /ĕ/ in the first syllable and the /ĭ/ in the second syllable. Now listen to *extra.* I stressed the first syllable. *Extra* has /ĕ/ in the first syllable and /ə/ in the second syllable. Repeat *exit* and *extra*, emphasizing each stressed syllable.

Next, say the words in the word list below, and have students raise hands to identify which syllable has the /ə/ sound. Remind students it is the syllable with the weaker sound.

parent (second)	water (second)
given (second)	compare (first)
adore (first)	Texas (second)

After you work through the exercise orally, you may wish to display Student Page S101 to extend the lesson, pointing out the syllables and where the /ə/ sound appears.

REMIND STUDENTS THAT...

- they can segment words into syllables.
- they can identify syllables with the /ə/ sound.

MONITOR PROGRESS Check students' progress with the words below. Listen carefully while I say each word. Tell me whether the first or the second syllable has the /ə/ sound.

nickel (second) melon (second) away (first)

IF... students cannot determine which syllable has the /ə/ sound,
THEN... review syllables and remind them that the /ə/ sound always appears in the weaker (unstressed) syllable.

Lesson 15 Schwa /ə/ Sound

REMIND STUDENTS THAT...

- they can segment words into syllables.
- they can identify syllables with the /ə/ sound.
- they can distinguish words with the /ə/ sound.

PRACTICE 3: Distinguish Words with the /ə/ Sound Invite students to listen for the /ə/ sound. I am going to say two words. Both words have two syllables, but only one word has the /ə/ sound in its unstressed syllable. After I say the words, I want you to tell me which one has the /ə/ sound. The first two words are *robin* and *rocky*. I'll say them again: *robin, rocky*. Which one has the /ə/ sound? (robin)

beanbag, bagel	salty, salad
able, airplane	cabin, cartwheel
person, pocket	extra, event

After you work through the exercise orally, you may wish to display Student Page S102 to extend the lesson. Remind students that any vowel can create the /ə/ sound.

✓ **INDEPENDENT PRACTICE** Check each student's independent progress with the words below. Listen carefully while I say each word. Tell me which words have the /ə/ sound.

mouthful, machine	about, anthill	matter, marry

IF... students cannot distinguish which words have the /ə/ sound,
THEN... model the correct response by saying both words, exaggerating the stressed and unstressed syllables in the word with the schwa.

Lesson 15 **Schwa /ə/ Sound**

At the Fruit Stand

Marta went to the fruit stand.
She saw a nice, ripe melon.
"Oh no!" Marta said.
She had left her basket at home.
"Later I will try again," she said.

Teacher: This Student Page is intended as an *optional extension* of the lesson. After teaching the phonological awareness lesson orally, you can distribute or display this page to connect the phonological awareness skills (sounds) to phonics skills (sound-spelling).

Lesson 15 Schwa /ə/ Sound

level	**buckle**
away	**careful**
open	**buses**

Teacher: This Student Page is intended as an *optional extension* of the lesson. After teaching the phonological awareness lesson orally, you can distribute or display this page to connect the phonological awareness skills (sounds) to phonics skills (sound-spelling).

Lesson 15 Schwa /ə/ Sound

parent	**water**
given	**compare**
adore	**Texas**

Teacher: This Student Page is intended as an *optional extension* of the lesson. After teaching the phonological awareness lesson orally, you can distribute or display this page to connect the phonological awareness skills (sounds) to phonics skills (sound-spelling).

Lesson 15 Schwa /ə/ Sound

beanbag, bagel	**salty, salad**
able, airplane	**cabin, cartwheel**
person, pocket	**extra, event**

Teacher: This Student Page is intended as an *optional extension* of the lesson. After teaching the phonological awareness lesson orally, you can distribute or display this page to connect the phonological awareness skills (sounds) to phonics skills (sound-spelling).

ASSESSMENT
LESSONS 14–15

Phonological Awareness

ASSESS MASTERY Use this checkpoint to assess students' mastery of the /oi/, /ow/, /o͝o/, and schwa (/ə/) sounds in spoken words.

ADMINISTER THE TEST Administer the Checkpoint to each student. For each item, model the process as described, and then have the student use the process to respond to your prompts. Record responses on the scoring chart on the next page.

RF.1.2.d Segment spoken single-syllable words into their complete sequence of individual sounds (phonemes).

1. Diphthongs and Variants (Lesson 14)
MODEL: I will say two words, and you will tell me which word has the /oi/ sound. For example, I could say *boy* and *boat*. Which word has the /oi/ sound? The word *boy* has the /oi/ sound.

ASSESS:	toy, tool	Jon, join	ball, boil

2. Diphthongs and Variants (Lesson 14)
MODEL: I will say two words, and you will tell me which word has the /ow/ sound. For example, I could say *town* and *tall*. Which word has the /ow/ sound? The word *town* has the /ow/ sound.

ASSESS:	brown, broom	now, not	crown, crow

3. Diphthongs and Variants (Lesson 14)
MODEL: I will say two words, and you will tell me which word has the /o͝o/ sound. For example, I could say *book* and *back*. Which word has the /o͝o/ sound? The word *book* has the /o͝o/ sound.

ASSESS:	pat, put	cook, cap	fat, foot

4. Schwa /ə/ Sound (Lesson 15)
MODEL: I will say a word, and you will tell me which syllable is unstressed. For example, I could say *bagel*. Which syllable is unstressed? The second syllable is unstressed.

ASSESS:	pickle	circus	afraid

5. Schwa /ə/ Sound (Lesson 15)
MODEL: I will say two words, and you will tell me which word has the /ə/ sound. For example, I could say *women* and *raincoat*. Which word has the /ə/ sound? The word *women* has the /ə/ sound.

ASSESS:	salad, sandwich	person, pancake	leopard, leaping

ASSESSMENT
LESSONS 14–15

Phonological Awareness

SCORING

SKILL/LESSON	SCORE
1. Diphthongs and Variants (Lesson 14) toy, tool *(toy)* Jon, join *(join)* ball, boil *(boil)*	___ / 3
2. Diphthongs and Variants (Lesson 14) brown, broom *(brown)* now, not *(now)* crown, crow *(crown)*	___ / 3
3. Diphthongs and Variants (Lesson 14) pat, put *(put)* cook, cap *(cook)* fat, foot *(foot)*	___ / 3
4. Schwa /ə/ Sound (Lesson 15) pickle *(second)* circus *(second)* afraid *(first)*	___ / 3
5. Schwa /ə/ Sound (Lesson 15) salad, sandwich *(salad)* person, pancake *(person)* leopard, leaping *(leopard)*	___ / 3

An overall score of 80% correct is typically considered mastery. Use your judgment and your individual students' needs as well to determine skill mastery.

IF...you determine that students have not demonstrated sufficient mastery of one or more skills,
THEN...review the skill(s), going back to the lessons to reteach and scaffold as needed.

Lesson 16 Common Consonant Digraphs 1

INTRODUCE Remind students that they can segment and blend sounds to say and read words with digraphs. A digraph is two consonants that stand for a single sound, for example, the letters *sh* make the single sound /sh/. Today we will learn to read and spell words with four digraphs that are used in many words.

MODEL Display or share copies of the passage "Home With a Cold" from Student Page S105, and read it aloud.

Home With a Cold

Kim feels sick.
She has a cough.
Her head throbs.
Her parents phone the school.

makes the /sh/ sound

makes the /th/ sound

makes the /f/ sound

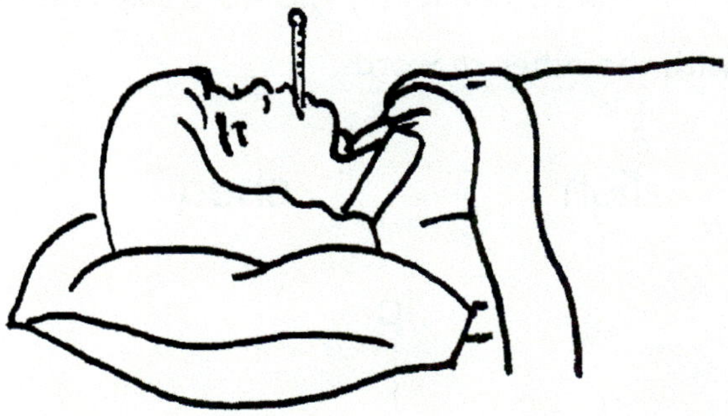

TEACH Point to and say each word with a digraph, emphasizing the single letter sounds: *sh* makes the /sh/ sound; *th* makes the /th/ sound; and *gh* and *ph* both make the /f/ sound. Have students repeat each word with you. Which two digraphs make the /f/ sound? (*gh, ph*) I know that each of these letter pairs makes one sound. I blend the digraph with other sounds to make a word. So, I can read and write words with these consonant digraphs correctly.

RF.1.3.a Know the spelling-sound correspondences for common consonant digraphs.

OBJECTIVES:

- Read and write words with the /sh/ *sh* digraph.
- Read and write words with the /th/ *th* digraph.
- Read and write words with the /f/ *ph* and *gh* digraphs.

Lesson 16 Common Consonant Digraphs 1

REMIND STUDENTS THAT...

- they can identify that the digraph *sh* makes the /sh/ sound.
- they can read words that begin or end with the digraph *sh*.
- they can write words that begin or end with the digraph *sh*.

PRACTICE 1: Consonant Digraph /sh/ *sh* Display Student Page S106. Use the following routine to guide students as they read and write words with the consonant digraph *sh*.

Routine

1. Model. Point to the word *ship*. Say it aloud several times. The first sound in *ship* is /sh/. Repeat the sound several times. Explain that /sh/ can be spelled *sh*. Have students say /sh/ several times as you point to the letters *sh*.

2. Model blending. Point to each part of the word and run your hand under *ship* as you blend the whole word. /sh//i//p/. Repeat the process by having students blend the word with you.

3. Write. Point to the Elkonin boxes. Ask students what letters you should write to complete the first set of boxes. Write *sh* in the box. What sound does *sh* make? Have students say the word *ship* and then write it.

Follow the routine with the other *sh* words.

ship fish shed cash

	ip	
f	i	
	ed	
c	a	

MONITOR PROGRESS Display the following sentences from Student Page S106. Have students identify the words with the consonant digraph *sh* and read them aloud.

Max makes a wish.
He wants red shoes.

IF...students cannot read a word correctly,
THEN...review that the two letters *sh* make the /sh/ sound. Guide students to blend the sounds to read the words. Then have them write the words.

Lesson 16 Common Consonant Digraphs I

PRACTICE 2: Consonant Digraph /th/ *th* Display the Student Page S107. Use the following routine to guide students as they read and write words with the consonant digraph *th*.

Routine

1. Model. Point to the word *thin*. Say it aloud several times. The first sound in *thin* is /th/. Repeat the sound several times. Explain that /th/ can be spelled *th*. Have students say /th/ several times as you point to the letters *th*.

2. Model blending. Point to each part of the word and run your hand under *thin* as you blend the whole word. /th//i//n/. Repeat the process by having students blend the word with you.

3. Write. Point to the Elkonin boxes. Ask students what letters you should write to complete the first set of boxes. Write *th* in the box. What sound does *th* make? Have students say the word *thin* and then write it.

Follow the routine with the other *th* words.

thin third both math

	in	
	ird	
b	o	
m	a	

REMIND STUDENTS THAT...

- they can identify that the digraph *th* makes the /th/ sound.
- they can read words that begin or end with the digraph *th*.
- they can write words that begin or end with the digraph *th*.

✓ **MONITOR PROGRESS** Display the following sentences from Student Page S107. Have students identify the words with the consonant digraph /th/ and read them aloud. Then have them spell each word.

Both boys like to read.
One boy is reading a book about Thor.

IF...students cannot read or spell a word correctly,
THEN...review that the two letters *th* make the /th/ sound. Guide students to blend the sounds to read the words. Then have them write the words. Have students think of another word that begins or ends with the /th/ sound.

Lesson 16 Common Consonant Digraphs I

REMIND STUDENTS THAT…

- they can identify that the letter pairs *ph* and *gh* make the /f/ sound.
- they can read words with the digraphs *ph* and *gh*.
- they can write words with the digraphs *ph* and *gh*.

PRACTICE 3: Consonant Digraphs /f/ *ph, gh* Display the Student Page S108. Use the following routine to help students practice the consonant digraphs *ph* and *gh*.

Routine

1. Model. Point to the word *phone*. Say it aloud several times. The first sound in *phone* is /f/. Repeat the sound several times. Explain that /f/ can be spelled *ph*. Have students say /f/ several times as you point to the letters *ph*.

2. Model blending. Point to *ph*: /f/. Point to *o*: /ō/. Point to *n*: /n/. Point out that the e is silent. Run your hand under *phone* as students slowly blend the whole word with you. /f//ō//n/. Repeat the process several times.

3. Write. Point to the Elkonin boxes. Ask students what letters you should write to complete the first set of boxes. Write *ph* in the box. What sound does *ph* make? (/f/) Have students say the word *phone* and then write it.

Follow the routine for the other words that have the /f/ sound. Point out that both *ph* and *gh* make the /f/ sound.

phone photo cough laugh

	one		
	o	t	o
c	ou		
l	au		

INDEPENDENT PRACTICE Display the following sentences from Student Page S108. Have students identify the words with the consonant digraphs *ph* and *gh* and read the words aloud. Then have them spell each word.

Mom talks on the phone.
She laughs.

IF…students cannot read or spell a word correctly,
THEN…review that the letters *ph* and *gh* make the /f/ sound. Guide students to blend the sounds to read the words. Then have them write the words.

Home With a Cold

Kim feels sick.
She has a cough.
Her head throbs.
Her parents phone the school.

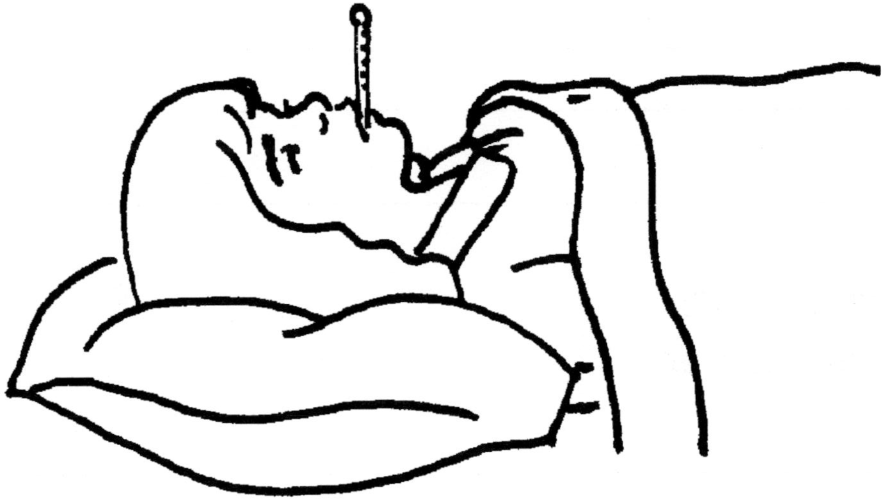

Lesson 16 Common Consonant Digraphs 1

ship fish shed cash

	ip	
f	i	
	ed	
c	a	

Max makes a wish.
He wants red shoes.

Lesson 16 Common Consonant Digraphs 1

thin third both math

	in	
	ird	
b	o	
m	a	

Both boys like to read.
One boy is reading a book about Thor.

Lesson 16 Common Consonant Digraphs 1

phone photo cough laugh

	one		
	o	t	o
c	ou		
l	au		

Mom talks on the phone.
She laughs.

Lesson 17 Common Consonant Digraphs 2

RF.1.3.a Know the spelling-sound correspondences for common consonant digraphs.

OBJECTIVES:

- Read and write words with the /ch/ *ch* digraph.
- Read and write words with the /ch/ *tch* digraph.
- Read and write words with the /wh/ *wh* digraph.

INTRODUCE Remind students that they know how to read and write words with the digraphs *sh, th, ph,* and *gh*. A digraph is two consonants that stand for a single sound. For example, in the word *shop*, the letters *sh* make the single sound /sh/. Today we will learn to read and spell words with three other digraphs that are used in many words.

MODEL Display or share copies of the passage "Chip the Dog" from Student Page S109, and read it aloud.

Chip the Dog

Chip the dog has an itch.
Where is it?
She bites her leg.
Much better!

makes the /ch/ sound

makes the /wh/ sound

TEACH Point to and say each word with a digraph, emphasizing the single letter sounds: *tch* makes the /ch/ sound; *wh* makes the /wh/ sound; and *ch*, like *tch*, makes the /ch/ sound. Have students repeat each word with you. Which two digraphs make the /ch/ sound? (*tch, ch*) Guide students to identify another word with the *ch* digraph. (*Much*) Circle *ch*. I know that each of these letter pairs make one sound. I blend the digraph with other sounds to make a word. So, I can read and write words with these consonant digraphs correctly.

Lesson 17 Common Consonant Digraphs 2

REMIND STUDENTS THAT...

- they can identify that the digraph *ch* makes the /ch/ sound.
- they can read words that begin or end with the digraph *ch*.
- they can write words that begin or end with the digraph *ch*.

PRACTICE 1: Consonant Digraph /ch/ *ch* Display Student Page S110. Use the following routine to guide students as they read and write words with the consonant digraph *ch*.

Routine

1. Model. Point to the word *chop*. Say it aloud several times. The first sound in *chop* is /ch/. Repeat it several times. Explain that /ch/ can be spelled *ch*. Have students say /ch/ several times as you point to the letters *ch*.

2. Model blending. Point to each part of the word and run your hand under *chop* as students slowly blend the whole word with you. /ch//o//p/.

3. Write. Point to the Elkonin boxes. Ask students what letters you should write to complete the first set of boxes. Write *ch* in the box. What sound does *ch* make? Have students say the word *chop* and then write it.

Follow the routine with the other *ch* words.

chop chat such rich

	op	
	at	
s	u	
r	i	

MONITOR PROGRESS Display the following sentence from Student Page S110. Have students identify the words with the consonant digraph *ch* and read them aloud.

Pat gets chips on his chin.

IF... students cannot read a word correctly,
THEN... review that the two letters *ch* make the /ch/ sound. Guide students to blend the sounds to read the words. Then have them write the words.

Lesson 17 Common Consonant Digraphs 2

PRACTICE 2: Consonant Digraph /ch/ *tch* Display Student Page S111. Use the following routine to guide students as they read and write words with the consonant digraph *tch*.

Routine

1. Model. Point to the word *catch*. Say it aloud several times. The last sound in *catch* is /ch/. Repeat the sound several times. Explain that /ch/ can be spelled *tch*. Have students say /ch/ several times as you point to the letters *tch*.

2. Model blending. Point to each part of the word and run your hand under *catch* as students slowly blend the whole word with you. /k/ /a/ /ch/.

3. Write. Point to the Elkonin boxes. Ask students what letters you should write to complete the first set of boxes. Write *tch* in the box. What sound does *tch* make? Have students say the word *catch* and then write it.

Follow the routine for the other *tch* words. Where does *tch* appear in all of these words? (at the end) Explain that the digraph *tch* often comes at the end of words but never at the beginning.

catch match watch pitch

c	a	
m	a	
w	a	
p	i	

REMIND STUDENTS THAT...

- they can identify that the digraph *tch* makes the /ch/ sound.
- they can read words that end with the digraph *tch*.
- they can write words that end with the digraph *tch*.

✔ **MONITOR PROGRESS** Display the following sentences from Student Page S111. Have students identify the words with the consonant digraph /ch/ and read them aloud. Then have them spell each word.

Ben made a batch of cookies.
Then he set his watch.

IF... students cannot read or spell a word correctly,
THEN... blend the words slowly with students and repeat the routine with the word *batch*.

Lesson 17 Common Consonant Digraphs 2

REMIND STUDENTS THAT…

- they can identify that the digraph *wh* makes the /wh/ sound.
- they can read words that begin with the digraph *wh*.
- they can write words that begin with the digraph *wh*.

PRACTICE 3: Consonant Digraphs /wh/ *wh* Display Student Page S112. Use the following routine to guide students as they read and write words with the consonant digraph *wh*.

Routine

1. Model. Point to the word *whale*. Say it aloud several times. The first sound in *whale* is /wh/. Repeat it several times. Explain that /wh/ can be spelled *wh*. Have students say /wh/ several times as you point to the letters *wh*.

2. Model blending. Point to *wh*: /wh/. Point to *a*: /ā/. Point to *l*: /l/. Point out that the e is silent. Run your hand under *whale* as students slowly blend the whole word with you. /wh//ā//l/.

3. Write. Point to the Elkonin boxes. Ask students what letters you should write to complete the first set of boxes. Write *wh* in the box. What sound does *wh* make? (/wh/) Have students say the word *whale* and then write it.

Follow the routine for the other *wh* words.

whale	why	when	what

	ale
	y
	en
	at

✔ **INDEPENDENT PRACTICE** Display the following sentences from Student Page S112. Have students identify the words with the consonant digraph *wh* and read the words aloud. Then have them spell each word.

Where did the white cat go?

IF… students cannot read or spell a word correctly,
THEN… review that the digraph *wh* make the /wh/ sound. Guide students to blend the sounds to read the words. Then have them write the words.

Lesson 17 **Common Consonant Digraphs 2**

Chip the Dog

Chip the dog has an itch.
Where is it?
She bites her leg.
Much better!

Lesson 17 Common Consonant Digraphs 2

chop **chat** **such** **rich**

	op	
	at	
s	u	
r	i	

Pat gets chips on his chin.

Lesson 17 Common Consonant Digraphs 2

catch match watch pitch

c	a	
m	a	
w	a	
p	i	

Ben made a batch of cookies.
Then he set his watch.

Lesson 17 Common Consonant Digraphs 2

whale why when what

	ale
	y
	en
	at

Where did the white cat go?

Lesson 18 Common Consonant Digraphs 3

INTRODUCE Remind students that they know how to read and write words with digraphs, such as *sh, tch, ph*, and *wh*. A digraph is two consonants that stand for a single sound, for example, in the word *match*, the letters *tch* make the single sound /ch/. Today we will learn to read and spell words with other consonant combinations.

MODEL Display or share copies of the following passage "A Rock Club" from Student Page S113, and read it aloud.

A Rock Club

Hank joins a rock club.
He gets a name badge.
It is on string.
He wears it around
his neck.

makes the /ngk/ sound
makes the /k/ sound
makes the /j/ sound
makes the /ng/ sound

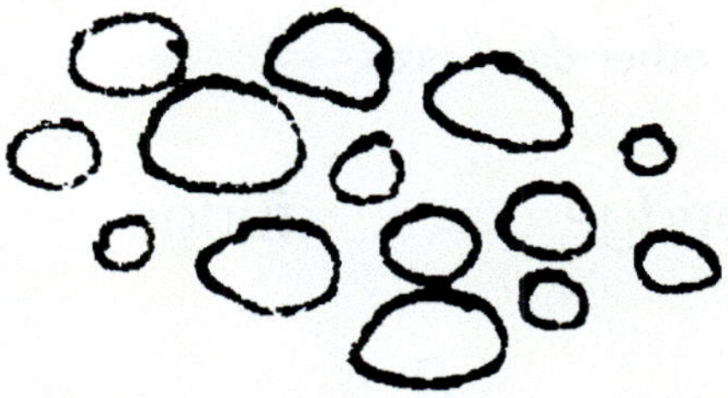

TEACH Read the passage aloud. Point to and say each word with circled letters, emphasizing the sound of the letter combinations: *nk* makes the /ngk/ sound; *ck* makes the /k/ sound; *dge* makes the /j/ sound, and *ng* makes the /ng/ sound. Have students repeat each word with you. Ask: Where do you hear /k/, /j/, /nk/, and /ngk/, at the beginning or end of the word? (end) Point out that final sounds can be spelled with a combination of letters. Guide students to identify another word that ends with a digraph. (neck) Circle *ck*. I know that each of these letter combinations makes one sound. I blend this sound with other sounds to make a word. Then I can read and write words that end with these letter combinations.

RF.1.3.a Know the spelling-sound correspondences for common consonant digraphs.

OBJECTIVES:

- Read and write words that end with the /j/ sound spelled *dge*.
- Read and write words with the /ng/ *ng* and /ngk/ *nk* digraphs.
- Read and write words with the /k/ *ck* digraph.

Lesson 18 Common Consonant Digraphs 3

REMIND STUDENTS THAT...

- they can identify that *dge* makes the /j/ sound.
- they can read words that end with *dge*.
- they can write words that end with *dge*.

PRACTICE 1: Consonant Digraph /j/ *dge* Display Student Page S114. Use the routine to teach the /j/ sound spelled *dge*.

Routine

1. Model. Point to and say the word *lodge*. If necessary, explain its meaning. Point to *dge* and say: The letters *dge* make the /j/ sound. Have students say /j/ several times as you point to the letters *dge*.

2. Model blending. Point to each part of the word and run your hand under *lodge* as students slowly blend the whole word with you. Repeat the process several times, making sure students blend the word without pausing between sounds.

3. Write. Point to the Elkonin boxes. Ask students what letters complete the first set of boxes. Write *dge* in the box. What sound does *dge* make? (/j/) Have students say and write the word *lodge*.

Follow the routine for the other *dge* words.

lodge bridge fudge ledge

l	o	
br	i	
f	u	
l	e	

MONITOR PROGRESS Display the following sentences from Student Page S114. Have students identify the words with the letter combination *dge* and read them aloud.

Ron and Jim sit at the edge of the lake.
Jim falls asleep.
Ron gives him a nudge.

IF... students cannot read a *dge* word correctly,
THEN... guide students to blend the sounds as you run your hand under the letters in the word.

Lesson 18 Common Consonant Digraphs 3

PRACTICE 2: Consonant Digraphs /ng/ *ng*, /ngk/ *nk* Display Student Page S115. Use the routine to teach the consonant digraphs *ng* and *nk*.

Routine

1. Model. Point to the word *king*. Say it aloud several times. The final sound in *king* is /ng/. Repeat it several times. Explain that /ng/ can be spelled *ng*. Have students say /ng/ several times as you point to the letters *ng*.

2. Model blending. Point to each part of the word and run your hand under *king* as students slowly blend the whole word with you. /k//i//ng/. Repeat the process several times.

3. Write. Point to the Elkonin boxes. Ask students what letters complete the first set of boxes. Write *ng* in the box. What sound does *ng* make? (/ng/) Have students say the word *king* and write it on their own paper.

Follow the routine using the word *junk* to explain that *nk* makes the /ngk/ sound. Then repeat the process for other *ng* and *nk* words.

king junk bank ring

k	i	
j	u	
b	a	
r	i	

REMIND STUDENTS THAT...

- they can identify that *ng* makes the /ng/ sound and *nk* makes the /ngk/ sound.
- they can read words that end with the digraphs *ng* and *nk*.
- they can write words that end with the digraphs *ng* and *nk*.

✔ **MONITOR PROGRESS** Display the following sentences from Student Page S115. Have students identify the words with the consonant digraphs *ng* and *nk* and read the words aloud. Then have them spell each word.

Po takes a long walk.
Then he sips a drink.
It is pink.

IF... students cannot spell a word correctly,
THEN... say /ng/ aloud as you point to *ng* or /ngk/ as you point to *nk*. Have students repeat the sound and the spelling with you.

Lesson 18 Common Consonant Digraphs 3

REMIND STUDENTS THAT...

- they can identify that the digraph *ck* makes the */k/ sound.*
- they can read words that end with the digraph *ck*.
- they can write words that end with the digraph *ck*.

PRACTICE 3: Consonant Digraph /k/ *ck* Display Student Page S116. Use the routine to teach the consonant digraph *ck*.

Routine

1. Model. Point to the word *truck*. Say it aloud several times. The letters *ck* make the /k/ sound. Have students say /k/ several times as you point to the letters.

2. Model blending. Run your hand under *truck* as students slowly blend the whole word with you. /tr//u//k/. Repeat the process several times.

3. Write. Point to the Elkonin boxes. Ask students what letters you should write to complete the first set of boxes. Write *ck* in the box. What sound does *ck* make? (/k/) Have students repeat the word *truck* with you.

Follow the routine with other *ck* words.

truck duck back block pick

tr	u	
d	u	
b	a	
bl	o	
p	i	

INDEPENDENT PRACTICE Display the following sentences from Student Page S116. Have students identify the words with the consonant digraph *ck* and read the words aloud. Then have them spell each word. Ask students to think of two more words that end with *ck*.

Pat does a trick with a stick.
With luck, I can learn it, too.

IF... students cannot read or spell a word correctly,
THEN... say /k/ aloud as you point to *ck*. Have students repeat the sound with you. Then guide them to blend the sounds to read the words as you run your hand under the letters. Ask students to spell the word.

Lesson 18 **Common Consonant Digraphs 3**

A Rock Club

Hank joins a rock club.
He gets a name badge.
It is on string.
He wears it around his neck.

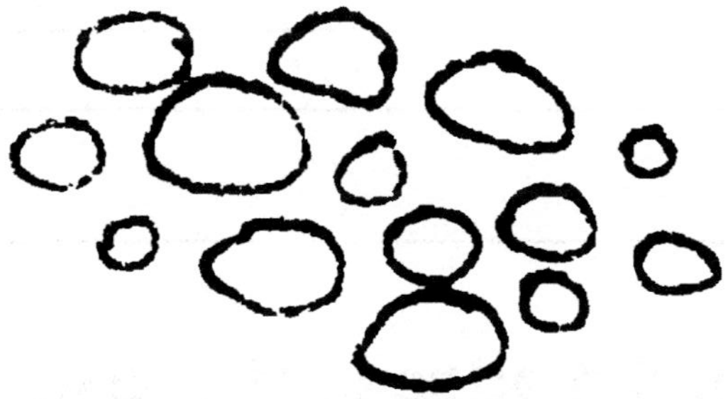

Lesson 18 Common Consonant Digraphs 3

lodge bridge fudge ledge

l	o	
br	i	
f	u	
l	e	

Ron and Jim sit at the edge of the lake.
Jim falls asleep.
Ron gives him a nudge.

Lesson 18 Common Consonant Digraphs 3

king junk bank ring

k	i	
j	u	
b	a	
r	i	

Po takes a long walk.
Then he sips a drink.
It is pink.

Lesson 18 Common Consonant Digraphs 3

truck duck back block pick

tr	u	
d	u	
b	a	
bl	o	
p	i	

Pat does a trick with a stick.
With luck, I can learn it, too.

Lesson 19 Common Consonant Digraphs 4

INTRODUCE Remind students that they know how to read and write words with digraphs such as *ck, nk, ph,* and *wh.* A digraph is two consonants that stand for a single sound. For example, in the word *stick,* the letters *ck* at the end of the word make the single sound /k/. Today we will learn to read and spell words with other digraphs that are used in many words.

MODEL Display or share copies of the following passage, "Rosa Gets Ready," from Student Page S117, and read it aloud.

Rosa Gets Ready

Rosa gets ready for a trip.
She packs her comb.
She also takes her knee socks and toy lamb.
She wraps the animal in a soft blanket.
It's time to go!

makes the /m/ sound

makes the /n/ sound

makes the /r/ sound

TEACH Point to and say each word with a highlighted digraph, emphasizing its sound: *mb* makes the /m/ sound; *kn* makes the /n/ sound; and *wr* makes the /r/ sound. Have students repeat each word with you.

Point out that in each of these digraphs, one letter is silent. Write out *comb* and cross out the silent letter *b*. The *b* in *comb* does not make a sound; it is silent. Let's say the word together, *comb.* Repeat this process for *knee* and *wraps*. Then guide students to identify another word in the passage with the digraph *mb*. (*lamb*) I know that each of these digraphs makes one sound. I blend this sound with other sounds to make a word.

RF.1.3.a Know the spelling-sound correspondences for common consonant digraphs.

OBJECTIVES:

- Read and write words that begin with the digraph /n/ *kn*.
- Read and write words that begin with the digraph /r/ *wr*.
- Read and write words with the digraph /m/ *mb*.

Lesson 19 Common Consonant Digraphs 4

REMIND STUDENTS THAT...

- they can identify that *kn* makes the /n/ sound.
- they can read words that begin with the digraph *kn*.
- they can write words that begin with the digraph *kn*.

PRACTICE 1: Consonant Digraph /n/ *kn* Display Student Page S118. Use the following routine to guide students as they read and write words that begin with the /n/ sound spelled *kn*.

Routine

1. Model. Point to the word *knock*. Say the word aloud several times. Point to *kn* and say: The letters *kn* make the /n/ sound. The *k* is silent. Elongate the /n/ sound for students. Then have students say /n/ as you point to the letters.

2. Model blending. Point to each part of the word and run your hand under *knock* as students blend the whole word with you. /n//o//k/ Repeat the process several times, making sure students blend the word without pausing between sounds.

3. Write. Point to the Elkonin boxes. Ask students what letters you should write to complete the first set of boxes. Write *kn* in the box. What sound does *kn* make? (/n/) Have students say the word *knock* and then write it.

Follow the routine for other *kn* words.

knock knee know knob

	ock
	ee
	ow
	ob

MONITOR PROGRESS Display the following sentences from Student Page S118. Have students identify the words with the consonant digraph *kn* and read them aloud. Have students think of another word that begins with *kn*.

The knight kneels down.
He picks up some rope.
He likes to tie knots.

IF... students cannot think of another *kn* word,
THEN... offer examples such as *knit*, *knew*, or *knuckle*. Demonstrate how to spell each word and have students blend the words with you slowly.

Lesson 19 Common Consonant Digraphs 4

PRACTICE 2: Consonant Digraph /r/ *wr* Display Student Page S119. Use the following routine to guide students as they read and write words with the consonant digraph *wr*.

Routine

1. Model. Point to the word *wraps*. Say it aloud several times. The beginning sound in *wraps* is /r/. Elongate the sound for students. Explain that /r/ can be spelled *wr*. Have students say /r/ several times as you point to the letters *wr*.

2. Model blending. Point to each part of the word and run your hand under *wraps* as students slowly blend the whole word with you: /r/ /a/ /p/ /s/. Repeat the process several times, making sure students blend the word without pausing between sounds.

3. Write. Point to the Elkonin boxes. Ask students to complete the first set of boxes. Write *wr* in the box. What sound does *wr* make? (/r/) Have students say the word *wraps* and then write it.

Follow the routine for other *wr* words.

wraps write wrist wrinkle

	ap	s
	ite	
	ist	
	ink	le

REMIND STUDENTS THAT...

- they can identify that *wr* makes the /r/ sound.
- they can read words that begin with the digraph *wr*.
- they can write words that begin with the digraph *wr*.

✔ **MONITOR PROGRESS** Display the following sentences from Student Page S119. Have students identify the words with the consonant digraph *wr* and read the words aloud. Then have them spell each word.

Will writes a story.
He tells how he broke his wrist.
It twisted the wrong way.

IF... students cannot read or spell a word correctly,
THEN... say /r/ aloud as you point to *wr*. Remind them that the *w* is silent. Then guide students to blend the sounds to read the words as you run your hand under the letters. Ask students to spell the words.

Lesson 19 Common Consonant Digraphs 4

REMIND STUDENTS THAT…

- they can identify that the digraph *mb* makes the /m/ *sound.*
- they can read words with the digraph *mb.*
- they can write words with the digraph *mb.*

PRACTICE 3: Consonant Digraphs /m/ *mb* Display Student Page S120. Use the following routine to guide students as they read and write words with the consonant digraph *mb.*

Routine

1. Model. Point to the word *lamb.* Say it aloud several times. The letters *mb* make the /m/ sound. The *b* is silent. Elongate the sound for students. Have students say /m/ several times as you point to *mb.*

2. Model blending. Point to each part of the word and run your hand under *lamb* as students slowly blend the whole word with you: /l//a//m/. Have students repeat the word several times.

3. Write. Point to the Elkonin boxes. Ask students what letters you should write to complete the first set of boxes. Write *mb* in the box. What sound does *mb* make? (/m/) Have students repeat the word *lamb* with you and then write it.

Follow the routine for other *mb* words.

lamb limb crumb climb

l	a	
l	i	
cr	u	
cl	i	

INDEPENDENT PRACTICE Display the following sentences from Student Page S120. Have students identify the words with the consonant digraph *mb*, and read the words aloud. Then have them spell each word. Ask students to think of one or two other words with the digraph *mb.*

The twins climb an icy tree.
Their thumbs are very cold.
They feel numb.

IF… students cannot think of another *mb* word,
THEN… offer examples such as *comb* or *crumb.* Demonstrate how to spell each word and have students blend the words with you slowly.

Rosa Gets Ready

Rosa gets ready for a trip.
She packs her comb.
She also takes her knee socks and toy lamb.
She wraps the animal in a soft blanket.
It's time to go!

Lesson 19 Common Consonant Digraphs 4

knock knee know knob

	ock
	ee
	ow
	ob

The knight kneels down.
He picks up some rope.
He likes to tie knots.

Lesson 19 Common Consonant Digraphs 4

wraps write wrist wrinkle

	ap	s
	ite	
	ist	
	ink	le

Will writes a story.
He tells how he broke his wrist.

Lesson 19 Common Consonant Digraphs 4

lamb **limb** **crumb** **climb**

l	a	
l	i	
cr	u	
cl	i	

The twins climb an icy tree.
Their thumbs are very cold.
They feel numb.

ASSESSMENT
LESSONS 16–19

Phonics and Word Recognition

ASSESS MASTERY Use this Checkpoint to assess students' mastery of common consonant digraphs.

ADMINISTER THE TEST Display or print the following page for students. Then administer the Checkpoint to each student. For each item, model the process as described, and then have the student use the process to respond to your prompts. Record responses on the scoring chart below.

MODEL: Identify the digraph and tell me what sound it makes. For example, if I showed the word *ship*, you would identify the digraph *sh* and the /sh/ sound.

RF.1.3.a Know the spelling-sound correspondences for common consonant digraphs.

1. Common Consonant Digraphs: *sh, th, ph, gh* (Lesson 16)

ASSESS:	both	cough	phone	fish

2. Common Consonant Digraphs: *ch, tch, wh* (Lesson 17)

ASSESS:	match	chip	when	rich

3. Common Consonant Digraphs: *dge, ng, nk, ck* (Lesson 18)

ASSESS:	ring	badge	luck	pink

4. Common Consonant Digraphs: *kn, wr, mb* (Lesson 19)

ASSESS:	write	lamb	know	comb

SCORING

SKILL/LESSON	SCORE
1. Common Consonant Digraphs: *sh, th, ph, gh* (Lesson 16) both (*th*, /th/); cough (*gh*, /f/); phone (*ph*, /f/); fish (*sh*, /sh/)	_____ / 8
2. Common Consonant Digraphs: *ch, tch, wh* (Lesson 17) match (*tch*, /ch/); chip (*ch*, /ch/); when (*wh*, /wh/); rich (*ch*, /ch/)	_____ / 8
3. Common Consonant Digraphs: *dge, ng, nk, ck* (Lesson 18) ring (*ng*, /ng/); badge (*dge*, /j/); luck (*ck*, /k/); pink (*nk*, /ngk/)	_____ / 8
4. Common Consonant Digraphs: *kn, wr, mb* (Lesson 16) write (*wr*, /r/); lamb (*mb*, /m/); know (*kn*, /n/); comb (*mb*, /m/)	_____ / 8

An overall score of 80% correct is typically considered mastery. Use your judgment and your individual students' needs as well to determine skill mastery.

IF...you determine that students have not demonstrated sufficient mastery of one or more skills,
THEN...review the skill(s), going back to the lessons to reteach as needed.

ASSESSMENT
LESSONS 16–19

Phonics and Word Recognition

1.	both	cough	phone	fish

2.	match	chip	when	rich

3.	ring	badge	luck	pink

4.	write	lamb	know	comb

Lesson 20 Decode Regularly Spelled VC and CVC Words

INTRODUCE Today we will listen to the sounds in short words and learn to recognize the letters that make the sounds. If I say the word *up*, the first sound I hear is /u/. The second sound I hear is /p/. /u/ /p/. Up. Many words use the same sounds and letters. Knowing letters and their sounds helps us read familiar and new words.

MODEL Display and read "Who Is Up?" from Student Page S123. Connect the /u/ and /p/ sounds to the letters. Hold up a letter *u* card. Point to *u* and say the sound. Hold up a letter *p* card. Point to *p* and say the sound. These sounds combine to make the word *up*. I see this word in the poem. Circle *up* in the title. Point to *up* and say the sounds and word: /u//p/. Up.

Who Is Up?

Who is up?
The sleepy pup.
Yip, yip, yip.
The sleepy pup
Is up!

TEACH Use the model to further teach the skill in context. We have learned the word *up* in this poem. I will say the sounds and the word. Then we will say them together. Point to *up* in the title. Say it with me: /u/. /p/. /u//p/. Say it with me: *up*. Repeat with *up* in lines 1 and 5.

But who is up? Prompt for *pup*. Yes! The pup is up. *Pup* has the same sounds as *up*. The first sound I hear is /p/. Say it with me: /p/. The next sound I hear is /u/. Say it with me: /u/. The last sound I hear is /p/. Say it with me: /p/. When I combine the sounds, I get *pup*. Say it with me: *pup*. Circle and say the sounds and words for each instance of *pup*. Have students say each sound and word after you do.

RF.1.3.b Decode regularly spelled one syllable words.

OBJECTIVES:

- Segment and blend one-syllable VC words.
- Segment and blend one-syllable CVC words.
- Connect the sounds to the letters in VC and CVC words.

Lesson 20 Decode Regularly Spelled VC and CVC Words

REMIND STUDENTS THAT...

- they have learned to connect sounds and their letters in short words.

PRACTICE 1 Display Student Page S124. Help students connect sounds and their letters in short words by first reviewing and modeling how to identify parts of a familiar VC word, such as *up*. Circle *up* on the Student Page. This is a familiar word. Say the word with me: *up*. I will say the sounds and the word again. Then we will say them together. Say it with me: /u/. /p/. Say it with me: *up*.

Next introduce a new VC word. Point to *at* in the second column. Let's learn the sounds and letters together. I will say each sound and the word. Then we will say them together. Say it with me: /a/. /t/. Say it with me: *at*. Repeat the steps for the remaining words.

Finally, have students practice VC words. Point to the words out of order. Have students say each word's sounds and say the word smoothly. Prompt and model as needed. Point to each word at least twice.

up		at		in		an		it	
u	p	a	t	i	n	a	n	i	t

To further students' learning, cut apart the cards. Cut each word apart from the two letters, but leave the letters together. Have students work in pairs to put the letter pairs with the correct word.

✔ **MONITOR PROGRESS** Point to each word. Have students sound out and say the word.

up	at	in	an	it

IF... students cannot say a word,
THEN... say the word slowly. Have students point and say each word with you.

Lesson 20 Decode Regularly Spelled VC and CVC Words

PRACTICE 2 Display Student Page S125. Help students connect sounds and their letters in short words by reviewing and modeling how to identify parts of a familiar CVC word, such as *pup*. Circle *pup* on the Student Page. *Pup*. This is a familiar word. Say the word with me: *pup*. I will say the sounds and the word again. Then we will say them together: /p/. /u/. /p/. /p//u//p/. Say it with me: *pup*.

Next, introduce and model new CVC words. Point to *hat* in the second column. Let's learn the sounds and letters together. I will say each sound and the word. Then we will say them together. Say it with me: /h/. /a/. /t/. /h//a//t/. Say it with me: *hat*. Repeat the steps for the remaining words.

Finally, have students practice CVC words. Point to the words out of order. Have students say each word's sounds and the word smoothly. Prompt and model as needed. Point to each word at least twice.

pup			hat			tan			sit			tin		
p	u	p	h	a	t	t	a	n	s	i	t	t	i	n

To further students' learning, cut apart each card. Cut each word apart from the three letters, but leave the letters together. Have students work in pairs to put the letters with the correct word.

MONITOR PROGRESS Point to each word. Have students sound out and say the word.

pup	hat	tin	tan	hit

IF... students cannot say a word,
THEN... say the word slowly, blending it for students. Guide students to point to and say the word independently. Then have them identify each sound.

REMIND STUDENTS THAT...

- they have learned to connect sounds and their letters in short words.

Lesson 20 Decode Regularly Spelled VC and CVC Words

REMIND STUDENTS THAT...

- they have learned to connect sounds and their letters in short words.

PRACTICE 3 Display Student Page S126. Review each word pair in the chart (*up/pup*). Point to and circle the words, sounds, and letters to model how to manipulate and decode words with shared letters. Point to and say *up* and *pup*. Have students read the words aloud several times.

Then point to *up* in the last row of the chart. Write the letter *c* in the blank box. I added /k/ in front of /u//p/. I will say the sounds and the word again. Then we will say them together. Cover the letter *c*. Say it with me: /u/. /p/. *Up*. Uncover the letter *c*. Say the word with me: /k/. /u/. /p/. *Cup*.

Finally, encourage students to use their knowledge to create new words. Recognizing letters and knowing their sounds is a good way to figure out new words. Now, we are going to figure out more new words. Say *at* and *hat*. Point to the empty cell in the third row below *hat*. I am thinking of a letter to add here that will create a word. What words end with /at/? Offer an example, such as *sat*. Model and practice saying the remaining word pairs in the chart.

up			at			an			it			in		
p	u	p	h	a	t	t	a	n	s	i	t	t	i	n
c	u	p	s	a	t	r	a	n	h	i	t	w	i	n

INDEPENDENT PRACTICE In random order, point to a VC word from Student Page S126. Hold up a letter card to create a related CVC word. Have students sound out and say the word. Write the letter in the appropriate cell after students create the word.

up			at			an			it			in		
p	u	p	m	a	t	c	a	n	p	i	t	b	i	n
c	u	p	c	a	t	m	a	n	b	i	t	f	i	n

IF... students cannot form words,
THEN... model how to add letters to create new words. Encourage students to think of rhyming words and nonsense words to help them think of their own new words.

Lesson 20 Decode Regularly Spelled VC and CVC Words

Who Is Up?

Who is up?
The sleepy pup.
Yip, yip, yip.
The sleepy pup
Is up!

Lesson 20 Decode Regularly Spelled VC and CVC Words

up		at		in		an		it	
u	p	a	t	i	n	a	n	i	t

up	at	in	an	it

Lesson 20 Decode Regularly Spelled VC and CVC Words

pup			hat			tan			sit			tin		
p	u	p	h	a	t	t	a	n	s	i	t	t	i	n

pup	hat	tin	tan	hit

Lesson 20 Decode Regularly Spelled VC and CVC Words

up		
p	u	p
	u	p

at		
h	a	t
	a	t

an		
t	a	n
	a	n

it		
s	i	t
	i	t

in		
t	i	n
	i	n

up		
	u	p
	u	p

at		
	a	t
	a	t

an		
	a	n
	a	n

it		
	i	t
	i	t

in		
	i	n
	i	n

Lesson 21 Decode Words: Initial Blends

INTRODUCE Today we will listen to the sounds at the beginning of words and learn to recognize the letters that make the sounds. If I say the word *like*, the first sound I hear is /l/. *Like*. If I say the word *rake*, the first sound I hear is /r/. *Rake*. If I say the word *song*, the first sound I hear is /s/. *Song*. Today we will practice words that blend the /l/, /r/, and /s/ sounds with another sound at the beginning of a word.

RF.1.3.b Decode regularly spelled one-syllable words.

OBJECTIVES:

- Segment and blend initial consonants in CCVC words.
- Connect the sounds to the letters in CCVC words.

MODEL Read the passage aloud and share the chart from Student Page S127. Point to each word and to each letter and sound combination as you say it. Elongate the blends. These are words that blend /l/, /r/, or /s/ with another letter sound at the beginning of a word. When two sounds are combined at the beginning of a word, we call it an initial blend. Listen carefully to how I blend the *p* and *l* when I say *plum*. /p//l//um/. *Plum*. Repeat the process for the two remaining words.

The Plum

Mr. Platt has a plum.

initial blends

He will drop the plum into the sack.

He will close the sack.

Tonight Mr. Platt will eat the plum for a snack.

plum	drop	snack
l	r	s
pl	dr	sn

TEACH Write out the blends as you model and practice each word in the chart. I will say each word slowly. Then we will say the word together very slowly. Listen for the initial sound that blends with the /l/, /r/, or /s/ sound. /P//l//um/. Say it with me slowly: /p//l//um/. What two sounds blend at the beginning of the word? Yes, the initial blend is /pl/. The word is /pl//u//m/. Say it with me: /p//l//u//m/, /pl//u//m/. *Plum*. Repeat the process with *drop* and *snack*. Tell students they will be learning more words with initial blends that include /l/, /r/, and /s/.

Lesson 21 Decode Words: Initial Blends

REMIND STUDENTS THAT…

- they learned to listen to initial blends.
- they learned a word with an initial *l* blend.
- they learned a word with an initial *r* blend.

PRACTICE 1: Initial *l* and *r* Blends Display the picture chart from Student Page S128. Review and model a previously learned initial *l* blend word, such as *plum*. Use the review to introduce and model new initial *l* blend words. Some words blend *l* with other letters. This word, *clam*, blends the *l* with *c*. Circle the *c* and *l*. Listen for the initial sound: /k//l//am/. Say it with me: /k//l//am/. *Clam*. Repeat this process to introduce students to *glass* and *blob*.

Next, have students review and model a previously learned initial *r* blend word, such as *drop*. Use the review to introduce and model new initial *r* blend words. Some words blend *r* with other letters. This word, *crab*, blends the *r* with *c*. Circle the *c* and *r*. Listen for the initial sound. /k//r//ab/. Say it with me: /k//r//ab/. *Crab*. Repeat this process to introduce and practice *frog* and *brick*.

l			r		
clam	glass	blob	crab	frog	brick
cl	gl	bl	cr	fr	br
					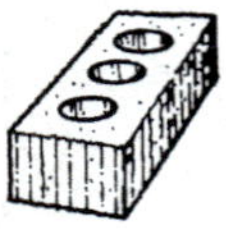

MONITOR PROGRESS Display the chart from Student Page S128. Read each of the word pairs below. Have students tell you which word includes the initial blend.

l	r
pan, plot	brag, bike
glad, go	dawn, draw
blur, best	crack, cake
cool, club	fee, free

IF… students cannot identify the initial blends,
THEN… review several words of each blend type by elongating the sounds. Have students say the blends with you and then independently.

Lesson 21 Decode Words: Initial Blends

PRACTICE 2: Initial *s* Blends Display the picture chart from Student Page S129. Review and model a previously learned word with an initial *s* blend, such as *snack.*

Next, introduce and model new words with an initial *s* blend, starting with the word *small.* Some words blend *s* with other letters. *Small* blends the *s* with *m.* Circle the *s* and *m.* Listen for the initial sound: /s//m/. Say it with me: /s//m/. The word is /sm//aw//l/, *small. Small.* Say it with me: /sm//aw//l/, *small.* Repeat this process to introduce *spot, swim,* and *star.*

REMIND STUDENTS THAT...

- they learned to listen to initial blends.
- they learned a word with an initial *s* blend.

s			
small	spot	swim	star
sm	sp	sw	st

To further learning, cut apart the cells in the third and fourth rows of the picture chart. Review each word with students. Have students work together in pairs to assemble the chart correctly.

MONITOR PROGRESS Read each word pair from the chart on Student Page S129. Have students tell you which word includes an *s* initial blend.

s
sack, smog
swan, send
seat, step
spin, sick

IF... students cannot identify the words with an initial *s* blend,
THEN... review several words with an initial *s* blend, elongating the sounds. Have students repeat the words after you and then repeat them with a partner.

Lesson 21 Decode Words: Initial Blends

REMIND STUDENTS THAT...

- they learned to listen to initial blends.
- they learned words with an initial s blends.

PRACTICE 3: Three-Letter Initial *s* Blends Review and model a previously learned word with an initial s blend, such as *spot* from Practice 2. We have learned words with initial *s* blends. *Spot*. This word has an initial *s* blend. It blends *s* with *p*. Listen for the initial sound: /s//p/. Say it with me: /s//p/. Now, say the word with me: /s//p//o//t/. /sp//o//t/. *Spot*. I circled the letters in this *s* blend: *s* and *p*. How many letters are in this *s* blend? Yes, this word has two letters in the initial *s* blend. Some words, though, have three letters in an initial *s* blend.

Next, display Student Page S130 to help introduce and model words with a three-letter initial *s* blend. *Spring*. This is a word with three letters in the initial *s* blend. Circle the *s*, the *p*, and the *r*. Elongate each sound individually. /s//p//r/. Listen carefully. /s//p//r/. Now say it with me: /s//p//r/. Listen carefully again: /spr//i//n//g/. Now say it with me: /spr//i//n//g/. Repeat this process to introduce *splash*, *stripe*, and *scrub*.

S _ _			
spring	splash	stripe	scrub
spr	spl	str	scr
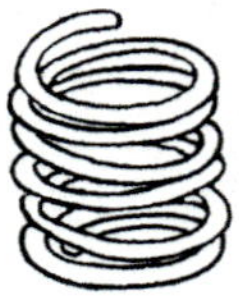			

To further learning, cut apart the cells in the third and last rows of the picture chart. Review each word with students. Have students work together in pairs to assemble the chart correctly.

✔ **INDEPENDENT PRACTICE** Read each of the word pairs from the chart on Student Page S130. Have students tell you which word includes an s initial *s* blend.

S_ _

split, sold
sick, straw
spray, set
sun, scrap

IF... students cannot identify the words with a three letter initial *s* blend, THEN... review several s-blend words, elongating the different sounds. Guide students to identify each initial blend and then have them blend the words independently. Offer corrective feedback as needed.

Lesson 21 **Decode Words: Initial Blends**

The Plum

Mr. Platt has a plum.
He will drop the plum into the sack.
He will close the sack.
Tonight Mr. Platt will eat the plum for a snack.

plum	drop	snack
l	r	s
pl	dr	sn

Lesson 21 Decode Words: Initial Blends

l		
clam	glass	blob
cl	gl	bl
		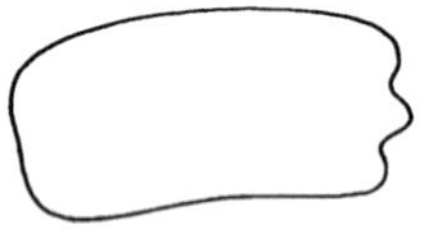

r		
crab	frog	brick
cr	fr	br
		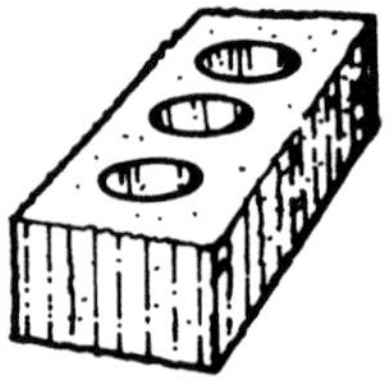

l

pan, plot
glad, go
blur, best
cool, club

r

brag, bike
dawn, draw
crack, cake
fee, free

Lesson 21 Decode Words: Initial Blends

S			
small	spot	swim	star
sm	sp	sw	st

S

sack, smog

swan, send

seat, step

spin, sick

Lesson 21 Decode Words: Initial Blends

S __ __			
spring	splash	stripe	scrub
spr	spl	str	scr

S __ __

split, sold

sick, straw

spray, set

sun, scrap

Lesson 22 Decode Words: Final Blends

INTRODUCE Today we will listen to the sounds at the end of words and learn to recognize the letters that make the sounds. If I say the word *top*, the last sound I hear is /p/. Emphasize the ending sound as you say /t//o//p/. Today, we will practice words that blend the sound of two letters at the end of a word, like /nd/ in the word *band*.

MODEL Display the passage and chart from Student Page S131. Point to each word and to each letter and sound combination as you say it. Two sounds are blended at the end of these words. These are called final blends. Listen carefully to how I blend the *n* and *d* when I say *hand*. /h//a//n//d/. /h//a//nd/. *Hand*. Repeat the process for the two remaining words.

Salt

"Hand me the salt," said Kent, my best friend.
"I lost it," I said.
"Don't worry," said Kent.
He added the word *salt* to his list.

hand	salt	list
nd	lt	st
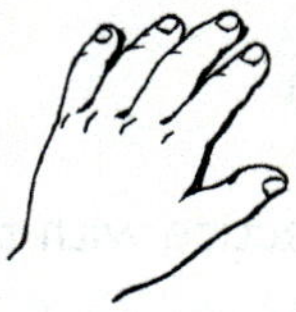		

TEACH I will say each word slowly. After I say a word, we will say the word together very slowly. Listen for the sounds that make up the blend at the end of the word. /H//a//n//d/. Say it with me slowly: /H//a//nd/. What is the final blend? Yes, /nd/. The word is /h//a//nd/. Say it with me: /h//a//nd/. *Hand*. Repeat the process with *salt* and *list*. Tell students they will be learning more words with final blends.

RF.1.3.b Decode regularly spelled one-syllable words.

OBJECTIVES:

- Segment and blend words with consonant blends.
- Segment and blend final consonants in CVCC and VCC words.
- Connect the sounds to the letters in CVCC and VCC words.

Lesson 22 Decode Words: Final Blends

REMIND STUDENTS THAT…

- they can segment and blend words with consonant blends.
- they learned to listen to final blends.
- they learned words with final blends.

PRACTICE 1: Final Blends *nd, nt, mp, ft* Display Student page S132 and use this routine to guide students.

Routine

1. Model. Display the *nd* card. Say: This is a blend of two sounds: /n/ and /d/. Listen to me say the blend: /n//d//, /nd/. Have students repeat after you as you point to the card. Write the word *hand*. Now I am going to say a word that blends the sounds of two letters at the end of the word. Listen for the blend: /h//a//nd/. Repeat the word several times as you run your finger under it. Now say the word slowly with me and then say the word normally: /h/ /a/ /nd/, hand. The blend is *nd*.

2. Guide practice. Write the word *send*. Elongate each sound and then gradually say the word normally: /s//e//n//d//, /s//e//nd/, *send*. Point to the word and have students read it aloud several times.

3. Review and practice. Display Student Page S132. Say each blend and the example word, and have students repeat after you.

nd	nt	mp	ft
lend	ant	jump	gift

Repeat the routine for each sound and word. Then practice with the word cards on Student Page S132. Now, I will say a word slowly. When I am done, point to the word I said.

✓ **MONITOR PROGRESS** Read each of the word pairs below from Student Page S132. Have students tell you which word includes the blend.

nd	nt	mp	ft
lend, let	pat, ant	jam, jump	goat, gift
bet, bend	sat, sent	bump, bit	stop, soft
hand, had	ant, ate	dot, damp	left, let

IF…students cannot distinguish the final blends,
THEN…review each sound and repeat the routine.

Lesson 22 Decode Words: Final Blends

PRACTICE 2: Final Blends *lt, ld, lp* Display Student Page S133 and use this routine to guide students.

Routine

1. Model. Display the *lt* card. Say: This is a blend of two sounds: /l/ and /t/. Listen to me say the blend: /l//t//, /lt/. Have students repeat after you as you point to the card. Now I am going to say a word that blends the sounds of two letters at the end of the word. Listen for the blend: /s//aw//lt/. Repeat the word several times as you run your finger under it. Now say the word slowly with me and then say the word normally: /s//aw//lt/, *salt*. The blend is *lt*.

2. Guide practice. Write the word *felt*. Elongate each sound and then gradually say the word normally: /f//e//l//t//, /f//e//lt/, *felt*. Point to the word and have students read it aloud several times.

3. Review and practice. Display Student Page S133. Say each blend and the example word, and have students repeat after you.

lt	ld	lp
belt	old	help

Repeat the routine for each sound and word. Then practice with the word cards on Student Page S133. Now, I will say a word slowly. When I am done, point to the word I said.

REMIND STUDENTS THAT...

- they can segment and blend words with consonant blends.
- they learned to listen to final blends.
- they learned words with final blends.

✓ **MONITOR PROGRESS** Read each of the word pairs below from Student Page S133. Have students tell you which word includes the blend.

lt	ld	lp
bet, belt	odd, old	get, gulp
salt, set	held, head	help, head
melt, map	white, wild	yelp, yet

IF... students cannot distinguish the final blends,
THEN... review each sound and repeat the routine.

Lesson 22 Decode Words: Final Blends

REMIND STUDENTS THAT...

- they can segment and blend words with consonant blends.
- they learned to listen to final blends.
- they learned words with final blends.

PRACTICE 3: Final Blends *sk, sp, st* Display Student Page S134 and use this routine to guide students.

Routine

1. Model. Display the *st* card. Say: This is a blend of two sounds: /s/ and /t/. Listen to me say the blend: /s//t/, /st/. Have students repeat after you as you point to the card. Write the word *rest*. Now I am going to say a word that blends the sounds of two letters at the end of the word. Listen for the blend: /r//e//st/. Repeat the word several times as you run your finger under it. Now say the word slowly with me and then say the word normally: /r/ /e/ /st/, *rest*. The blend is *st*.

2. Guide practice. Write the word *must*. Elongate each sound and then gradually say the word normally: /m//u//s//t/, /m//u//st/, *must*. Point to the word and have students read it aloud several times.

3. Review and practice. Display Student Page S134. Say each blend and the example word, and have students repeat after you.

sk	sp	st
desk	wasp	list

Repeat the routine for each sound and word. Then practice with the word cards on Student Page S134. Now, I will say a word slowly. When I am done, point to the word I said.

INDEPENDENT PRACTICE Read each of the word pairs below. Have students tell you which word includes the blend.

sk	sp	st
dress, desk	wasp, want	sis, best
mask, mat	crisp, Chris	rest, root
ask, act	gap, gasp	cat, cost

IF...students cannot distinguish the final blends,
THEN...review each sound and repeat the routine.

Lesson 22 Decode Words: Final Blends

Salt

"Hand me the salt," said Kent, my best friend.
"I lost it," I said.
"Don't worry," said Kent.
He added the word *salt* to his list.

hand	salt	list
nd	lt	st
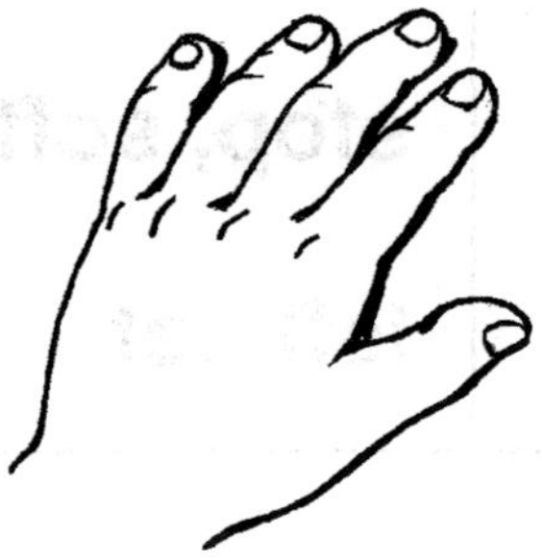		

Lesson 22 Decode Words: Final Blends

nd	nt	mp	ft
lend	ant	jump	gift

nd	nt	mp	ft
lend, let bet, bend hand, had	pat, ant sat, sent ant, ate	jam, jump bump, bit dot, damp	goat, gift stop, soft left, let

Lesson 22 Decode Words: Final Blends

lt	ld	lp
belt	old	help

lt	ld	lp
bet, belt salt, set melt, map	odd, old held, head white, wild	get, gulp help, head yelp, yet

Lesson 22 Decode Words: Final Blends

sk	sp	st
desk	wasp	list

sk	sp	st
dress, desk mask, mat ask, act	wasp, want crisp, Chris gap, gasp	sis, best rest, root cat, cost

ASSESSMENT
LESSONS 20–22

Phonics and Word Recognition

ASSESS MASTERY Use this Checkpoint to assess students' mastery of decoding words by segmenting and blending VC and CVC words and words with initial and final consonant blends.

RF.1.3.b Decode regularly spelled one-syllable words.

ADMINISTER THE TEST Administer the Checkpoint to each student. For each item, model the process and have the student use the process to respond to your prompts. Record responses on the scoring chart on the next page.

1. Decode One-Syllable VC Words (Lesson 20)
MODEL: I will say the sounds in a word. Point to the word with the sounds.

ASSESS: it at up an

2. Decode One-Syllable CVC Words (Lesson 20)
MODEL: I will say the sounds in a word. Point to the word with the sounds.

ASSESS: can sit bin cat cup bat

3. Initial Blends: *l*, *r*, and *s* Blends (Lesson 21)
MODEL: I will say the initial sound in a word. Point to the word that begins with that sound. For example, if I say /pl/, you would point to the word that begins with the letters that make the /pl/ sound, such as the word *play*.

ASSESS: club drip swell

4. Initial Blends: Three-Letter *s* Blends (Lesson 21)
MODEL: I will say the beginning sound in a word. Point to the word that begins with that sound.

ASSESS: straw spry split scrap

5. Final Blends: *nd*, *nt*, *mp*, and *ft* Blends (Lesson 22)
MODEL: I will say the final sound in a word. Point to the word that ends with that sound. For example, if I say /nd/, you would point to the word that ends with the letters that make the /nd/ sound, such as the word *band*.

ASSESS: send pant dump sift

6. Final *l* and *s* Blends: *lt*, *ld*, *lp*, *sk*, *sp*, and *st* Blends (Lesson 22)
MODEL: I will say the final sound in a word. Point to the word that ends with that sound.

ASSESS: felt cold scalp risk gasp best

ASSESSMENT
LESSONS 20–22

Phonics and Word Recognition

SCORING

SKILL/LESSON	SCORE
1. One-Syllable VC Words (Lesson 20) /i//t/ (it); /a//t/ (at); /u//p/ (up); /a//n/ (an)	_____ / 4
2. One-Syllable CVC Words (Lesson 20) /c//a//n/ (can); /s//i//t/ (sit); /b//i//n/ (bin); /c//a//t/ (cat); /c//u//p/ (cup); /b//a//t/ (bat)	_____ / 6
3. Initial Blends: *l, r, s* (Lesson 21) /kl/ (club); /dr/ (drip); /sw/ (swell)	_____ / 3
4. Initial Blends: Three-letter *s* (Lesson 21) /str/ (straw); /spr/ (spry); /spl/ (split); /skr/ (scrap)	_____ / 4
5. Final Blends: *nd, nt, mp,* and *ft* (Lesson 22) /nd/ (send); /nt/ (pant); /mp/ (dump); /ft/ (sift)	_____ / 4
6. Final *l* and *s* Blends: *lt, ld, lp, sk, sp,* and *st* (Lesson 22) /lt/ (felt); /ld/ (cold); /lp/ (scalp); /sk/ (risk); /sp/ (gasp); /st/ (best)	_____ / 6

An overall score of 80% correct is typically considered mastery. Use your judgment and your individual students' needs as well to determine skill mastery.

IF... you determine that students have not demonstrated sufficient mastery of one or more skills,
THEN... review the skill(s), going back to the lessons to reteach and scaffold as needed.

Lesson 23 Long Vowels and the Silent e Rule

INTRODUCE Remind students they have learned words with short vowel sounds (e.g., *cap* and *can*). Today we will learn words with these vowel sounds: /ā/, /ī/, /ē/, /ō/, and /ū/. These vowel sounds have the same sound as their letter names. For example, listen for *a* in these words. *Cape. Cane.*

MODEL Display "I Had a Cap" from Student Page S137. Read the passage, pointing to each word as you read. *Cap. Cape.* /k/ /ă/ /p/. /k/ /ā/ /p/. How did e give the child a cape? The final letter e changed the short *a* sound to the long *a* sound. Write the letters in the blanks to complete *cap*. Say *cap*, drawing out the sounds. Write the letters in the blanks to complete *cape*. Say *cape*, drawing out the sounds. Circle each relevant letter and word as you explain: When we see the letter e at the end of a word after a consonant, the first vowel in the word sounds like the letter's name. *Cape.* /k/ /ā/ /p/.

I Had a Cap

I had a cap.
I had a can.
Then e gave me a cape and cane!

_ a _ → _ a _ e

_ a _ → _ a _ e

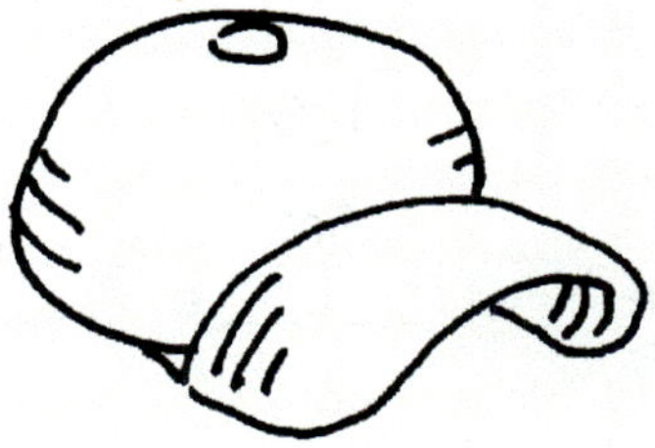

TEACH We have learned that e at the end of a word after a consonant makes the first vowel in the word a long vowel. Now, we will say and write /k//ă//n/ and /k//ā//n/. Hold your marker over the blank for letter *c* in *can*. Ask students what letter you should write. Prompt and repeat for the letter *n* in *can*. Now I will say the word and then we will say it together. /k/. /ă/. /n/. Say it with me: /k/ /ă/ /n/. Repeat with *cane*. After saying *cane*, circle the silent e and repeat the rule.

RF.1.3.c Know final -e and common vowel team conventions for representing long vowel sounds.

RF.1.3.b Decode regularly spelled one-syllable words.

OBJECTIVES:

- Introduce the concept of the long vowel sound and silent e rule for single-syllable VC words that end in e.
- Introduce segmenting and blending *a_e* patterns.
- Apply the silent e rule to reading and writing spelling correspondences for single-syllable VCe words.

Lesson 23 Long Vowels and the Silent e Rule

REMIND STUDENTS THAT...

- they can say a long vowel sound because it is the same as the letter name.
- they can apply the silent e rule to words spelled *a*_e and *i*_e.

PRACTICE 1: Long *a* and Long *i* (Spelled *a*_e, *i*_e) Use the following routine to help students recognize long *a* and long *i* sounds.

Routine

1. Review. Write the word *cape*. Cover the final e. The final letter e is gone. Now the word does not have a long *a* sound. What is this word now? /K/. /ă/. /p/. Say it with me: /k//ă//p/. Reveal the e. /k//ā//p/.

2. Introduce new long *a* words. Display and refer to Student Page S138. Point to *a*_e at the top of the first chart. Many words use the sound /ā/ when there is the letter *a*, a consonant, and then the letter e. Introduce the word *cake*. /K/. /ā/. /k/. Listen for the /ā/ sound. Say it with me: /ā/. /k//ā//k/. *Cake*.

3. Practice long *a* words. Fill in the chart as you draw out the sounds for the word *cake*. Say it with me: /k//ā//k/. *Cake*. Introduce and practice *safe* and *game*.

Repeat the routine with *i*_e and the words *kite*, *bike*, and *fire*.

a_e	a_e	a_e
cake _c_ a _k_ e	safe _s_ a _f_ e	game _g_ a _m_ e
i_e	i_e	i_e
kite _k_ i _t_ e	bike _b_ i _k_ e	fire _f_ i _r_ e

MONITOR PROGRESS Point to *a*_e on Student Page S138. Say the *a*_e words, and ask the student to point to and say each word. Repeat with *i*_e.

a_e	i_e
cake	kite
safe	bike
game	fire

IF... students cannot identify a word,
THEN... say the word, drawing out the /ā/ or /ī/ sound as you run your finger under the related letters.

Lesson 23 Long Vowels and the Silent e Rule

PRACTICE 2: Long *o* and Long *e* (Spelled *o_e*, *e_e*) Use the following routine to help students recognize long *o* and long *e* sounds.

REMIND STUDENTS THAT...

- they can say a long vowel sound because it is the same as the letter name.
- they can apply the silent *e* rule to words spelled *o_e* and *e_e*.

Routine

1. Introduce the long *o* sound spelled *o_e*. Display and refer to Student Page S139. Point to *o_e* at the top of the first chart. Many words use the sound /ō/ when there is the letter *o*, a consonant, and then the letter *e*. Ask students to name the picture of the *bone*. Then point to the word *bone*. Listen for the /ō/ sound. /B/. /ō/. /n/.

2. Model the long *o* sound spelled *o_e*. Circle the letters *o* and *e* in *bone* and blend the word slowly. /B/. /ō/. /n/. Have students repeat the word as you point to it.

3. Practice the long *o* sound spelled *o_e*. Fill in the chart for the word *bone* as you draw out the sounds in *bone*. Say it with me: /b/. /ō/. /n/. Repeat the process with the words *rope* and *nose*.

Repeat the routine with *e_e* and the words *Zeke*, *Pete*, and *Eve*.

o_e	o_e	o_e
bone	rope	nose
_b_ o _n_ e	_r_ o _p_ e	_n_ o _s_ e
e_e	e_e	e_e
Zeke	Pete	Eve
_Z_ e _k_ e	_P_ e _t_ e	E _v_ e

✔ **MONITOR PROGRESS** Point to *o_e* on Student Page S139. Tell the student you will say an *o_e* word. Say the word and ask the student to point to and say the word. Repeat with *e_e*.

o_e	e_e
bone	Zeke
rope	Pete
nose	Eve

IF... students cannot identify a word,
THEN... say the word, drawing out the long vowel sound as you run your finger under the related letters.

Lesson 23 Long Vowels and the Silent e Rule

REMIND STUDENTS THAT...

- they can say a long vowel sound because it is the same as the letter name.
- they can apply the silent *e* rule to words spelled *u_e*.

PRACTICE 3: Long *u* (Spelled *u_e*) Use the following routine to help students recognize the long *u* sound.

Routine

1. Introduce the long *u* sound spelled *u_e*. Display and refer to Student Page S140. Many words use the sound /ū/ when there is the letter *u*, a consonant, and then the letter *e*. Point to the word *mule* and to the picture of the mule. Listen for the long *u* sound. */M/. /ū/. /l/. Mule.*

2. Practice the /ū/ sound spelled *u_e*. Point to the word *mule*. Write the missing letters on the chart as you draw out the sounds. Say it with me: */m/. /ū/. /l/. Mule.* Repeat the process with the words *cube* and *cute*.

u_e	u_e	u_e
mule _ u _ e	cube _u_e	cute _ u _ e

To further students' learning, provide word cards of introduced words and additional /ū/ words (e.g., *huge, use*). Have students decode the words as a group with you, or in small groups independently.

✓ **INDEPENDENT PRACTICE** Point to *u_e* on Student Page S140. Tell the student you will say a *u_e* word. Say the word and ask the student to point to and say the word.

u_e
mule
cube
cute

IF... students cannot identify a word,
THEN... say the word, drawing out the /ū/ sound as you run your finger under the related letters.

Lesson 23 **Long Vowels and the Silent e Rule**

I Had a Cap

I had a cap.
I had a can.
Then *e* gave me a cape and cane!

_____ **a** _____ → _____ **a** _____ **e**

_____ **a** _____ → _____ **a** _____ **e**

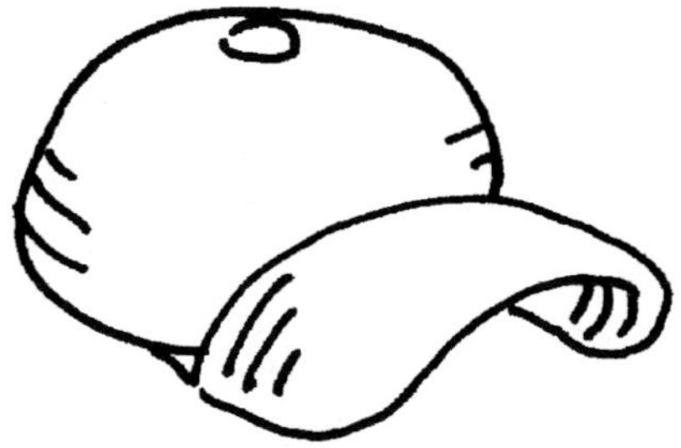

Lesson 23 Long Vowels and the Silent e Rule

a__e	a__e	a__e
cake __a__e	safe __a__e	game __a__e

i__e	i__e	i__e
kite __i__e	bike __i__e	fire __i__e

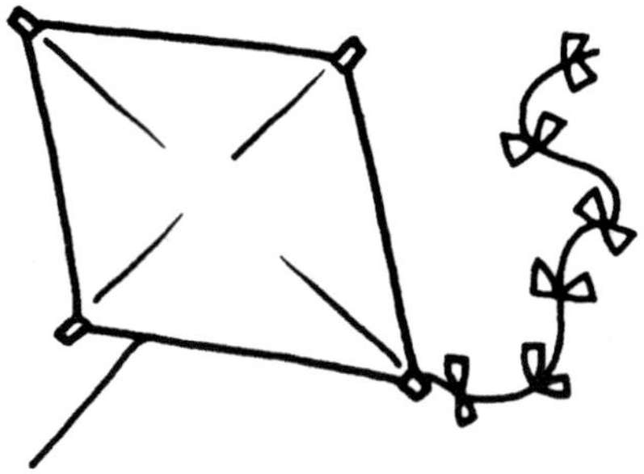

a_e
cake
safe
game

i_e
kite
bike
fire

Lesson 23 Long Vowels and the Silent e Rule

o__e	o__e	o__e
bone __o__e	rope __o__e	nose __o__e

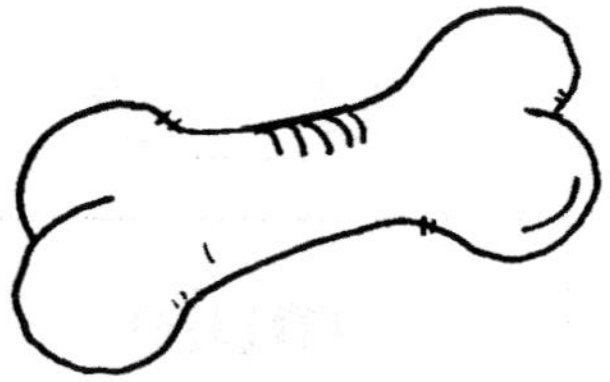

e__e	e__e	e__e
Zeke __e__e	Pete __e__e	Eve E__e

o_e
bone
rope
nose

e_e
Zeke
Pete
Eve

Lesson 23 Long Vowels and the Silent e Rule

u__e	u__e	u__e
mule __u__e	cube __u__e	cute __u__e

u_e
mule cube cute

Lesson 24 Long Vowel Patterns

INTRODUCE Remind students that long vowel sounds sound like the letter name. Remind students they have learned to recognize and say words with long vowel sounds in words with a silent final e. Today we will learn to recognize words with these long vowel sounds—/ē/, /ō/, and /ī/—that are spelled differently.

MODEL Display Student Page S141. Read aloud the first two sentences in the passage. Point to the word *she*, read it aloud, and have students repeat after you. Point to the letter e. *She* is a word with a long e sound that is spelled differently from the word *Pete*.

Hi!

She is a young girl.
Pete is a cold boy.
The young girl says hi to the cold boy.
The boy is too cold to say hi back!

e	o	i
she	cold	hi

TEACH Direct students' attention to the chart and run your finger under relevant letters and words as you read it aloud. Draw out and blend the sounds. Say the long *e* sound with me: /ē/. Say the word with me: /Sh//ē/. Point to the drawing of snowflakes falling. Is it warm outside? No! It is cold. /K/. /ō/. /ld/. *Cold* uses a long *o* sound, but it is spelled differently from *bone*. Say the long *o* sound with me: /ō/. Now say the word with me: /c//ō//ld/. Point to the word *hi* in the last column. *Hi* uses a long *i* sound, but it is spelled differently from *kite*. Say the long *i* sound with me: /ī/. Now say the word with me: /h//ī/.

RF.1.3.c Know final -e and common vowel team conventions for representing long vowel sounds.

RF.1.3.b Decode regularly spelled one-syllable words.

OBJECTIVE:

- Learn spelling correspondences for long vowel VCe words spelled *e*, *o*, *i*, and *y*.

Lesson 24 Long Vowel Patterns

REMIND STUDENTS THAT…

- they can say a long vowel sound because it is the same as the letter name.
- they can say the /ē/, /ō/, and /ī/ sounds.
- they can say words with these sounds.

PRACTICE 1: Long e, o, and *i* (Spelled e, o, *i*) Use the following routine to help students recognize long e, o, and *i* sounds spelled e, o, and *i*.

Routine

1. Review a familiar long e word. Display a word card for *she* from Student Page S142. The e in /sh/ /ē/ says its letter name: /ē/. Say it with me: /ē/. /Sh/. /ē/. Many words use the letter *e* to make this sound.

2. Introduce and practice new long e words. Point to e at the top of the first chart on Student Page S142. The e in the word *me* includes the sound of its letter name: /ē/. Say the word with me: /m//ē/. Use the same procedure to introduce *he* and *we*.

Use the routine to review the word *cold* and introduce new long *o* words from column two of the chart.

Then repeat the routine with the word *hi* and introduce new long *i* words from column three of the chart.

e	o	i
me	most	find
he	told	kind
we	go	mind
she	cold	hi

MONITOR PROGRESS Point to e on Student Page S142. Tell the student you will say a word with the /ē/ sound. Say a word and ask the student to point to and say the word. Repeat with at least two long e words. Repeat for long *o* and *i* words.

e	we	he	me	she
o	go	cold	told	most
i	mind	hi	find	kind

IF… students cannot identify a word,
THEN… say the word, drawing out the long vowel sound as you run your finger under the related letters.

Lesson 24 Long Vowel Patterns

PRACTICE 2: Long *i* (Spelled *y*) Use the following routine to help students recognize words with the long vowel *i* sound spelled *y*.

Routine

1. Review the long *i* sound.

Write the word *hi*.
This is a word we know. Say it with me: /h//ī/. The last sound in this word is the sound of the letter *i*. Many words use this sound. Today we will learn words with the /ī/ sound that are spelled differently.

2. Introduce a word with long *i* spelled with *y*.

Display a word card for *sky* from Student Page S143. /sk/. /ī/. Say it with me: /sk//ī/. The last sound in this word is the sound of the letter *i*. In this word, the letter *y* is used to make the /ī/ sound. Many words use the letter *y* to make the /ī/ sound.

3. Introduce and practice new long *i* words spelled with a *y*.

Point to the picture on Student Page S143 that is associated with *fly*. Follow Step 2 to introduce and practice *fly*. Repeat for *why* and *try*.

fly	why	try	sky

REMIND STUDENTS THAT...

- they can say a long vowel sound because it is the same as the letter name.
- they can say the /ī/ sound.
- they can say words with this sound that use the letter *i*.

✔ **MONITOR PROGRESS** Read the sentence from Student Page S143. Tell the student you will say a word with the sound of the letter *i* that is spelled with a *y*. In random order, say a long *i* word in the sentence. Ask the student to point to the word in the sentence and say the word. Repeat the steps for all long vowel *i* words spelled with a *y* in the sentence. (Alternative: Point to a word. Ask the student to say the word.)

Why try to fly in the sky?

IF... students cannot identify a word,
THEN... say the word, drawing out the long *i* sound as you run your finger under the related letter.

Lesson 24 Long Vowel Patterns

REMIND STUDENTS THAT...

- they can say a long vowel sound because it is the same as the letter name.
- they can say the /ē/ sound.
- they can say words with this sound that use the letter e.

PRACTICE 3: Long e (Spelled y) Use the following routine to help students recognize words with the long vowel e sound spelled *y*.

Routine

1. Review the long e sound. Display a word card for *she*. Draw out and blend the sounds as indicated. This is a word we know. /sh/. /ē/. Say it with me: /sh//ē/. The last sound in this word is the sound of the letter e. Many words use this sound. Today we will learn words with the long e sound that are spelled differently.

2. Introduce a word with long e spelled with y. Display a word card for *lady*. /l//ā/. /d/. /ē/. Say it with me: /l//ā//d//ē/. Say the last sound with me: /ē/. In this word, the letter *y* is used to make the /ē/ sound. Many words use the letter *y* to make the /ē/ sound.

3. Practice new long e words spelled with a y. Display Student Page S144. Point to *silly*. Follow Step 2 to introduce and practice *silly*. Repeat for *baby* and *happy*.

lady	silly	baby	happy

✓ **INDEPENDENT PRACTICE** Read the sentence from Student Page S144. Tell the student you will say a word with the sound of the letter e that is spelled with a *y*. In random order, say a long e word in the sentence. Ask the student to point to the word in the sentence and say the word. Repeat the steps for all long vowel e words spelled with a *y* in the sentence.

I saw a <u>happy</u> <u>baby</u> with a <u>silly</u> <u>lady</u>.

IF... students cannot identify a word,
THEN... say the word, drawing out the long e sound as you run your finger under the related letter.

Lesson 24 Long Vowel Patterns

Hi!

She is a young girl.
Pete is a cold boy.
The young girl says hi to the cold boy.
The boy is too cold to say hi back!

e	o	i
she	cold	hi

Lesson 24 Long Vowel Patterns

e
me
he
we
she

o
most
told
go
cold

i
find
kind
mind
hi

e	we	he	me	she
o	go	cold	told	most
i	mind	hi	find	kind

Lesson 24 Long Vowel Patterns

fly	why	try	sky

Why try to fly in the sky?

Lesson 24 Long Vowel Patterns

lady	silly	baby	happy

I saw a happy baby with a silly lady.

Lesson 25 Vowel Teams

INTRODUCE Remind students that long vowel sounds say the letter name. Remind students they have learned to recognize and say words with long vowel sounds that use different letters to make the same sound. For example, we learned the words *Pete* and *me*. Both words use the /ē/ sound. Hold up word cards for *Pete* and *me*. These words both have the long e sound. *Pete* has the letter *t* followed by a silent e. *Me* has the long e sound at the end of the word. Today we will learn to recognize words with these long vowel sounds—/ē/, /ā/, and /ō/—that are spelled differently from other words we have learned.

RF.1.3.c Know final -e and common vowel team conventions for representing long vowel sounds.

RF.1.3.b Decode regularly spelled one-syllable words.

OBJECTIVE:

- Introduce spelling correspondences for long vowel teams spelled *ee, ea, ai,* and *oa.*

MODEL Display, point to, and read "The Bee" from Student Page S145. In many words the letters ee make the /ē/ sound. Hold up a letter card with ee. I see these letters in this word: /b/. /ē/. Draw out the sound. Run your fingers under the letters as you say the sound. /b/. /ē/. Now listen carefully as I say the word: /b//ē/.

The Bee

The bee can eat and sleep in the tree.
He can stay all day, in the sun or the rain.
He can float like a boat in the sea.

TEACH We have learned that the letters ee can say the name of the letter e. Say the sound with me: /ē/. I will say each word and then we will say it together. Say the /ē/ sound before you say each word. Run your fingers under the letters ee as you say the word. Begin with *bee*: /ē/. Now say the word with me: /b//ē/. Use the same steps to introduce and practice *sleep* and *tree*. Read the first sentence again, drawing out the sounds. Then repeat the process with the other words that have vowel teams *ea* (*eat*), *ai* (*rain*), and *oa* (*float*).

Lesson 25 Vowel Teams

REMIND STUDENTS THAT...

- they can say words that use different letters to make the /ē/ sound.
- they can say words that use *ee* and *ea* to make the /ē/ sound.

PRACTICE 1: Long e (Spelled *ee, ea*) Use the following routine to help students recognize words with long e spelled *ee, ea.*

Routine

1. Review a familiar long e word spelled ee.

Write *bee.* The e in /b/ /ē/ says its letter name: /ē/. Say it with me: /ē/. /B/. /ē/. Many words use the letter e to make this sound. Say the word and repeat it with students. Display Student Page S146. Read the ee poem. Draw your finger under each long e sound as you read. In this poem, the letters ee say the letter name. I will read the sentence again and underline the words with the long e sound. Then we will say each word together.

2. Introduce and practice new words with the long e sound spelled ee.

Display Student Page S146. Read the ee poem. Draw your finger under each long e sound as you read. In this poem, the letters ee say the letter name. I will read the sentence again and underline the words with the long e sound. Then we will say each word together.

Then repeat the routine to introduce and practice *ea* words.

ee	ea
Keep a seed. Plant it deep. Grow a tree For a bee!	Sneak to the sea To beat the heat! Sit on a seat. Have a bite to eat!

MONITOR PROGRESS Display the following words from Student Page S146. Say a word. Ask the student to point to and say the word.

sea	tree	deep	heat	bee
keep	seat	seed	beat	eat

IF... students cannot identify a word,
THEN... say the word, drawing out the long e sound as you run your finger under the related letters.

Lesson 25 Vowel Teams

PRACTICE 2: Long *a* (Spelled *ai*) Use the following routine to help students recognize words with long *a* spelled *ai.*

Routine

1. Review long *a* words.

Write the word *cape.* This is a familiar word: /k/. /ā/. /p/. Say it with me: /k/ /ā/ /p/. This is a word with a long *a* sound that has a silent e at the end of the word. Today we will learn words with the /ā/ sound that are spelled differently.

2. Introduce and model long *a* words spelled *ai.*

Write or display the letters *ai.* Point to the letters and say the sound. Ask students to say the sound with you. In many words, the letters *ai* make the /ā/ sound. Write the word *mail.* In *mail*, the letters *ai* make the long *a* sound. Run your fingers under the letters as you draw out the sounds in the word: /m/. /ā/. /l/. Say it with me: /m//ā//l/. *Mail.*

3. Practice words with the long *a* sound spelled *ai.*

Display Student Page S147. Read the poem. I will underline the words with the long *a* sound. Then we will say each word together.

ai

A snail
on a pail
in the rain
waits for
its mail.

REMIND STUDENTS THAT…

- they can say the long vowel sound /ā/.
- they can identify words that use the /ā/ sound spelled *ai.*

MONITOR PROGRESS Display the following words from Student Page S147. Say a word. Ask the student to point to and say the word. Repeat for at least three words.

mail	rain	snail
nail	pail	wait

IF… students cannot identify a word,
THEN… say the word, drawing out the long *a* sound as you run your finger under the related letters.

Lesson 25 Vowel Teams

REMIND STUDENTS THAT…

- they can say the long vowel sound /ō/.
- they can identify words that use the /ō/ sound spelled *oa*.

PRACTICE 3: Long *o* (Spelled *oa*) Use the following routine to help students recognize words with long *o* spelled *oa*.

Routine

1. Practice a long *o* word.

Write the word *bone*. This is a familiar word: /b/. /ō/. /n/. Say it with me: /b//ō//n/. This is a word with the long *o* sound that has a silent e at the end of the word. Today we will learn words with the /ō/ sound that are spelled differently.

2. Introduce and model long *o* words spelled *oa*.

Write the letters *oa*. Point to the letters and say the sound. Ask students to say the sound with you. In many words, the letters *oa* make the /ō/ sound. Write the word *boat*. In /b/ /ō/ /t/, the letters *oa* make the /ō/ sound. Run your fingers under the letters as you draw out each sound in the word: /b/. /ō/. /t/. Say it with me: /b//ō//t/. *Boat*.

3. Practice new words with the long *o* sound spelled *oa*.

Display Student Page S148. Read the poem. I will read the poem again slowly. I will underline the words with the /ō/ sound. Then we will say each /ō/ word together.

oa

A goat
who ate toast
liked to float
on a boat.

INDEPENDENT PRACTICE Display the following words from Student Page S148. Say a word. Ask the student to point to and say the word. Repeat for at least three words.

float	soap	goat	toast	boat

IF… students cannot identify a word,
THEN… say the word, drawing out the /ō/ sound as you run your finger under the related letters.

The Bee

The bee can eat and sleep in the tree.
He can stay all day, in the sun or the rain.
He can float like a boat in the sea.

Lesson 25 Vowel Teams

ee	ea
Keep a seed. Plant it deep. Grow a tree For a bee!	Sneak to the sea To beat the heat! Sit on a seat. Have a bite to eat!

sea	tree	deep	heat	bee
keep	seat	seed	beat	eat

Lesson 25 Vowel Teams

ai

A snail
on a pail
in the rain
waits for
its mail.

mail	rain	snail
nail	pail	wait

Lesson 25 Vowel Teams

oa

A goat
who ate toast
liked to float
on a boat.

float soap goat toast boat

ASSESSMENT
LESSONS 23–25

Phonics and Word Recognition

ASSESS MASTERY Use this Checkpoint to assess students' mastery of long vowels and the silent e rule, long vowel patterns, and vowel teams.

ADMINISTER THE TEST Administer the Checkpoint orally to each student. For each item, model the process as described, and then have the student use the process to respond to your prompts. Record responses on the scoring chart on the next page.

RF.1.3.c Know final -e and common vowel team conventions for representing long vowel sounds.
RF.1.3.b Decode regularly spelled one-syllable words.

1. Long Vowels and the Silent e Rule (Lesson 23)

MODEL: Repeat the word with the long vowel sound. For example, if I say *tape* and *tap,* then you would repeat the word *tape.*

ASSESS:	fire, fir	hat, hate	kit, kite
	cub, cube	hot, hole	hug, huge

2. Long Vowel Patterns (Lesson 24)

MODEL: Repeat the word that makes the long vowel sound /ē/, /ō/, or /ī/ with only one letter.

ASSESS:	coal, sold	he, heat	find, file

3. Long Vowel Patterns (Lesson 24)

MODEL: Repeat the word that makes the long vowel sound /ē/ or /ī/ with the letter *y.*

ASSESS:	my, mine	shine, shy	cream, candy	party, peel

4. Vowel Teams (Lesson 25)

MODEL: Repeat the word with the long vowel sound /ē/ spelled with ee or *ea.*

ASSESS:	**ee:** she, seen	heel, he	**ea:** be, beat	seat, see

5. Vowel Teams (Lesson 25)

MODEL: Repeat the word with the long vowel sound /ā/ spelled *ai,* or point to the word with the long vowel sound /ō/ spelled *oa.*

ASSESS:	**ai:** hay, hail	sail, say	**oa:** boat, bow	so, soak

ASSESSMENT
LESSONS 23–25

Phonics and Word Recognition

SCORING

SKILL/LESSON	STANDARD	SCORE
1. Long Vowels and the Silent e Rule (Lesson 23) fire, fir (fire) hat, hate (hate) kit, kite (kite) cub, cube (cube) hot, hole (hole) hug, huge (huge)	**RF.1.3.c** Know final -e and common vowel team conventions for representing long vowel sounds.	_____ / 6
2. Long Vowel Patterns (Lesson 24) coal, sold (sold) he, heat (he) find, file (find)	**RF.1.3.b** Decode regularly spelled one-syllable words.	_____ / 3
3. Long Vowel Patterns (Lesson 24) my, mine (my) shine, shy (shy) cream, candy (candy) party, peel (party)		_____ / 4
4. Vowel Teams (Lesson 25) ee: she, seen (seen) ee: heel, he (heel) ea: be, beat (beat) ea: seat, see (seat)		_____ / 4
5. Vowel Teams (Lesson 25) ai: hay, hail (hail) ai: sail, say (sail) oa: boat, bow (boat) oa: so, soak (soak)		_____ / 4

An overall score of 80% correct is typically considered mastery. Use your judgment and your individual students' needs as well to determine skill mastery.

IF...you determine that students have not demonstrated sufficient mastery of one or more skills,
THEN...review the skill(s), going back to the lessons to reteach and scaffold as needed.

Lesson 26 Understand Syllables

INTRODUCE Explain that syllables are parts of words. Today we are going to clap the syllables in words. Say *num•ber* slowly, holding up your thumb for *num* and your index finger for *ber.* Now clap with me for each syllable: *num•ber.*

MODEL Display or share copies of the passage "The Picnic" from Student Page S151. Read it aloud and clap as you say each syllable.

The Picnic

Jo and Polly had a picnic.
Jo ate a turkey leg.
Polly drank a soda.
A little insect came along, so they went inside.

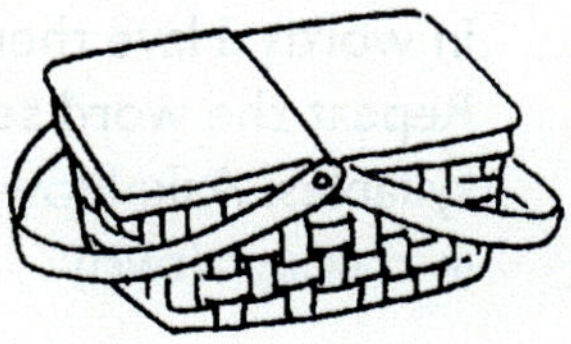

TEACH Point out that the separate word parts students can hear are syllables. Many short words, such as *the,* have one syllable; other short words, such as *picnic,* have two syllables. Now clap with me as I read aloud "The Picnic."

Next, point to *leg* and explain that some spelling patterns signal a short vowel sound. Point to *ate* to demonstrate that the consonant-vowel-e spelling pattern shows a long vowel sound.

Use the routines that follow to help students understand syllables and recognize closed syllables and open syllables.

RF.1.3.d Use knowledge that every syllable must have a vowel sound to determine the number of syllables in a printed word.

OBJECTIVES:

- Demonstrate that words can be divided into parts or chunks called syllables (e.g., clap and identify syllables).
- Identify vowel sounds in syllables (e.g., in /ĭ/ • sect /ĕ/).
- Understand that a closed syllable has a single vowel with a consonant after it, making the vowel sound short (e.g., *map, sit, stop*).
- Understand that an open syllable contains a vowel at the end of the syllable and the vowel is usually long (e.g., *we, go, hi, she*).
- Understand that the final -e in a vowel-consonant-e (VCe) syllable makes the vowel long or "say its own name" (e.g., *make, time, cute*).

Lesson 26 Understand Syllables

REMIND STUDENTS THAT...

- they can divide words into parts called syllables.
- they can clap while saying a word to count the number of syllables.

WORD LIST

- tiny
- pencil
- very
- robot
- over

PRACTICE 1: Understand and Count Syllables Use the following routine to help students understand and count syllables.

Routine

1. Introduce the strategy. Explain that students' names have syllables. You can clap the syllables, or word parts, that you hear in your own name.

2. Model the strategy. Choose a student's name that has one syllable. Say the name and clap one time. Then choose a name with two syllables and use your thumb to show the first syllable and your index finger to show the second syllable as you say the name.

3. Guide practice. Point out that students can use the separate word parts they hear to understand syllables in words. Have them listen as you say *cowboy*. Repeat the word several times, segmenting the syllables. Ask: How many syllables do you hear in *cowboy?* (two)

For additional practice with two-syllable words, follow the same procedure with the words *doctor* (doc•tor) and *busy* (bus•y), or use the Word List in the side column and ask students to clap the syllables as you say the words.

apple	plum	cracker	lemon
milk	tea	popcorn	carrot

Next, have students cut apart the word cards. Individuals take turns choosing a card and saying the name of the item. The class repeats the word and claps the number of syllables they hear.

✔ **MONITOR PROGRESS** Display and read aloud the sentences from Student Page S152. Have students clap the syllables they hear in each word.

Where are the little kittens?
They are in the bottom of the picnic basket.

IF... students do not clap each syllable,
THEN... offer corrective feedback and practice with one- and two-syllable words.

Lesson 26 Understand Syllables

PRACTICE 2: Closed Syllables Use this routine to introduce closed syllables.

Routine

1. Introduce the strategy. Explain that many words are spelled with a single vowel followed by a consonant. Sometimes the spelling pattern of vowels and consonants in a word helps you sound out and read the word.

2. Model the strategy. Write the words *map* and *sit*. Point out that the spellings: *m-a-p* and *s-i-t*. The final letters *p* and *t* are consonants. In *map*, *p* follows *a*. In *sit*, *t* follows *i*. Are *a* and *i* vowels or consonants? (vowels) This spelling pattern of one vowel followed by a consonant usually signals a short sound of the vowel.

3. Guide practice. Write the words *at*, *mud*, and *zip*. Look at the spelling pattern in these words. The final letters *t*, *d*, and *p* are consonants. A vowel comes before the final consonant in each word. What can you predict about the sound of the vowel in the word? (It will be a short vowel sound.)

For additional practice, use the Word List in the side column. Have students identify the vowel sound and use the word in an oral sentence.

Have students use Student Page S153 to build words with short vowel sounds. First have them write letters *a* and *m* in the boxes to make the words *ham*, *jam*, and *Sam*. Then have them write the letters *i* and *t* in the boxes to make the words *bit*, *sit*, and *hit*.

MONITOR PROGRESS Display the following sentences from Student Page S153 and ask students to identify the words with a short vowel sound spelled with a vowel followed by a consonant.

Nan did not grab an apple.
She got grapes.

IF... students do not identify *Nan*, *did*, *not*, *grab*, *an*, and *got*,
THEN... review the routine and provide additional sentences for practice.

REMIND STUDENTS THAT...

- they can identify vowels and consonants.
- they can identify vowel sounds in words.
- they can differentiate between long and short vowel sounds.

WORD LIST

- hot
- mad
- big
- web
- sum

Lesson 26 Understand Syllables

REMIND STUDENTS THAT...

- they can identify vowels and consonants.
- they can identify vowel sounds in words.
- they can differentiate between long and short vowel sounds.
- they can look for spelling patterns to see whether a word has a long or short vowel sound.
- they can use the final -e as a sign of a long vowel sound.

WORD LIST

- no
- late
- tune
- be
- mine

PRACTICE 3: Open Syllables Use this routine to introduce open syllables.

Routine

1. Introduce the strategy. Explain that sometimes spelling patterns can help you sound out and read a word. Syllables with the vowel at the end and syllables with a vowel followed by a consonant and *e* usually have the long vowel sound.

2. Model the strategy. Write the word *go*. Explain that this word has one syllable. Point to the final *o* at the end of *go*. This spelling pattern of a vowel at the end of a syllable usually signals a long vowel sound. Repeat this process with the word *gate*.

3. Guide practice. Write the words *hi, she, bite,* and *rule*. What vowel sound do you hear in the words—long or short vowels? (long vowel) In *bite* and *rule,* the vowel is followed by a consonant and silent *e*.

For additional practice with one-syllable words ending with a consonant-vowel or with a vowel-consonant-e, use the Word List in the side column. Have students identify the vowel sound and use the word in an oral sentence.

a	e	i	o
b	m	n	t

Have students cut out the letter cards and work in pairs to put the letters together to form different words that have a long vowel sound.

✓ **INDEPENDENT PRACTICE** Display the following sentences from Student Page S154 and ask students to identify the words with a long vowel sound spelled with a consonant-vowel or a vowel-consonant-e.

Nate made Bo a fine gift.
She did not like it.
What a shame!

IF... students do not identify the words with the long vowel sound,
THEN... review the routine and provide additional words for practice.

Lesson 26 **Understand Syllables**

The Picnic

Jo and Polly had a picnic.
Jo ate a turkey leg.
Polly drank a soda.
A little insect came along, so they went inside.

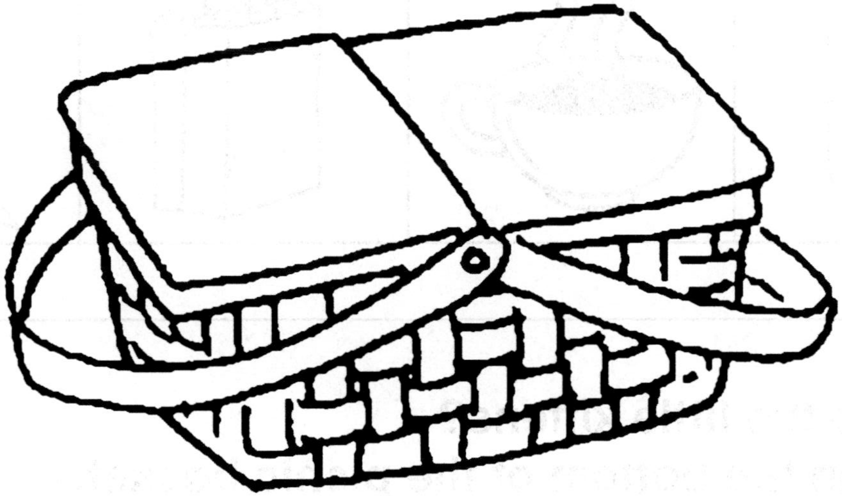

Lesson 26 Understand Syllables

apple 	plum 	cracker 	lemon 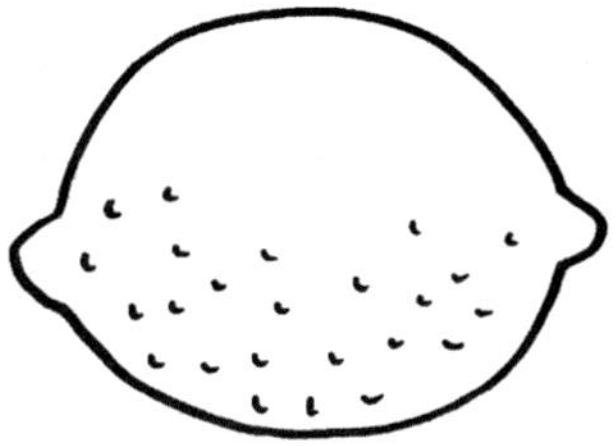
milk 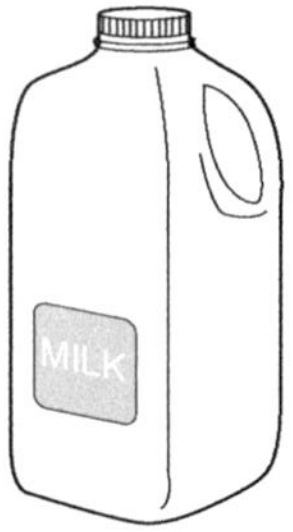	tea 	popcorn 	carrot 

Where are the little kittens?
They are in the bottom of the picnic basket.

Lesson 26 Understand Syllables

am

h		
j		
S		

it

b		
s		
h		

Nan did not grab an apple.
She got grapes.

Lesson 26 Understand Syllables

a	e	i	o
b	m	n	t

Nate made Bo a fine gift.
She did not like it.
What a shame!

Lesson 27 Syllable Patterns

INTRODUCE Remind students that words have small parts, or syllables. They have already practiced clapping the syllables in words. Today we will look at spelling patterns to learn how some words are broken into syllables.

MODEL Display or share copies of the following passage "Find the Dragons" from Student Page S155, and read it aloud. Some words in this passage have the patterns we will learn for finding syllables.

Find the Dragons

Seven little dragons are hidden in a picture.
One peeks from under a table.
Find the rest.
You will get a bonus.

TEACH Remind students that they have been identifying syllables and vowels in syllables. Explain that some syllable patterns will help them read words. The word *little* shows one pattern. Write *little*. When I see a word with two consonants in the middle, I divide the word after the first consonant. Cover *tle*. Say the first syllable with me: *lit*. Then cover *lit* and read the final syllable aloud: *tle*. Now read the syllables one after the other to say the word. The syllables are *lit* and *tle*. I read: *lit, tle, little.*

Use the routines that follow for the spelling patterns VC/CV, V/CV, and VC/V.

RF.1.3.e Decode two-syllable words following basic patterns by breaking the words into syllables.

OBJECTIVES:

- Distinguish between syllable types.
- Demonstrate knowledge of syllabication rules.

Lesson 27 Syllable Patterns

REMIND STUDENTS THAT...

- they can distinguish between syllable types.
- they can demonstrate knowledge of syllabication rules.

WORD LIST

- rabbit
- basket
- sister
- napkin
- yellow

PRACTICE 1: Syllable Pattern VC/CV Follow the routine to teach the VC/CV syllable pattern.

Routine

1. Introduce the strategy. Write and read aloud *hidden* and *picture* and have students say the words several times. These words have two syllables. The words can be divided between the two consonants.

2. Model the strategy. Circle each *d* in *hidden*. For a word with two consonants in the middle, divide the word after the first consonant. Cover *den*. Say the first syllable: *hid*. Cover *hid*. Read the second syllable: *den*. Now read one syllable after the other: *hidden*.

3. Guide practice. Write *picture*. Where would you break the word into parts? (between *c* and *t*) Say the syllables: *pic•ture*. Now blend the syllables and say the word: *picture*. Repeat with *under, kitten,* and *picnic*.

For additional practice, use the Word List in the side column.

Have students cut apart the word cards. Have pairs read each word, decide where it breaks into syllables, and draw a line between the syllables.

rabbit	panda	mitten
dinner	hello	inside
cupcake	hammer	sentence

✔ **MONITOR PROGRESS** Display and read aloud the sentences from Student Page S156. Have students identify the words with two syllables.

> What will happen if I walk in a puddle?
> I will get my new cotton pants wet!

IF... students do not recognize *happen, puddle,* and *cotton,*
THEN... review the routine and the practice words in the lesson.

Lesson 27 Syllable Patterns

PRACTICE 2: Syllable Pattern V/CV Follow the routine to teach the V/CV syllable pattern.

Routine

1. Introduce the strategy. We will learn to divide words with one consonant between vowels. Write *paper* and *student*. Have students say them several times. These words have two syllables. They can be divided after the first vowel.

2. Model the strategy. Point to *paper*. To divide a word with a consonant between two vowels, the consonant (point to *p*) may go with the second syllable. The first vowel (point to the *a*) is usually long. Cover *per*. Read *pa*. What vowel sound do you hear? (long *a*) Cover *pa*. Read *per*. Repeat for *student*.

3. Guide practice. Write *motel, music,* and *pretend*. Have students read *motel*. Where would you break it into parts? (between *o* and *t*) What is the vowel sound of *o*? (long *o*) Continue with *music* and *pretend*.

For additional practice, use the Word List in the side column.

pilot	polar	silent
final	pilot	behind
open	silent	polar
behind	final	open

Have partners cut the word cards and put them face down. Pick two cards. If the words match, keep them. If they don't match, put them back.

✔ **MONITOR PROGRESS** Display and read aloud the sentence from Student Page S157. Have students identify the words with the V/CV pattern.

The tiger and the spider are toy robots.

IF… students cannot identify *tiger, spider,* and *robots,*
THEN… review the routine and the practice words in the lesson.

REMIND STUDENTS THAT…

- they can distinguish between syllable types.
- they can demonstrate knowledge of syllabication rules.

WORD LIST

- motor
- open
- even
- bonus
- robot

Lesson 27 Syllable Patterns

REMIND STUDENTS THAT…

- they can distinguish between syllable types.
- they can demonstrate knowledge of syllabication rules.

WORD LIST

- finish
- river
- visit
- wagon
- robin

PRACTICE 3: Syllable Pattern VC/V Follow the routine to teach the VC/V syllable pattern.

Routine

1. Introduce the strategy. With some words that have the pattern vowel-consonant-vowel, such as *paper,* divide the word after the first vowel. With other words, divide the word after the consonant.

2. Model the strategy. Write *seven.* If I divide *seven* after the first vowel, the e has a long sound: /ē/. /s//ē//v//e//n/. That does not sound right. If I divide it after *v,* the vowel in the first syllable is short. Say /s//ĕ//v/. Have students say the word with you: *sev•en, seven.* That sounds right.

3. Guide practice. Write *clever, dragons,* and *lemon.* Have students read *clever* and identify the two syllables. Where would you break it into parts? (after *v*) What is the vowel sound of the first *e?* (short e) Continue with the other words.

For additional practice with VC/V words, use the Word List in the side column.

never	punish	cabin
model	menu	pedal

Have students cut apart the word cards. Put them in a bowl. Pick a card, read it aloud, and use it in a sentence. Discuss where to draw a line to show the syllables.

✔ **INDEPENDENT PRACTICE** Display the following sentences from Student Page S158 and ask students to identify the words with a short vowel sound spelled with a vowel-consonant-vowel pattern.

> Never make a promise you cannot keep.
> We found a lizard in the closet.

IF… students do not identify *never, promise, lizard,* and *closet,*
THEN… review the routine and the practice words.

Find the Dragons

Seven little dragons are hidden in a picture.
One peeks from under a table.
Find the rest.
You will get a bonus.

Lesson 27 Syllable Patterns

rabbit	panda	mitten
dinner	hello	inside
cupcake	hammer	sentence

What will happen if I walk in a puddle?
I will get my new cotton pants wet!

Lesson 27 Syllable Patterns

pilot	polar	silent
final	pilot	behind
open	silent	polar
behind	final	open

The tiger and the spider are toy robots.

Lesson 27 Syllable Patterns

never	punish	cabin
model	menu	pedal

Never make a promise you cannot keep.
We found a lizard in the closet.

Lesson 28 Syllable Patterns: R-Controlled Vowels

RF.1.3.e Decode two-syllable words following basic patterns by breaking the words into syllables.

OBJECTIVES:

- Recognize that an *r*-controlled syllable is a vowel plus *r* (e.g., *for, star, first*).
- Use syllabication rules.

INTRODUCE Remind students that the sounds of vowels change when they are followed by the letter *r*. Write *ban/barn* and say each word aloud, emphasizing the sound *ar* makes. An *r*-controlled syllable is a syllable that contains a vowel followed by *r*. The *r* makes the vowel sound different. Say the sound /ar/ several times and have students repeat after you. Say: Today we will learn how to use vowel + *r* sounds to help us decide where to break words into syllables.

MODEL Display or share copies of "A Storm from the North" from Student Page S159 and read it aloud. The words in this passage have the /r/ sound you hear in *car, more,* and *her.*

A Storm from the North

I hear thunder.
A storm from the north is on the way.
I am sorry.
We cannot go to the market.

TEACH Write *ar*. Have students say /ar/ several times as you point to *ar*. Together the letters *ar* spell the single sound /ar/. Point to *market* and say it aloud slowly, emphasizing the two syllables. Then have students repeat the word several times. Ask: Where do you hear the /ar/ sound? Is it in the first or second syllable? (first) Circle the letters *ar*. Remember that *ar* makes the single sound /ar/. When we divide a word into syllables, we keep the vowel plus *r* together. Remind students of the VC/CV pattern. Use your knowledge about syllables to break apart the word. Remember to keep the *ar* sound together. Draw a line between the syllables in *market*. Follow this procedure with the sound /or/ in *sorry* and the sound /ur/ in *thunder*.

Use the routines to teach and practice syllable patterns for the *r*-controlled vowels /ar/ spelled *ar*, /or/ spelled *or, ore, oar,* and /ur/ spelled *er, ir, ur*.

Lesson 28 Syllable Patterns: *R*-Controlled Vowels

REMIND STUDENTS THAT...

- they can recognize that an *r*-controlled syllable is a vowel plus *r* (e.g., *for, star, first*).
- vowel sounds change when the vowel is followed by /r/.
- they can use syllabication rules.

PRACTICE 1: *R*-Controlled Vowel /ar/ Spelled *ar* Follow the routine to teach the syllable pattern of /ar/ spelled *ar*.

Routine

1. Model the strategy. Write the word *dollar*. Point to the word and say it slowly, pausing between the syllables. I hear the sound /ar/. I have to figure out if /ar/ is in the first syllable or the second. Say the word again and have students repeat after you. The /ar/ sound is in the second syllable. When I break the syllable, I know to keep the *a* and *r* together. Circle *ar*. Remind students of the VC/CV pattern, and draw a line between the syllables in *dollar*.

2. Guide practice. Display the word card for *polar* from Student Page S160. Read aloud the word slowly, pausing between syllables, and have students repeat after you. Ask: Where is the /ar/ sound? Is it in the first or second syllable? (second) What letters make the /ar/ sound? (*ar*) Circle *ar*. We know to keep these letters together in the syllable. Then we use what we already know about syllables to break the word apart. Have students draw a line between the syllables in *polar*.

polar	lizard	alarm	garden

Have students cut apart the word cards and read them aloud with a partner. Then have students identify the syllable that contains the /ar/ sound and use what they already know about syllables to draw a line between the syllables, making sure to keep the /ar/ sound together.

✔ **MONITOR PROGRESS** Have students read the sentences from Student Page S160 and identify the syllables with /ar/ spelled *ar*.

Martin is having a party.
Bart and I will go.

IF... students do not identify syllables that contain the /ar/ sound,
THEN... provide feedback and review the routine.

Lesson 28 Syllable Patterns: *R*-Controlled Vowels

PRACTICE 2: *R*-Controlled Vowel /or/ Spelled *or, ore, oar* Use the word *for* to teach the sound /or/.

Routine

1. Model the strategy. Write the word *before*. Point to the word and say it slowly, pausing between the syllables. I hear the sound /or/. I have to figure out if /or/ is in the first syllable or the second. Say the word again and have students repeat after you. The /or/ sound is in the second syllable. When I break the syllable, I know to keep the *o, r,* and *e* together. Circle *or*. Remind students of the V/CV pattern, and draw a line between the syllables in *before*.

2. Guide practice. Display the word card for *doctor* from Student Page S161. Read aloud the word slowly, pausing between syllables, and have students repeat after you. Ask: Where is the /or/ sound? Is it in the first or second syllable? (second) What letters make the /or/ sound? (*or*) Circle *or*. We know to keep these letters together in the syllable. Then we use what we already know about syllables to break the word apart. Have students draw a line between the syllables in *doctor*.

doctor	condor	afford
support	soaring	boredom

Have students cut apart the word cards, mix them, and sort them into three groups: words spelled *or*, words spelled *ore*, and words spelled *oar*.

REMIND STUDENTS THAT…

- they can recognize that an *r*-controlled syllable is a vowel plus *r* (e.g., *for, star, first*).
- vowel sounds change when the vowel is followed by /r/.
- they can use syllabication rules.

✓ **MONITOR PROGRESS** Display the sentences from Student Page S161 and have students identify words with /or/ spelled *or, ore,* or *oar*.

The boar is snoring and snorting.
What a boring chore to feed him more!

IF… students do not identify *boar, snoring, snorting, boring, chore,* and *more,*
THEN… review the three different spellings of /or/.

Lesson 28 Syllable Patterns: R-Controlled Vowels

REMIND STUDENTS THAT...

- they can recognize that an *r*-controlled syllable is a vowel plus *r* (e.g., *for, star, first*).
- vowel sounds change when the vowel is followed by /r/.
- they can use syllabication rules.

PRACTICE 3: *R*-Controlled Vowel /ur/ Spelled *er, ir, ur* Use the word *her* to teach the sound of /ur/.

Routine

1. Model the strategy. Write the word *butter*. Point to the word and say it slowly, pausing between the syllables. I hear the sound /ur/. I have to figure out if /ur/ is in the first syllable or the second. Say the word again and have students repeat after you. The /ur/ sound is in the second syllable. When I break the syllable, I know to keep the *e* and *r* together. Circle *er*. Remind students of the VC/CV pattern, and draw a line between the syllables in *butter*.

2. Guide practice. Display the word card for *thirsty* from Student Page S162. Read aloud the word slowly, pausing between syllables, and have students repeat after you. Ask: Where is the /ur/ sound? Is it in the first or second syllable? (first) What letters make the /ur/ sound? (*ir*) Circle *ir*. We know to keep these letters together in the syllable. Then we use what we already know about syllables to break the word apart. Have students draw a line between the syllables in *thirsty*.

thirsty	desert	burning	baker
certain	curly	blurted	dirty

Have students cut apart the word cards, mix them, and sort them into three groups: words spelled *er*, words spelled *ur*, and words spelled *ir*.

✔ **INDEPENDENT PRACTICE** Display the sentences from Student Page S162 and have students identify words with /ur/.

The dancer is turning and twirling.
She is swirling across the desert!

IF... students do not identify *dancer, turning, twirling, swirling,* and *desert,*
THEN... provide feedback and review the routine.

Lesson 28 **Syllable Patterns: *R*-Controlled Vowels**

A Storm from the North

I hear thunder.
A storm from the north is on the way.
I am sorry.
We cannot go to the market.

Lesson 28 Syllable Patterns: *R*-Controlled Vowels

polar	lizard
alarm	garden

Martin is having a party.
Bart and I will go.

Lesson 28 Syllable Patterns: *R*-Controlled Vowels

doctor	condor	afford
support	soaring	boredom

The boar is snoring and snorting.
What a boring chore to feed him more!

Lesson 28 Syllable Patterns: *R*-Controlled Vowels

thirsty	desert	burning	baker
certain	curly	blurted	dirty

The dancer is turning and twirling.
She is swirling across the desert!

ASSESSMENT
LESSONS 26–28

Phonics and Word Recognition

ASSESS MASTERY Use this Checkpoint to assess students' mastery of syllables and syllable patterns.

ADMINISTER THE TEST Administer the Checkpoint orally to each student. Give each student a copy of the next page. Instruct students as follows.

RF.1.3.d Use knowledge that every syllable must have a vowel sound to determine the number of syllables in a printed word.

RF.1.3.e Decode two-syllable words following basic patterns by breaking the words into syllables.

1. Understand Syllables (Lesson 26)
MODEL: I will say a word. Clap the syllables and tell me if it has one or two syllables.

ASSESS: set puppy come hotel seven

2. Syllable Patterns VC/CV, V/CV, VC/V (Lesson 27)
MODEL: I will read these words twice. Draw a line to divide the syllables.

ASSESS: bottom pilot middle metal cabin

3. Syllable Patterns: *R*-Controlled Vowels (Lesson 28)
MODEL: I will say two words that have a vowel with *r*. Tell me if the words have the same sound or a different sound.

ASSESS: turn, north storm, corn curb, term mart, more

SCORING

SKILL/LESSON	SCORE
1. Understand Syllables (Lesson 26) set (1); puppy (2); come (1); hotel (2); seven (2)	_____ / 5
2. Syllable Patterns VC/CV, V/CV, VC/V (Lesson 27) bottom (between *t* and *t*); pilot (between *i* and *l*); middle (between *d* and *d*); metal (between *t* and *a*); cabin (between *b* and *i*)	_____ / 5
3. Syllable Patterns *R*-Controlled Vowels (Lesson 28) turn, north (different); storm, corn (same); curb, term (same); mart, more (different)	_____ / 4

An overall score of 80% correct is typically considered mastery. Use your judgment and your individual students' needs as well to determine skill mastery.

IF... you determine that students have not demonstrated sufficient mastery of one or more skills,
THEN... review the skill(s), going back to the lessons to reteach and scaffold as needed.

ASSESSMENT
LESSONS 26–28

Phonics and Word Recognition

1.	**set**	**puppy**	**come**	**hotel**	**seven**
2.	**bottom**	**pilot**	**middle**	**metal**	**cabin**

3. **turn, north** **storm, corn**
curb, term **mart, more**

Lesson 29 Inflectional Endings

RF.1.3.f Read words with inflectional endings.

OBJECTIVES:

- Decode letter-sound correspondences for common inflectional endings (e.g., *-es*, *-ed*, *-ing*).
- Read fluently root words that can have common inflectional endings added to them (e.g., *add, fox, open, play, jump*).
- Recognize inflectional endings on words.

INTRODUCE Remind students that many words are made up of smaller word parts. In this lesson, you will learn to read words with the word parts *-s, -es, -ed,* and *-ing* and to add endings to words to make new words.

MODEL Display or share copies of the passage "The Cooks" from Student Page S165, and read it aloud. Say: The words in this story have the endings *-s, -es, -ed,* and *-ing.*

The Cooks

Mai has fixed the grill.
Sal is mixing the batter.
I am tossing the salad.
Kim moved away and misses us.

TEACH Point to the title and the word *Cooks.* An *-s* added to the end of *cook* makes a new word. Cover the word part -*s* and read the root word aloud: *cook.* Then cover the root word and read the word part -*s* aloud: /s/. The *s* in *cooks* makes the sound /s/. *Cooks* means "more than one cook." The letter *s* can have the sound /s/ as in *cooks* or the sound /z/ as in *legs.*

Explain that action words such as *fix, mix, toss, move,* and *miss* have endings to show when actions happen. Then point to *fixed* and *mixing* in the story and read the words aloud. Say: When we add *-ed* or *-ing* to action words, like *fix* or *mix,* we tell when actions happen.

Lesson 29 Inflectional Endings

REMIND STUDENTS THAT...

- they can connect letters and sounds.
- they can recognize inflectional endings on words.

WORD LIST

- tugs
- hands
- taxes
- stops
- messes

PRACTICE 1: Inflectional Endings -s, -es Introduce the strategy by writing the word *runs*. This word has two parts: *run* and *-s*. When we add *-s* to an action word, we make it agree with the person doing the action. Write: *Ben runs. Ben and Pete run.* Underline *runs* and *run*. One person *runs*, but two or more people *run*. Write *fixes* and circle the *x*. For some words, like *fix*, we write -es instead of -s.

Next, model blending by writing the word *licks*. When I see this word with *-s* at the end, I notice the two parts of the word, *lick* and *-s*. Let's read the parts one after the other to say the word: /l/ /i/ /k/ /s/, *licks*. In this word the *s* has the sound /s/. Repeat this procedure with the words *adds, legs,* and *cuts* and note that *s* has the sound /z/ in *adds* and *legs*.

Finally, point to the word *misses* in the passage from Student Page S165. Run your hand under the word as you pronounce it, blending the sounds. Say the word with me: *misses*. What ending is added to *miss?* (-es) Write the following words and have students identify the ending *-s* or *-es*: *tells, passes, mixes,* and *ships*.

Have students cut apart the word cards. Ask them to read each word and then sort the cards into two piles: words that end in -s and words that end in -es.

sips	foxes	picks
dresses	kisses	tags
digs	hops	buses

MONITOR PROGRESS Display the sentences from Student Page S166. Have individuals identify the words that end in -s and -es.

Jim passes the drum to Kim.
Kim hits it.
Jim nods and hums.

IF... students do not identify -es and -s endings,
THEN... guide students in additional practice using the Word List in the sidebar.

Lesson 29 Inflectional Endings

PRACTICE 2: Inflectional Ending *-ed* Introduce the strategy by writing the word *fix* and saying it aloud. We can add *-ed* to *fix* to make a new word. Add *-ed*. Say: The word *fixed* shows when the action happened. He fixed *the car yesterday.*

Run your hand under the word as you say the word /f/ /i/ /x/ /t/ and ask students to say the word with you: *fixed*. The *-ed* in *fixed* makes the sound /t/. To demonstrate *-ed* with the sound /d/, write the word *filled* and say it aloud. Have students say the word with you: /f/ /i/ /l/ /d/. The *-ed* in *filled* makes the sound /d/.

Today we will make new words by adding *-ed* to words we know. Write the word *play*. Run your hand under the word as you pronounce it, blending the sounds. Say the word with me: *play*. Now let's add *-ed* to *play*. What is the new word? Yes, *played*. We pronounce this word /p/ /l/ /ā/ /d/. I played *a game last night.* Follow the same procedure with the words *help*, *open*, and *toss*.

Have students say each word and write *-ed* on the lines to build new words. Ask them to use the new words in oral sentences.

kiss ________

buzz ________

mix ________

yell ________

spell ________

REMIND STUDENTS THAT…

- they can connect letters and sounds.
- they can recognize inflectional endings on words.

WORD LIST

- kick
- miss
- ask
- jump
- pick

MONITOR PROGRESS Display the sentences from Student Page S167. Have students identify the words with *-ed* endings.

Pat packed a box.
She filled it with socks.

IF… students do not identify the *-ed* endings for the words *packed* and *filled*, THEN… practice adding *-ed* to other words by using the words from the Word List in the sidebar.

Lesson 29 Inflectional Endings

REMIND STUDENTS THAT…

- they can connect letters and sounds.
- they can recognize inflectional endings on words.

WORD LIST

- eating
- adding
- calling
- jumping
- telling

PRACTICE 3: Inflectional Ending *-ing* Introduce the strategy by writing *mix* and saying it aloud. We can add *-ing* to *mix* to make a new word. Add *-ing*. Say: The word *mixing* shows when the action happens. *I am* mixing *the paint now.*

Run your hand under the word as you say it: /m//i//x//i//n//g/ and ask students to say the word with you: *mixing*. The *-ing* in *mixing* spells the sound /i//n//g/. The word *jumping* has the same /i//n//g/ sound at the end.

Today we will make new words by adding *-ing* to words we know. Write the word *rest*. Say the word with me: *rest*. Now let's add *-ing* to *rest*. What is the new word? (*resting*) Follow the same procedure with the words *end, look,* and *toss*. Explain that adding *-ing* to a word changes it from one syllable to two syllables. Clap the syllables: *end•ing, look•ing, toss•ing.*

Read the words in the Word Bank and have students say them after you. Ask students to identify the pictures on Student Page S168 and the word from the Word Bank that goes with the picture. Then have them the word.

licking	mixing	fixing	buzzing

✔ **INDEPENDENT PRACTICE** Display the sentences from Student Page S168. Have students identify the words with *-ing* endings.

> Mom is passing the beans.
> Dad is adding pepper to his meat.

IF… students do not identify words with *-ing* endings,
THEN… provide the Word List in the sidebar for additional practice.

Lesson 29 **Inflectional Endings**

The Cooks

Mai has fixed the grill.
Sal is mixing the batter.
I am tossing the salad.
Kim moved away and misses us.

Lesson 29 Inflectional Endings

sips	foxes	picks
dresses	kisses	tags
digs	hops	buses

Jim passes the drum to Kim.
Kim hits it.
Jim nods and hums.

Lesson 29 Inflectional Endings

kiss ________

buzz ________

mix ________

yell ________

spell ________

Pat packed a box.
She filled it with socks.

Lesson 29 Inflectional Endings

licking **mixing** **fixing** **buzzing**

____

____

____

____

Mom is passing the beans.
Dad is adding pepper to his meat.

Lesson 30 Irregular Spellings

INTRODUCE Explain that the spelling of some words does not match the sounds the letters usually stand for. We learn to read some words by saying the sounds that the letters stand for. Other words have spellings that do not match the sounds we hear in the words.

MODEL Display or share copies of "Being a Big Brother" from Student Page S169 and read it aloud.

Being a Big Brother

The baby could not walk.
Then he had one birthday.
He could walk everywhere.
His big brother had to watch him!

Point out the words *could, walk,* and *one.* This passage has different spellings for some sounds you know.

TEACH Write the words *could, one,* and *walk.* Point out *could.* Underline the letters *ld* and say the word. Have students say it after you. Ask: What sound do you hear at the end of *could?* (/d/) Do you hear the sound /l/ in the word? (no) The letters *ld* sometimes have the sound /d/.

Follow the same procedure for *one* pronounced with the /w/ sound for *o* and *walk* pronounced with the /k/ sound for *lk.* You learn words like *could, one,* and *walk* by remembering the letters.

RF.1.3.g Recognize and read grade-appropriate irregularly spelled words.

OBJECTIVES:

- Recognize that some words cannot be decoded using one-to-one correspondence (e.g., *could, one, walk*).
- Use high-frequency sight words.

Lesson 30 Irregular Spellings

REMIND STUDENTS THAT...

- they can recognize that some words cannot be decoded using one-to-one correspondence (e.g., *could, one, walk*).
- they can use high-frequency sight words.

PRACTICE 1: Sound /d/ (Spelled *ld*) Sometimes two letters together have more than one sound. In the word *cold,* the letters *ld* have the sound /ld/. Today we will learn a new sound for *ld.* Follow the routine to teach the sound /d/ spelled *ld.*

Routine

1. Model the strategy. Write *could.* Point to the letters *ld* in *could.* Together the letters *ld* can make the sound /d/. Run your hand under *could* and say the word. Have students say the word with you several times.

2. Guide practice. Write the word *should.* Have students point to the letters *ld* and identify the sound /d/ that the letters spell. Now say the word after me: *should.* Have students say the word several times to reinforce that *ld* in *should* has the sound /d/. Repeat the procedure with the word *would.*

3. Extend practice. Write the words *could, would,* and *should.* Provide oral examples of sentences: *I could come at five. He would like to go to the movie. She should pick up after herself.* Then ask individuals to point to one word, say the word, and use it in an oral sentence.

told	could	would
should	held	cold

Distribute Student Page S170. Have students cut apart the word cards. Have them sort the cards into two piles, one with /d/ spelled *ld* and the other with /ld/ spelled *ld.*

MONITOR PROGRESS Display the following sentences from Student Page S170. Ask students to identify the words with the sound /d/ spelled *ld.*

He could not come.
It was too cold.
He would miss a good time.

IF... students do not respond correctly,
THEN... model blending each *ld* word from the sentences. Ask: Do you hear the /l/ sound in this word? Do you hear the /d/ sound in this word? Guide students to identify the two words with the /d/ sound spelled *ld.*

Lesson 30 Irregular Spellings

PRACTICE 2: Sound /k/ (Spelled *lk*) Sometimes two letters together have more than one sound. In the word *milk*, the letters *lk* have the sound /lk/. Today we will learn a new sound for *lk*. Follow the routine to teach the sound /k/ spelled *lk*.

Routine

1. Model the strategy. Write *walk*. Point to the letters *lk* in *walk*. Together the letters *lk* can spell the sound /k/. Run your hand under *walk* and say the word. Have students say the word with you several times.

2. Guide practice. Write the word *talk*. Have students point to the letters *lk* and identify the sound /k/ that the letters spell. Now say the word after me: *talk*. Have students say the word several times to reinforce that *lk* in *talk* has the sound /k/. Repeat the procedure with the word *chalk*.

3. Extend practice. Write the words *walk, talk,* and *chalk*. Provide oral examples of sentences: *I will walk home. He will talk with Ms. Peters. She found some chalk.* Then ask individuals to point to one of the words, say the word, and use it in an oral sentence.

talk	silk	chalk
milk	walk	bulk

Distribute Student Page S171. Have students cut apart the word cards. Have them sort the cards into two piles, one with /k/ spelled *lk* and the other with /lk/ spelled *lk*.

REMIND STUDENTS THAT...

- they can recognize that some words cannot be decoded using one-to-one correspondence (e.g., *could, one, walk*).
- they can use high-frequency sight words.

✓ **MONITOR PROGRESS** Display the following sentences from Student Page S171. Have students identify the words with /k/ spelled *lk*.

Bill and Val walk and talk.
Sometimes they walk to get milk.

IF… students do not respond correctly,
THEN… help them blend each *lk* word from the sentences. Ask: Do you hear the /l/ sound in this word? Do you hear the /k/ sound in this word? Guide students to identify the two words with the /k/ sound spelled *lk*.

Lesson 30 Irregular Spellings

REMIND STUDENTS THAT...

- they can recognize that some words cannot be decoded using one-to-one correspondence (e.g., *could, one, walk*).
- they can use high-frequency sight words.

PRACTICE 3: Sound /w/ (Spelled *o*) You have been learning some sounds that are not spelled in the regular way. Today we will learn a new sound for the letter *o*. Follow the routine to teach the sound /w/ spelled *o*.

Routine

1. Model the strategy. Write *once*. Point to the letter *o* at the beginning of *once*. In the word *once*, the letter *o* spells the sound /w/. Ask students to say the word with you. Do you hear the sound /w/ in *once*? Say the word *once* again and listen to the beginning sound.

2. Guide practice. Write the word *one*. Have students point to the letter *o* and identify the sound /w/ that the letter spells. Now say the word after me: *one*. Have students say the word several times to reinforce that *o* in *one* has the sound /w/.

3. Extend practice. Write the words *once* and *one*. Provide oral examples of sentences: *I went to that store only* once. *The show lasts* one *hour.* Then ask individuals to point to one of the words, say the word, and use it in an oral sentence.

on	one	win
off	out	once

Distribute Student Page S172. Have students cut the word cards. Have them pick the cards with /w/ spelled *o*.

✔ **INDEPENDENT PRACTICE** Display the following sentences from Student Page S172. Have students identify the words with /w/ spelled *o*.

We like that song.
Sing it one more time.
Walt wants to hear it once again.

IF... students do not respond correctly,
THEN... help them blend each word with the letter *o*. Ask: Do you hear the /w/ sound in this word? Guide students to identify the two words with the /w/ sound spelled *o*.

Lesson 30 **Irregular Spellings**

Being a Big Brother

The baby could not walk.
Then he had one birthday.
He could walk everywhere.
His big brother had to watch him!

Lesson 30 Irregular Spellings

told	could	would
should	held	cold

He could not come.
It was too cold.
He would miss a good time.

Lesson 30 Irregular Spellings

talk	silk	chalk
milk	walk	bulk

Bill and Val walk and talk.
Sometimes they walk to get milk.

Lesson 30 Irregular Spellings

on	one	win
off	out	once

We like that song.
Sing it one more time.
Walt wants to hear it once again.

ASSESSMENT
LESSONS 29–30

Phonics and Word Recognition

ASSESS MASTERY Use this Checkpoint to assess students' mastery of the inflectional endings *-s, -es, -ed, -ing* and the irregular spellings *ld* /d/, *lk* /k/, and *o* /w/.

ADMINISTER THE TEST Administer the Checkpoint orally to each student. For each item, model the process as described, and then have the student use the process to respond to your prompts. Record responses on the scoring chart on the next page.

RF.1.3.f Read words with inflectional endings.
RF.1.3.g Recognize and read grade-appropriate irregularly spelled words.

1. Inflectional Endings *-s, -es* (Lesson 29)
MODEL: I will say three words. You tell me which two words have an *-s* or *-es* ending.

ASSESS:	add, yells, jumps	hands, can, fans	kisses, fusses, foot

2. Inflectional Ending *-ed* (Lesson 29)
MODEL: I will say two words, and you will tell me which one has an *-ed* ending. For example, I could say *fix* and *kicked*. The word *kicked* has the ending *-ed*.

ASSESS:	moves, tossed	hopped, shops	fix, mixed

3. Inflectional Ending *-ing* (Lesson 29)
MODEL: I will say three words and you will tell which one has the *-ing* ending. For example, I could say *acted, acts, acting*. The word *acting* has an *-ing* ending.

ASSESS:	bumps, bumping, bumped	cooking, cooks, cooked
	using, uses, used	

4. Irregular Spelling *ld* /d/ (Lesson 30)
MODEL: I will say two words. You tell me which one has the sound /d/. For example, I could say *shell* and *should*. The word *should* has the sound /d/.

ASSESS:	wall, would	call, could	should, ship

5. Irregular Spelling *lk* /k/ (Lesson 30)
MODEL: I will say two words. You tell me which one has the sound /k/. For example, I could say *wall* and *walk*. The word *walk* has the sound /k/.

ASSESS:	talk, tall	stall, stalk	walk, wall

6. Irregular Spelling *o* /w/ (Lesson 30)
MODEL: I will say three words. You tell me which one has the sound /w/. For example, I could say *owl*, *one*, and *odd*. The word *one* has the sound /w/. It is spelled with the letter *o*.

ASSESS:	once, oak, oh	old, on, oneself	our, one, open

ASSESSMENT
LESSONS 29–30

Phonics and Word Recognition

SCORING

SKILL/LESSON	STANDARD	SCORE
1. Inflectional Endings *-s, -es* (Lesson 29) add, yells, jumps *(yells; jumps)* hands, can, fans *(hands; fans)* kisses, fusses, foot *(kisses; fusses)*	**RF.1.3.f** Read words with inflectional endings.	_____ / 3
2. Inflectional Ending *-ed* (Lesson 29) moves, tossed *(tossed)* hopped, shops *(hopped)* fix, mixed *(mixed)*		_____ / 3
3. Inflectional Ending *-ing* (Lesson 29) bumps, bumping, bumped *(bumping)* cooking, cooks, cooked, *(cooking)* using, uses, used *(using)*		_____ / 3
4. Irregular Spelling *ld* /d/ (Lesson 30) wall, would *(would)* call, could *(could)* should, ship *(should)*	**RF.1.3.g** Recognize and read grade-appropriate irregularly spelled words.	_____ / 3
5. Irregular Spelling *lk* /k/ (Lesson 30) talk, tall *(talk)* stall, stalk *(stalk)* walk, wall *(walk)*		_____ / 3
6. Irregular Spelling *o* /w/ (Lesson 30) once, oak, oh (*once*) old, on, oneself (*oneself*) our, one, open (*one*)		_____ / 3

An overall score of 80% correct is typically considered mastery. Use your judgment and your individual students' needs as well to determine skill mastery.

IF... you determine that students have not demonstrated sufficient mastery of one or more skills,
THEN... review the skill(s), going back to the lessons to reteach and scaffold as needed.

Lesson 31 Determine Genre and Purpose

INTRODUCE Say: A purpose is a reason for doing something. We read for different purposes. For example, sometimes we read when we want to laugh. Sometimes we read to find the answer to a question.

Review the difference between nonfiction and fiction. Nonfiction tells about real places, people, or things. Fiction tells made-up stories.

Then connect genres to purpose. We read different kinds of texts for different reasons. For example, if I want to find out what polar bears eat, should I read a fiction or nonfiction book? Pause for responses. Right, I should read a nonfiction book. It will tell me what real polar bears eat.

MODEL Tell students that they will read about a polar bear. Explain that their reading purpose is to find the answer to this question, "Why was Knut the polar bear famous?"

Read aloud the following passage from Student Page S175.

Knut, the Famous Polar Bear

Knut was a baby polar bear born at a zoo.
When he was born, he was the size of a ball of snow.
A person at the zoo took care of him.
Knut was the first baby polar bear to live and grow up at the zoo in many years.
Knut was famous!
People around the world heard about him.

Find parts of the passage that help answer the question.

TEACH Explain to students that the passage is an article. An article is nonfiction. Remind students that their reading purpose is to find the answer to a question.

Look at sentences that help answer the question. We want to find out why Knut was so famous. Reread the article with students. Point out the longest sentence and reread it. This sentence explains why Knut was famous.

Ask students how a reading purpose helped them understand what they read.

RF.1.4.a Read on-level text with purpose and understanding.

OBJECTIVES:

- Understand various reasons for reading.
- Recognize characteristics of common genres.
- Identify different reasons for reading different kinds of texts.

Lesson 31 Determine Genre and Purpose

REMIND STUDENTS THAT…

- fiction tells made-up stories.
- nonfiction tells about real people, places, and things.
- there are different reasons for reading different kinds of texts.

PRACTICE 1 Say: Remember that fiction tells made-up stories. The characters are the people or animals in a story. Sometimes the animals talk. Can animals talk in real life? (no) Provide examples of fictional stories with talking animals, such as "The Three Pigs."

Explain that fiction can tell about fantastical things. Fiction stories can tell about things that would never happen in real life. For example, think about the story of Cinderella. Can a pumpkin really turn into a carriage? No.

Then share several examples of nonfiction texts from your classroom library. Nonfiction is the opposite of fiction. It tells about real people, places, and things. Show students a biography. For example, a biography tells the true story of someone's life.

Write or display the following paragraph from Student Page S176. Read to answer the question, "Is this fiction or nonfiction?" Read aloud the passage with students.

> Lala the polar bear likes to skate.
> "Look how fast I can go!" Lala says.
> She skates down the hill.
> She zigs and zags all the way home.

Who is this passage about? (Lala the polar bear) What does Lala do? (skate and talk) Is this passage fiction or nonfiction? Pause for responses. Right, it's fiction. How do you know? (talking animals, skating polar bears)

✔ **MONITOR PROGRESS** Distribute the following passage from Student Page S176 and ask: Is this fiction or nonfiction?

> Polar bears can swim.
> They use their front legs to swim.
> They swim to hunt for food.
> They can swim very far.

IF…students have difficulty distinguishing between fiction and nonfiction, THEN…ask guiding *yes-no* questions, such as: Do polar bears swim? Do polar bears hunt? Does the passage give only true information about polar bears?

Lesson 31 Determine Genre and Purpose

PRACTICE 2 Say: A short story is a type of fiction. It has characters, or the people or animals in the story. It has a setting, or when and where a story happens. Then write this passage and read it aloud: Max ran in the mushy grass. He got mud on his tail. He knew he had to find the other cubs. It was late and he had to get home.

Ask: Was this real or made-up? (made-up) How do you know? (It tells how a bear feels.) Who is the character? (Max) When and where does this take place? (late outside in a muddy place) This is a short story. It is fiction and has characters and a setting. I read a short story like this to be entertained.

Explain some characteristics of a nonfiction text. A science article is nonfiction. Some science articles have headings, which tell what each section is about.

Display this text from Student Page S177. Help students identify the heading and its purpose.

Sun Bears

Sun bears are the smallest kind of bear.
Sun bears rest in the day.

What Sun Bears Eat

Sun bears eat bugs and berries.

Say: We can read a science article to learn something new, find the answer to a question, or learn why or how something happened.

REMIND STUDENTS THAT...

- fiction tells made-up stories.
- nonfiction tells about real people, places, and things.
- there are many kinds of fiction and nonfiction texts.
- there are different reasons for reading different kinds of texts.

MONITOR PROGRESS Distribute this passage from Student Page S177. Ask: What kind of text is this? What is one purpose for reading it?

Koalas are called "bears," but they are not bears at all.
Koalas have more in common with kangaroos.
Do you know what animal has more in common with bears?
Dogs!

IF...students have difficulty identifying the kind of text,
THEN...review the characteristics of fiction and nonfiction.

Lesson 31 Determine Genre and Purpose

REMIND STUDENTS THAT...

- they can identify several purposes for reading.
- they can recognize characteristics of common genres.
- they read different kinds of texts for different reasons.

PRACTICE 3 Tell students you will talk about different kinds of texts and different reasons for reading them. Then read aloud with students the following chart from Student Page S178.

Purpose	Kind of Text
to find the answer to a question	news story, article, history book, science book
to be entertained	story, poem, article
to learn why or how something happened	science book, history book, article
to learn how to do or make something	instructions, how-to book

Write the following paragraph and read it aloud with students.

Black bears eat grass and fish.
Black bears can run fast.
They stand up to smell things that are far away.
Black bears rest in the winter.
They live in caves.

Ask: Is this fiction or nonfiction? How do you know? What kind of text is it? What are different reasons you might read a text like this?

✓ **INDEPENDENT PRACTICE** Distribute the following passage from Student Page S178. Have students identify whether it is fiction or nonfiction, the kind of text it is, and different reasons for reading it.

Brown bears are as big as polar bears.
Brown bears are also called grizzly bears.
They can run fast and swim.
They are bigger than many animals that live on land.
Some brown bears can be 10 feet tall!

IF...students have difficulty thinking of multiple reasons for reading a science article such as this,
THEN...review the kinds of purposes and texts listed in the chart.

Lesson 31 Determine Genre and Purpose

Knut, the Famous Polar Bear

Knut was a baby polar bear born at a zoo.
When he was born, he was the size of a ball of snow.
A person at the zoo took care of him.
Knut was the first baby polar bear to live and grow up at the zoo in many years.
Knut was famous!
People around the world heard about him.

Lesson 31 Determine Genre and Purpose

Lala the polar bear likes to skate.
"Look how fast I can go!" Lala says.
She skates down the hill.
She zigs and zags all the way home.

Polar bears can swim.
They use their front legs to swim.
They swim to hunt for food.
They can swim very far.

Lesson 31 **Determine Genre and Purpose**

Sun Bears

Sun bears are the smallest kind of bear.
Sun bears rest in the day.

What Sun Bears Eat

Sun bears eat bugs and berries.

Koalas are called "bears," but they are not bears at all.
Koalas have more in common with kangaroos.
Do you know what animal has more in common with bears?
Dogs!

Lesson 31 Determine Genre and Purpose

Purpose	Kind of Text
to find the answer to a question	news story, article, history book, science book
to be entertained	story, poem, article
to learn why or how something happened	science book, history book, article
to learn how to do or make something	instructions, how-to book

Brown bears are as big as polar bears.
Brown bears are also called grizzly bears.
They can run fast and swim.
They are bigger than many animals that live on land.
Some brown bears can be 10 feet tall!

ASSESSMENT
LESSON 31

Fluency

RF.1.4.a Read on-level text with purpose and understanding.

ASSESS MASTERY Use this Checkpoint to assess students' mastery of reading on-level text with a purpose and understanding.

ADMINISTER THE TEST Administer the Checkpoint to each student.
1. Give each student a copy of the following page.
2. Echo read the passage twice with students.
3. For each item, model the process as described, and then have the student use the process to respond to your prompts. Record responses on the scoring chart.

1. Determine Genre and Purpose (Lesson 31)
MODEL: Read the passage. Is this fiction or nonfiction? How do you know?

2. Determine Genre and Purpose (Lesson 31)
MODEL: Read the passage again. Is this a poem, a short story, or an article?

3. Determine Genre and Purpose (Lesson 31)
MODEL: Read the passage once more. What are different reasons you might read a text like this?

SCORING

SKILL/LESSON	SCORE
1. Determine Genre and Purpose (Lesson 31) Nonfiction; it tells about real things (animals)	_____ / 1
2. Determine Genre and Purpose (Lesson 31) Science article	_____ / 1
3. Determine Genre and Purpose (Lesson 31) To learn something new or find the answer to a question	_____ / 1

An overall score of 80% correct is typically considered mastery. Use your judgment and your individual students' needs as well to determine skill mastery.

IF...you determine that students have not demonstrated sufficient mastery of one or more skills,
THEN...review the skill(s), going back to the lessons to reteach and scaffold as needed.

ASSESSMENT
LESSON 31

Fluency

A polar bear is the biggest kind of bear.
There are other animals even bigger than a polar bear.
One kind of snake is an anaconda.
An anaconda is as long as a small plane.
An African elephant is very big.
It is as heavy as nine polar bears.
A blue whale is the biggest animal ever.
Its heart is as big as a car!

Lesson 32 Read Accurately

INTRODUCE Tell students that to read fluently, they have to practice. Today we're going to practice reading a story until we can read all the words accurately. We'll check our comprehension as we read.

MODEL Display or share copies of the following passage, "At Bat," from Student Page S181. Read the story once accurately.

At Bat

Pig is at bat.
Can Pig get a hit?
Pig got a hit.
Pig ran and ran.

Dog is at bat.
Can Dog get a hit?
Dog got a hit.
Dog ran and ran.

Cat is at bat.
But can Cat get a hit?
Cat got a hit!
Will Pig, Dog, and Cat win?

TEACH Explain that reading accurately means paying close attention to the words and reading each word. Briefly point out that periods, question marks, and other punctuation show where students should pause in a text. Then model the skill, starting with the first four sentences. Before I read aloud, I will take a moment to read the sentences to myself. This helps me become familiar with the words. Pause to read to yourself.

Have students follow along as you model reading the first four sentences with no mistakes, pointing to each word as you read it aloud. Read each word clearly and deliberately to model reading accurately. Remind students to check their comprehension as they read by asking questions about what they just read, such as Who is batting first? (Pig)

Have students follow along as you model reading the rest of the story with no mistakes. Then, model checking your comprehension aloud to help students connect accurate reading with understanding what they read. Which characters got a hit? (Pig, Dog, and Cat)

RF.1.4.b Read on-level text orally with accuracy, appropriate rate, and expression on successive readings.

OBJECTIVES:

- Read every word accurately.
- Read without adding or skipping words.
- Pause after periods.

Lesson 32 Read Accurately

REMIND STUDENTS THAT...

- they should read every word accurately.

PRACTICE 1 Display the passage "Six Big Frogs" from Student Page S182.

Six Big Frogs

Six big frogs hop on one big stick.
Six big frogs spot six big bees.

Six big bees fly around the big stick.
They fly away when they see the frogs.

Six big frogs hop as fast as they may.
They try to catch the bees that flew away.

Six big frogs open their mouths.
They snap!
The six big bees never had a chance.

Read the first two sentences aloud to model reading accurately. Show students how to pause to read the sentences silently. Then, read the sentences aloud using correct pronunciation and without skipping words. Remind students to ask questions to check their comprehension as they read using questions such as Where are the frogs? (on a big stick)

Then, prepare for a choral reading of "Six Big Frogs."

Routine	**Choral Reading**
1. Read together.	Have students read aloud with you.
2. Reread.	Then have students read aloud without you. For optimal fluency, students should reread three or four times.
3. Provide feedback.	Listen to students and provide corrective feedback. Point out any words students read incorrectly.

✔ **MONITOR PROGRESS** Have students read the last two sentences from "Six Big Frogs" on Student Page S182. Check that they read accurately. Then ask a question to model checking comprehension, such as What happened to the six bees? (The six frogs ate them.)

IF...students cannot read a particular word,
THEN...have them blend decodable words. Guide students by running your hand below a word as they blend the sounds first with you and then without you.

Lesson 32 Read Accurately

PRACTICE 2 Display "Jen the Vet" from Student Page S183.

REMIND STUDENTS THAT...
- they should read every word accurately.
- they should not add or skip words.

Jen the Vet

Jen the vet likes hens.
She feeds a hen named Ben.
Jen pets Ben the hen.

Jen the vet likes pigs too.
She met Blue the pig at a zoo.
Jen pets and feeds Blue too.

Jack is my pet cat.
Jen always gives Jack a snack.
She likes to pet Jack on his back.

Jen the vet feeds Ben, Blue, and Jack.
She pets their heads and backs.
Ben, Blue, and Jack love Jen the vet.

Read the first three sentences silently and then aloud. Next, have students read the sentences aloud with you. Ask: What animal does Jen like? (hens)

Pair students to do an oral reading of "Jen the Vet." Use this routine.

Routine	**Paired Reading**
1. Reader 1 begins.	Reader 1 reads the story to Reader 2.
2. Reader 2 begins.	Reader 2 reads the story to Reader 1.
3. Reread.	Have students reread three to four times.
4. Provide feedback.	Listen and provide corrective feedback.

✔ **MONITOR PROGRESS** Have students read the last three sentences from "Jen the Vet." Ask: Why do the pets like Jen? (She feeds and pets them.)

IF...students substitute a word,
THEN...point to the misread word, sound it out, and read it correctly. Then model the sentence and have students repeat it after you.

Lesson 32 Read Accurately

REMIND STUDENTS THAT...

- they should read every word accurately.
- they should not add or skip words.
- they should pause when they see a period.

PRACTICE 3 Display "Luke and Jack See Granddad" from Student Page S184.

Luke and Jack See Granddad

Dad, Luke, and Jack ride in a jeep.
They are on a trip to see Granddad.

"See that?" asks Dad.
"Yes, I can see six sheep!" calls Luke.

"See that?" asks Dad.
"Yes, I can see two trucks," Jack tells him.

"See that bobcat?" Jack asks Luke.
"It is behind that tree."
The bobcat jumps out and runs by the jeep.

"I wish Granddad could see that!" Luke yells.

Give students time to read the first four sentences silently. Then read the sentences as a class. Ask a question to model checking comprehension.

Give students a few moments to read the rest of the passage silently. Then pair students for the paired reading routine.

Routine	Paired Reading
1. Reader 1 begins.	Reader 1 reads the story to Reader 2.
2. Reader 2 begins.	Reader 2 reads the story to Reader 1.
3. Reread.	For optimal fluency, students should reread three to four times.
4. Provide feedback.	Listen to students read and provide corrective feedback regarding their fluency and their decoding.

✔ **INDEPENDENT PRACTICE** Have students read the last five sentences from "Luke and Jack See Granddad." Check that they have read accurately. Then ask a question to remind students to check their comprehension: What do Luke and Jack see? (six sheep, two trucks, and a bobcat)

IF...students have difficulty reading with accuracy,
THEN...have them point to problem words and read them first with you.

Lesson 32 **Read Accurately**

At Bat

Pig is at bat.
Can Pig get a hit?
Pig got a hit.
Pig ran and ran.

Dog is at bat.
Can Dog get a hit?
Dog got a hit.
Dog ran and ran.

Cat is at bat.
But can Cat get a hit?
Cat got a hit!
Will Pig, Dog, and Cat win?

Lesson 32 **Read Accurately**

Six Big Frogs

Six big frogs hop on one big stick.
Six big frogs spot six big bees.

Six big bees fly around the big stick.
They fly away when they see the frogs.

Six big frogs hop as fast as they may.
They try to catch the bees that flew away.

Six big frogs open their mouths.
They snap!
The six big bees never had a chance.

Lesson 32 **Read Accurately**

Jen the Vet

Jen the vet likes hens.
She feeds a hen named Ben.
Jen pets Ben the hen.

Jen the vet likes pigs too.
She met Blue the pig at a zoo.
Jen pets and feeds Blue too.

Jack is my pet cat.
Jen always gives Jack a snack.
She likes to pet Jack on his back.

Jen the vet feeds Ben, Blue, and Jack.
She pets their heads and backs.
Ben, Blue, and Jack love Jen the vet.

Lesson 32 **Read Accurately**

Luke and Jack See Granddad

Dad, Luke, and Jack ride in a jeep.
They are on a trip to see Granddad.

"See that?" asks Dad.
"Yes, I can see six sheep!" calls Luke.

"See that?" asks Dad.
"Yes, I can see two trucks," Jack tells him.

"See that bobcat?" Jack asks Luke.
"It is behind that tree."
The bobcat jumps out and runs by the jeep.

"I wish Granddad could see that!" Luke yells.

Lesson 33 Read with Appropriate Rate

INTRODUCE Tell students that rate means the speed of reading. Explain that they will practice reading at the same speed they use when speaking. Instead of rushing through reading or reading very slowly, read as if you are talking. Remember, it takes practice to sound natural when reading. Point out reading at an appropriate rate makes a story easier to understand.

MODEL Display the following passage from Student Page S185. Before I read, I will read the sentences to myself to make sure I know all the words. When I finish, I will ask a question to make sure you understand the story.

Read aloud the story at an appropriate rate as students follow along.

Little Sister

I have a little sister.
What is her name?
Her name is Eva.

Eva is pretty.
She is a baby.
Her eyes are blue.

Can Eva play with toys?
She plays with a ball.
She plays with a bear.
I like to play with Eva.

TEACH After you read, emphasize that reading at an appropriate rate requires knowing the words. Take time to read to yourself before reading aloud to learn the words.

Point out that punctuation tells when to pause. Periods and question marks end a sentence and tell you to pause before you continue reading the next sentence. Remind students to breathe naturally, taking a breath at end punctuation.

Demonstrate these techniques as you reread the story. Check comprehension. What color are Eva's eyes? (blue)

RF.1.4.b Read on-level text orally with accuracy, appropriate rate, and expression on successive readings.

OBJECTIVE:
- Read fluently at a natural speaking rate.

Lesson 33 Read with Appropriate Rate

REMIND STUDENTS THAT...

- they should read every word in the passage and read words correctly.
- they should read the sentences to themselves to become familiar with the words.
- they should pause when they see a period, question mark, or exclamation point at the end of a sentence.

PRACTICE 1 Display and distribute to students the story "Hot Rod" from Student Page S186.

Hot Rod

Dad got Dan a hot rod.
Dan got in it.
Kim can hop in it.
Pat and Nan hop in it.

Can Dot get in it?
Can Mac fit in it?
They can fit.
They got in.

The hot rod cannot go.
Did Dad get gas?

Say: I want to read as if I were talking to someone, so I will take time to read silently first to learn the words. Tell students they will have a chance to read the text. When it is your turn to read aloud, try to read at the same speed you normally speak. Then, use the routine to guide Choral Reading.

Routine	Choral Reading
1. Model.	Instruct students to track the print, pointing to each word as you read it aloud.
2. Read together.	Next, have students read aloud with you.
3. Reread.	Then, have students read aloud without you. For optimal fluency, students should reread three or four times.
4. Provide feedback.	Listen to students and provide corrective feedback. Make suggestions for pausing, speeding up, or slowing down the rate.

✓ **MONITOR PROGRESS** Have students read the last four sentences of "Hot Rod" from Student Page S186. Check that they read accurately at an appropriate rate. Check comprehension. What is the problem with the hot rod? (It cannot go because it has no gas.)

IF...students cannot read a word,
THEN...have them blend decodable words or say and spell high-frequency words.

Lesson 33 Read with Appropriate Rate

PRACTICE 2 Display and distribute "Duck Pond" from Student Page S187. Read the first four sentences aloud as students track the text.

Duck Pond

The sun is hot.
It is hot at Duck Pond.

Ducks land on Duck Pond with a big splash!
Ducks like to swim.

Ducks jump in Duck Pond and get wet.
Ducks go *splat!*

Ducks get small fish to eat in Duck Pond.
Ducks snack on bugs!

Ducks rest at Duck Pond.
Ducks pick snug resting spots and nap.

It is fun at Duck Pond.

Model reading the text. Then have students read with partners. Allow time for students to read silently and clarify unfamiliar words before they read aloud.

Routine	Paired Reading
1. Reader 1 begins.	Reader 1 reads the story to Reader 2.
2. Reader 2 begins.	Reader 2 reads the story to Reader 1.
3. Reread.	For optimal fluency, students should reread three or four times.
4. Provide feedback.	Listen as students read and provide corrective feedback. Point out if students read too fast or too slow.

MONITOR PROGRESS Have students read the last three sentences of "Duck Pond." Emphasize that they should pause only at end punctuation. Check comprehension. Name two things ducks do at Duck Pond. (swim, eat, rest)

IF...students cannot read fluently alone,
THEN...have them read the story with you before reading it with partners.

REMIND STUDENTS THAT...

- they should read at the same rate that they normally speak.
- sometimes a sentence continues onto the next line.
- they can pause and take a breath when they see a period, question mark, or exclamation point.

Lesson 33 Read with Appropriate Rate

REMIND STUDENTS THAT...

- they should read at the same speed that they would speak.
- commas note a short pause and end punctuation marks a longer pause.
- quotation marks show the words characters say, which might be complete sentences within a longer sentence.

PRACTICE 3 Distribute Student Page S188. Model reading at an appropriate rate. Have students read the text silently and then in pairs.

Dean's Cast

Dean and Sid like to race on sleds.
When they race, Sid likes to beat Dean.

One time, Dean went very fast.
"Look how fast I am going!" called Dean.
Then Dean's sled tipped.
Dean's leg was hurt.

Dad took Dean to see Doc Jean.
She looked at his leg.
"Bones are like a frame.
They don't bend," Doc Jean said.
"You broke your leg.
I will put it in a cast.
That will help it heal."

Dean had the cast for six weeks.
There were no more sled rides that winter!

Routine	Paired Reading
1. Reader 1 begins.	Reader 1 reads the story to Reader 2.
2. Reader 2 begins.	Reader 2 reads the story to Reader 1.
3. Reread.	For optimal fluency, students should reread three or four times.
4. Provide feedback.	Provide corrective feedback.

✓ **INDEPENDENT PRACTICE** Have students read the last two paragraphs of the passage. Monitor rate and attention to punctuation. Check comprehension. Why were there no more sled rides that winter? (His leg was in a cast.)

IF...students cannot read at an appropriate rate,
THEN...model reading a paragraph and then have students read with you.

Lesson 33 **Read with Appropriate Rate**

Little Sister

I have a little sister.
What is her name?
Her name is Eva.

Eva is pretty.
She is a baby.
Her eyes are blue.

Can Eva play with toys?
She plays with a ball.
She plays with a bear.
I like to play with Eva.

Lesson 33 **Read with Appropriate Rate**

Hot Rod

Dad got Dan a hot rod.
Dan got in it.
Kim can hop in it.
Pat and Nan hop in it.

Can Dot get in it?
Can Mac fit in it?
They can fit.
They got in.

The hot rod cannot go.
Did Dad get gas?

Lesson 33 **Read with Appropriate Rate**

Duck Pond

The sun is hot.
It is hot at Duck Pond.

Ducks land on Duck Pond with a big splash!
Ducks like to swim.

Ducks jump in Duck Pond and get wet.
Ducks go *splat!*

Ducks get small fish to eat in Duck Pond.
Ducks snack on bugs!

Ducks rest at Duck Pond.
Ducks pick snug resting spots and nap.

It is fun at Duck Pond.

Lesson 33 **Read with Appropriate Rate**

Dean's Cast

Dean and Sid like to race on sleds.
When they race, Sid likes to beat Dean.

One time, Dean went very fast.
"Look how fast I am going!" called Dean.
Then Dean's sled tipped.
Dean's leg was hurt.

Dad took Dean to see Doc Jean.
She looked at his leg.
"Bones are like a frame.
They don't bend," Doc Jean said.
"You broke your leg.
I will put it in a cast.
That will help it heal."

Dean had the cast for six weeks.
There were no more sled rides that winter!

Lesson 34 Read with Appropriate Expression

INTRODUCE Explain reading with expression to students. Reading with expression simply means reading with feeling in our voices. Reading with feeling makes the story come alive. You can create feeling by reading loudly or quietly, quickly or slowly. You can also create feeling by making your voice go up and down like you do when you talk.

MODEL Display the passage "Fred the Frog" from Student Page S189. Tell students they will practice reading stories with expression. Read the story with expression as students follow along.

Fred the Frog

Jesse has a pet frog.
His name is Fred.

He is green with spots.
Fred has webbed toes.
He lives in a glass box in Jesse's room.
Fred says, "Ribbit!"

Fred likes to swim!
He swims in his box.

Fred also hops!
Sometimes Jesse lets him hop
around the room.

"Ribbit! Ribbit!" says Fred as he hops.

TEACH Point out that some sentences end with an exclamation mark. Students should read these sentences in an excited voice. When I read in an excited voice, I speak quickly and make my voice go up. Model reading sentence seven with excitement. Then model reading it in a monotone. Ask students to note the difference.

Remind students that before reading aloud they should always take the time to read silently to make sure they know the words.

Ask questions about content to check comprehension. What does Fred like to do? (swim)

RF.1.4.b Read on-level text orally with accuracy, appropriate rate, and expression on successive readings.

OBJECTIVES:

- Read with expression so the passage is interesting and easy to understand.
- Use intonation, volume, and rate to create expression in reading.

Lesson 34 Read with Appropriate Expression

REMIND STUDENTS THAT...

- quotation marks show a character is speaking.
- they should read with feeling in their voices.
- they can create feeling by making their voices go up and down or fast and slow.

PRACTICE 1 Display the story "Hide and Seek" from Student Page S190.

Hide and Seek

James wants to play hide and seek.
"Will you play hide and seek with me?"
James asks Tasha.

"No," Tasha says. "I am reading a book."

James asks Lee and Will to play.
"No," says Lee. "I am playing kickball."

"I will play with you!" Will says.
"Can I hide first?"

"Yes! I will find you," James says.

Remind students that quotation marks show a character's words. I want to read with expression. I will read the characters' words the same way they would say them. Review the other punctuation marks. Remember, a comma means a short pause and a period shows a longer pause. Question marks mean your voice should go up at the end of the sentence. Exclamation marks tell you to show excitement when you read.

Allow time for students to read silently in preparation for the routine.

Routine	**Choral Reading**
1. Model.	Have students track the print as you read aloud.
2. Read together.	Next, have students read aloud with you.
3. Reread.	Have students read aloud without you, three times.
4. Provide feedback.	Listen to students and provide corrective feedback.

MONITOR PROGRESS Have students read the last two sentences from "Hide and Seek." Make sure that they read with appropriate expression. Check comprehension. Who plays hide and seek with James? (Will)

IF...students cannot read a word,
THEN...help them blend decodable words or identify high-frequency words.

Lesson 34 Read with Appropriate Expression

PRACTICE 2 Display and distribute copies of "Whales" from Student Page S191.

Whales

Whales live in the water.
Most whales are very big.
Some whales are as big as a bus!
Some whales have teeth,
and some whales do not.
All whales have fins.
They use their fins to swim.

Whales have holes on top.
The hole is like a nose.
Whales use the hole to get air.
When whales go under water, the hole closes.
Whales like to swim and have fun!

Instruct students to track the text as you model reading the first paragraph. First, read in a monotone. Then, read with appropriate expression. Which reading did you like the most? Why? Then have students read the text silently.

Routine	**Paired Reading**
1. Reader 1 begins.	Reader 1 reads the story to Reader 2.
2. Reader 2 begins.	Reader 2 reads the story to Reader 1.
3. Reread.	For optimal fluency, students should reread three or four times.
4. Provide feedback.	Listen as students read and provide corrective feedback. Point out if students read without expression or with inappropriate expression.

MONITOR PROGRESS Have students read the last paragraph of the passage from Student Page S191. Listen for appropriate expression. Check comprehension. Why do whales have holes on top? (to get air)

IF...students are unaware of their inexpressive reading,
THEN...model each sentence and have students echo until they match your expression.

REMIND STUDENTS THAT...

- they should read every word accurately at an appropriate rate.
- they should read with feeling in their voices.
- they can create feeling by making their voices go up and down or fast and slow.

Lesson 34 Read with Appropriate Expression

REMIND STUDENTS THAT …

- they should read with accuracy and appropriate expression.
- they can create expression by varying their intonation and reading rate.
- when they see an exclamation mark, they should use their voices to show excitement or surprise.

PRACTICE 3 Display and distribute copies of "Fun at Pine Lake" from Student Page S192. Discuss reading with appropriate expression.

Fun at Pine Lake

Mom, Dad, and I go to Pine Lake.
Pine Lake is fun!

Mom and I like to walk,
hike, and run at Pine Lake.
We hike for miles.
I pick up big pine cones.

Dad and I dive, swim, and fish.
We get lots of fish.
I like fish from Pine Lake!

At home, we eat, talk, and laugh
about the day at Pine Lake.
That place is fun!

Allow students time to read through the passage silently before the routine.

Routine	**Paired Reading**
1. Reader 1 begins.	Reader 1 reads the story to Reader 2.
2. Reader 2 begins.	Reader 2 reads the story to Reader 1.
3. Reread.	Have students read aloud three times.
4. Provide feedback.	Listen as students read and provide corrective feedback.

☑ **INDEPENDENT PRACTICE** Have students read the last two paragraphs of the passage from Student Page S192. Listen for appropriate rate, intonation, and expression. Check comprehension. What does the family do at the end of the day? (eat dinner and talk about the day)

IF…students have difficulty reading with expression,
THEN…have them tell you something interesting that happens and then have students echo read as you model the paragraph containing the event.

Lesson 34 **Read with Appropriate Expression**

Fred the Frog

Jesse has a pet frog.
His name is Fred.

He is green with spots.
Fred has webbed toes.
He lives in a glass box in Jesse's room.
Fred says, "Ribbit!"

Fred likes to swim!
He swims in his box.

Fred also hops!
Sometimes Jesse lets him hop around the room.
"Ribbit! Ribbit!" says Fred as he hops.

Lesson 34 **Read with Appropriate Expression**

Hide and Seek

James wants to play hide and seek.
"Will you play hide and seek with me?" James asks Tasha.

"No," Tasha says. "I am reading a book."

James asks Lee and Will to play.
"No," says Lee. "I am playing kickball."

"I will play with you!" Will says.
"Can I hide first?"

"Yes! I will find you," James says.

Lesson 34 **Read with Appropriate Expression**

Whales

Whales live in the water.
Most whales are very big.
Some whales are as big as a bus!
Some whales have teeth,
and some whales do not.
All whales have fins.
They use their fins to swim.

Whales have holes on top.
The hole is like a nose.
Whales use the hole to get air.
When whales go under water, the hole closes.
Whales like to swim and have fun!

Lesson 34 **Read with Appropriate Expression**

Fun at Pine Lake

Mom, Dad, and I go to Pine Lake.
Pine Lake is fun!

Mom and I like to walk,
hike, and run at Pine Lake.
We hike for miles.
I pick up big pine cones.

Dad and I dive, swim, and fish.
We get lots of fish.
I like fish from Pine Lake!

At home, we eat, talk, and laugh
about the day at Pine Lake.
That place is fun!

ASSESSMENT Fluency

LESSONS 32–34

ASSESS MASTERY Use this Checkpoint to assess students' mastery of reading accurately and reading with appropriate rate and expression.

ADMINISTER THE TEST Administer the Checkpoint to each student. Give each student a copy of the following page. Then, echo read the passage twice with students. For each item, model the process below. Then have students read aloud the passage on their own, focusing on the skill described.

RF.1.4.b Read on-level text orally with accuracy, appropriate rate, and expression on successive readings.

1. Read Accurately (Lesson 32)
MODEL: Now you will read the passage aloud on your own. Remember to read accurately. Do not skip words or add words. Pause when you see punctuation. Listen to me read a few sentences accurately.

2. Read with Appropriate Rate (Lesson 33)
MODEL: You will read the passage again. Remember to read as if you are talking. Do not read too quickly or slowly. Listen to me read a few sentences that way.

3. Read with Appropriate Expression (Lesson 34)
MODEL: As you read the passage again, remember to read with feeling. Make your voice go up and down like you do when you talk. Listen to me read a few sentences that way.

SCORING

SKILL/LESSON	ANSWER	SCORE
1. Read Accurately (Lesson 32)	• Does not skip words. • Does not add words. • Sounds out words correctly. • Pauses for punctuation.	____ / 4
2. Read with Appropriate Rate (Lesson 33)	• Does not skip words. • Does not read too quickly. • Does not read too slowly. • Reads at conversational pace.	____ / 4
3. Read with Appropriate Expression (Lesson 34)	• Reads with expression and inflection. • Reads naturally. • Varies voice to match meaning of text.	____ / 4

An overall score of 80% correct is typically considered mastery. Use your judgment and your individual students' needs as well to determine skill mastery.

IF...you determine that students have not demonstrated sufficient mastery of one or more skills,
THEN...review the skill(s), going back to the lessons to reteach as needed.

ASSESSMENT
LESSONS 32–34

Fluency

Bub Is Hungry

"Stop!" yells Max.
Bub looks at Max and wags his tail.
"Bub, spit that out now!"

But Bub runs away and hides.
Max cuts Bub off in the hall.

"Ha! I got you!" yells Max.
Bub has mushy gum on his face.
Max has gum on his hands.

All Mom sees is a lot of gum.
"What in the world…?" asks Mom.
"What happened?" she asks.

"I think Bub really likes gum," Max tells her.

"Oh Bub!" smiles Mom.
She rubs his tummy.
"Time to go to the vet!"

Lesson 35 Use a Dictionary and Glossary

INTRODUCE Display a dictionary. Explain that people use dictionaries to find information about the words, such as how to spell them and what they mean.

MODEL Tell students that you will be reading a story that might have some unfamiliar words. Read the story from Student Page S195 aloud.

Joanna's Books

Joanna loved to read.
She had lots of books of her own.
She borrowed books from friends.
She borrowed from the library!
She made a stack of the books she read.
The stack was taller than she was!

TEACH Tell students that you will use the dictionary to find the meaning of the word *stack*. Explain that the words in a dictionary are arranged alphabetically, or from *A* to *Z*. Words that start with *S* should be near the end of the book, because *S* is near the end of the alphabet.

Move through the pages to the middle of the dictionary, reading a few words aloud and then coming to a word beginning with S. Now I look for a word beginning with *s-t*. The letter *t* is near the end of the alphabet. I'll look near the end of the words beginning with *S*. Find the word *stack*. Show students the word in the book and explain that the word is followed by its meaning and its pronunciation. Now I understand what *stack* means. A *stack* is a pile or a large amount of something. I know that Joanna has a lot of books, so I know that is a large amount. Emphasize that using the dictionary helped you understand the story better. Point out that sometimes books have small dictionaries of their own called glossaries.

RF.1.4.c Use context to confirm or correct word recognition and understanding, rereading as necessary.

L.1.4 Determine or clarify the meaning of unknown and multiple-meaning words and phrases based on grade 1 content, choosing flexibly from an array of strategies.

OBJECTIVES:

- Determine when words in a text are not understood.
- Use a dictionary to find the meaning of unknown or unfamiliar words.
- Use a glossary to find the meaning of unknown or unfamiliar words.

Lesson 35 Use a Dictionary and Glossary

REMIND STUDENTS THAT...

- they can use a dictionary or a glossary to help them understand unfamiliar words.
- they can understand a text better if they know what all of the words mean.

PRACTICE 1 Tell students that they are going to read a text and find words that they do not know. When you read, look for words you don't know yet. Later, you can look them up in a dictionary or glossary.

Display the text from Student Page S196. Read it aloud, skipping the words *every* and *nothing*.

> I love to read!
> Reading takes me to new places.
> It helps me learn lots of new words.
> I read every book I can find.
> Nothing is more fun than reading.
> I am in the middle of a book right now!

Point to several of the two- and three-letter words in the story, such as *fun, to,* and *new*. Ask students to read these words. Then ask them to read words with four letters, such as *read* and *lots*. You did a good job of reading those words. But some of the longer words are harder. Which words were harder to read and to understand? Have students point out words they do not find familiar, by touching them, spelling out the first few letters, or describing where on the projectable they can be found. Circle these words. If students do not include *every* and *nothing*, add those words to the list.

Wrap up by reviewing the words that have been circled, identifying all the words except *every* and *nothing*. Emphasize that deciding which words you know and which ones you do not know is an important step in understanding a text.

✓ **MONITOR PROGRESS** Have students look at the following sentence from Student Page S196. Ask students to identify words they do not know in the sentence.

> Tom likes apples, boysenberries, peaches, and bananas.

IF...students say they know all the words,
THEN...check their level of awareness by asking them to read and define *boysenberries*.

Lesson 35 Use a Dictionary and Glossary

PRACTICE 2 Tell students that they are going to find the meanings of two of the words in the text they read in the previous part of the lesson. Let's look again at the text we read last time. This time we'll look up some of the unfamiliar words.

Display the text from Student Page S197. Point out that there are small numbers next to two of the words. Those little numbers mean that these words are in the glossary. Remember, a glossary is like a little dictionary. It gives the meanings of hard words in the text.

Have students read the text with you.

I love to read!
Reading takes me to new places.
It helps me learn lots of new words.
I read every[1] book I can find.
Nothing[2] is more fun than reading.
I'm in the middle of a book right now!

Glossary

1. every: [EV-ree] each one; all
2. nothing: [NUH-thing] not anything

Next, have students look at the glossary. Point out that the two words with the small numbers are there. Show students that the pronunciation and the definition of each word is given. Ask students to identify the words and read the definitions.

Have students read the two sentences that include *every* and *nothing*. Ask students to restate the sentences using their own words. Review that they used a glossary to help them identify the words and better understand the text.

REMIND STUDENTS THAT...

- they can identify words in a text that they do not already know.
- they can understand a text better if they know the meaning of all the words.

✔ **MONITOR PROGRESS** Ask students to explain how they can use a glossary if one is provided in a text.

IF...students are not sure how to begin their explanations,
THEN...provide a prompt by telling them that the first step is to find the word in the glossary. Have students use the prompt to continue the explanation. Offer additional guidance as needed.

Lesson 35 Use a Dictionary and Glossary

REMIND STUDENTS THAT…

- they can identify words in a text that they do not already know.
- they can understand a text better if they know the meaning of all the words.
- they can use a glossary to help them understand the meaning of unfamiliar words.

PRACTICE 3 Explain that while some books have glossaries, many do not. You can use a dictionary to look up words you don't know. Display the text from Student Page S198. Read it aloud, emphasizing the word *enough*.

We have a library in our town.
The library is not very big.
In fact, it's kind of small!
I don't think the library has enough books.
I gave some of my old books to the library.
Maybe other people will do the same thing.

Point to the word *enough*. Explain that students can look this word up in the dictionary because the text does not have a glossary. Guide students to look up words in a classroom dictionary, starting with the word *enough*. Is the letter *E* closer to the beginning, middle, or end of the alphabet? (beginning) Have a volunteer look in the beginning of the dictionary for words beginning with *E*. Next, ask students to identify the second letter of the word and use that letter to find *enough* in the *E* section.

When students find the word, help them identify the pronunciation and definition. Then return to the sentence with *enough* in the text. Have students read it chorally. Ask them to put the sentence into their own words.

INDEPENDENT PRACTICE Ask students to look through books in the classroom to find a word they do not know or are unsure that they know. Have them use a dictionary to look up the word and find its meaning.

IF…students cannot read the definition easily,
THEN…provide the words they do not know. Then guide students to look up these words to reinforce the skill.

Lesson 35 **Use a Dictionary and Glossary**

Joanna's Books

Joanna loved to read.
She had lots of books of her own.
She borrowed books from friends.
She borrowed from the library!
She made a stack of the books she read.
The stack was taller than she was!

Lesson 35 Use a Dictionary and Glossary

I love to read!
Reading takes me to new places.
It helps me learn lots of new words.
I read every book I can find.
Nothing is more fun than reading.
I am in the middle of a book right now!

Tom likes apples, boysenberries, peaches, and bananas.

Lesson 35 Use a Dictionary and Glossary

I love to read!
Reading takes me to new places.
It helps me learn lots of new words.
I read every[1] book I can find.
Nothing[2] is more fun than reading.
I'm in the middle of a book right now!

Glossary

1. every: [EV-ree] each one; all
2. nothing: [NUH-thing] not anything

Lesson 35 Use a Dictionary and Glossary

We have a library in our town.
The library is not very big.
In fact, it's kind of small!
I don't think the library has enough books.
I gave some of my old books to the library.
Maybe other people will do the same thing.

Lesson 36 Use Context Clues: Definition

RF.1.4.c Use context to confirm or correct word recognition and understanding, rereading as necessary.

OBJECTIVES:

- Understand that the word *context* refers to other text near a word, including the title of a passage.
- Use context to determine the meaning of unfamiliar words.

INTRODUCE Tell students that they may find words in text that they do not recognize or do not know the meaning of. You can sometimes use context clues to figure out the meaning of a word you do not know.

MODEL Display or share copies of the following passage "Birds" from Student Page S199. Ask students what they think the text will be about based on the title and the images. Then read the passage aloud.

Birds

The owl flies at night.
The cardinal is all red.
The robin pulls up worms.
The kiwi cannot fly at all!

TEACH Reread the sentence with the word *cardinal*. I'm going to look at the context of this word. That means looking at the words in the text that are near this word. I start by looking at the title. The title of the passage is *Birds*, so I can guess that *cardinal* is the name of a bird. Next, I look at the rest of the sentence. Underline the title and the words *is all red*. Based on these clues, I think that a cardinal is a red bird. You may wish to model looking up *cardinal* in the dictionary to check its meaning, or display a photograph of a cardinal. Repeat this process with the word *kiwi*.

Lesson 36 Use Context Clues: Definition

REMIND STUDENTS THAT...

- they can use the words near a word to help them understand the meaning of an unfamiliar word.
- they can use the title of a passage to help them understand the meaning of an unfamiliar word.

PRACTICE 1 Display the passage from Student Page S200 and read it aloud, emphasizing the word *condor.*

More About Birds

A sparrow is a small bird.
A **condor** has big, long wings.
A crow is all black, and it caws.
A loon can swim in the lake.

Have students identify words that might help them understand what a *condor* could be. Let's look for context clues. What words and sentences will help us find the meaning of *condor*?

Point to the title. Will the title help us? How? (Yes, it will give us an idea of what all the sentences will be about.) Help students see that the title suggests that all the information in the passage will be about birds, so a *condor* is probably a bird. Underline the title.

Will the first sentence help us? Guide students to understand that the first sentence is not about a *condor* and will not help readers know the meaning of *condor*. What other clues could help us? Guide students to determine that the rest of the sentence that contains *condor* will also provide important clues. Underline the remaining words in the second sentence. Establish with students that the words in this sentence will help them understand that a condor is a bird with enormous wings.

✔ **MONITOR PROGRESS** Ask students to look at the final sentence of Projectable S200. Have them tell which words they would use to help them identify what a *loon* is.

IF...students cannot quickly identify context clues,
THEN...ask: Will the title help you determine the meaning of *loon*? What about the first sentence or the second sentence? Pause for student responses and offer corrective feedback as needed.

Lesson 36 Use Context Clues: Definition

PRACTICE 2 Display the passage from Student Page S201. Read the title and text aloud, emphasizing the word *mallard*.

Birds That Swim

Some birds are very good swimmers.
Here are some of these birds.
A penguin is black and white.
A **mallard** can have a green head.
A goose makes a honking sound.

Invite students to tell you what clues they would use from the text to help them define the word *mallard*. Draw out that the title and the sentence that includes the word *mallard* provide important context clues to help students determine the meaning.

Have students use the information in the title and the passage to draw a simple picture of a *mallard* doing something it knows how to do. Check that the *mallard* has a green head and is shown in the water. Then use the following questions to go over the assignment. What did you learn from the title? (That the mallard is a bird that knows how to swim) What did you learn from the sentence that contains the word *mallard*? (That some mallards have green heads)

REMIND STUDENTS THAT...

- they can find words in a text to help them learn the meaning of an unfamiliar word.
- they can use the title of a passage as well as other words in a sentence to help them.

✓ **MONITOR PROGRESS** Ask students what they can tell about the meaning of the word *goose* based on the passage.

IF...students give information that is not present in the text,
THEN...help them identify information from the text related to the word *goose*. Ask: How do these clues help you understand what a goose is? Reinforce the skill by asking students to find clues about the word *penguin*.

Lesson 36 Use Context Clues: Definition

REMIND STUDENTS THAT...

- they can find words in a text to help them learn the meaning of an unfamiliar word.
- they can use the title of a passage as well as other words in a sentence to help them.

PRACTICE 3 Explain that sometimes readers can use context clues from more than one sentence to help them identify the meaning of an unfamiliar word. Display the passage from Student Page S202. Read the title and text aloud, emphasizing the word *orioles*.

All About Orioles

Orioles are birds.
They are orange and black.
They can fly, but they cannot swim.
Orioles sing songs.
They make nests and sit on them.

Remind students that they can use context clues from more than one sentence. Have students use these clues to draw pictures of orioles. Then review what an oriole is by asking questions, such as *What can an oriole do?* and *What color is an oriole?* Offer corrective feedback as needed.

☑ **INDEPENDENT PRACTICE** Ask students to use all the sentences in the text below to tell what the word *albatross* means.

The Albatross

An albatross is a big bird.
Most albatrosses are white.
An albatross likes to eat fish.
It flies above the ocean.
It can live for 50 years!

IF...students have trouble reading the words,
THEN...read the words aloud and have students repeat after you. After reading the text once together, have students read the passage independently, blending the difficult words slowly as needed. Prompt correct pronunciation, if needed.

Lesson 36 **Use Context Clues: Definition**

Birds

The owl flies at night.
The cardinal is all red.
The robin pulls up worms.
The kiwi cannot fly at all!

Lesson 36 **Use Context Clues: Definition**

More About Birds

A sparrow is a small bird.
A **condor** has big, long wings.
A crow is all black, and it caws.
A loon can swim in the lake.

Lesson 36 **Use Context Clues: Definition**

Birds That Swim

Some birds are very good swimmers.
Here are some of these birds.
A penguin is black and white.
A **mallard** can have a green head.
A goose makes a honking sound.

Lesson 36 **Use Context Clues: Definition**

All About Orioles

Orioles are birds.
They are orange and black.
They can fly, but they cannot swim.
Orioles sing songs.
They make nests and sit on them.

The Albatross

An albatross is a big bird.
Most albatrosses are white.
An albatross likes to eat fish.
It flies above the ocean.
It can live for 50 years!

ASSESSMENT
LESSONS 35–36

Fluency

ASSESS MASTERY Use this Checkpoint to assess students' mastery of using dictionaries, glossaries, and context clues to determine meanings of unfamiliar words.

ADMINISTER THE TEST Administer the Checkpoint orally to each student. Give each student a copy of the next page. Instruct students as follows.

1. Use a Glossary (Lesson 35)
MODEL: I will read the passage aloud. Then you will use the glossary to tell me what the words *troublesome* and *enjoyable* mean.

2. Use a Dictionary (Lesson 35)
MODEL: Look at the sentence. Tell me where you would look in a dictionary for the two bold words: at the beginning, in the middle, or at the end.

3. Use Context Clues (Lesson 36)
MODEL: Look at the sentences. Use context clues to tell me what you think the word *birch* means.

RF.1.4.c Use context to confirm or correct word recognition and understanding, rereading as necessary.

L.1.4 Determine or clarify the meaning of unknown and multiple-meaning words and phrases based on grade 1 content, choosing flexibly from an array of strategies.

SCORING

SKILL/LESSON	SCORE
1. Use a Glossary (Lesson 35) troublesome; enjoyable (2 words)	_____ / 2
2. Use a Dictionary (Lesson 35) wonder (end); chalk (beginning)	_____ / 2
3. Use Context Clues (Lesson 36) (Sample answer: kind of tree, white bark)	_____ / 2

An overall score of 80% correct is typically considered mastery. Use your judgment and your individual students' needs as well to determine skill mastery.

IF...you determine that students have not demonstrated sufficient mastery of one or more skills,
THEN...review the skill(s), going back to the lessons to reteach and scaffold as needed.

ASSESSMENT
LESSONS 35–36

Fluency

1. It can be troublesome[1] to have a pet dog. But having a pet dog can be enjoyable,[2] too.

Glossary

1. troublesome [TRUH-bul-sum] a problem
2. enjoyable [in-JOI-uh-bul] fun

2. I **wonder** where I put my **chalk.**

3. One kind of tree is called a **birch** tree.
Many birch trees have bark that is white.
Their leaves turn colors in the fall.

READING, WRITING, AND LANGUAGE

PART 2

Lesson 37 Ask and Answer Questions About a Story

DIRECTIONS Look at the title of the story and the picture. Then follow along as your teacher reads aloud "Rainy-Day Cookies."

Rainy-Day Cookies

Gina and her dad planned to go to the zoo on Saturday. Gina was glad. She loved the zoo. But the sky was cloudy on Saturday morning. Soon it was raining cats and dogs!

"Oh, well," said Dad. "We will go to the zoo next weekend."

Gina tried not to look sad.

"Hey! I have a great idea!" Dad said. "What if I show you how to make my amazing Chunky and Chewy Chocolate Chip Cookies?"

"Yes, please! That is a great idea, Dad," said Gina.

Dad told Gina what they needed to make cookies. First, they got butter and eggs. Next, they found the flour and sugar and the other ingredients.

Dad explained, "First we mix up the butter and the sugar. Next we add eggs."

Crack! He tapped an egg on the rim of a cup. He opened the shell. *Plop!* The yolk and white dropped into the cup.

Dad poured the egg into the bowl. "You do the second egg, Gina," he said.

Crack! Plop! Gina's egg dropped into the cup. She poured it into the bowl.

Dad showed Gina his baking tricks.

"I like to add two pinches of salt. Like this!" he said. He acted like a magician as he tossed salt into the bowl.

Lesson 37 **Ask and Answer Questions About a Story**

Rainy-Day Cookies, *continued*

Gina added the chocolate chips. "Look! I am a cookie-making machine," she said. She stirred the dough round and round. She moved and acted like a robot.

After that, they used spoons to drop blobs of dough onto baking pans. Then they put the cookies into the oven.

Soon the kitchen filled with the smell of cookies.

They baked the cookies for ten minutes. Then they put them on racks to cool.

Gina and her dad sat together in the kitchen. They listened to the rain fall on the roof.

Gina felt cozy and happy.

"This is just as much fun as the zoo, Dad," said Gina.

Dad smiled. "It's a rainy-day adventure, isn't it?"

"Yes. And now it's time to eat the cookies!" Gina laughed.

Lesson 37 Ask and Answer Questions About a Story

INTRODUCE Explain to students that asking and answering questions about what they read is great way to check their understanding. I like to stop every now and then when I read and ask myself, "What exactly is going on here? Why did this event happen? Why did that character do what she did?" I may not be able to figure out the answers yet. I might have to keep on reading. But I might find the answer to a question I had earlier.

MODEL Display or distribute the following section from "Rainy-Day Cookies" on Student Page S207. After reading it aloud, guide students through the process of asking and answering questions about the story.

characters

Rainy-Day Cookies

problem

Gina and her dad planned to go to the zoo on Saturday. Gina was glad. She loved the zoo. But the sky was cloudy on Saturday morning. Soon it was raining cats and dogs!

"Oh, well," said Dad. "We will go to the zoo next weekend."

Gina tried not to look sad.

TEACH Ask: Does this passage give facts and information, or tell a story? How do you know? Students should note the characters, setting, and sequence of events. What is a question we could ask about this story? How about *Who are the characters in this story?* Invite students to answer. Writers usually introduce the main characters at the beginning of the story. Stories also usually have a problem. What problem does Gina have? Pause for student responses. She's sad because the weather is too rainy to go to the zoo that day.

RL.1.1 Ask and answer questions about key details in a text. ***See also*** **RL.1.5, L.1.4.a**

OBJECTIVES:

- Understand and explain differences between fiction and nonfiction texts.
- Ask questions about key details such as characters, settings and events.
- Answer questions about key details such as characters, settings and events.

BUILD VOCABULARY

Use Context Clues

Point out the word *ingredients* on Teacher Page T205.

Explain: When you find a word you don't know, look at the words around it for clues to the word's meaning. What clues here can help me with *ingredients*?

First Dad tells Gina what they need to make cookies. They get butter and eggs, then flour, sugar, and other ingredients. I think *ingredients* means "things you need to cook something."

Have students use this strategy to determine the meaning of *yolk*.

Lesson 37 Ask and Answer Questions About a Story

REMIND STUDENTS THAT...

- some texts tell stories, while other texts give information.
- readers can figure out whether a text is telling a story or giving information.
- knowing whether a text tells a story or gives information will help them to understand it better.

PRACTICE 1: Explain the Difference Between Stories and Informational Text

Say: "Rainy-Day Cookies" is a story, not a text written to give information. Display or distribute copies of Student Page S208. Read it aloud.

> Dad explained, "First we mix up the butter and the sugar. Next we add eggs."
>
> *Crack!* He tapped an egg on the rim of a cup. He opened the shell. *Plop!* The yolk and white dropped into the cup.
>
> Dad poured the egg into the bowl. "You do the second egg, Gina," he said.

Ask: What kinds of writing give information? Help students to think of nonfiction genres and talk about the kind of information they provide; examples include history, newspaper articles, biography, cookbooks, and instruction manuals. Remember, though, stories can still contain information. What information is in this part of the story? (how to make cookies) A story may give information, but it also contains made-up parts. What parts seem made up? Responses may include the characters Gina and Dad (note that real people are usually introduced by full name and described in terms of something they did); dialogue; description, figurative language, onomatopoeia (*crack* and *plop*).

✓ **MONITOR PROGRESS** Ask students to think about the whole story and to identify more made-up details (for example, Dad pretending to be a magician).

IF... students struggle to identify the fictional aspects of the story,
THEN... show them a recipe for cookies from a cookbook or online source. Talk about how the two texts are different.

Lesson 37 Ask and Answer Questions About a Story

PRACTICE 2: Ask Questions About Key Details Say: As you read a story, questions help you keep track of the characters (people or animals), setting (where they are), and events (the things that happen). One good question to ask often is, *What is happening right now?* Display or distribute copies of Student Page S209. Read it aloud.

> "I like to add two pinches of salt. Like this!" he said. He acted like a magician as he tossed salt into the bowl.
>
> Gina added the chocolate chips. "Look! I am a cookie-making machine," she said. She stirred the dough round and round. She moved and acted like a robot.

Ask: What is happening in this section? (The characters are mixing ingredients to make cookies. Dad adds salt, and he acts like a magician; Gina adds chocolate chips, and she acts like a robot.)

Say: The author uses comparisons to help you imagine what is happening. What does that make you wonder? Guide students to see that they could ask *How would a magician throw salt?* and *How would a robot stir dough?* Invite volunteers to act out the events for the class.

✔ MONITOR PROGRESS Write *who, what, when, where, why,* and *how* on the board. Ask students to recall the whole story and ask a question that begins with one of these words. Invite volunteers to share questions.

IF... students have difficulty forming questions about key details,
THEN... have students make statements and work backwards to phrase them as questions. *Gina stirred the dough. Who stirred the dough?*

REMIND STUDENTS THAT...

- readers can ask questions about a text while they are reading it.
- stories include key details about characters, settings, and events.
- having questions about what they are reading will make it easier for students to focus on and enjoy the story.

Lesson 37 Ask and Answer Questions About a Story

REMIND STUDENTS THAT…

- they can ask questions about the key details in a story.
- they may find the answers to their questions during a first or second reading.
- asking and answering questions about a story helps readers to understand it better and enjoy it more.

PRACTICE 3: Answer Questions About Key Details Say: You will understand a story better after you answer questions about it. Reread the story to focus on finding answers.

Display or distribute copies of Student Page S210. Read it aloud.

Gina and her dad sat together in the kitchen. They listened to the rain fall on the roof.

Gina felt cozy and happy.

"This is just as much fun as the zoo, Dad," said Gina.

Dad smiled. "It's a rainy-day adventure, isn't it?"

"Yes. And now it's time to eat the cookies!" Gina laughed.

Ask: Why is Gina "cozy and happy"? (She is having fun with her dad inside, while the weather outside is bad.) What does the phrase "a rainy-day adventure" mean? (It is an adventure you can have even though it is raining.)

✓ **INDEPENDENT PRACTICE** Ask students to think back on the whole story. Pose questions to individual students. For example, How have things changed for Gina since the beginning? (At first she was sad, but now she is happy.) Why does Gina mention the zoo? (She and her dad were supposed to go to the zoo, but they make cookies instead.) Gina says she's having fun. What details also show this? (Gina pretended to be a robot while stirring; at the end, she laughs.)

IF… students cannot answer questions about key details,
THEN… choose three *who, what, when, where, why,* or *how* questions to focus on, then reread the story to students, pausing to point out answers to the questions.

Lesson 37 **Ask and Answer Questions About a Story**

Rainy-Day Cookies

Gina and her dad planned to go to the zoo on Saturday. Gina was glad. She loved the zoo. But the sky was cloudy on Saturday morning. Soon it was raining cats and dogs!

"Oh, well," said Dad. "We will go to the zoo next weekend."

Gina tried not to look sad.

Lesson 37 Ask and Answer Questions About a Story

Dad explained, “First we mix up the butter and the sugar. Next we add eggs.”

Crack! He tapped an egg on the rim of a cup. He opened the shell. *Plop!* The yolk and white dropped into the cup.

Dad poured the egg into the bowl. “You do the second egg, Gina,” he said.

Lesson 37 Ask and Answer Questions About a Story

"I like to add two pinches of salt. Like this!" he said. He acted like a magician as he tossed salt into the bowl.

Gina added the chocolate chips. "Look! I am a cookie-making machine," she said. She stirred the dough round and round. She moved and acted like a robot.

Lesson 37 Ask and Answer Questions About a Story

Gina and her dad sat together in the kitchen. They listened to the rain fall on the roof.

Gina felt cozy and happy.

“This is just as much fun as the zoo, Dad,” said Gina.

Dad smiled. “It’s a rainy-day adventure, isn’t it?”

“Yes. And now it’s time to eat the cookies!” Gina laughed.

Lesson 38 Retell Stories

DIRECTIONS Look at the title and illustration. Then follow along as your teacher reads aloud "Susie Goes to a Party."

Susie Goes to a Party

Susie opened the colorful envelope that her friend Ann handed her. It was an invitation to a birthday party. Ann told Susie, "My party will have games, music, and pizza. Then we will eat cake and ice cream. I hope you can come."

Susie ran home from school with the party invitation. She showed it to her mom. "May I go to Ann's birthday party, Mom?" she asked.

Mom said, "Let's see. Today is Wednesday. The party is on Friday. You may go if you walk the dog each day until then." Susie agreed. She would take her puppy, Bruno, outside for a walk every day after school.

The days went by, and Susie did as she had promised. However, on Friday morning, Susie started to feel sick. Her head hurt, and she felt hot all over. Susie's mom felt Susie's forehead.

"I'm sorry, Susie. You have to stay home from school today," Mom said.

"But Ann's party is this afternoon," Susie said. She felt unhappy that she was sick. Susie stayed in bed. She coughed and sneezed.

Susie fell asleep. When she woke up, it was night. Susie thought, "Ann opened gifts and ate pizza. I was not there. I want to redo this day. I don't want to be sick!"

Susie's mom came to the door with hot soup. She said, "You were asleep all day. Please eat this soup." Susie disliked soup, but she felt hungry. She ate a little and went right back to sleep.

Lesson 38 Retell Stories

Susie Goes to a Party, *continued*

The next day, Susie felt better. She got up and walked down the stairs. Her parents sat at the table and ate breakfast. Susie frowned. "I feel better," she said, "but I missed the fun party. There were games, music, and pizza." Her family tried to cheer her up. Dad made silly faces. Bruno chased his tail. But Susie was still sad.

Mom said, "It's too bad that you had to miss Ann's birthday party, but I have an idea! Wait here." A little while later, Susie's mom called her into the living room.

The room had been transformed with bright banners and streamers, and a stack of games was on the table. "We can play games and listen to music here. We can eat pizza, too." Mom played some music, and the whole family danced.

Susie forgot about being sick. She was happy again.

Lesson 38 Retell Stories

INTRODUCE Remind students that a story is made up of several events. When you read, look for events and other details in the story. Pay attention to what happens to Susie.

MODEL Display or distribute Student Page S213. After students read it, draw their attention to important parts of the story and the central message.

Susie Goes to a Party

key details

Susie opened the colorful envelope that her friend Ann handed her. It was an invitation to a birthday party. Ann told Susie, "My party will have games, music, and pizza. Then we will eat cake and ice cream. I hope you can come."

Susie ran home from school with the party invitation. She showed it to her mom. "May I go to Ann's birthday party, Mom?" she asked.

Mom said, "Let's see. Today is Wednesday. The party is on Friday. You may go if you walk the dog each day until then." Susie agreed.

TEACH Begin by asking students to describe the events in the paragraphs above. What event do the characters talk about here? Guide students to explain that Susie has been invited to Ann's birthday party. How does Susie feel about this? Pause for responses. She feels excited. What happens next? Point out that Susie gets permission to go to Ann's party.

Guide students to review events in the rest of the "Susie Goes to a Party." Ask: Why doesn't Susie go to Ann's party? What happens instead? Students should point out that Susie gets sick and that she has to stay home from school. Next, point to the last paragraphs on Teacher Page T212. How does Susie feel at the end of the story? What events make her feel that way? Finally, link the events to the message of the story. How do people in a family take care of each other? Guide students to form a message statement such as *Families spend time together and do things to make each other feel better based* on events in the story.

RL.1.2 Retell stories, including key details, and demonstrate understanding of their central message or lesson. ***See also*** **RL.1.5, L.1.4.b**

OBJECTIVES:

- Identify important parts of the story.
- Identify central message or lesson.
- Retell a story and its message.

BUILD VOCABULARY

Use Prefixes

Point out the word *disliked* on Teacher Page T212.

Say: A prefix is placed at the beginning of a word to change its meaning. The word *disliked* has a prefix, *dis-*. What do you think *dis-* means? Susie dislikes soup. She eats only a little. Do you think she likes soup? No, because *dis-* means "not." Susie does not like soup.

Have students use the same strategy to find the meanings of other words with prefixes, such as *unhappy* and *redo*.

Lesson 38 Retell Stories

REMIND STUDENTS THAT...

- a retelling of a story includes the characters, the main events, and the key details.
- the events in a story happen in order, or sequence.
- readers use a story's events and key details to figure out its central message.

PRACTICE 1: Identify Important Parts of a Story Tell students that some events in a story are more important than others. Ask: Which one of these events is more important to the story? *Susie opened an envelope that her friend gave her. Susie stayed home because she was sick.* Guide students to understand that retelling a story means telling the most important events.

Display or hand out copies of Student Page S214. Remind students that the middle of a story often has more events than the beginning and end. Say: For instance, the beginning of a story introduces a problem. In the middle, the problem may get worse in several linked events. In the end, readers learn how the problem is solved.

Prompt students to use the graphic organizer to keep track of important story events. Remind them that most, but not all, stories describe events in time order, or the order they took place.

Beginning	Middle	End
gets invited to a party	gets permission to go to a party	family throws a "party" at home
	walks the dog as promised	feels good again
	gets sick misses the party	

✔ **MONITOR PROGRESS** Call attention to the third and fourth paragraphs on Teacher Page T211. What did Susie do on Wednesday and Thursday? What happened on Friday? How do you know?

IF... students cannot recount what Susie did on each day,
THEN... guide students to underline action words in sentences and to rephrase sentences in their own words.

Lesson 38 Retell Stories

PRACTICE 2: Identify a Central Message Say: You can find a central message in a story by considering the events and key details. Think about "Susie Goes to a Party." What are some changes that happened in the story? Changes are often clues to the central message. Display or distribute Student Page S215.

Middle	End
feels sick, coughs, sneezes	forgets about her cold
feels sad for missing the party	feels happy
Central Message	
Families take care of each other.	

Have students complete the graphic organizer to explain how Susie felt in the middle of the story, and how she felt at the end. Guide students to see that the actions of her family caused Susie to feel better. Follow up by asking: What message about *family* is the story making? What can we say about *making people feel better* based on the story?

MONITOR PROGRESS Point out that interactions between characters are often important story events. Have students review the story. Ask students to explain how the passage relates to the central message *Families take care of each other.*

IF... students cannot relate Mom's caring actions to Susie's cheering up, THEN... have them fill in the *End* column on the graphic organizer on Student Page S215 with the events that happen between Susie becoming ill and the end of the story.

REMIND STUDENTS THAT...

- the events in a story happen in order, or sequence.
- readers use a story's events and key details to figure out its central message.
- a central message is a general statement about life.

Lesson 38 Retell Stories

REMIND STUDENTS THAT...

- readers use a story's events and key details to figure out its central message.
- a central message is a general statement about life that the author wants to share.
- when you retell a story, you include the characters, story events, and central message.

PRACTICE 3: Retell a Story and Determine Central Message Have students reread "Susie Goes to a Party." Explain that stories can have more than one message. Ask students to name the important ideas in the story and key events or character actions that relate to those ideas. A central message is a general statement about life that the author wants to share with the reader.

Display or hand out copies of Student Page S216.

The characters in the story are ____________.

The events at the beginning of the story are ____________.

The events in the middle of the story are ____________.

The events at the end of the story are ____________.

The most important events in the story are about ____________.

The story's central message is ____________.

Help students use the sentence frames to retell the story, including only the most important details. In addition, guide them to use the sentence frames to identify important ideas (such as *family* or *taking care of people*) and a message about those ideas. They can retell the story orally and/or record written responses on Student Page S216.

✔ **INDEPENDENT PRACTICE** Ask students independently to retell the story in their own words. Ask: What big event happens to Susie in the story? What happens first? What happens next? What happens last?

IF... students cannot retell the story and its central message,
THEN... have students cross out sentences in the story that are unimportant or do not belong in a retelling. Have them highlight or circle words and phrases that are important and do belong in a retelling.

Susie Goes to a Party

Susie opened the colorful envelope that her friend Ann handed her. It was an invitation to a birthday party. Ann told Susie, "My party will have games, music, and pizza. Then we will eat cake and ice cream. I hope you can come."

Susie ran home from school with the party invitation. She showed it to her mom. "May I go to Ann's birthday party, Mom?" she asked.

Mom said, "Let's see. Today is Wednesday. The party is on Friday. You may go if you walk the dog each day until then." Susie agreed.

Lesson 38 Retell Stories

Beginning	Middle	End

Lesson 38 Retell Stories

Middle	End

Central Message

Lesson 38 Retell Stories

The characters in the story are ____________________

____________________.

The events at the beginning of the story are ____________________

____________________.

The events in the middle of the story are ____________________

____________________.

The events at the end of the story are ____________________

____________________.

The most important events in the story are about ____________________

____________________.

The story's central message is ____________________

____________________.

ASSESSMENT
LESSONS 37–38

Reading Literature

ASSESS MASTERY Use this Checkpoint to assess students' mastery of the Level B Reading standards listed here.

ADMINISTER THE TEST Administer the Checkpoint orally to each student.

1. Read aloud the story on the following page.
2. Read questions 1–4 and have students respond. Check their answers using the Scoring chart.

SCORING

SKILL/LESSON	STANDARD	ANSWER	SCORING
1. Ask and Answer Questions About a Story (Lesson 37)	**RL.1.1**	Sample response: Who are the story characters? The first sentence of the story names the characters.	_____ / 2
2. Ask and Answer Questions About a Story (Lesson 37)	**RL.1.1**	The problem is that characters don't want to eat their own lunches.	_____ / 1
3. Ask and Answer Questions About a Story (Lesson 37)	**RL.1.1** **RL.1.5**	"Lunch Time" is a made-up story. A text about how to make lunch would have facts and how-to steps.	_____ / 1
4. Retell Stories (Lesson 38)	**RL.1.2**	Answers will vary, but should include: no one likes his/her original lunch; Josie suggests a trade; after the trade, everyone is happy.	_____ / 1

An overall score of 80% is typically considered mastery. Use your judgment and your individual students' needs as well to determine skill mastery.

IF...you determine that students have not demonstrated sufficient mastery of one or more skills,
THEN...review needed skills, going back to the lessons to reteach and scaffold as needed.

RL.1.1 Ask and answer questions about key details in a text.

RL.1.2 Retell stories, including key details, and demonstrate understanding of their central message or lesson.

RL.1.5 Explain major differences between books that tell stories and books that give information, drawing on a wide reading of a range of text types.

ASSESSMENT
LESSONS 37–38

Reading Literature

Lunch Time

Kara, Wes, Nico, and Josie were best friends. Every day at lunch, they sat together and talked happily. But today, the four friends were not happy.

Kara pulled a sandwich out of her lunchbox and groaned. "Peanut butter and jelly and an apple again!"

Wes replied, "You're lucky, Kara. I got last night's beef stew and a pear!"

Josie said, "Beef stew, yum! That sounds way better than my tuna fish sandwich and banana!"

"Well, tuna doesn't sound so bad to me," said Nico. "All I've got is a turkey sandwich and a box of raisins."

The four friends were quiet for a moment. Then Josie said, "Kara, why don't you trade lunches with Wes, and I'll trade lunches with Nico? If we share, we'll all be happy!"

"Great idea!" said Kara. Wes and Nico nodded in agreement. So Kara and Wes swapped lunches and so did Josie and Nico. As the four friends munched on their new lunches, they talked happily about their day.

1. What question could you ask about "Lunch Time" to help you understand it? What text detail helps you answer this question?
2. What problem do the characters have?
3. How is "Lunch Time" different from a text about how to make lunch?
4. Retell the major story events in order.

Lesson 39 Describe Characters, Settings, and Major Events

DIRECTIONS Follow along as your teacher reads aloud the story. Listen for information about the characters, setting, and major events.

A Camping Adventure

The woods were pretty. Benny could see the tall trees. Jack could smell the flowers.

Benny and Jack were dogs. Benny was big. Jack was small. They were on a camping trip with their family. They were on a walk, just the two of them.

The path went left. Then it went right. It passed by a big tree stump. It went up a hill and beside a creek.

"The woods are great," thought Jack. "But it's probably time to turn around. We don't want to be late for lunch!"

Benny stopped. He sniffed the air. He smelled something. Was it their boy, Don? He sniffed again. No. It was something else.

Now Jack barked. It was a warning. "Look out for the bear!" it said.

A bear! Benny did not wait. He ran as fast as he could. So did Jack. They ran up a hill and past a big rock. At first they could hear the bear running, too. But the bear could not catch up to them. When they stopped to rest, the bear was gone. Now the dogs could relax.

Benny and Jack looked around. They sniffed the air. They smelled the dirt. None of it looked familiar. None of it smelled familiar.

"Uh-oh," Jack thought. "We're lost!"

"Which way is camp?" Jack asked.

Benny did not know.

Lesson 39 **Describe Characters, Settings, and Major Events**

A Camping Adventure, *continued*

The dogs sniffed the air again. They ran here and there. At last they started to walk downhill. They knew the camp was by a river. Maybe the river would be at the bottom of the hill.

They walked and they walked. The sun was bright. The sky was blue. But the dogs did not care. They wanted to get back to the camp.

Benny barked. "Left or right?"

Jack did not know. But the path on the left was bigger, so the dogs went left.

The day got hot. The trees got taller. Benny and Jack saw some mud. Jack barked. He thought the mud meant that they were getting close to the river. He hoped so. Both of them needed a drink of water!

Now it was Benny's turn to bark. "The river!" Together they ran down the path. There were ducks. There were fish. First, they drank. Then they looked around.

Jack barked. He could see the camp on the other side. "All we need to do is to swim across!"

So they did. They shook the water out of their fur and ran to the tent. Their people were glad to see them. And they were just in time for lunch.

Lesson 39 Describe Characters, Settings, and Major Events

INTRODUCE Explain that almost all stories have characters, a setting, and events. Characters are the people or animals who appear in the story. The setting is where the story happens. Major events are the important things that happen in the story.

MODEL Display or distribute Student Page S221. After students read it, draw their attention to the names Benny and Jack. The story tells what Benny and Jack do on the camping trip, so they are the characters.

A Camping Adventure

characters

The woods were pretty. Benny could see the tall trees. Jack could smell the flowers.

Benny and Jack were dogs. Benny was big. Jack was small. They were on a camping trip with their family. They were on a walk, just the two of them.

setting

The path went left. Then it went right. It passed by a big stump. It went up a hill and beside a creek.

TEACH Call students' attention to the words that describe the setting. Read the words aloud. Ask students to picture in their heads where the story takes place. Does the story happen inside or outside? Does it happen in a city or in the country? Guide students to recognize that words like *trees, flowers,* and *creek* show that the story takes place outside in the woods. When you read closely, you can tell who the characters are and where the story takes place. You can also tell what important things happen in the story. Briefly discuss the scene in which the dogs run away from the bear. Explain that this is a major event in the story.

RL.1.3 With prompting and support, identify characters, settings, and major events in a story. ***See also* RL.1.7, L.1.4.c**

OBJECTIVES:

- Identify characters, settings, and major events in a story.
- Use key details to describe a story's important characters, settings, and major events.
- Use illustrations to describe a story's important characters, settings, and major events.

BUILD VOCABULARY

Use Base Words

Point out the word *warning* on Teacher Page T219.

Say: The simplest form of a word is called the *base word.* Beginnings and endings can be added to base words.

The base word in *warning* is *warn.* When you warn someone, you tell him or her about nearby danger. So a *warning* is a message about something dangerous.

Have students use the same strategy to determine the meaning of *sniffed.*

Lesson 39 Describe Characters, Settings, and Major Events

REMIND STUDENTS THAT...

- characters in a story are the people or animals that the story is mostly about.
- the setting of a story is where it happens.
- authors use descriptive words to depict settings and major events.

PRACTICE 1: Identify Characters, Settings, and Major Events Display or distribute Student Page S222. Read the top excerpt aloud with students. Review that there are two main characters in the story, and have students find the characters' names.

Benny barked. "Left or right?" *characters*

Jack did not know. But the path on the left was bigger, so the dogs went left.

The day got hot. The trees got taller. Benny and Jack saw some mud. Jack barked. He thought the mud meant that they were getting close to the river. He hoped so. Both of them needed a drink of water! *setting details*

Now ask students to form a picture in their minds of where this scene takes place. Say: You already know that the story takes place outdoors in the woods. Let's look for words in the story that tell what the place looks like. Guide students to identify the words *path, trees,* and *mud.* Explain that these words help students figure out the setting of the story.

Then remind students that stories are made up of events, or things that happen. What is happening in this scene? What are the dogs doing?

✓ **MONITOR PROGRESS** Read aloud the bottom passage on Student Page S222. Ask students what major event in the story is being described. (The dogs swim across the river.)

Jack barked. He could see the camp on the other side. "All we need to do is to swim across!"

So they did.

IF... students cannot identify the major event,
THEN... review that an event is something that happens in a story and that a major event is an important thing that happens.

Lesson 39 Describe Characters, Settings, and Major Events

PRACTICE 2: Use Key Details to Describe Characters, Settings, and Major Events Tell students that they can use important details in a story to help them understand more about the characters, setting, and major events. Display or distribute Student Page S223 and read the top excerpt aloud.

Benny stopped. He sniffed the air. He smelled something. Was it their boy, Don? He sniffed again. No. It was something else.

Now Jack barked. It was a warning. "Look out for the bear!" it said.

A bear! Benny didn't wait. He ran as fast as he could. So did Jack. They ran up a hill and past a big rock. At first they could hear the bear running, too. But the bear could not catch up to them.

character details

Tell students that this passage gives some key details about the story's characters. You already know that Benny and Jack are dogs, and Benny is big and that Jack is little. Now you can tell some more things about them. Benny smells the air to learn about the world around him. Jack barks to warn Benny about a bear. What else can you learn about the dogs? Have students look at the third paragraph of the above excerpt. Guide students to recognize that these details suggest the dogs are fast runners.

Repeat with the setting and the major event of the dogs encountering a bear.

REMIND STUDENTS THAT...

- a story contains characters, settings, and major events.
- authors use names to identify characters.
- authors use descriptive words to depict settings and major events.

✓ **MONITOR PROGRESS** Have students read the bottom excerpt on Student Page S223. Ask students what they can learn about the setting from the text on the page.

"The river!" Together they ran down the path. There were ducks. There were fish.

IF... students cannot identify details about the setting,
THEN... ask students to draw a picture of the setting, emphasizing the animals described, and point out that students can use these details to help them understand the setting.

Lesson 39 Describe Characters, Settings, and Major Events

REMIND STUDENTS THAT...

- a story contains characters, settings, and major events.
- authors use key details to depict characters, settings, and major events.
- illustrations give information about characters, settings, and events.

PRACTICE 3: Use Illustrations to Describe Characters, Settings, and Major Events Remind students that they can learn important details about setting, characters, and events by looking closely at illustrations. Many stories have pictures, which are also called illustrations. You can learn a lot about the characters, settings, and events of a story by looking closely at the pictures, too.

Display or distribute Student Page S224. Have students describe what they see.

Say: You can see in the picture that one of the dogs is big and the other one is small, which is also a detail in the text. But you can also see something else that is not in the text. Ask students how wide the river is. The text doesn't give you an idea of how wide the river is. The picture helps you understand that it is not very wide, and they might be able to swim across.

Wrap up by having students discuss how illustrations can assist their understanding of major events in a story.

✓ **INDEPENDENT PRACTICE** Ask students what they can tell about the family's campsite by looking at the picture.

IF... students cannot say anything about the campsite,
THEN... ask guiding questions, such as *Is it a house or a tent?* to help them understand what they are seeing.

Lesson 39 **Describe Characters, Settings, and Major Events**

A Camping Adventure

The woods were pretty. Benny could see the tall trees. Jack could smell the flowers.

Benny and Jack were dogs. Benny was big. Jack was small. They were on a camping trip with their family. They were on a walk, just the two of them.

The path went left. Then it went right. It passed by a big tree stump. It went up a hill and beside a creek.

Lesson 39 Describe Characters, Settings, and Major Events

Benny barked. “Left or right?”

Jack did not know. But the path on the left was bigger, so the dogs went left.

The day got hot. The trees got taller. Benny and Jack saw some mud. Jack barked. He thought the mud meant that they were getting close to the river. He hoped so. Both of them needed a drink of water!

Jack barked. He could see the camp on the other side. “All we need to do is to swim across!”

So they did.

Lesson 39 **Describe Characters, Settings, and Major Events**

Benny stopped. He sniffed the air. He smelled something. Was it their boy, Don? He sniffed again. No. It was something else.

Now Jack barked. It was a warning. "Look out for the bear!" it said.

A bear! Benny didn't wait. He ran as fast as he could. So did Jack. They ran up a hill and past a big rock. At first they could hear the bear running, too. But the bear could not catch up to them.

"The river!" Together they ran down the path. There were ducks. There were fish.

Lesson 39 Describe Characters, Settings, and Major Events

Lesson 40 Identify the Meanings of Words

DIRECTIONS Follow along as your teacher reads the story aloud. Listen for unfamiliar words.

The Missing Piggy Bank

"I got here as soon as I could," said Lucy. "What's the problem?"

"The problem is my piggy bank," said Jane. She looked like she had been crying. "It's gone!"

"That's a problem, all right," Lucy agreed.

Lucy was nine years old. She was a detective. She loved to help people solve problems. "I am a great detective," Lucy liked to tell people. "If you have a problem, you can come to me!"

Jane's dog, Wolf, dashed up. Wolf was very large. Her teeth were huge. She had a big toy bone in her mouth. Wolf dropped the bone, and it bounced at Lucy's feet.

"Hi, Wolf," Lucy said. She smiled and bent down to touch the dog's soft fur.

"She likes it when you throw the toy," Jane said.

Lucy picked up the bone. It was soaking wet from Wolf's mouth. It was heavy, too. She tossed the bone over Jane's bed. "Go get it!" she said.

Wolf barked three times. Then she ran around the bed. Her toenails scratched on the floor as she ran. Lucy grinned.

"Can you help me?" Jane asked.

"Of course I can help you," said Lucy. She opened her notebook, which smelled like flowers. She wrote "Piggy Bank" at the top of the page. "When did you last see it?"

Lesson 40 **Identify the Meanings of Words**

The Missing Piggy Bank, *continued*

"It was here this morning," said Jane. She tapped a low table near her bed. "Where could it have gone?"

Lucy wrote quickly. "Who has been in your room?" she asked.

"No one," Jane said sadly. "My mom has been downstairs all day. And my dad and sister are out of town."

Lucy licked the end of her pen. This was a big mystery. And she loved big mysteries. "Did you go downstairs this morning?" she asked.

"I went down to eat," Jane said. "When I came back, the piggy bank had vanished."

There was a bark from under the bed. Suddenly, Lucy had an idea. She was excited. "Wolf!" she called.

Wolf came out from under Jane's bed. Wolf wagged her tail. "Where did Wolf put the toy bone?" Lucy asked.

"Under the bed," Jane told her. "Wolf takes toys and hides them down there."

Lucy nodded. "Would you get the bone for me, please?" she asked.

Jane frowned. She reached under her bed. Then she opened her mouth in surprise.

"You found the piggy bank," Lucy said.

Jane pulled out her piggy bank. She stood up, pumped her fists, and began to dance. "Thanks!" she said. "How did you know it was there?"

"Wolf took it and put it under your bed," Lucy thought to herself. But she told Jane, "When you're a great detective, you know things!"

Lesson 40 Identify the Meanings of Words

INTRODUCE Tell students that authors choose their words carefully. Say: When you read, it's important to understand the meanings of the words in the text. You should also look for words that help you understand what the characters are thinking and feeling. Add that words often appeal to the senses.

MODEL Display or distribute Student Page S227, and read it aloud. Ask: What does the word *huge* mean? Elicit or explain that it means "very large." Highlight *very large*, *huge*, and *big*. Explain that these words mean almost the same thing, but *huge* has a different shade of meaning: *huge* suggests something even bigger than *big* or *very large*.

> **The Missing Piggy Bank**
>
> Jane's dog, Wolf, dashed up. Wolf was very large. Her teeth were huge. She had a big toy bone in her mouth. Wolf dropped the bone, and it bounced at Lucy's feet.
>
> "Hi, Wolf," Lucy said. She smiled and bent down to touch the dog's soft fur.

TEACH Have students identify what Lucy is doing. (petting the dog) Ask if they can tell what the dog's fur feels like. How do you know that it is soft? Guide students to find the word *soft*. That descriptive detail appeals to your sense of touch. It helps you imagine what petting Wolf would be like and what the dog's fur would feel like.

Ask: How do you think Lucy is feeling when she sees and pats Wolf? How do you know? Point out the clue word *smiled*. Guide students to understand that Lucy probably feels happy because people smile when they are happy. Explain that clues like this can help students determine the meaning of words they do not know.

RL.1.4 Identify words and phrases in stories or poems that suggest feelings or appeal to the senses. ***See also*** **L.1.4, L.1.5.d**

OBJECTIVES:

- Define unfamiliar words in a story.
- Identify words that suggest feeling and emotion.
- Identify words that appeal to the senses.

BUILD VOCABULARY

Shades of Meaning

Point out the word *tossed* on Teacher Page T225.

Say: Some words have meanings that are almost but not quite the same. We say they have different shades of meaning. The sentence says that Lucy tossed the bone. *Toss* has a similar meaning to *throw*. But when you *toss* something, you don't throw it very hard. That word creates a picture in my mind of Lucy lightly throwing the bone. Model by pantomiming a gentle throw.

Have students talk through the meanings of *dashed* and *grinned*, which have meanings similar to "ran" and "smiled."

Lesson 40 Identify the Meanings of Words

REMIND STUDENTS THAT...

- readers need to know what the words in a story mean.
- clues from the story can help them determine the meaning of words they do not know.

PRACTICE 1: Define Unfamiliar Words Display or distribute Student Page S228. Read it with students. Point out that there are several words in the text that students may not know or be familiar with.

> Lucy licked the end of her pen. This was a big mystery. And she loved big mysteries. "Did you go downstairs this morning?" she asked.
>
> "I went down to eat," Jane said. "When I came back, the piggy bank had vanished."
>
> There was a bark from under the bed.

unfamiliar word (mystery)

multiple-meaning word (bark)

Call students' attention to the word *mystery*. Ask students if they know what a mystery is. Tell students that, if they do not know the word, they can use what they know about the story to help them. You already know that Lucy is a detective. A detective solves problems. Detectives figure out the answers to puzzles. So it makes sense that a *mystery* is a puzzle.

Explain that some words are difficult because they have more than one meaning. Point out the word *bark*. Tell students that *bark* has more than one meaning: it can mean "the outside covering of a tree," or it can mean "a noise that dogs make." Which meaning is used in this sentence? (a noise a dog makes) How do you know? (Jane has a dog named Wolf.) If time permits, repeat with *pen*. ("something to write with" or "a place to keep animals")

✓ MONITOR PROGRESS Read the sentence from Student Page S228 that includes the word *vanished*. Ask students what they think the word means and why they think so.

IF... students cannot give the meaning of the word,
THEN... model how to use context clues to determine the word's meaning.

Lesson 40 Identify the Meanings of Words

PRACTICE 2: Identify Sensory Words and Phrases Say: Authors often use words and phrases that appeal to the senses, or help the reader feel as if he or she can see, hear, or even smell what the writer is describing. Explain that good stories usually appeal to the senses in some way. Then display or distribute Student Page S229 and read it aloud.

REMIND STUDENTS THAT...

- clues from the story can help them determine the meaning of words they do not know.
- words can appeal to the senses.

Lucy picked up the bone. It was soaking wet from Wolf's mouth. It was heavy, too. She tossed the bone over Jane's bed. "Go get it!" she said.

Wolf barked three times. Then she ran around the bed. Her toenails scratched on the floor as she ran. Lucy grinned.

"Can you help me?" Jane asked.

"Of course I can help you," said Lucy. She opened her notebook, which smelled like flowers.

Tell students that this part of the text includes some words that appeal to the senses. Look at the phrase "soaking wet." Show me how you would hold something that is soaking wet. What would it look like? What would it feel like? Why do you think the author chose to use that phrase? Draw out that the phrase "soaking wet" helps the reader picture what the dog's bone looks and feels like. Repeat with "heavy," "barked three times," "toenails scratched on the floor," and "smelled like flowers." Make sure that students identify the correct sense the word and phrases appeal to.

✔ **MONITOR PROGRESS** Have students identify which sentence appeals to their sense of hearing:

The sleek black cat ran inside. The mouse squeaked loudly.

IF... students cannot identify the second sentence as correct,
THEN... ask students to make the noise the mouse makes, guiding them to see that the word *squeaked* appeals to their sense of hearing.

Lesson 40 Identify the Meanings of Words

REMIND STUDENTS THAT...

- they need to know the meanings of unfamiliar words and phrases to understand a story.
- some words in a story appeal to the senses.

PRACTICE 3: Understand Sensory Details Tell students that just as words and phrases appeal to the senses, they can also give information about what characters are thinking and feeling. Say: At the beginning of the story, the author tells readers that Jane looks "like she had been crying." What does that suggest about how Jane is feeling? (It suggests that she is feeling sad.) Point out that the author does not directly say that Jane is sad. Explain that readers use context clues to draw that conclusion.

Display or distribute Student Page S230. Read it with students.

> Jane frowned. She reached under her bed. Then she opened her mouth in surprise.
>
> "You found the piggy bank," Lucy said.
>
> Jane pulled out her piggy bank. She stood up, pumped her fists, and began to dance. "Thanks!" she said. "How did you know it was there?"

Point out the word *frowned*, and have students determine or explain the meaning. Let me see you frown. What are people usually feeling when they frown? (sad, angry, or worried) Repeat with "opened her mouth in surprise." How do you look and act when you are surprised? What are you thinking or feeling? Guide students to see that this phrase suggests that something good happened. Continue with the sentence "She stood up, pumped her fists, and began to dance." Verify that students understand the meaning of *pumped* and have a volunteer demonstrate Jane's actions.

✓ **INDEPENDENT PRACTICE** Say the following sentences from the text, and ask students which sentence helps the reader know what Wolf is feeling.

Wolf came out from under Jane's bed. Wolf wagged her tail.

IF... students cannot identify the second sentence as a clue to Wolf's feelings, THEN... ask guiding questions, such as *What do dogs do when they are happy?* to help them identify the correct answer.

Lesson 40 **Identify the Meanings of Words**

The Missing Piggy Bank

Jane's dog, Wolf, dashed up. Wolf was very large. Her teeth were huge. She had a big toy bone in her mouth. Wolf dropped the bone, and it bounced at Lucy's feet.

"Hi, Wolf," Lucy said. She smiled and bent down to touch the dog's soft fur.

Lesson 40 Identify the Meanings of Words

Lucy licked the end of her pen. This was a big mystery. And she loved big mysteries. "Did you go downstairs this morning?" she asked.

"I went down to eat," Jane said. "When I came back, the piggy bank had vanished."

There was a bark from under the bed.

Lesson 40 Identify the Meanings of Words

Lucy picked up the bone. It was soaking wet from Wolf's mouth. It was heavy, too. She tossed the bone over Jane's bed. "Go get it!" she said.

Wolf barked three times. Then she ran around the bed. Her toenails scratched on the floor as she ran. Lucy grinned.

"Can you help me?" Jane asked.

"Of course I can help you," said Lucy. She opened her notebook, which smelled like flowers.

Lesson 40 Identify the Meanings of Words

Jane frowned. She reached under her bed. Then she opened her mouth in surprise.

"You found the piggy bank," Lucy said.

Jane pulled out her piggy bank. She stood up, pumped her fists, and began to dance. "Thanks!" she said. "How did you know it was there?"

Lesson 41 **Analyze Characters' Experiences**

DIRECTIONS Follow along as your teacher reads the story aloud.

Toby in Charge

Toby the dog was asleep. She was dreaming. She was having a great dream!

Toby dreamed that she was on a spaceship. She was blasting off into the deep blue sky. But the dream did not stop there. In Toby's dream, the spaceship went past the rocky moon. Then it went past the brilliant sun. And the dream kept getting better.

Toby dreamed that the spaceship went to the stars. But the dream was even better than that, because Toby was not just on the spaceship. She was in charge. She was the captain of the spaceship. She was the captain even though she was a dog.

"Turn to the left!" Toby called to a cat. The cat turned the spaceship to the left.

"Turn off the lights!" Toby said to a bird. The bird turned off the lights.

The spaceship came up to a star. Toby looked out the window. The star was a gigantic ball of fire. It was blue and red. It was the most beautiful thing she had ever seen.

"Take a picture of the star!" Toby said to a fox. The fox took a picture of the star.

Toby sat down and opened her laptop. She found the picture of the star. Then she put the picture on her blog. She wrote about how it felt to look at the star—

Toby woke up. Her phone was ringing.

Lesson 41 **Analyze Characters' Experiences**

Toby in Charge, *continued*

Miles away, at mission control, a man named Dr. Wills walked back and forth. He was worried. He was about to send a spaceship into outer space. But the pilot was sick.

"Who else can I send?" he asked his friends. "I need someone who can be in charge."

"You should ask Toby," said Dr. Banks. He found a picture of Toby on his laptop. "She is a dog, but she is smart and loves outer space."

Dr. Mays nodded her head. "Yes, Toby is a good choice."

"I'll call her right now!" said Dr. Wills. He clapped his hands together. He found Toby's phone number and made the call.

"Hello," said a voice that sounded like a dog.

"Hello," said Dr. Wills. "Is this Toby the dog?"

"Yes, it is," said Toby. "Who is this?"

"This is Dr. Wills," said Dr. Wills. He was excited. But he was worried that Toby might say no. "We are sending up a spaceship. Would you like to be in charge?"

Dr. Wills held his phone tight. He felt scared. What if Toby didn't want to go?

"It's okay," Dr. Banks whispered. He smiled at Dr. Wills.

"I would love to go!" said Toby. "When do we blast off?"

"The day after tomorrow!" said Dr. Wills. He grinned at Dr. Mays and Dr. Banks. "We will see you then!"

Lesson 41 Analyze Characters' Experiences

INTRODUCE Tell students that characters are different in some ways and alike in other ways. When you read a story carefully, you can see how characters are alike and how they are different.

MODEL Display or distribute Student Page S233. Have students read it, and ask them to identify the two characters. (Dr. Wills and Toby) You learned earlier that Toby was a dog. That fact comes up again in this part of the story because the text says that Toby had "a voice that sounded like a dog" and Dr. Wills asks, "Is this Toby the dog?"

characters

details

"I'll call her right now!" said Dr. Wills. He clapped his hands together. He found Toby's phone number and made the call.

"Hello," said a voice that sounded like a dog.

"Hello," said Dr. Wills. "Is this Toby the dog?"

"Yes, it is," said Toby. "Who is this?"

TEACH Tell students that they can learn about the other character, Dr. Wills, by examining the details of the story. Ask: Is Dr. Wills a dog like Toby? How do you know? Guide students to recognize that Dr. Wills is not a dog. One clue is that he "clapped his hands together." What else can you tell about Dr. Wills? Help students recognize that Dr. Wills is a man because the story states that he is a man. Point out that the sentence "He was about to send a spaceship into outer space" suggests that he is in charge of making sure the mission runs smoothly. Review with students that they can find important information about each character by looking for details in the whole story.

RL.1.6 Identify who is telling the story at various points in the story.

RL.1.9 Compare and contrast the adventures and experiences of characters in stories.

See also **L.1.5.d**

OBJECTIVES:

- Identify which character is telling a story.
- Identify the experiences of different characters in a story.
- Compare and contrast the experiences of different characters in a story.

BUILD VOCABULARY

Shades of Meaning

Point out the word *gigantic* on Teacher Page T231.

Ask: What does *gigantic* mean? What words have meanings that are similar to *gigantic*?

The word *gigantic* is similar in meaning to the word *big*. The story tells about a star that is not just big; it is very, very, very big. The word *gigantic* means "very, very big."

Have students use the same strategy to determine the meaning of *brilliant*.

Lesson 41 Analyze Characters' Experiences

REMIND STUDENTS THAT...

- the story may be told by a character inside the story or a narrator not in the story.

PRACTICE 1: Identify Who Is Telling a Story Display or distribute Student Page S234. Read it with students. Explain that these excerpts are from two different pages of the story.

> The spaceship came up to a star. Toby looked out the window. The star was a gigantic ball of fire. It was blue and red. It was the most beautiful thing she had ever seen.

> Miles away, at mission control, a man named Dr. Wills walked back and forth. He was worried. He was about to send a spaceship into outer space. But the pilot was sick.

Say: Sometimes a story is told by a character in the story. If so, the character will use *I* and *me* to tell about his or her thoughts and feelings. Sometimes the story is told by a narrator who is not a character in the story. Then the narrator will use *he*, *she*, *him*, and *her* to describe what the characters say, do, and feel. Have students reread the first paragraph above. Who is this part of the story about? (Toby) Readers learn what Toby thinks about the star, but is Toby telling the story? (no) You can tell because the author says, "Toby looked out the window," not "I looked out the window." The story is told by a narrator who is not a character in the story. Repeat this process with the next paragraph, guiding students to see that the same narrator is telling the story even though the second paragraph is about Dr. Wills.

✔ **MONITOR PROGRESS** Read aloud the following text from Teacher Page T232: *Dr. Wills held his phone tight. He felt scared. What if Toby didn't want to go?*

Then ask: Which character is this part of the story about? (Dr. Wills) Who is telling the story? (a narrator) Is the teller of the story a character in the story? (no) How do you know? (The narrator says, "He felt scared." If Dr. Wills were telling the story, he would say, "I felt scared.")

IF... students cannot identify that an outside narrator is telling this part of the story, THEN... review how to use information about characters sharing their thoughts and feelings with the reader.

Lesson 41 Analyze Characters' Experiences

PRACTICE 2: Distinguish Characters Tell students that every character in a story has his or her own experiences. Explain that these experiences might or might not be the same as those of another character.

Display or distribute Student Page S235 and have students follow along as you read the first excerpt aloud.

> "This is Dr. Wills," said Dr. Wills. He was excited. But he was worried that Toby might say no. "We are sending up a spaceship. Would you like to be in charge?"
>
> Dr. Wills held his phone tight. He felt scared. What if Toby didn't want to go?

Point out the highlighted words. Help students understand that the words *excited*, *worried*, and *scared* all tell something about how Dr. Wills feels. You can understand Dr. Wills better because of what these words tell about him. Why is Dr. Wills feeling excited? Why is he feeling worried or scared? Have students discuss these questions with a partner; then have them share their thinking with the class. Ask students what else they remember about Dr. Wills's experiences from other parts of the story.

REMIND STUDENTS THAT...

- the story may be told by a character inside the story or a narrator not in the story.
- characters are alike in some ways and different in others.

✔ **MONITOR PROGRESS** Have students read the second excerpt on Student Page S235. What does the text tell you about the character Toby and her experiences?

> Toby was not just on the spaceship. She was in charge. She was the captain of the spaceship. She was the captain even though she was a dog.

IF... students cannot identify information about Toby's character and experiences,
THEN... review with students how they learned about Dr. Wills's character and experiences.

Lesson 41 Analyze Characters' Experiences

REMIND STUDENTS THAT...

- the story may be told by a character inside the story or a narrator not in the story.
- the story tells about a character's experiences.
- they can compare and contrast characters to see how they are alike and different.

PRACTICE 3: Compare and Contrast Characters Tell students that they can use what they learn about a story's characters to compare and contrast the characters. If necessary, explain that comparing things shows how they are alike, and contrasting things shows how they are different. You can use a graphic organizer to compare and contrast characters.

Display or distribute Student Page S236. Help students read the labels on the organizer.

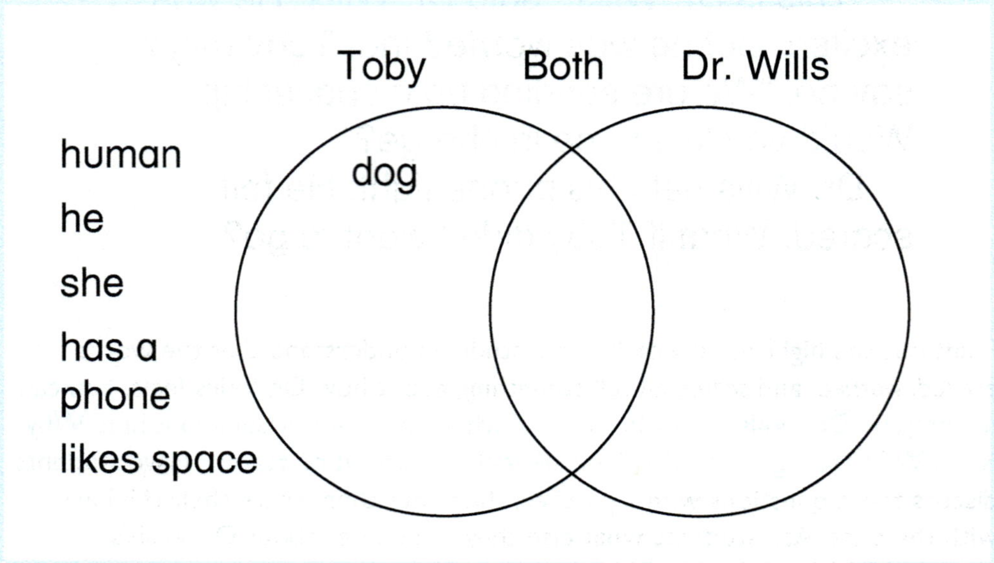

Tell students that the organizer has one circle for Toby. Outline the circle with your finger. In this circle we can write everything we know about Toby. You can see that one thing is already in the circle: dog. Tap the words *human*, *he*, and *she*, and read them aloud. Ask which of these words applies to Toby. (*she*) Write *she* in the left circle.

Repeat for Dr. Wills, writing *human* and *he* in the right circle. Then point out the overlap. This area is in the circle marked *Toby*. It's also in the circle for Dr. Wills. Anything we write in this area has to be true of both of these characters. Tap and read the two phrases "has a phone" and "likes space." Where should we put these? How do you know? Guide students to understand that the phrases describe both Toby and Dr. Wills and should go in the overlapping section of the organizer.

✓ **INDEPENDENT PRACTICE** Ask students where they would put the phrase "walks back and forth" in the above organizer.

IF... students cannot indicate that the phrase should go in the right circle, THEN... review with students how the graphic organizer works and how the labels for the circles can help them correctly place information.

Lesson 41 Analyze Characters' Experiences

"I'll call her right now!" said Dr. Wills. He clapped his hands together. He found Toby's phone number and made the call.

"Hello," said a voice that sounded like a dog.

"Hello," said Dr. Wills. "Is this Toby the dog?"

"Yes, it is," said Toby. "Who is this?"

Lesson 41 Analyze Characters' Experiences

The spaceship came up to a star. Toby looked out the window. The star was a gigantic ball of fire. It was blue and red. It was the most beautiful thing she had ever seen.
Miles away, at mission control, a man named Dr. Wills walked back and forth. He was worried. He was about to send a spaceship into outer space. But the pilot was sick.

Lesson 41 Analyze Characters' Experiences

"This is Dr. Wills," said Dr. Wills. He was excited. But he was worried that Toby might say no. "We are sending up a spaceship. We need someone to be in charge. Would you be in charge?"

Dr. Wills held his phone tight. He felt scared. What if Toby didn't want to go?

Toby was not just on the spaceship. She was in charge. She was the captain of the spaceship. She was the captain even though she was a dog.

Lesson 41 Analyze Characters' Experiences

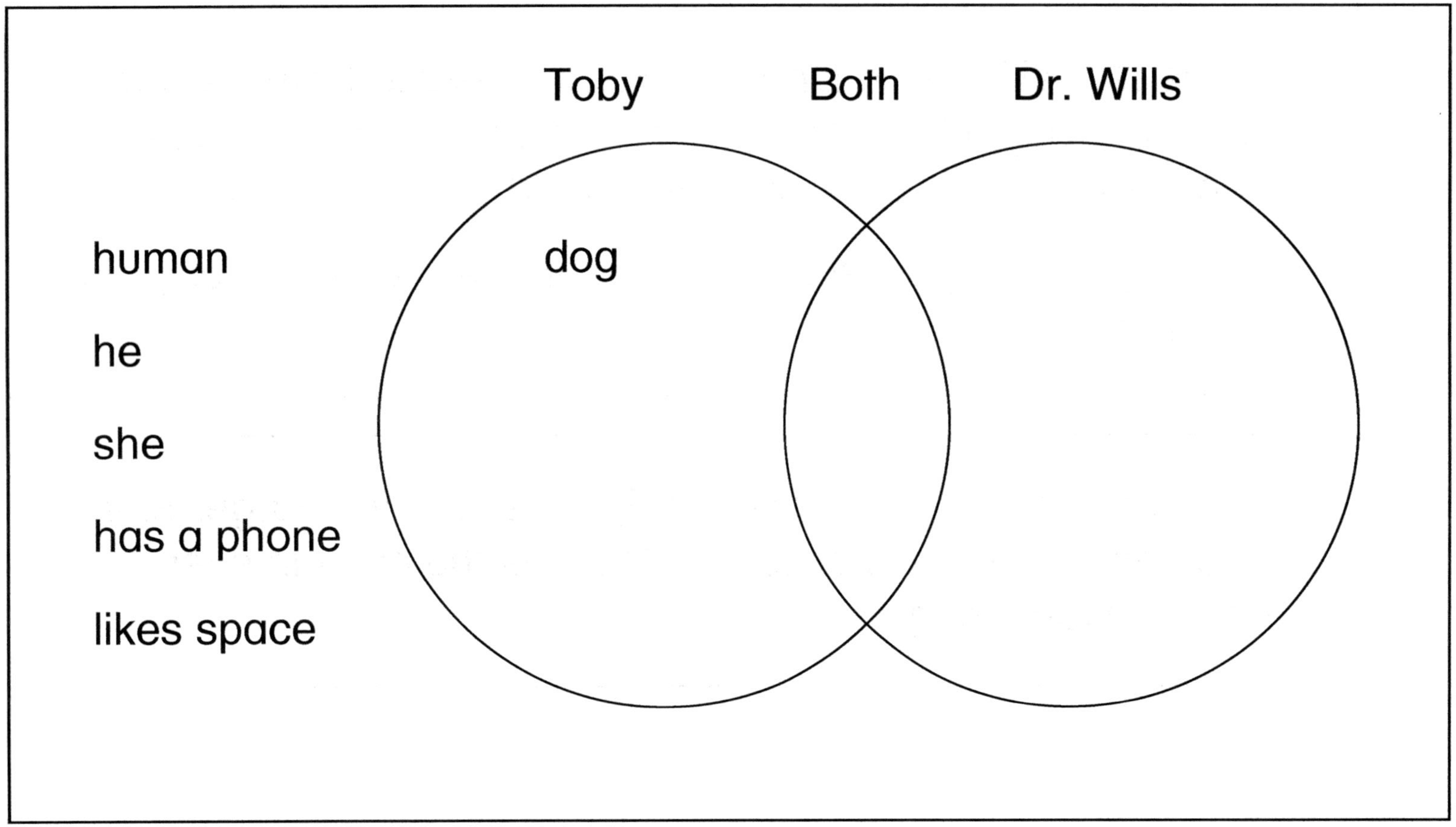

ASSESSMENT
LESSONS 39–41

Reading Literature

ASSESS MASTERY Use this Checkpoint to assess students' mastery of the Level B Reading standards listed here.

ADMINISTER THE TEST Read aloud Teacher Page T238 and the following questions. Have each student respond. Check answers using the Scoring chart.

1. Who is the main character? What is the setting? What major event does the illustration show?
2. Which of the following appeals to the reader's sense of touch: "She climbed up the smooth stalks" or "Jackie's dad was mad"?
3. How are Jackie and the giant different?
4. Is the person telling the story a character in the story? How do you know?

SCORING

SKILL/LESSON	STANDARD	ANSWER	SCORING
1. Describe Characters, Settings, and Main Events (Lesson 39)	**RL.1.3** **RL.1.7**	Jackie; around Jackie's home and in the clouds; the giant gives Jackie a golden egg	_____ / 3
2. Identify the Meaning of Words (Lesson 40)	**RL.1.4** **L.1.4**	She climbed up the smooth stalks	_____ / 1
3. Analyze Characters' Experiences (Lesson 41)	**RL.1.9**	Possible answers: They live in different places; the giant has a goose	_____ / 2
4. Analyze Characters' Experiences (Lesson 41)	**RL.1.6**	No; the person telling the story doesn't use *I*, *me*, or *my*	_____ / 2

An overall score of 80% is typically considered mastery. Use your judgment and your individual students' needs as well to determine skill mastery.

IF...you determine that students have not demonstrated sufficient mastery of one or more skills,
THEN...review needed skills, going back to the lessons to reteach and scaffold as needed.

RL.1.3 With prompting and support, identify characters, settings, and major events in a story.

RL.1.4 Identify words and phrases in stories or poems that suggest feelings or appeal to the senses.

RL.1.6 Identify who is telling the story at various points in a text.

RL.1.7 Use illustrations and details in a story to describe its characters, setting, or events.

RL.1.9 Compare and contrast the adventures and experiences of characters in stories.

L.1.4 Determine or clarify the meaning of unknown and multiple-meaning words and phrases based on grade 1 reading and content, choosing flexibly from an array of strategies.

ASSESSMENT
LESSONS 39–41

Reading Literature

Jackie and the Beanstalk

Jackie had a cow. Her dad told her to sell it for a high price. No one in town wanted to buy Jackie's cow. But a little girl said she would give Jackie special beans for it. Jackie said yes.

Jackie's dad was mad when he found out. He threw the beans out the window. Later that day, the beanstalks grew. Then they grew some more. Soon they were as tall as the house. They even went up past the clouds! Jackie decided to see who lived up there. She climbed up the smooth stalks.

Soon she got to the top. There was a big castle. And outside the castle was a goose—and a giant! Jackie explained to him how she got special beans instead of money for selling a cow and then climbed the beanstalk. The giant told the goose to lay an egg. The goose laid an egg that was made of gold!

The giant picked up the egg. "This is for you," he said with a smile. "You can sell it."

Jackie thanked him and climbed back down the beanstalk. She sold the egg, and she and her dad had the money they needed.

Lesson 42 Identify Main Topic and Key Details

DIRECTIONS Follow along as your teacher reads "The Truth About Koalas" aloud. Look at the subtitles in bold and view the picture.

The Truth About Koalas

What Do Koalas Look Like?

Some people think koalas are bears, but this is not true! Koalas are from the same family as the wombat. They look a lot like wombats. Koalas can be brown or grey. They have large black noses and thick fur. They have claws for climbing trees.

What Makes Koalas So Special?

A koala is a marsupial. A marsupial is an animal with a pouch. Koala mothers have a pouch to carry their young. The pouch keeps the growing koala warm and safe. A baby koala is called a joey.

When a joey is born, it is tiny. It can't see. It has no fur. It is about the size of a jellybean! The joey crawls into its mother's pouch to stay safe. It stays in the pouch for the next six months.

Lesson 42 **Identify Main Topic and Key Details**

The Truth About Koalas, *continued*

What Is a Koala's Life Like?

Koalas eat tree leaves. They have to eat leaves all the time to stay healthy. This takes a lot of energy. When koalas are not eating, they are sleeping. Some koalas sleep twenty hours a day.

Lesson 42 Identify Main Topic and Key Details

INTRODUCE Guide students to the understanding that the main topic of a text is what that text is all about. Ask: If I want to know the *main topic* of what I am reading, what do I want to know about it? (what person, place, or thing the text is about) Tell students that today they are going to learn how to tell about the main topic of the texts they read, using important details they find in in the texts.

MODEL Have students view the picture and subheadings, then display or distribute Student Page S241. Ask students what they think the text will be about. Then read it aloud.

The Truth About Koalas

detail

What Do Koalas Look Like?

Some people think koalas are bears, but this is not true! Koalas are from the same family as the wombat. They look a lot like wombats. Koalas can be brown or grey. They have large black noses and thick fur. They have claws for climbing trees.

TEACH Reread the title of the text aloud. Underline the word *Koalas*. This text must be all about koalas, just like the title says. Then point to the word *Truth*. In this text, what is one thing you learn that isn't true about koalas? Guide students to answer that koalas are not bears. Underline the text that says this. Explain that this small, important part of the text is called a *detail*. Then work together with students to identify other important details in the selection.

RI.1.1 Ask and answer questions about key details in a text.

RI.1.2 Identify the main topic and retell key details of a text.

See also **L.1.4.a**

OBJECTIVES:

- Ask and answer questions about the main topic of a text.
- Ask and answer questions about key details in a text.
- Retell the text's main topic and key details.

BUILD VOCABULARY

Context Clues

Point out the word *marsupial* on Teacher Page T239.

Ask: Sometimes difficult words are explained right in the text. How can I use context clues, or words and sentences around the word, to understand what *marsupial* means?

Say: In the next sentence it says what a marsupial is. It says that a marsupial is "an animal with a pouch."

Direct students to use the same strategy to determine the meaning of the word *joey*.

Lesson 42 Identify Main Topic and Key Details

REMIND STUDENTS THAT...

- the smaller, important parts of the text are called details.
- the details in the text help tell about the main topic.

PRACTICE 1: Ask and Answer Questions About the Main Topic Explain that the main topic of a text is what the key details will tell about. To determine the main topic, readers can figure out what most of the details are related to. Display or pass out Student Page S242. Say: First you will determine what this text is about, or what its main topic is.

The Truth About Koalas

What Do Koalas Look Like?
What Makes Koalas So Special?
What Is a Koala's Life Like?

Have students use a Web graphic organizer. Invite students to identify the main topic based on the title, headings, and picture. Write *koalas* in the center circle. Say: Headings tell what the sections of a text are about. The writer uses questions as headings. They are all questions about the main topic. You can use information, or details, in the text to answer those questions. Write one heading in each circle connected to the center circle.

Have students write details in the outer circles of the graphic organizer. Point out that the details do not all connect with each other, but that all the details connect to the main topic of the passage.

MONITOR PROGRESS Have students generate and answer a question about the text's main topic.

IF... students struggle to identify the text's main topic,
THEN... provide sentence frames such as these: *A word that appears in the title and in the headings is _______. The first section is about _______, the second section is about _______, and the third section is about _______. The picture shows a _______.*

Lesson 42 Identify Main Topic and Key Details

PRACTICE 2: Ask and Answer Questions About Key Details Display the passage from Student Page S243. Point to the heading, or title of this section. Ask: What kinds of details do you think you will find in this text based on the heading, or title of this section? Affirm that there will probably be details about what makes koalas special. Tell students to listen for these details as you read aloud.

What Makes Koalas So Special?

A koala is a marsupial. A marsupial is an animal with a pouch. Koala mothers have a pouch to carry their young. The pouch keeps the growing koala warm and safe. A baby koala is called a joey.

Point to the word *marsupial* in the first sentence. Ask students to read the sentence aloud. That seems like an important detail. What questions could you ask about marsupials? Guide students to generate questions using *who, what, when, where, why,* and *how*. What does the text say makes marsupials special? Ask students to point out details about the marsupial's pouch in the text. Can we use those details to answer any of our questions?

REMIND STUDENTS THAT...

- small bits of information in a text are called details.
- the main topic of a text is what that text is all about.

✔ **MONITOR PROGRESS** Ask students to review Student Page S243 and tell what other details the writer includes to explain why a koala is special.

IF... students are unable to identify key details and/or explain why they are important to the rest of the text,
THEN... Ask: What words do you see repeated in the paragraph? What information in the paragraph answers the question *What makes koalas so special?* Pause for student responses and offer guidance as needed.

Lesson 42 Identify Main Topic and Key Details

REMIND STUDENTS THAT...

- the important details in a text support the text's main topic.
- identifying the details in a text can help them understand the text's main topic.

PRACTICE 3: Retell Main Topic and Key Details Explain to students that they have had practice determining a text's main topic and identifying the details in a text. Tell students they will practice retelling the main topic and details to show that they understand what they are reading. Display or distribute Student Page S244. Read the title and text aloud.

What Is a Koala's Life Like?

Koalas eat tree leaves. They have to eat leaves all the time to stay healthy. This takes a lot of energy. When koalas are not eating, they are sleeping. Some koalas sleep twenty hours a day.

Remind students that identifying the details in the text will help them determine the text's main topic, or what the text is all about.

Have students reread what you have just read quietly with a partner, and work together to create a list of the paragraph's important details, or what they learn. Say: As you think about what details are important, consider the questions the author has answered about the topic, such as *What do koalas eat?* and *Why do they sleep all the time?*

✔ **INDEPENDENT PRACTICE** Ask students to review "The Truth About Koalas" and state the text's main topic and list key details.

IF... students have trouble retelling the main topic and key details,
THEN... have students work in pairs to ask and answer questions using words and phrases from the passage. Guide students in using the key details that make up the questions and answers to identify the main topic.

Lesson 42 Identify Main Topic and Key Details

The Truth About Koalas

What Do Koalas Look Like?

Some people think koalas are bears, but this is not true! Koalas are from the same family as the wombat. They look a lot like wombats. Koalas can be brown or grey. They have large black noses and thick fur. They have claws for climbing trees.

Lesson 42 Identify Main Topic and Key Details

The Truth About Koalas

What Do Koalas Look Like?
What Makes Koalas So Special?
What Is a Koala's Life Like?

Lesson 42 **Identify Main Topic and Key Details**

What Makes Koalas So Special?

A koala is a marsupial. A marsupial is an animal with a pouch. Koala mothers have a pouch to carry their young. The pouch keeps the growing koala warm and safe. A baby koala is called a joey.

Lesson 42 **Identify Main Topic and Key Details**

What Is a Koala's Life Like?

Koalas eat tree leaves. They have to eat leaves all the time to stay healthy. This takes a lot of energy. When koalas are not eating, they are sleeping. Some koalas sleep twenty hours a day.

Lesson 43 Connect Information in a Text

DIRECTIONS Look at the passage and the illustration. Follow along as your teacher reads aloud "How the Wright Brothers Learned to Fly."

How the Wright Brothers Learned to Fly

One hundred and twenty years ago, airplanes were a just a dream. People dreamed of being able to fly like birds. Some were not sure that flying was possible. They had ideas about how to fly but none of them worked. Then the Wright brothers came along.

Orville and Wilbur Wright were not only brothers. They were friends, and they both loved birds. They spent a lot of time watching birds in action. They dreamed of discovering the birds' secret of flight. They wanted to build a machine that could fly.

Lesson 43 **Connect Information in a Text**

How the Wright Brothers Learned to Fly, *continued*

At first, Orville and Wilbur only made bicycles. They were good at it. Learning to make bicycles taught them all kinds of important things. It taught them how gears work. It also taught them important new ideas about motion. It gave them ideas about how to fly.

Building bicycles gave the brothers ideas about how to build the first airplane. But birds gave them the best idea. The brothers saw that when birds fly into the wind, the wind lifts them into the air. They saw how birds change the shape of their wings to fly faster or in another direction. This gave the brothers an idea. They built an airplane with wings that could catch the wind and change shape. The idea worked! The Wright brothers' airplane made its first flight on December 17, 1903.

Lesson 43 Connect Information in a Text

INTRODUCE Remind students that facts in a text are connected. Say: When you read, think about what you learn. Try to remember the most important information and how pieces of information are connected.

MODEL Display or distribute Student Page S247. Ask students what information they think they will find based on the illustration and title. Then ask students to listen for ideas as you read the passage aloud.

How the Wright Brothers Learned to Fly

title

One hundred and twenty years ago, airplanes were just a dream. People dreamed of being able to fly like birds. Some were not sure that flying was possible. They had ideas about how to fly but none of them worked. Then the Wright brothers came along.

text

illustration

TEACH Point out the different parts of the text—the title of the text, the illustration, and the text itself. Ask students to tell what information can be found in each part of the text. What did you learn from the title of this text? What does the illustration show? What does the writer tell about in this paragraph? Affirm the information students correctly identify and write it on the board.

Once the list is complete, review it with students. Remind them that when they read, it's important to think about how the information they find is connected. The title tells me this text will be about how the Wright Brothers learned to fly. The text says that lots of people wanted to fly like birds. The picture shows people looking at flying birds. What is the connection between these things? Guide students to explain that all the parts of the text are related to flight, the Wright brothers are in the title, the text, and the illustration, and that the Wright brothers learned to fly like birds do.

RI.1.3 Describe the connection between two individuals, events, ideas, or pieces of information in a text.

RI.1.5 Know and use various text features (e.g., headings, tables of content, glossaries, electronic menus, icons) to locate key facts or information in a text.

See also L.1.4.b

OBJECTIVES:

- Use text features to find information.
- Gather important information.
- Describe the connection between pieces of information.

BUILD VOCABULARY

Use Suffixes

Point out *ideas* in paragraph 1.

Say: When you want to say there is more than one of something, add an s at the end of a word. Adding an s means there is more than one. That makes the word plural.

If I put my finger over the s in *ideas*, I have the word *idea*. That's one idea. Adding an s makes the word plural, or more than one idea.

Direct students to identify other plural words. *(airplanes, brothers, birds)*

Lesson 43 Connect Information in a Text

REMIND STUDENTS THAT…

- they can look at all parts of the text, including the title and pictures, when gathering information.
- it is important to think about how the information in a text is connected.

PRACTICE 1: Use Text Features to Find Information Display or distribute Student Page S248.

Orville and Wilbur Wright were not only brothers. They were friends, and they both loved birds. They spent a lot of time watching birds in action. They dreamed of discovering the birds' secret of flight. They wanted to build a machine that could fly.

Point out that the paragraph tells the reader about the Wright Brothers and how they both loved watching birds. Ask: What else do you see that can help you understand the text? What information can you get from the picture? Guide students to note that the picture shows two people. What can you say about how the people are dressed? (They are wearing suits and old-fashioned hats.) What are they doing? (They watch a bird in flight. One points to it, as if they are studying and discussing the bird's flight.) What are they holding? (Both men have bicycles.)

MONITOR PROGRESS Discuss the image in more detail. Ask: What else do you see in this picture? Prompt students to consider the identity and relationship of the people shown. Students should also recognize that the picture shows an outdoor landscape, with large rolling fields in the background.

IF… students have trouble identifying the information in the picture, THEN… guide students to "read" the picture from left to right, top to bottom. What is in the top left corner? (a flying bird, far in the distance) What is shown in the top half of the picture? (the sky, flying birds, distant fields)

Lesson 43 Connect Information in a Text

PRACTICE 2: Gather Important Information Say: Some details are more important than others in a text. Important details are related to the topic of the text and directly support the writer's main ideas. You will learn how to focus on the most important information in the text. Display or distribute copies of Student Page S249. Read the text aloud.

> At first, Orville and Wilbur only made bicycles. They were good at it. Learning to make bicycles taught them all kinds of important things. It taught them how gears work. It also taught them important new ideas about motion. It gave them ideas about how to fly.

Ask: How can you tell what information is important? Explain that information is important if it helps readers better understand what the text is all about. Remind students that this text is all about how the Wright brothers learned to fly. This section of text gives information about how the brothers built bicycles. That is important because building bicycles helped them understand how to fly.

REMIND STUDENTS THAT...

- readers gather information as they read.
- they can gather information from all parts of the text and illustrations.
- some details are more important than others.

✔ **MONITOR PROGRESS** Review Student Page S249. Ask: What is the topic of this text? What information in this paragraph is about that topic? How do you know?

IF... students struggle to correctly identify important information or to explain their choices,
THEN... refer students to the title of text and review what the text is all about. Ask students to underline any information that is about the Wright brothers, learning, or flying.

Lesson 43 Connect Information in a Text

REMIND STUDENTS THAT...

- important information in a text directly supports the writer's main ideas.
- connections between pieces of information help readers better understand a topic.

PRACTICE 3: Describe Connections Between Information Display or distribute copies of Student Page S250 and read it aloud. Ask students to listen for important information.

1. Building bicycles gave the brothers ideas about how to build an airplane.
2. But birds gave them the best idea.
3. The brothers saw that when birds fly into the wind, the wind lifts them into the air.
4. They saw how birds change the shape of their wings to fly faster or in another direction.
5. This gave the brothers an idea.
6. They built an airplane with wings that could catch the wind and change shape.
7. The idea worked!
8. The Wright brothers' airplane made its first flight on December 17, 1903.

Say: According to the information in the text, two things gave the brothers ideas about flying. What are they? Affirm that building bicycles and watching birds helped the brothers learn to fly. Point out that you are making a connection between pieces of information from this text to answer the question. How would you explain the connection between these two pieces of information to someone else? Affirm that you could explain by saying both experiences helped the brothers discover the secret of flight.

✔ **INDEPENDENT PRACTICE** Direct students to items 3 and 4. Have students echo-read the lines with you. Ask individual students to identify information they can connect and explain how it connects.

IF... students struggle to explaining how the information is connected, THEN... have students restate the main topic of the text—how the Wright brothers learned to fly, and discuss how each piece of information relates to that topic.

How the Wright Brothers Learned to Fly

One hundred and twenty years ago, airplanes were just a dream. People dreamed of being able to fly like birds. Some were not sure that flying was possible. They had ideas about how to fly but none of them worked. Then the Wright brothers came along.

Lesson 43 Connect Information in a Text

Orville and Wilbur Wright were not only brothers. They were friends, and they both loved birds. They spent a lot of time watching birds in action. They dreamed of discovering the birds' secret of flight. They wanted to build a machine that could fly.

Lesson 43 Connect Information in a Text

At first, Orville and Wilbur only made bicycles. They were good at it. Learning to make bicycles taught them all kinds of important things. It taught them how gears work. It also taught them important new ideas about motion. It gave them ideas about how to fly.

Lesson 43 Connect Information in a Text

1. Building bicycles gave the brothers ideas about how to build an airplane.
2. But birds gave them the best idea.
3. The brothers saw that when birds fly into the wind, the wind lifts them into the air.
4. They saw how birds change the shape of their wings to fly faster or in another direction.
5. This gave the brothers an idea.
6. They built an airplane with wings that could catch the wind and change shape.
7. The idea worked!
8. The Wright brothers' airplane made its first flight on December 17, 1903.

ASSESSMENT
LESSONS 42–43

Reading Informational Text

ASSESS MASTERY Use this Checkpoint to assess students' mastery of the Level B Reading standards listed here.

ADMINISTER THE TEST Administer the Checkpoint orally to each student.

1. Read aloud the story on the following page.
2. Read questions 1–3 and have students respond. Check their answers using the Scoring chart.

SCORING

SKILL/LESSON	STANDARD	ANSWER	SCORING
1. Identify Main Topic and Key Details (Lesson 42)	**RI.1.1** **RI.1.2**	Main Topic: Cheetahs Key Details: Fastest animal on Earth, has excellent eyesight, quietest big cat	_____ / 4
2. Connect Information in a Text (Lesson 43)	**RI.1.5**	Title tells important fact. Picture shows what a cheetah looks like. Text gives facts about the cheetah.	_____ / 6
3. Connect Information in a Text (Lesson 43)	**RI.1.3**	The title helps support the fact in the text that cheetahs are one of the fastest animals on Earth.	_____ / 1

An overall score of 80% is typically considered mastery. Use your judgment and your individual students' needs as well to determine skill mastery.

IF... you determine that students have not demonstrated sufficient mastery of one or more skills,
THEN... review needed skills, going back to the lessons to reteach and scaffold as needed.

RI.1.1 Ask and answer questions about key details in a text.

RI.1.2 Identify the main topic and retell key details of a text

RI.1.3 Describe the connection between two individuals, events, ideas, or pieces of information in a text.

RI.1.5 Know and use various text features (e.g., headings, tables of content, glossaries, electronic menus, icons) to locate key facts or information in a text.

ASSESSMENT
LESSONS 42–43

Reading Informational Text

The Fastest Cat on the Block

What has pointy ears and a spotted yellow coat? What purrs but doesn't roar? What can run faster than a car driving through your town? It's the fastest cat on the block. A cheetah!

The cheetah is one of the fastest animals on Earth. It can run as fast as 70 miles per hour. That's the speed cars drive on the highway!

Speed isn't all there is to this amazing cat. Cheetahs have excellent eyesight, too. If you had eyes like a cheetah, you would be able to see the lines on a football from four football fields away!

The cheetah is also one of the quietest big cats. They are the only big cat that can't roar. But like house cats, cheetahs can purr. Just like our cats at home, cheetahs like to purr when they are happy.

1. What are the main topic and key details of this text?
2. What are the parts of this text? What information did you learn from each part?
3. What information in the first paragraph relates to the title? How is the information connected?

Lesson 44 Understand Illustrations in a Text

DIRECTIONS Look at the passage and study the illustrations. Follow along as your teacher reads aloud "Change of Season."

Change of Season

There are four seasons. They are spring, summer, fall, and winter. What happens in each season? The magic of nature happens. Each season is special.

In spring, the air gets warmer. It rains. The rain feeds the plants. Everything turns green.

People plant seeds in their gardens. Seeds sprout and plants start to grow. Flowers bloom. Grass covers your yard. Trees get their leaves.

Birds lay and hatch their eggs. Animal babies are born. Days get longer.

Next comes summer. The sun shines bright and warms the air. Oceans and lakes warm up as the sun hits the water. Flowers keep blooming. Vegetables grow and soon they are ready to eat.

Trees give shade from the hot sun. Sometimes it thunders and rains hard. Lightning strikes. Weather can be hot and sunny. It can be rainy and wild, too.

Lesson 44 Understand Illustrations in a Text

Change of Season, *continued*

As summer ends, fall begins. Days grow shorter. Vegetables stop growing, and plants start to die. Grass turns brown. Flowers quit blooming. The leaves turn bright colors before they drop from trees.

Many birds fly south. Animals collect food to get ready for winter. The weather changes. Some days are sunny and warm. Others are cool and windy.

By the end of fall, the wind blows from the north. It gets so cold it could snow. Fall reminds you winter is coming.

Winter brings cold and snow. The days are the shortest in the year. The ground is frozen. It is often covered in snow. Nothing grows in winter.

The trees have no leaves. Only pine trees stay green. Some animals sleep all winter.

Most animals have to hunt for food. Food is hard to find. But spring will come again soon.

What makes each season special? Spring brings new life. Summer has the hot sun and warm water. Fall means the leaves change color and drop from the trees. Winter is cold and snowy. Next spring, the seasons will start over again.

Lesson 44 Understand Illustrations in a Text

INTRODUCE Tell students that when they read informational text, they should pay attention to the text and the illustrations. Say: Authors share information in words and in pictures. Explain that pictures can help them better understand the information in the text. By adding illustrations, authors "show" important ideas.

MODEL Distribute or display the passage from Student Page S255. Read aloud the text as students follow along. Draw students' attention to the illustration and its contents.

Change of Season

There are four seasons. They are spring, summer, fall, and winter. What happens in each season? The magic of nature happens. Each season is special.

In spring, the air gets warmer. It rains. The rain feeds the plants. Everything turns green.

TEACH Ask: What do you learn about seasons from the text? Model identifying important details and recording them in a T-Chart. Distribute or display the chart on Student Page S255. Ask: How does the illustration help you understand these ideas? Help students look closely at the illustration. How does the illustration help you understand what is special about spring?

Ideas from Text	Ideas from Illustrations
Spring, summer, fall, and winter are the four seasons. Each is special.	Spring is when leaves start to grow on trees.
Spring is when it gets warmer and things turn green.	

Tell students they will read the rest of the text later and continue to use the illustrations to help them understand key ideas. Instruct students to create and fill in their own T-Charts. They will continue to use them throughout the lesson.

RI.1.6 Distinguish between information provided by pictures or other illustrations and information provided by the words in a text.

RI.1.7 Use the illustrations and details in a text to describe its key ideas.

See also **L.1.5.a**

OBJECTIVES:

- Identify information in the text and the illustrations.
- Distinguish between information provided in illustrations and in words.
- Use information from the illustrations to better understand the text's key ideas.

BUILD VOCABULARY

Sort Words

Point out the noun *plants* in the second paragraph.

Ask: How can I sort words to help me better understand the word *plants*?

If I look at the third paragraph, I see that plants come from seeds. I will try to find words that name plants. *Flowers, grass,* and *trees* are all plants. By sorting these words into the *plant* group, I can figure out that *plants* grow in the ground, have leaves or flowers, and need rain to grow.

Have students use the same strategy with *weather.*

Lesson 44 Understand Illustrations in a Text

REMIND STUDENTS THAT…

- they can find information in text and illustrations.
- they should be able to identify whether the information comes from the text or from the illustrations.

PRACTICE 1: Identify Important Ideas Say: We will look for important ideas in the text and pictures in "Change of Season." Display and distribute copies of Student Page S256.

In spring, the air gets warmer. It rains. The rain feeds the plants. Everything turns green.

People plant seeds in their gardens. Seeds sprout and plants start to grow. Flowers bloom. Grass covers your yard. Trees get their leaves.

Birds lay and hatch their eggs. Animal babies are born. Days get longer.

Read the first paragraph of the excerpt. Ask students to identify information from the paragraph. Say: This paragraph says that it rains a lot in spring. It also says that everything turns green. Draw a T-Chart and label the columns *Text* and *Illustrations*. Record the information in the Text column for students to see. Then have students copy this information in their own T-Chart.

Next, identify information from the illustration of spring. I see the tree is starting to bud. It looks like grass is growing. Point out information that appears in both the text and the illustration. Write this information in the T-Chart.

Finally, pair students. Say: Listen to the next paragraph, look at the picture, and talk with your partner about what else happens in spring, according to the text. Allow time for students to discuss their ideas. Then discuss the ideas as a class and encourage students to record the information in their T-Charts.

✔ **MONITOR PROGRESS** Have students point out the source of each detail listed in their T-Charts.

IF… students have difficulty finding information in illustrations,
THEN… ask them to simply describe what they see in the illustration. Offer corrective feedback, if needed.

Lesson 44 Understand Illustrations in a Text

PRACTICE 2: Identify Important Ideas in Text and Illustrations Review the T-Charts you made with students in Practice 1. Then say: You will continue to add information to your charts from the text and the illustrations. You will talk about how the illustrations highlight key ideas in the text. Display or distribute Student Page S257.

Next comes summer. The sun shines bright and warms the air. Oceans and lakes warm up as the sun hits the water. Flowers keep blooming. Vegetables grow and soon they are ready to eat.

Trees give shade from the hot sun. Sometimes it thunders and rains hard. Lightning strikes. Weather can be hot and sunny. It can be rainy and wild, too.

Read aloud the paragraphs. Pair students and have them continue discussing ideas from the text and illustrations.

Display or distribute Teacher Page T253. Guide the class to identify the information from the text that the first two illustrations emphasize. Both pictures show a boy and his dad looking up at a tree. In the first picture, the boy holds a tiny puppy and the leaves of the tree are just starting to show. In the second picture, the puppy is walking on a leash and the boy and his dad are wearing sunglasses. I can tell it is getting warmer outside and that the tree is growing even more. These are key ideas about summer. They are found in the text and in the changes between the illustrations. Have students add relevant information to their T-Charts.

REMIND STUDENTS THAT...

- they can find information in text and illustrations.
- they should be able to identify whether the information comes from the text or from the illustrations.
- they can use information from the illustrations to identify and understand the text's key ideas.

✓ **MONITOR PROGRESS** Ask students to list key ideas about spring and summer.

IF... students have difficulty identifying key ideas,
THEN... ask: What is the most important thing about this season? Point out key parts of the text and the illustrations to guide students.

Lesson 44 Understand Illustrations in a Text

REMIND STUDENTS THAT...

- they can identify whether the information comes from the text or from the illustrations.
- they can use information from the illustrations to identify and understand the text's key ideas.

PRACTICE 3: Compare Ideas in Text and Illustrations Say: Today you will finish your T-charts about this passage and its illustrations. Distribute or display Student Page S258. Read the paragraphs aloud to students.

As summer ends, fall begins. Days grow shorter. Vegetables stop growing, and plants start to die. Grass turns brown. Flowers quit blooming. The leaves turn bright colors before they drop from trees.

Many birds fly south. Animals collect food to get ready for winter. The weather changes. Some days are sunny and warm. Others are cool and windy.

By the end of fall, the wind blows from the north. It gets so cold it could snow. Fall reminds you winter is coming.

Pair students and have them discuss ideas from the text and ideas from the illustrations and identify the sources of each idea. Display or distribute Teacher Page S253. Guide the class to identify the information from the text that the first three illustrations emphasize. Record the information for the class in a T-Chart. Encourage students to copy the information into their own T-Charts. Help students compare ideas in the text with ideas in the illustrations.

Expand the activity by having students work independently or with a partner to find information about winter in the last paragraphs and the last illustration.

✔ **INDEPENDENT PRACTICE** Have students briefly summarize the text, explaining its key ideas and telling how these ideas are supported by the illustrations.

IF... students have difficulty identifying key ideas,
THEN... help them identify information that is presented in both the text and the illustrations. Point out that repeated or highlighted information provides a clue to the key ideas.

Lesson 44 **Understand Illustrations in a Text**

Change of Season

There are four seasons. They are spring, summer, fall, and winter. What happens in each season? The magic of nature happens. Each season is special.

In spring, the air gets warmer. It rains. The rain feeds the plants. Everything turns green.

Ideas from Text	Ideas from Illustrations

Lesson 44 Understand Illustrations in a Text

In spring, the air gets warmer. It rains. The rain feeds the plants. Everything turns green.

People plant seeds in their gardens. Seeds sprout and plants start to grow. Flowers bloom. Grass covers your yard. Trees get their leaves.

Birds lay and hatch their eggs. Animal babies are born. Days get longer.

Lesson 44 Understand Illustrations in a Text

Next comes summer. The sun shines bright and warms the air. Oceans and lakes warm up as the sun hits the water. Flowers keep blooming. Vegetables grow and soon they are ready to eat.

Trees give shade from the hot sun. Sometimes it thunders and rains hard. Lightning strikes. Weather can be hot and sunny. It can be rainy and wild, too.

Lesson 44 Understand Illustrations in a Text

As summer ends, fall begins. Days grow shorter. Vegetables stop growing, and plants start to die. Grass turns brown. Flowers quit blooming. The leaves turn bright colors before they drop from trees.

Many birds fly south. Animals collect food to get ready for winter. The weather changes. Some days are sunny and warm. Others are cool and windy.

By the end of fall, the wind blows from the north. It gets so cold it could snow. Fall reminds you winter is coming.

Lesson 45 Determine Reasons

DIRECTIONS Follow along as your teacher reads aloud "Breakfast Is Best." Look for important points and the reasons that support them.

Breakfast Is Best

Breakfast is the best meal of the day.

Breakfast gets my day off to a great start. A healthy breakfast gives my body what it needs to grow. Breakfast gives me energy to get ready for school. Eating breakfast helps keep me awake. With a full stomach, I can listen and learn.

I can eat my favorite foods at breakfast. Some mornings I eat cereal with milk. Some mornings I eat toast with jelly. Some mornings I eat eggs and fruit. I can drink my favorite drinks, too. Some mornings I drink orange juice. Some mornings I drink apple juice. Some mornings I drink milk. These are my favorite foods and drinks.

It does not take too long to eat breakfast. I can eat a bowl of cereal or a piece of toast quickly. I make sure to chew every bite!

Lesson 45 **Determine Reasons**

Breakfast Is Best, *continued*

Breakfast is better than lunch. We eat lunch in the middle of the day. If I eat lunch at school, I do not get to have cereal or toast. I have to sit inside and wait. It takes a long time before the teachers let us outside to play. Lunch takes too much time.

Breakfast is better than dinner, too. We eat dinner at the end of the day. My whole family eats dinner together. We do not have cereal or toast for dinner. We do not drink orange juice for dinner. I have to sit at the table for a very long time. Dinner is even longer than lunch. My little brother chews with his mouth open. Yuck!

Breakfast is the best meal of the day. I can eat my favorite foods. I can drink my favorite drinks. Breakfast makes me feel good. And it doesn't take too long to eat breakfast!

Lesson 45 Determine Reasons

INTRODUCE Explain that opinion pieces tell how an author feels about a topic. Say: Authors should give reasons for their opinions. It is your job to find the opinions and decide if the reasons for them make sense.

MODEL Display the following section of "Breakfast Is Best" from Student Page S261. Read aloud as students follow along.

> **Breakfast Is Best**
>
> Breakfast is the best meal of the day. Breakfast gets my day off to a great start. A healthy breakfast gives my body what it needs to grow. Breakfast gives me energy to get ready for school. Eating breakfast helps keep me awake. With a full stomach, I can listen and learn.
>
> main opinion
>
> reasons
>
> important point

TEACH Reread the main opinion. Then say: The author believes "Breakfast Is Best." What important points does the author use to support this opinion? Draw students' attention to the highlighted text. The author claims, "Breakfast gets my day off to a great start." Let's look for reasons breakfast is a good start to the day.

Read the paragraph again. Underline and number each reason. One, breakfast gives the body what it needs to grow. Two, breakfast gives the author energy.

When you finish identifying reasons, model evaluating them. Ask: Are these good reasons the author likes breakfast best? I know that eating healthy food is good for you, and food gives you energy. I think those are good reasons to like breakfast.

Tell students they will reread the rest of the text later. They will continue marking up text to identify important points and reasons. Then they will learn to evaluate reasons.

RI.1.8 Identify the reasons an author gives to support points in a text. ***See also*** **L.1.5.a**

OBJECTIVES:

- Identify important points in an opinion text.
- Identify reasons that support important points.
- Ask questions to evaluate supporting reasons.

BUILD VOCABULARY

Word Categories

Point out the word *best* in the title and in the first sentence.

Say: By sorting words into groups, you can better understand what they have in common.

Read and display paragraph 2. Which word belongs in the same group as *best*? My favorite things are things I like best, so I will put *favorite* in the group. *Best* and *favorite* both describe good things.

Have students continue listing words for the *best* group from the rest of the opinion piece. Challenge them to arrange the linearly to show the relationships among the words and their meanings. Have volunteers explain the placements of their words.

Lesson 45 Determine Reasons

REMIND STUDENTS THAT...

- authors support their opinions with important points and reasons.
- most paragraphs share important points.
- they can identify important points by thinking about how ideas connect to the main opinion.

PRACTICE 1: Identify Important Points Remind students of the main opinion: "Breakfast is the best meal of the day." You already noted that "breakfast gets my day off to a great start" is an important point. What other important points can you find?

Display and distribute copies of Student Page S262. Read the excerpt aloud as students follow along.

important points

I can eat my favorite foods at breakfast. Some mornings I eat cereal with milk. Some mornings I eat toast with jelly. Some mornings I eat eggs and fruit. I can drink my favorite drinks, too. Some mornings I drink orange juice. Some mornings I drink apple juice. Some mornings I drink milk. These are my favorite foods and drinks.

It does not take too long to eat breakfast. I can eat a bowl of cereal or a piece of toast quickly. I make sure to chew every bite!

Say: Look at how the writing is divided into paragraphs. Authors often start a new paragraph when they want to share another important point. Look at the second paragraph of this excerpt. What is the most important point in it? Invite student input. To figure out the important points, ask, *Does this tell why breakfast is the best meal?* If you answer yes, then you have found an important point.

✔ **MONITOR PROGRESS** Instruct students to summarize the important points they have identified so far. Ask them to explain why the points are important.

IF... students have difficulty identifying important points,
THEN... have them read each paragraph slowly and find the sentence that directly supports the author's opinion.

Lesson 45 Determine Reasons

PRACTICE 2: Identify Supporting Reasons Tell students they will have more practice identifying important points and the reasons that support them.

Display and distribute Student Page S263. Display the main opinion, "Breakfast is the best meal of the day," on the board.

supporting reasons

Breakfast is better than lunch. We eat lunch in the middle of the day. If I eat lunch at school, I do not get to have cereal or toast. I have to sit inside and wait. It takes a long time before the teachers let us outside to play. Lunch takes too much time.

Breakfast is better than dinner, too. We eat dinner at the end of the day. My whole family eats dinner together. We do not have cereal or toast for dinner. We do not drink orange juice for dinner. I have to sit at the table for a very long time. Dinner is even longer than lunch. My little brother chews with his mouth open. Yuck!

Next, pair students and have them highlight the important point in the first paragraph. (Sentence 1) Say: Remember, the important point is that breakfast is better than lunch. What do you think the author will describe in this paragraph? Ask students to share their ideas.

Then say: Once you figure out the important point, look for the reasons the author includes to support that point. What is one reason the author does not like lunch as much as breakfast? Model underlining and numbering sentence 3. Say: The first reason the author does not like lunch is because the author does not get to eat cereal or toast. Have partners work together to continue finding evidence and marking up the first paragraph.

REMIND STUDENTS THAT...

- they can identify important points by thinking about how ideas connect to the main opinion.
- they should look for reasons that support important points.

✔ **MONITOR PROGRESS** Have students mark up the second paragraph on Student Page S263. Make sure students understand that this paragraph consists of reasons breakfast is better than dinner.

IF... students have difficulty identifying reasons,
THEN... ask, *Why does the author think breakfast is better than dinner?* Guide students to identify each answer given in the second paragraph.

Lesson 45 Determine Reasons

REMIND STUDENTS THAT...

- they can identify important points by thinking about how ideas connect to the main opinion.
- they can identify reasons that support important points.
- they can ask questions to evaluate the reasons the author gives.

PRACTICE 3: Ask Questions to Evaluate Supporting Reasons Review the important points and reasons students identified on Student Page S262. Display the marked up example on Student Page S264. Say: Today you will learn how to ask questions to evaluate the reasons the author used to support his or her opinion about breakfast.

important points

reasons

I can eat my favorite foods at breakfast. [1] Some mornings I eat cereal with milk. [2] Some mornings I eat toast with jelly. [3] Some mornings I eat eggs and fruit. I can drink my favorite drinks, too. [1] Some mornings I drink orange juice. [2] Some mornings I drink apple juice. [3] Some mornings I drink milk. These are my favorite foods and drinks.

It does not take too long to eat breakfast. [1] I can eat a bowl of cereal or a piece of toast quickly. I make sure to chew every bite!

Read aloud the first reason in the first paragraph of the excerpt, "Some mornings I eat cereal with milk." What does this tell you about why the author thinks breakfast is the best meal of the day? Allow students to respond. It tells that the author sometimes eats cereal for breakfast. This is a good reason because cereal is one of the author's favorite foods.

Continue asking questions about how each reason supports the important point. Help students understand that a good reason tells something specific about the important point. Encourage student participation in forming questions and answers.

✓ **INDEPENDENT PRACTICE** Read aloud the last paragraph of "Breakfast Is Best" from Teacher Page T260. Have students follow along and mark up the main point and supporting reasons in the paragraph. Then have them ask and answer questions to evaluate each reason.

IF... students have difficulty evaluating reasons,
THEN... help them create a question, such as *Does this tell how breakfast is best? How?*

Lesson 45 **Determine Reasons**

Breakfast Is Best

Breakfast is the best meal of the day.

Breakfast gets my day off to a great start. A healthy breakfast gives my body what it needs to grow. Breakfast gives me energy to get ready for school. Eating breakfast helps keep me awake. With a full stomach, I can listen and learn.

Lesson 45 Determine Reasons

I can eat my favorite foods at breakfast. Some mornings I eat cereal with milk. Some mornings I eat toast with jelly. Some mornings I eat eggs and fruit. I can drink my favorite drinks, too. Some mornings I drink orange juice. Some mornings I drink apple juice. Some mornings I drink milk. These are my favorite foods and drinks.

It does not take too long to eat breakfast. I can eat a bowl of cereal or a piece of toast quickly. I make sure to chew every bite!

Lesson 45 Determine Reasons

Breakfast is better than lunch. We eat lunch in the middle of the day. If I eat lunch at school, I do not get to have cereal or toast. I have to sit inside and wait. It takes a long time before the teachers let us outside to play. Lunch takes too much time.

Breakfast is better than dinner, too. We eat dinner at the end of the day. My whole family eats dinner together. We do not have cereal or toast for dinner. We do not drink orange juice for dinner. I have to sit at the table for a very long time. Dinner is even longer than lunch. My little brother chews with his mouth open. Yuck!

Lesson 45 **Determine Reasons**

I can eat my favorite foods at breakfast. **[1]** Some mornings I eat cereal with milk. **[2]** Some mornings I eat toast with jelly. **[3]** Some mornings I eat eggs and fruit. I can drink my favorite drinks, too. **[1]** Some mornings I drink orange juice. **[2]** Some mornings I drink apple juice. **[3]** Some mornings I drink milk. These are my favorite foods and drinks.

It does not take too long to eat breakfast. **[1]** I can eat a bowl of cereal or a piece of toast quickly. I make sure to chew every bite!

Breakfast Is Best

Breakfast is the best meal of the day. I can eat my favorite foods. I can drink my favorite drinks. Breakfast makes me feel good. And it doesn't take too long to eat breakfast!

Lesson 46 Compare Two Texts

DIRECTIONS Follow along as your teacher reads aloud "Good Morning" and "Good Night." Think about how the texts are similar and how they are different.

Good Morning
by Ericka Gordon

Morning is my favorite time. I really like sunny mornings. Rainy mornings are okay, too. I am happy to start the day. Mornings are exciting and fun.

I love my bed. My blanket is warm. My pillow is soft. The sun shines on my bed in the morning. I can make shadow puppets on the wall. Waking up is fun.

I get up and eat a delicious breakfast. Dad makes eggs and toast. Mom gives me yogurt and bananas. Breakfast is my favorite meal.

I pick out my clothes. I love my dinosaur shirt. Mom or Dad helps me get dressed. My dog steals my socks. I chase him. I grab my socks. We play and laugh.

I am ready to go to school. What fun it will be! I wait for the bus. My best friend rides the same bus. We play games and talk. Morning is the best part of the day.

Lesson 46 Compare Two Texts

Good Night
by Roberto Garcia

The day is over. Homework is done. Chores are done. I can relax. I like getting ready for bed. It is time for rest. Night is the best part of the day.

Before bed I have a bath. I soak in the warm water. Bubbles tickle my nose. I scrub off the dirty day. I am squeaky clean.

After my bath, I put on pajamas. I get in bed. I love my bed. It feels warm and soft. My cat curls up with me. It feels great to lie down. I am tired. Bedtime is the best.

Dad reads me a book. Sometimes Mom tells me a story. We talk about the day. I tell what I liked best. We make plans for tomorrow.

The lights are out. I hear my cat purr. The soft covers are snuggly. I close my eyes and fall asleep. Good dreams are coming. What a great time night is!

Lesson 46 Compare Two Texts

INTRODUCE Tell students they will learn to compare and contrast texts. Say: First, you need to find texts that share a topic. Then you can look for ways the texts are the same and ways they are different.

MODEL Display and read aloud Student Page S267.

Good Morning

Morning is my favorite time. I really like sunny mornings. Rainy mornings are okay, too. I am happy to start the day. Mornings are exciting and fun.

Each text tells the author's favorite time of day.

Good Night

The day is over. Homework is done. Chores are done. I can relax. I like getting ready for bed. It is time for rest. Night is the best part of the day.

TEACH After reading, model identifying the shared topic. One text is called "Good Morning," and the other is "Good Night." The first part of each text tells which time of the day the author likes best. The shared topic is "The best time of day." One likes morning, and the other likes night. Create a Three-Column Chart and record the shared topic. Have students create their own charts.

Good Morning	Both	Good Night
Morning is best.	the best time of day	Night is best.
like sunny and rainy mornings	tell how they feel	homework, chores are done
happy to start the day		can relax and rest

Continue the comparison by discussing the ideas each author shares. The author of "Good Morning" describes the type of mornings she likes. In "Good Night," on the other hand, the author tells why he likes nights. They both tell how they feel. Model filling the information into the chart.

RI.1.9 Identify basic similarities in and differences between two texts on the same topic (e.g., in illustrations, descriptions, or procedures).

OBJECTIVES:
- Identify texts with similar topics.
- Compare texts to identify similarities.
- Contrast texts to identify differences.

BUILD VOCABULARY

Real-Life Connections

Point out the words *exciting* and *fun* in "Good Morning."

Say: If I connect words in a text to my life, I will better understand the text.

The first author writes, "Mornings are exciting and fun." What exciting and fun things do I do in the morning? I go to the gym. I exercise and talk to my friends there. That is fun. I think about the good things that might happen today. That is exciting.

Have students use the same strategy to list things that are "relaxing" to help them understand how the author of "Good Night" feels.

Lesson 46 Compare Two Texts

REMIND STUDENTS THAT...

- some texts share the same topic.
- topics do not have to be the same to compare and contrast texts.
- texts with shared topics can have other similarities.

PRACTICE 1: Compare Texts Review Student Page S267 and students' charts. Say: When looking for texts with shared topics, you have to think about the big picture. Here, the big picture is "the best time of day." Now you can look for how each author uses reasons to explain why morning or night is best. You can also see how the writing is similar and different. Let's start by looking for things that are the same.

Display and distribute Student Page S268. Read aloud as students follow along.

Good Morning

I love my bed. My blanket is warm. My pillow is soft. The sun shines on my bed in the morning. I can make shadow puppets on the wall. Waking up is fun.

Good Night

After my bath, I put on pajamas. I get in bed. I love my bed. It feels warm and soft. My cat curls up with me. It feels great to lie down. I am tired. Bedtime is the best.

Have students return to their charts. Ask: What is one thing that is similar in both passages? Circle "I love my bed" in both passages. Model recording it in the chart.

Pair students. Say: Look for and write other things that are similar. Look for words, but also think about big ideas and the way information is shared.

✔ **MONITOR PROGRESS** Have each student name one shared element. Invite students to share their charts.

IF... students have difficulty identifying similarities,
THEN... guide identification by asking questions: *Which words appear in both passages? What types of reasons do the authors use?*

Lesson 46 Compare Two Texts

PRACTICE 2: Contrast Texts Briefly review students' charts. Say: You have found things that are similar. Now you'll learn to find things that are different.

Display and distribute Student Page S269. Read aloud the first set of paragraphs as students follow along.

Good Morning

I get up and eat a delicious breakfast. Dad makes eggs and toast. Mom gives me yogurt and bananas. Breakfast is my favorite meal.

Good Night

Before bed I have a bath. I soak in the warm water. Bubbles tickle my nose. I scrub off the dirty day. I am squeaky clean.

Explain that identifying differences can be more challenging than similarities. Say: Think about the big picture to find differences. Let's start by telling what each paragraph describes. "Good Morning" describes what happens *after* the author gets *out* of bed. "Good Night" tells what happens *before* the author gets *into* bed. Model recording the ideas.

Distribute Teacher Pages T265–T266, and pair students. Have them read the fourth paragraphs of "Good Morning" and "Good Night." Say: Look for differences. Write them in your charts.

✔ **MONITOR PROGRESS** Have students identify and share another difference between the texts.

IF... students have difficulty identifying differences,
THEN... have them write one-sentence paragraph summaries for each text. They can contrast the summaries to identify differences in content.

REMIND STUDENTS THAT...

- some texts share the same topic.
- texts with shared topics can have other similarities.
- texts with shared topics have differences.

Lesson 46 Compare Two Texts

REMIND STUDENTS THAT...

- some texts share the same topic.
- texts with shared topics can have other similarities as well as differences.
- comparing texts helps the reader better understand them.

PRACTICE 3: Compare and Contrast Texts Say: Identifying similarities and differences between texts can help you better understand the authors' ideas. First you will work independently to identify things that are the same and different. Then the class will talk about how looking at these things helped you understand the texts.

Distribute Student Page S270.

Good Morning

I am ready to go to school. What fun it will be! I wait for the bus. My best friend rides the same bus. We play games and talk. Morning is the best part of the day.

Good Night

The lights are out. I hear my cat purr. The soft covers are snuggly. I close my eyes and fall asleep. Good dreams are coming. What a great time night is!

✔ **INDEPENDENT PRACTICE** Instruct students to independently identify at least two similarities and two differences in the paragraphs and record them in their charts.

After students finish the Independent Practice, discuss students' findings. Ask: What did you learn from comparing the texts? What types of reasons did the authors give? Did both authors use plenty of reasons to support their opinions? Which author do you think made the best argument? Why?

IF... students have difficulty answering the questions,
THEN... suggest they review their completed charts to determine what they learned.

Lesson 46 Compare Two Texts

Good Morning

Morning is my favorite time. I really like sunny mornings. Rainy mornings are okay, too. I am happy to start the day. Mornings are exciting and fun.

Good Night

The day is over. Homework is done. Chores are done. I can relax. I like getting ready for bed. It is time for rest. Night is the best part of the day.

Good Morning	Both	Good Night

Lesson 46 Compare Two Texts

Good Morning

I love my bed. My blanket is warm. My pillow is soft. The sun shines on my bed in the morning. I can make shadow puppets on the wall. Waking up is fun.

Good Night

After my bath, I put on pajamas. I get in bed. I love my bed. It feels warm and soft. My cat curls up with me. It feels great to lie down. I am tired. Bedtime is the best.

Lesson 46 Compare Two Texts

Good Morning

I get up and eat a delicious breakfast. Dad makes eggs and toast. Mom gives me yogurt and bananas. Breakfast is my favorite meal.

Good Night

Before bed I have a bath. I soak in the warm water. Bubbles tickle my nose. I scrub off the dirty day. I am squeaky clean.

Lesson 46 Compare Two Texts

Good Morning

I am ready to go to school. What fun it will be! I wait for the bus. My best friend rides the same bus. We play games and talk. Morning is the best part of the day.

Good Night

The lights are out. I hear my cat purr. The soft covers are snuggly. I close my eyes and fall asleep. Good dreams are coming. What a great time night is!

ASSESSMENT
LESSONS 44–46

Reading Informational Text

ASSESS MASTERY Use this Checkpoint to assess students' mastery of the Level B Reading standards listed here.

ADMINISTER THE TEST Administer the Checkpoint orally to each student.

1. Read aloud the story on the following page.
2. Read questions 1–5 and have students respond. Check their answers using the Scoring chart.

SCORING

SKILL/LESSON	STANDARD	ANSWER	SCORING
1. Understand Illustrations in Text (Lesson 44)	**RI.1.6**	going down a slide	_____ / 1
2. Understand Illustrations in Text (Lesson 44)	**RI.1.7**	Playing outside is good exercise and is fun.	_____ / 1
3. Determine Reasons (Lesson 45)	**RI.1.8**	Moving around is important; the library has information about different subjects.	_____ / 2
4. Determine Reasons (Lesson 45)	**RI.1.8**	Possible answers: is good exercise, is fun; has different information, is quiet, read whatever you want	_____ / 2
5. Compare Two Texts (Lesson 46)	**RI.1.9**	Both are about taking a break from school/class; one is about recess, the other is about the library.	_____ / 2

An overall score of 80% is typically considered mastery. Use your judgment and your individual students' needs as well to determine skill mastery.

IF... you determine that students have not demonstrated sufficient mastery of one or more skills,
THEN... review needed skills, going back to the lessons to reteach and scaffold as needed.

RI.1.6 Distinguish between information provided by pictures or other illustrations and information provided by the words in a text.

RI.1.7 Use the illustrations and details in a text to describe its key ideas.

RI.1.8 Identify the reasons an author gives to support points in a text.

RI.1.9 Identify basic similarities in and differences between two texts on the same topic (e.g., in illustrations, descriptions, or procedures).

ASSESSMENT
LESSONS 44–46

Reading Informational Text

Yes to Recess

School is for learning. But taking a break is important. Recess is a great break. Moving around is important!

Playing outside is great exercise. You can run, shout, and jump rope. You can race, play ball, or climb a tree. Exercise will keep you fit and it's fun!

Yes to the Library

Learning in class is important. But you can't learn everything in class. The library has information about different subjects.

The library gives you a break from class. It is quiet and you can read about whatever you want. The library will exercise your brain.

1. What idea does the picture show that the text does not?
2. What is a key idea that the text and picture share?
3. What are the most important points in each text?
4. What reason supports each important point?
5. How are the texts similar? How are they different?

Lesson 47 Use a Prompt to Identify a Writing Topic

INTRODUCE Say: Writing assignments contain instructions you should follow. The assignments also give you the topic about which to write.

MODEL Distribute Student Page S273 for students. Read aloud the prompt and complete the chart together.

Opinion Writing

Prompt: Write an opinion piece about why people should learn more about animals that live in their area.

What kind of writing is it?	What is the topic?	Are there details I must include?
opinion piece	why people should learn more about animals that live in their area	yes: reasons that support my opinion

TEACH Say: When you get a writing assignment, you have to figure out exactly what to do. First, make sure you understand all parts of the assignment. Read the prompt again. In this assignment, what is your purpose, or reason for writing? (to give an opinion) What are you supposed to give an opinion about? (why people should learn more about animals that live in their area) *Why people should learn more about animals that live in their area* is the topic of the assignment.

Ask: Do you think people should learn more about animals that live in their area, or not? Why do you think that? Reread the prompt and have students discuss their thoughts with you, with a partner, or in a group. Point out that the prompt assumes students will agree that people should learn more about these animals. If students disagree with that assumption, they should give reasons for people not to learn more.

W.1.1 Write opinion pieces in which they introduce the topic or name the book they are writing about, state an opinion, supply a reason for the opinion, and provide some sense of closure.

W.1.2 Write informative/explanatory texts in which they name a topic, supply some facts about the topic, and provide some sense of closure.

W.1.3 Write narratives in which they recount two or more appropriately sequenced events, include some details regarding what happened, use temporal words to signal event order, and provide some sense of closure.

W.1.5 With guidance and support from adults, focus on a topic, respond to questions and suggestions from peers, and add details to strengthen writing as needed.

OBJECTIVES:

- Find the key parts of a writing prompt.
- Determine a topic from a writing prompt.

Lesson 47 Use a Prompt to Identify a Writing Topic

REMIND STUDENTS THAT...

- they can look at each part of a writing assignment.
- they can determine the topic of a writing assignment.

PRACTICE 1: Opinion Writing Say: Review each part of a writing assignment to be sure you know what it says. Distribute or display Student Page S274. Read the prompt aloud.

Opinion Writing

Prompt: Write an opinion piece about what kind of exercise is the most fun. Include reasons to support your opinion.

Ask: You know that the prompt contains the word *opinion*. What should the opinion be about? Focus attention on the phrase "kind of exercise." Brainstorm with students several kinds of exercise, such as playing on a sports team, dancing, and indoor exercise routines. Reread the prompt. Choose the kind of exercise that you think is the most *fun*. Your opinion will be based on your own experiences. When you know your opinion, think of reasons you can give to explain it.

✔ **MONITOR PROGRESS** Using the prompt above, have students fill in the chart on Student Page S274. You may wish to read the prompt and chart headings aloud and have students respond orally if needed.

What kind of writing is it?	What is the topic?	Are there details I must include?
opinion piece	what kind of exercise is the most fun	yes: reasons that support my opinion

IF... students cannot identify that the topic is the kind of exercise they find most fun,
THEN... reread the prompt and ask: How does the assignment say you should choose a kind of exercise to write about?

Lesson 47 Use a Prompt to Identify a Writing Topic

PRACTICE 2: Informative/Explanatory Writing Say: Assignments often give you tips to help you think about the topic. When you read an assignment and find the topic, look for instructions that will help you focus on the topic and write about it.

Distribute or display Student Page S275 and read it aloud.

Informative/Explanatory Writing

Prompt: Write an informative/explanatory text about where you live. How would you describe it to someone who has never been there? What information could you include that might show readers why your town or city is so interesting?

Ask: What is the topic? (where I live) What tips does the assignment give to help you write about the topic? Guide students to understand that the assignment asks them to imagine a reader who is a person who has never visited the town or city.

REMIND STUDENTS THAT...

- they can analyze a writing assignment piece by piece.
- they can determine the topic of a writing assignment.

MONITOR PROGRESS Using the prompt above, have students complete the chart on Student Page S275. You may wish to read the prompt and chart headings aloud and have students respond orally if needed. Encourage them to pay extra attention to the third column.

What kind of writing is it?	What is the topic?	Are there tips to help me focus on the topic?
informative/ explanatory (describe)	where I live	yes: describe it to someone who has never been there; encourage a person to visit

IF... students do not understand how the tips will help them focus their writing, THEN... pose several questions to demonstrate what the prompt does *not* ask, such as Are you writing for your friends and neighbors? Are you telling about problems in your town or city?

Lesson 47 Use a Prompt to Identify a Writing Topic

REMIND STUDENTS THAT...

- they can analyze a writing assignment piece by piece.
- they can determine the topic of a writing assignment.
- assignments often include tips that help writers focus on the topic.

PRACTICE 3: Narrative Writing Say: Writing assignments often include ideas or questions to help you start. When the assignment is to write a story, for example, it might include some ideas for the characters or events that happen in the story. Distribute or display Student Page S276 and read it aloud.

Narrative Writing

Prompt: Write a story about a child with an invisible friend. What kind of adventures would they have? Think about what problems they might have because one of them is invisible.

Guide students to recognize the topic as "a child with an invisible friend." How many characters are in the story? (two) What ideas does the assignment give for events in the story? (the pair's adventures; problems because one of them is invisible)

✓ **INDEPENDENT PRACTICE** Using the prompt above, have students complete the chart on Student Page S276. You may wish to read the prompt and chart headings aloud and have students respond orally if needed.

What kind of writing is it?	What is the topic?	Are there tips to help me focus on the topic?
narrative (story)	a child with an invisible friend	yes: adventures; problems they might have because one of them is invisible

IF... students have difficulty identifying the topic,
THEN... pose questions to help them focus on the characters, such as Whose adventures should the story be about?

Lesson 47 **Use a Prompt to Identify a Writing Topic**

Opinion Writing

Prompt: Write an opinion piece about why people should learn more about animals that live in their area.

What kind of writing is it?	What is the topic?	Are there details I must include?

Lesson 47 **Use a Prompt to Identify a Writing Topic**

Opinion Writing

Prompt: Write an opinion piece about what kind of exercise is the most fun. Include reasons to support your opinion.

What kind of writing is it?	What is the topic?	Are there details I must include?

Lesson 47 Use a Prompt to Identify a Writing Topic

Informative/Explanatory Writing

Prompt: Write an informative/explanatory text about where you live. How would you describe it to someone who has never been there? What information could you include that might show readers why your town or city is so interesting?

What kind of writing is it?	What is the topic?	Are there tips to help me focus on the topic?

Lesson 47 Use a Prompt to Identify a Writing Topic

Narrative Writing

Prompt: Write a story about a child with an invisible friend. What kind of adventures would they have? Think about what problems they might have because one of them is invisible.

What kind of writing is it?	What is the topic?	Are there tips to help me focus on the topic?

Lesson 48 Recall and Gather Information About a Topic

INTRODUCE Say: School assignments will ask you to write about a topic. Usually, you will already know something about the topic.

MODEL Distribute Student Page S277 and read the prompt aloud.

Opinion Writing

Prompt: Write an opinion piece about why people should learn more about animals that live in their area.

My area ______________________________

Animals that live in the area __________

What I already know _______________

Where to get more information _________

TEACH Say: To write about a topic, first think about what you already know. In an opinion piece, you will need to include information connected to reasons. Discuss the first two items with students and have them agree on information to include. Ask: What else do you already know? Have students share answers. Then briefly brainstorm additional sources of information.

Help students focus on the prompt. Remember that this assignment asks for an opinion. Decide before you write: Should people know about animals in the area? Why or why not? After students respond, guide them to recognize that what they already know, as well as the availability of additional information, has helped them form their opinions on this topic.

W.1.5 With guidance and support from adults, focus on a topic, respond to questions and suggestions from peers, and add details to strengthen writing as needed.

W.1.8 With guidance and support from adults, recall information from experiences or gather information from provided sources to answer a question.

See also W.1.1, W.1.2, W.1.3

OBJECTIVES:

- Focus on the topic of a prompt.
- Recall information from experiences.
- Identify possible sources of additional information.

Lesson 48 Recall and Gather Information About a Topic

REMIND STUDENTS THAT...

- they can focus on the topic of an assignment.
- they can recall information about the topic from their own experiences.
- they can think of sources of additional information about the topic.

PRACTICE 1: Opinion Writing Say: You may already know a lot about the topic of a writing assignment. If you don't know much about the topic, you can think of ways to find information.

Distribute or display Student Page S278 and read the prompt aloud.

Opinion Writing

Prompt: Write an opinion piece about what kind of exercise is the most fun. Include reasons to support your opinion.

Ask: What does this assignment ask you to do? (give my opinion about what kind of exercise is the most fun) *Exercise* means to actively move the body. When have you had fun exercising? Have students recall fun, active experiences. Then ask: If you wanted to learn new information about the topic, how could you find out more about fun kinds of exercise? Guide students to suggest that they might ask other people about their experiences or explore books, pictures, or video of people who are having fun while exercising.

MONITOR PROGRESS Using the prompt above, have students complete the following sentence frames from Student Page S278.

My fun exercise experiences include _______.

The kind of exercise I think is the most fun is _______.

I think this kind of exercise is the most fun because _______.

IF... students do not choose a single kind of exercise to write about, THEN... have them list words and phrases that explain why one or two kinds of exercise are fun, and then select the exercise activity that goes with the longest list.

Lesson 48 Recall and Gather Information About a Topic

PRACTICE 2: Informative/Explanatory Writing Say: You may already know about the topic of a writing assignment. However, the assignment may ask you to include details that you don't know much about. In that case, you can find information in sources. Distribute or display Student Page S279 and read it aloud.

Informative/Explanatory Writing

Prompt: Write an informative/explanatory text about where you live. How would you describe it to someone who has never been there? What information could you include that might show readers why your town or city is so interesting?

Say: You definitely know something about this topic, even if you just moved here! The assignment asks you to give information. You can focus the information to inform and interest a person who has not been here before. Have students offer ideas of information to include.

Read the prompt aloud again. Display sources, such as the website for a local library, a pamphlet for a museum, or pictures of a local park. What details from these sources about events and attractions would encourage someone to visit? Guide students to identify information in the sources that is relevant to the writing assignment.

REMIND STUDENTS THAT...

- they can focus on the topic of an assignment.
- they can recall information about the topic from their own experiences.
- they can think of sources of additional information about the topic.

✔ **MONITOR PROGRESS** Using the prompt above, have students complete the following sentence frames from Student Page S279.

A good place to find information about our area is _______.
Someone who has never been here should know that _______.
A very interesting fact about our area is _______.

IF... students have trouble using a source to select information for their writing,
THEN... have them practice posing and responding to questions using information gathered from an outside source.

Lesson 48 Recall and Gather Information About a Topic

REMIND STUDENTS THAT...

- they can focus on the topic of an assignment.
- they can recall information about the topic from their own experiences.
- they can think of sources of additional information about the topic.

PRACTICE 3: Narrative Writing Say: You may already know some information that can help you write about a topic. For example, you can use your experiences to imagine events for a story. Display or distribute Student Page S280 and read it aloud.

> **Narrative Writing**
>
> **Prompt:** Write a story about a child with an invisible friend. What kind of adventures would they have? Think about what problems they might have because one of them is invisible.

Say: The topic of this assignment is a pair of friends. What is unusual about this pair? (One of them is invisible.) What ideas does the assignment give for events the story could include? (adventures; problems the friends might have because one of them is invisible)

Have a volunteer name an activity that friends do together. Ask: What would that activity be like if one person could move and talk but was invisible? After some discussion, ask: What would be a problem for an invisible person doing that activity? What would be a problem for the invisible person's friends? Encourage discussion.

✓ **INDEPENDENT PRACTICE** Using the prompt above, have students complete the following sentence frames from Student Page S280.

> I can tell about two friends having an adventure when they ______.
>
> An invisible person would make that adventure ______.
>
> The friends would have a problem when ______.

IF... students struggle to identify relevant experiences,
THEN... have them describe books they have read or stories they know that feature a pair of friends doing activities together.

Lesson 48 **Recall and Gather Information About a Topic**

Opinion Writing

Prompt: Write an opinion piece about why people should learn more about animals that live in their area.

My area ____________________

Animals that live in the area ____________________

____

What I already know ____________________

____

Where to get more information ____________________

____

Lesson 48 **Recall and Gather Information About a Topic**

Opinion Writing

Prompt: Write an opinion piece about what kind of exercise is the most fun. Include reasons to support your opinion.

My fun exercise experiences include ______________________________

____.

The kind of exercise I think is the most fun is _____________________

____.

I think this kind of exercise is the most fun because _______________

____.

Lesson 48 **Recall and Gather Information About a Topic**

Informative/Explanatory Writing

Prompt: Write an informative/explanatory text about where you live. How would you describe it to someone who has never been there? What information could you include that might show readers why your town or city is so interesting?

A good place to find information about our area is ______________

____.

Someone who has never been here should know that ______________

____.

A very interesting fact about our area is ______________

____.

Lesson 48 **Recall and Gather Information About a Topic**

Narrative Writing

Prompt: Write a story about a child with an invisible friend. What kind of adventures would they have? Think about what problems they might have because one of them is invisible.

I can tell about two friends having an adventure when they ______

______________________________.

An invisible person would make that adventure ______________

______________________________.

The friends would have a problem when ________________

______________________________.

Lesson 49 Add Specific Details to Support Ideas

INTRODUCE Say: You can strengthen your writing by adding details.

MODEL Distribute Student Page S281 and read the prompt aloud. Then have students read the student draft aloud with you.

Opinion Writing

Prompt: Write an opinion piece about why people should learn more about animals that live in their area.

Draft: I think people should learn more about animals that live in their area. They should learn more so they can protect the animals.

TEACH Say: This draft is a good start, but more detail would make it more interesting to read. To find details to add, the writer could answer questions about the draft. What questions could we ask? Reread the second sentence of the draft. Here's a question: *Why do animals need protection?* Pause for responses. The writer could tell *why*. That would make the writing stronger.

Say: A good way to add details is to add examples. The writer could begin a new sentence with "For example." After that, the writer could add "animals might need protection wherever new buildings are being built." Read aloud the following updated draft:

Updated Draft: I think people should learn more about animals that live in their area. They should learn more so they can protect the animals. For example, animals might need protection wherever new buildings are being built.

W.1.5 With guidance and support from adults, focus on a topic, respond to questions and suggestions from peers, and add details to strengthen writing as needed.

See also **W.1.1, W.1.2, W.1.3**

OBJECTIVES:

- Identify opportunities to add details to writing.
- Identify details that will strengthen writing.

Lesson 49 Add Specific Details to Support Ideas

REMIND STUDENTS THAT...

- they can strengthen their writing by adding details.
- asking and answering questions will help them decide where to add details.
- asking and answering questions will also help them think of details to add.

PRACTICE 1: Opinion Writing Say: In opinion writing, add details, such as facts and examples, to support your opinion. Distribute or display Student Page S282 and read it aloud with students.

Opinion Writing

Prompt: Write an opinion piece about what kind of exercise is the most fun. Include reasons to support your opinion.

Draft: Exercising alone is the most fun. This is because you can always try to do better than you did the last time.

Ask: What questions do you have for this writer? Help students identify details that are missing from the draft, such as *What type of exercise? (yoga? shooting baskets? swimming? running?)* and *How can you determine whether you did better?* Point out that the writer could replace *Exercising* with a more specific kind of exercise. The writer could also replace *do better* with a more specific detail about improving.

MONITOR PROGRESS Have students revise the draft above by replacing *Exercising* and *do better* with specific details. Use the following sentence frames from Student Page S282:

_______ alone is the most fun. This is because you can always try to _______ than you did the last time.

IF... students struggle with adding details by answering questions,
THEN... guide them to pose questions and then answer the questions by rephrasing the question in the form of a statement and adding a detail.

Lesson 49 Add Specific Details to Support Ideas

PRACTICE 2: Informative/Explanatory Writing Say: In informative writing, add details, such as facts, examples, and descriptions, to strengthen your writing. Distribute or display Student Page S283 and read it aloud with students.

Informative/Explanatory Writing

Prompt: Write an informative/explanatory text about where you live. How would you describe it to someone who has never been there? What information could you include that might show readers why your town or city is so interesting?

Draft: I live in Smithtown. It started as a place for cowboys to rest during cattle drives. There are ranches all around. Visitors come to see the rodeo each summer.

Say: The assignment asks for a description. Does the draft help us form a clear picture of Smithtown in our minds? What could we ask the writer to describe? Give other examples for students, such as additional facts, examples, and other details. Encourage students to suggest several questions for the writer.

MONITOR PROGRESS Have students pose three questions to the writer of the draft above that would elicit a description, an example, and an explanation to make the draft stronger. Help students record their questions using the following checklist from Student Page S283.

- ☐ Description ______________________________
- ☐ Example ______________________________
- ☐ Explanation ______________________________

IF... students struggle to generate questions,
THEN... remind them of the 5Ws and H, and help them use those words to form questions such as How do people in Smithtown spend their weekends?

REMIND STUDENTS THAT...

- they can strengthen their writing by adding details.
- asking and answering questions will help them decide where to add details.
- asking and answering questions will also help them think of details to add.

Lesson 49 Add Specific Details to Support Ideas

REMIND STUDENTS THAT...

- they can strengthen their writing by adding details.
- details may include facts, examples, explanations, and descriptions.

PRACTICE 3: Narrative Writing Say: Descriptive details that appeal to the five senses make stories stronger. They help readers imagine the setting, characters, and events. Distribute or display Student Page S284. Read the draft aloud.

Narrative Writing

Prompt: Write a story about a child with an invisible friend. What kind of adventures would they have? Think about what problems they might have because one of them is invisible.

Draft: Jay and his invisible friend Lyle like the state fair. They go on rides together, but they only pay for one seat. They are waiting for the Ferris wheel to start and someone tries to sit in Lyle's seat! Lyle yells "ouch!" and the person gets scared and jumps out.

Remind students that readers learn about characters from how they look, what they say, and how others respond to them. Ask: What details could the writer add about the characters?

✔ **INDEPENDENT PRACTICE** Have students suggest a detail about the setting and a detail about the events in the story that would make the story stronger. Help students record details using the following checklist from Student Page S284.

- ☐ Detail about the setting ____________________
- ☐ Detail about the event ____________________

IF... students have difficulty suggesting a new detail about events,
THEN... have them imagine the steps the friends followed to get into their seats, and help them turn the steps into a detail for the story.

Lesson 49 Add Specific Details to Support Ideas

Opinion Writing

Prompt: Write an opinion piece about why people should learn more about animals that live in their area.

Draft: I think people should learn more about animals that live in their area. They should learn more so they can protect the animals.

Updated Draft: I think people should learn more about animals that live in their area. They should learn more so they can protect the animals. For example, animals might need protection wherever new buildings are being built.

Lesson 49 **Add Specific Details to Support Ideas**

Opinion Writing

Prompt: Write an opinion piece about what kind of exercise is the most fun. Include reasons to support your opinion.

Draft: Exercising alone is the most fun. This is because you can always try to do better than you did the last time.

____________________ alone is the most fun. This is because you can always try to ____________________ than you did the last time.

Lesson 49 **Add Specific Details to Support Ideas**

Informative/Explanatory Writing

Prompt: Write an informative/explanatory text about where you live. How would you describe it to someone who has never been there? What information could you include that might show readers why your town or city is so interesting?

Draft: I live in Smithtown. It started as a place for cowboys to rest during cattle drives. There are ranches all around. Visitors come to see the rodeo each summer.

- ☐ Description ______________________
- ☐ Example ______________________
- ☐ Explanation ______________________

Lesson 49 **Add Specific Details to Support Ideas**

Narrative Writing

Prompt: Write a story about a child with an invisible friend. What kind of adventures would they have? Think about what problems they might have because one of them is invisible.

Draft: Jay and his invisible friend Lyle like the state fair. They go on rides together, but they only pay for one seat. They are waiting for the Ferris wheel to start and someone tries to sit in Lyle's seat! Lyle yells "ouch!" and the person gets scared and jumps out.

☐ Detail about the setting ______________________________

☐ Detail about the event ______________________________

ASSESSMENT Writing

LESSONS 47–49

ASSESS MASTERY Use this Checkpoint to assess students' mastery of the Level B Writing standards listed here.

ADMINISTER THE TEST Administer the Checkpoint orally to each student.

1. Read aloud the prompt on the following page.
2. Read questions 1–3 and have students respond. Check their answers using the Scoring chart.
3. Read aloud the draft on the following page and have students respond to question 4. Check their answers using the Scoring chart.

SCORING

SKILL/LESSON	STANDARD	ANSWER	SCORING
1. Use a Prompt to Identify a Writing Topic (Lesson 47)	**W.1.3** **W.1.5**	narrative	_____ / 1
2. Use a Prompt to Identify a Writing Topic (Lesson 47)	**W.1.3** **W.1.5**	an adventure of pet animals; where they live, problems or dangers they might encounter	_____ / 2
3. Recall and Gather Information About a Topic (Lesson 48)	**W.1.3** **W.1.5** **W.1.8**	having or reading about pet animals	_____ / 1
4. Add Specific Details to Support Ideas (Lesson 49)	**W.1.3** **W.1.5**	a description of the danger the gerbil faced	_____ / 1

An overall score of 80% is typically considered mastery. Use your judgment and your individual students' needs as well to determine skill mastery.

IF... you determine that students have not demonstrated sufficient mastery of one or more skills,
THEN... review needed skills, going back to the lessons to reteach and scaffold as needed.

W.1.3 Write narratives in which they recount two or more appropriately sequenced events, include some details regarding what happened, use temporal words to signal event order, and provide some sense of closure.

W.1.5 With guidance and support from adults, focus on a topic, respond to questions and suggestions from peers, and add details to strengthen writing as needed.

W.1.8 With guidance and support from adults, recall information from experiences or gather information from provided sources to answer a question.

ASSESSMENT
LESSONS 47–49

Writing

Prompt: Write an adventure narrative about some pet animals. Consider where they live and what problems or dangers they might encounter.

Draft: The gerbil and the cat wanted an adventure. The gerbil got on the cat's back. The cat ran down the stairs. The gerbil fell off! The cat didn't notice and ran out the door.

1. What kind of writing does the assignment call for?
2. What is the topic, and what tips will help writers focus on the topic?
3. Which experiences would help you write about the characters in this story?
4. Which one of the following details should be added to make the draft stronger?

   a description of the staircase
   a description of the danger the gerbil faced
   an example of another adventure the animals have had
   facts about the animals' ages

Lesson 50 Use Subject-Verb Agreement

INTRODUCE Read aloud and discuss the definitions for *subject, singular subject, plural subject, pronoun,* and *verb.* Say: Today you will practice matching subjects and verbs.

MODEL Display or distribute Student Page S287 and read it aloud. Ask: What is this text about? (pets)

Pets

Ana thinks cats are great pets. She calls her cat Puff. Puff purrs. Ana pets his soft fur.

Jim likes dogs more than cats. Jim and his dogs play ball. He throws the ball into the air. The dogs jump up to catch it. Then they bark.

Ted had a pet bird. One day, he took the bird outside. It flew away. Ted will keep his next bird inside!

TEACH Point out the subject *Ana* in the first sentence. Ana is one person, so the subject is singular. A singular subject needs a singular verb. Then point out the verb *thinks.* Singular verbs that tell what happens in the present end in *s* or *es. Thinks* ends in an *s*, so it matches the singular subject *Ana.* Repeat this process for the next three sentences.

Then say: Plural verbs that tell what happens in the present do not end in *s* or *es.* Point out that *Jim and his dogs* is a plural subject. Tell students that two nouns connected by *and* form a plural subject. The subject *dogs* in the eighth sentence is a plural subject, too. The verbs play and jump are plural verbs that match the plural subjects.

Point out that the verbs in the last paragraph describe actions in the past or future. In this case, the same verb matches both singular and plural subjects.

Review the definition of *pronouns.* Identify and discuss the singular subject pronouns *she, he,* and *it;* the plural subject pronoun *they;* and the possessive pronouns *her* and *his.*

L.1.1 Demonstrate command of the conventions of standard English grammar and usage when writing or speaking.

L.1.1.c Use singular and plural nouns with matching verbs in basic sentences.

L.1.1.d Use personal, possessive, and indefinite pronouns.

L.1.1.e Use verbs to convey a sense of past, present, and future.

OBJECTIVES:

- Identify singular and plural nouns, pronouns, and verbs.
- Identify past, present, and future verbs.
- Correctly match nouns and pronouns to verbs.

DEFINITIONS:

subject: describes a person, place, or thing that does or is something

singular subject: a word or words that refer to one person, place, or thing

plural subject: a word or words that refer to more than one person, place, or thing

pronoun: a word that stands for one or more nouns

verb: describes what the subject does or is

Lesson 50 Use Subject-Verb Agreement

L.1.1.c Use singular and plural nouns with matching verbs in basic sentences.

REMIND STUDENTS THAT...

- singular subjects match verbs that end with *s* or *es*.
- plural subjects match verbs that don't end in *s* or *es*.
- two nouns connected by *and* form a plural subject.

PRACTICE 1: Agreement with Singular and Plural Nouns Review with students the definitions in the sidebar on Teacher Page T288. Then distribute Student Page S288.

1. Jane (visit, visits) the zoo.
2. Ned and his dad (like, likes) pizza.
3. My friends (ride, rides) to school with me.
4. Alex (eat, eats) the apple.
5. The bus (drive, drives) down our street.
6. My mom and I (go, goes) to the store.

Read aloud sentence 1. Point out that *Jane* is the subject. Is the subject singular or plural? (singular) I know that singular verbs end in *s* or *es*. Which verb choice is singular? (visits) Have students circle *visits*.

Read aloud sentence 2. What is the subject? (Ned and his dad) Is the subject singular or plural? (plural) Why? (It is about more than one person) Which verb choice is plural? (like) Have students circle *like*.

Have students work in groups to read sentences 3 and 4, identify the subject, and circle the correct verb. Circulate and ask questions to help them recognize singular and plural subjects. What is the subject in sentence 3? (friends) Is the subject singular or plural? (plural) What will the matching verb look like? (It won't end in *s* or *es*.) Follow the same procedure for sentence 4.

✓ **MONITOR PROGRESS** Have groups identify the subjects and circle the correct verbs in sentences 5 and 6 on Student Page S288.

IF... students choose incorrect verbs in either sentence,
THEN... ask: Does the subject describe one person or thing or more than one person or thing? How does that help you choose the matching verb? Pause for student responses and offer corrective feedback as needed.

Lesson 50 Use Subject-Verb Agreement

PRACTICE 2: Agreement with Pronouns Remind students that they have encountered the pronouns *she, he, it,* and *they* in the passage "Pets" on Teacher Page T287. Discuss other familiar pronouns, such as *we, I,* and *you*. Then distribute Student Page S289.

1. He (draw, draws) funny cartoons.
2. They (work, works) at the pet shop.
3. We (ride, rides) our bikes to school.
4. You (read, reads) three books a week.
5. She (jump, jumps) rope every day.
6. I (play, plays) in the yard after school.

Help students recall that the pronouns *she, he,* and *it* refer to a single person or thing, so they are singular. Pronouns such as *we* and *they* refer to more than one thing, so they are plural. Explain that the rules for the pronouns *you* and *I* are different. Say: Both pronouns are singular, but they match with the same verb as plural subjects.

Have students read sentences 1–4. Say: First, decide if the subject is singular or plural. Then choose the matching verb. Work through sentences 1 and 2 with students, modeling the steps. Circle the correct verb in each sentence. Then have students work with a partner to select the correct verbs in sentences 3 and 4. Circulate to ask questions and make suggestions, as needed.

✔ MONITOR PROGRESS Have partners select the correct verbs in sentences 5 and 6 on Student Page S289.

IF... students consistently select the wrong verb,
THEN... help them create a chart showing singular pronouns on one side and plural pronouns on the other to use as a reference.

L.1.1.d Use personal, possessive, and indefinite pronouns.

REMIND STUDENTS THAT...

- pronouns are words that stand for one or more nouns.
- pronouns may be singular or plural.

Lesson 50 Use Subject-Verb Agreement

L.1.1.e Use verbs to convey a sense of past, present, and future.

REMIND STUDENTS THAT...

- verbs describe what the subject does or is.
- verbs can describe past, present, or future actions or states of being.

PRACTICE 3: Agreement with Nouns and Past, Present, and Future Verbs
Say: Verbs that describe past actions often end in *ed.* Verbs that describe future actions have the word *will* before the verb. Distribute Student Page S290.

1. Kim (walk, walks) home. (present)
2. Ann and Juan (walk, walks) home. (present)
3. Kim walked home. (past)
4. Ann and Juan walked home. (past)
5. Kim will walk home. (future)
6. Ann and Juan will walk home. (future)
7. We (play, plays, played) soccer yesterday.
8. The dogs (will learn, will learns) a new trick.

Read aloud sentences 1 and 2. Both sentences describe a present action; it is happening now. Have students underline the correct verbs. Then say: Look at sentences 3 and 4. Point out the underlined *walked* in each sentence. The verb *walked* describes something that happened in the past; it happened yesterday or earlier in the past. What happens to the verb when the subject changes from singular to plural? (It stays the same.) Repeat the process for sentences 5 and 6. Then have students underline the correct verbs in sentences 7 and 8.

✔ **INDEPENDENT PRACTICE** Read the following sentences aloud. For each sentence, name a verb tense. Have individual students identify the correct verb.

1. Sally's mom (move, moves, moved, will move) her car. (past)
2. I (clean, cleans, cleaned, will clean) my room. (future)
3. Turtles (crawl, crawls, crawled, will crawl) on the ground. (present)

IF... students choose the incorrect verb form,
THEN... model the steps in selecting the correct verb form for a few sentences. Urge students to say the steps aloud as they try again.

Lesson 50 Use Subject-Verb Agreement

Pets

Ana thinks cats are great pets. She calls her cat Puff. Puff purrs. Ana pets his soft fur.

Jim likes dogs more than cats. Jim and his dogs play ball. He throws the ball into the air. The dogs jump up to catch it. Then they bark.

Ted had a pet bird. One day, he took the bird outside. It flew away. Ted will keep his next bird inside!

Lesson 50 Use Subject-Verb Agreement

1. Jane (visit, visits) the zoo.
2. Ned and his dad (like, likes) pizza.
3. My friends (ride, rides) to school with me.
4. Alex (eat, eats) the apple.
5. The bus (drive, drives) down our street.
6. My mom and I (go, goes) to the store.

Lesson 50 Use Subject-Verb Agreement

1. He (draw, draws) funny cartoons.
2. They (work, works) at the pet shop.
3. We (ride, rides) our bikes to school.
4. You (read, reads) three books a week.
5. She (jump, jumps) rope every day.
6. I (play, plays) in the yard after school.

Lesson 50 Use Subject-Verb Agreement

1. Kim (walk, walks) home. (present)

2. Ann and Juan (walk, walks) home. (present)

3. Kim walked home. (past)

4. Ann and Juan walked home. (past)

5. Kim will walk home. (future)

6. Ann and Juan will walk home. (future)

7. We (play, plays, played) soccer yesterday.

8. The dogs (will learn, will learns) a new trick.

Lesson 51 Produce and Expand Sentences

INTRODUCE Read aloud and discuss with students the terms and definitions in the sidebar.

MODEL Display or distribute Student Page S291 and read it aloud.

interrogative sentences

declarative sentences

Recess Is Fun!

What do you like to do during recess? I like to climb on the monkey bars and play tag with my friends. I also like the big, shiny, yellow slide, but so do my friends. Let me have a turn!

My friend, Jamal, brings a book to recess. Doesn't he want to run around? Hey, Jamal. Let's race! He just smiles and waves. I guess he thinks reading is more fun.

I'm heading back to the monkey bars, or maybe the slide. Yippee!

exclamatory sentence

imperative sentence

TEACH Reread the title. Is the title a sentence? (yes) Why does it end in an exclamation point? (to show the writer's excitement about having fun) What other sentence shows excitement? ("Let's race!" "Yippee!") Then reread the first sentence. Why does the sentence end in a question mark? (It asks a question.) What other sentence asks a question? ("Doesn't he want to run around?") Use the same process to help students identify declarative and imperative sentences.

Point out and discuss the use of the gray highlighted conjunctions *and, but,* and *or* to join parts of a simple sentence into a longer one. Then discuss the use of the green highlighted prepositions *during, on, with,* and *to.*

Use the third sentence to discuss expanding sentences by using adjectives. Read the sentence first without and then with the blue highlighted *big, shiny, yellow.* Why do you think the writer added these words before *slide?* (They help me picture the slide.) Discuss why the adjectives are separated by commas.

L.1.1.f Use frequently occurring adjectives.

L.1.1.g Use frequently occurring conjunctions.

L.1.1.i Use frequently occurring prepositions.

L.1.1.j Produce and expand complete simple and compound declarative, interrogative, imperative, and exclamatory sentences in response to prompts.

***See also* L.1.1, L.1.2, L.1.2.b, L.1.2.c**

OBJECTIVES:

- Correctly punctuate declarative, interrogative, imperative, and exclamatory sentences.
- Use conjunctions and commas to expand sentences.
- Use adjectives and prepositions to expand sentences.

DEFINITIONS:

declarative sentence: states a fact or an opinion; ends with a period

interrogative sentence: asks a question; ends with a question mark

imperative sentence: a command or polite request; ends with an exclamation point or period

exclamatory sentence: expresses excitement or strong emotion; ends with an exclamation point

Lesson 51 Produce and Expand Sentences

L.1.1.j Produce and expand complete simple and compound declarative, interrogative, imperative, and exclamatory sentences in response to prompts.

L.1.2.b Use end punctuation for sentences.

REMIND STUDENTS THAT…

- a declarative sentence ends with a period.
- an interrogative sentence ends with a question mark.
- an imperative sentence ends with an exclamation point or period.
- an exclamatory sentence ends with an exclamation point.

PRACTICE 1: Choose Punctuation Review the definitions of the four types of sentences. Then distribute Student Page S292.

1. What games do you like?
2. Our car is blue.
3. I like apples more than oranges.
4. Please give me that book.
5. Wow, that's great!
6. Why is your dog barking?
7. My sister's name is Rana.

Write out or point to sentence 1. Read it aloud, using intonation to suggest a question. What is the purpose of the sentence? (It asks a question.) What punctuation should go at the end of the sentence? (a question mark) Add a question mark to the end of sentence 1 and have students put a question mark on their copies of the student page. Repeat the process for sentence 2. Then have partners use the same process to add the correct end punctuation to sentence 3. Ask: What punctuation did you add? How did you decide? (Sentence 3 states an opinion. Facts and opinions take periods.)

Read aloud sentences 4 and 5, changing your intonation to reflect a polite request and an exclamation. Help students use the clues *Please* and *Wow* to select a period for sentence 4 and an exclamation point for sentence 5.

MONITOR PROGRESS Have students read sentences 6 and 7 on Student Page S292 and write the correct end punctuation marks.

IF… students don't write a question mark and a period,
THEN… ask: How did you decide what mark to use? Listen to their answers, and give feedback as needed. If necessary, review the hints in the "Remind Students That . . ." section.

Lesson 51 Produce and Expand Sentences

PRACTICE 2: Join Sentences Say: You can use joining words, or conjunctions, such as *and, but,* and *or* to connect two short sentences. Display or distribute Student Page S293. Point out the two short sentences in each item.

1. Which dog is yours?
   What is the dog's name? — and but
2. Our car is blue.
   It has black tires. — or and
3. Shut the door!
   Wipe your feet first! — but or
4. You can have an apple.
   You can have a banana. — or but
5. I'm hungry.
   I don't have time to eat now. — but or

Read aloud the two sentences in item 1. Point out the two conjunctions, or joining words—*and* and *but.* Read the two sentences joined by *and.* Then read them joined by *but.* Which joining word makes more sense? (*and*)

Say: Write the new sentence. What punctuation mark goes at the end of the joined sentence? (question mark) Why? (Both sentences are questions.) Repeat this process for items 2 and 3.

Invite students to combine the sentences in item 4 on their own. Then have them compare their new sentences. If students disagree on what conjunction to use, have them explain how they chose their words. Clarify any misconceptions.

✓ MONITOR PROGRESS Ask students which joining word they would use to connect the sentences in item 5.

IF... students choose *or* instead of *but,*
THEN... model the decision process. Read aloud the first sentence. Then read aloud the second sentence. Discuss how the two sentences are related. How does the second sentence affect the first sentence? (When you're hungry you want to eat. The person doesn't have time to eat.) What joining word matches this idea? (*but*)

L.1.1.g Use frequently occurring conjunctions.

L.1.1.j Produce and expand complete simple and compound declarative, interrogative, imperative, and exclamatory sentences.

L.1.2.b Use end punctuation for sentences.

REMIND STUDENTS THAT...

- they can use joining words such as *and, but,* and *or* to connect two simple sentences into a longer sentence.
- they should write a period, question mark, or exclamation point at the end of the new sentence.

Lesson 51 Produce and Expand Sentences

L.1.1.j Produce and expand complete simple and compound declarative, interrogative, imperative, and exclamatory sentences in response to prompts.

See also **L.1.1.f, L.1.1.i, L.1.2.c**

REMIND STUDENTS THAT...

- they can use words to tell something more about nouns.
- they can use words such as *on, with,* or *to* to give more information.
- they can use commas to separate lists of things.

PRACTICE 3: Expand Sentences Present items 1–4 aloud to students. Model expanding the sentences in steps using adjectives and prepositional phrases.

1. The black, shiny car turned the corner. The ___big___, black, shiny car turned the corner.
2. Tim threw the ball.
   Tim threw the ball ___to his friend___.
3. Jen walked her dog.
   Jen walked her ___furry___ dog.
   Jen walked her dog ___on the sidewalk___.
   Jen walked her ___furry___ dog ___on the sidewalk___.
4. I ate a banana.
   I ate a ___yellow___ banana.
   I ate a banana ___with my lunch___.
   I ate a ___yellow___ banana ___with my lunch___.

Read aloud the first sentence in item 1. The words *black* and *shiny* describe the car. What other word might give more information about the car? (big) Write *big* in the blank. Point out the commas separating the three adjectives. Repeat the process for items 2–4, showing how to use adjectives and prepositions to expand sentences.

INDEPENDENT PRACTICE Distribute Student Page S294. Have students complete the activity independently.

Do you have pets ___?___
I have ___two___ pets ___.___
One is a ___noisy___, ___little___, fluffy dog named Max.
Max chases me ___around the yard___.
Stop it, Max ___!___
My other pet is a mouse ___with gray fur___, ___but___ it doesn't play.

IF... students make an incorrect choice,
THEN... review selecting appropriate end punctuation, adjectives, prepositional phrases, and conjunctions and have them try again.

Lesson 51 **Produce and Expand Sentences**

Recess Is Fun!

What do you like to do during recess? I like to climb on the monkey bars and play tag with my friends. I also like the big, shiny, yellow slide, but so do my friends. Let me have a turn!

My friend, Jamal, brings a book to recess. Doesn't he want to run around? Hey, Jamal. Let's race! He just smiles and waves. I guess he thinks reading is more fun.

I'm heading back to the monkey bars, or maybe the slide. Yippee!

Lesson 51 Produce and Expand Sentences

1. What games do you like _____
2. Our car is blue _____
3. I like apples more than oranges _____
4. Please give me that book _____
5. Wow, that's great _____
6. Why is your dog barking _____
7. My sister's name is Rana _____

Lesson 51 Produce and Expand Sentences

1. Which dog is yours? What is the dog's name?	and	but
2. Our car is blue. It has black tires.	or	and
3. Shut the door! Wipe your feet first!	but	or
4. You can have an apple. You can have a banana.	or	but
5. I'm hungry. I don't have time to eat now.	but	or

Lesson 51 **Produce and Expand Sentences**

Do you have pets _____

I have ___________ pets_____

One is a ___________, ___________, fluffy dog named Max.

Max chases me ___________.

Stop it, Max _____

My other pet is a mouse ___________, ___________ it doesn't play.

Answer Choices

.	around the yard	noisy
?	but	two
!	little	with big eyes

Lesson 52 Understand Spelling Patterns

INTRODUCE Say: Remember, some letters work together to make a single sound. For example, the word *show* begins with the letters *sh*, but it has one sound: /sh/. The word *team* contains the letters e and *a*, but it has one sound: /ē/. Today you'll practice spelling words like this.

MODEL Display or distribute Student Page S295 and read it aloud. Point to each word with a highlighted consonant digraph. Say each word aloud, stressing the blended sound, and have students echo you. Repeat this process for the words with highlighted vowel teams.

The Spelling Bee

Phil and Joan each spelled two words right. Phil spelled the words *both* and *neat*. Joan spelled the words *tooth* and *where*. Would she spell the next word right? Phil waited.

The teacher said, "tape."

Joan spelled, "t-a-p." The class moaned.

Phil's knees shook. He did not want to fail. Then he spelled, "t-a-p-e." The class cheered.

TEACH Point out that *ph, th, wh, sh,* and *ch* all have a consonant followed by the letter *h*. Then remind students that vowels—*a, e, i, o,* and *u*—can also form teams that make one sound. Review the sound made by each highlighted consonant digraph and vowel team.

Reread the last paragraph. Which words have two consonants that together form one sound? (*Phil's, shook, Then, The, cheered*) What words have vowel teams? (*knees, shook, fail, cheered*) Have students identify the consonant digraph and/or vowel team in each word.

Ask: How did Phil spell *tape?* (t-a-p-e) Why did Joan spell the word wrong? (She forgot the silent e rule.) Point to the silent e in *tape* and repeat the rule.

If necessary, review Lessons 16 and 17 (consonant digraphs), Lesson 23 (silent e rule), Lesson 24 (long vowel patterns), and Lesson 25 (vowel teams) before continuing.

L.1.2 Demonstrate command of the conventions of standard English capitalization, punctuation, and spelling when writing.

L.1.2.d Use conventional spelling for words with common spelling patterns and for frequently occurring irregular words.

OBJECTIVES:

- Spell words that contain the *sh, th, ph, ch,* and *wh* diagraphs.
- Spell words using the long vowel sound and silent e rule.
- Spell words that contain vowel teams (*ee, ea, ai, oa*).

Lesson 52 Understand Spelling Patterns

L.1.2.d Use conventional spelling for words with common spelling patterns and for frequently occurring irregular words.

REMIND STUDENTS THAT…

- a digraph is two consonants that stand for a single sound.
- they can spell words that begin or end with a digraph.

PRACTICE 1: Recognize and Spell Words With Common Consonant Digraphs Display or distribute Student Page S296. Explain that in this lesson students will practice using digraphs to spell words. Say: A digraph is two consonants that stand for a single sound.

1. Model.	Point to and say the four listed digraphs: *ch, sh, th, wh.* Have students echo you as you say the sound of each digraph. Then point to the first incomplete word in the chart: _ _ irt. Say: You can spell a familiar word by adding a digraph to the two empty spaces.
2. Model testing digraphs.	Read aloud the result of adding each digraph to *irt: chirt, shirt, thirt, whirt.* Ask: Which digraph works with *irt* to make a familiar word? (*sh*)
3. Write and pronounce.	Write *shirt* on the board. Have students pronounce and spell the word.

Follow the routine with the remaining incomplete words in the four-column chart.

Digraphs	ch, sh, th, wh

s h irt	mou t h	c h air	w h ite
wat c h	t h umb	pu s h	lun c h

✔ **MONITOR PROGRESS** Have students fill in the digraphs of the two incomplete words at the bottom of Student Page S296 to make familiar words. Then have them pronounce and spell the words.

w h ich	cra s h

IF… students choose the incorrect digraphs,
THEN… ask: Why did you choose that digraph? Listen to their answers, and remind them to try each of the four digraphs to see which one sounds like a familiar word.

Lesson 52 Understand Spelling Patterns

PRACTICE 2: Use the Silent e Rule Display or distribute Student Page S297. Point out that the words in the first column have a CVC pattern and the words in the third column end in e. Say: Remember that this is a "silent" e. You don't hear it, but the silent e makes the vowel in the word say its name.

L.1.1.d Use conventional spelling for words with common spelling patterns and for frequently occurring irregular words.

REMIND STUDENTS THAT...

- the sound of a long vowel is the same as the letter name.
- they can apply the silent e rule to words spelled *a_e*, *e_e*, *i_e*, *o_e*, and *u_e*.

Silent *e* Examples

Word	Vowel Sound	Word	Vowel Sound
cap	short	cape	long
pet	short	Pete	long
kit	short	kite	long
rod	short	rode	long
cut	short	cute	long

Write the following sentences on the board.

1. The candy cost a (dim, dime).
2. Please give me that (can, cane) of peas.
3. I (hop, hope) I can go to the party.
4. The cat (hid, hide) under the bed.
5. Do you have the (tap, tape)?
6. The (tub, tube) is full of water.
7. Let's play a (gam, game)!

Read aloud sentence 1, emphasizing the word *dime*. Model choosing the correct spelling: The *i* in the word says its name, so there must be a silent e at the end of the word. The correct spelling is *d-i-m-e*. Circle *d-i-m-e*. Repeat this process for sentences 2–4.

Read aloud sentences 5 and 6. Have students select the words that correctly complete the sentences.

MONITOR PROGRESS Read sentence 7 aloud. Have students select the word that correctly completes the sentence.

IF... students choose *gam*,
THEN... reread the sentence aloud. Ask: What is the vowel sound in *gam*? (short) What is the vowel sound in *game*? (long) Which of the two is the correct spelling of *game*? (g-a-m-e)

Lesson 52 Understand Spelling Patterns

L.1.2.d Use conventional spelling for words with common spelling patterns and for frequently occurring irregular words.

REMIND STUDENTS THAT...

- vowels (*a*, *e*, *i*, *o*, and *u*) can form teams that make one sound.
- they can spell words with vowel teams.

PRACTICE 3: Recognize and Spell Words With Vowel Teams Display or distribute Student Page S298. Review the chart.

Vowel Team	Vowel Sound	Examples
ee	long e	feet, seed
ea	long e	each, team
ai	long a	rain, wait
oa	long o	goat, toast

1. Take a seat in this chair.
2. Did you mail the card?
3. Tad got soap in his eyes.
4. Nan beat Jill in the race.
5. That dog has a long tail.
6. Try on your new winter coat.

Word Bank

coat	soap
seat	tail
mail	beat

Have students complete sentences 1–6 with a word from the Word Bank. Read aloud sentence 1, emphasizing the long e sound. Which two words have the long e sound? (*seat, beat*) Which one makes sense in the sentence? (*seat*) Repeat for sentences 2–4. Then have students complete sentences 5 and 6 independently.

INDEPENDENT PRACTICE List *chain, coat, goat, heat, meet, seat, seeds, train* on the board. Then write these frames.

1. We took a ______ to the farm.
2. There, we saw a ______eating grass.
3. The farmer grows some plants from ______.
4. The summer ______ helps some plants grow.

Have individual students complete each frame with a word from the list. Write the correct word in each blank. Then have students identify the vowel team in each word and say and spell the word aloud.

IF... students cannot identify the vowel team in a word,
THEN... ask: What are the five vowels? What two vowels do you see in the word? What sound do they make?

Lesson 52 **Understand Spelling Patterns**

The Spelling Bee

Phil and Joan each spelled two words right. Phil spelled the words *both* and *neat.* Joan spelled the words *tooth* and *where.* Would she spell the next word right? Phil waited.

The teacher said, "tape."

Joan spelled, "t-a-p." The class moaned.

Phil's knees shook. He did not want to fail. Then he spelled, "t-a-p-e." The class cheered.

Lesson 52 Understand Spelling Patterns

Digraphs	ch, sh, th, wh

__ __ irt	mou __ __	__ __ air	__ __ ite
wat __ __	__ __ umb	pu __ __	lun __ __

__ __ ich	cra __ __

Lesson 52 Understand Spelling Patterns

Silent *e* Examples			
Word	**Vowel Sound**	**Word**	**Vowel Sound**
cap	short	cape	long
pet	short	Pete	long
kit	short	kite	long
rod	short	rode	long
cut	short	cute	long

Lesson 52 Understand Spelling Patterns

Vowel Team	Vowel Sound	Examples
ee	long e	feet, seed
ea	long e	each, team
ai	long a	rain, wait
oa	long o	goat, toast

1. Take a ___ ea ___ in this chair.
2. Did you ___ ai ___ the card?
3. Tad got ___ oa ___ in his eyes.
4. Nan ___ ea ___ Jill in the race.
5. That dog has a long ___ ai ___.
6. Try on your new winter ___ oa ___.

Word Bank

coat	soap
seat	tail
mail	beat

ASSESSMENT
LESSONS 50–52

Language

ASSESS MASTERY Use this Checkpoint to assess students' mastery of the Level B Language standards listed here.

ADMINISTER THE TEST Administer the Checkpoint to each student. Display or distribute copies of the following student page. Model each process described below. Then have students use the process to respond to each set of questions.

MODEL 1: I will read aloud sentences with different forms of the same verb. You will tell me which verb matches the subject.
MODEL 2: You will see sentences with missing parts. Then you will choose the missing part from the Answer Bank.
MODEL 3: You will see four words. I will ask you questions about the spellings of the words. Say the word or words that answer each question. (Questions: Which word and letters spell the *sh* sound? Which word and letters spell the long *a* sound? Which word and letters spell the long *o* sound?)

1. Work through sets 1–3 on the following page.
2. Have students respond. Check their answers using the Scoring chart.

L.1.1 Demonstrate command of the conventions of standard English grammar and usage when writing or speaking.

L.1.2 Demonstrate command of the conventions of standard English capitalization, punctuation, and spelling when writing.

See also **L.1.1.c, L.1.1.d, L.1.1.e, L.1.1.f, L.1.1.g, L.1.1.i, L.1.1.j, L.1.2, L.1.2.b, L.1.2.c, L.1.2.d**

SCORING

SKILL/LESSON	STANDARD	ANSWER	SCORING
1. Use Subject-Verb Agreement (Lesson 50)	**L.1.1**	*played; likes; bark; will stay*	_____ / 4
2. Produce and Expand Sentences (Lesson 51)	**L.1.1** **L.1.2**	*?; or; green; in the water*	_____ / 4
3. Understand Spelling Patterns (Lesson 52)	**L.1.2**	*shop, sh; rain, ai; hope, o_e*	_____ / 3

An overall score of 80% is typically considered mastery. Use your judgment and your individual students' needs as well to determine skill mastery.

IF... you determine that students have not demonstrated sufficient mastery of one or more skills,
THEN... review needed skills, going back to the lessons to reteach and scaffold as needed.

ASSESSMENT
LESSONS 50–52

Language

1.a. I (play, plays, played) with my dogs at the lake yesterday.
1.b. The brown dog (like, likes, will like) to get wet.
1.c. Both dogs (bark, barks) at squirrels and cats.
1.d. The dogs and I (stay, stays, will stay) home tomorrow.

2.a. Where is my book ________
2.b. Do you like red best ________ do you like blue best?
2.c. The ________ turtle swims ________.

Answer Bank

.	and	green
?	but	purple
!	or	in the water
		up a tree

3.

what	shop	hope	rain